Baedeker

Cyprus

Hints for using the Guide

Following the tradition established by Karl Baedeker in 1844, build-ings and works of art, places of natural beauty and sights of particular interest are distinguished by one ★ or two ★★.

To make it easier to locate the various places listed in the "A to Z" section of the Guide, their co-ordinates are shown in red at the head of each entry: e.g., Páphos A/B 4.

Coloured lines down the right-hand side of the page are an aid to finding the main heading in the Guide: blue stands for the Introduction (Nature, Culture, History, etc.), red for the "A to Z" section, and yellow indicates Practical Information.

Only a selection of hotels, restaurants and shops can be given; no reflec-tion is implied therefore on establishments not included.

In a time of rapid change it is difficult to ensure that all the information given is entirely accurate and up-to-date, and the possibility of error can never be entirely eliminated.

Although the publishers can accept no responsibility for inaccuracies and omissions, they are constantly endeavouring to improve the quality of their Guides and are therefore always grateful for criticisms, corrections and suggestions for improvement.

Preface

This guide to Cyprus is one of the new generation of Baedeker guides.

These guides, illustrated throughout in colour, are designed to meet the needs of the modern traveller. They are quick and easy to consult, with the principal places of interest described in alphabetical order, and the information is presented in a format that is both attractive and easy to follow.

This guide covers the whole of the Mediterranean island of Cyprus, including both the Greek part, the Republic of Cyprus, which under international law covers the whole island, and the Turkish Republic of North Cyprus, which is recognised only by Turkey.

The guide is in three parts. The first part gives a general account of Cyprus, its topography, climate, flora and fauna, population, religion, government and society, economy, history, famous people, art and culture. A selection of literary quotations and a number of suggested

Close to the south-eastern point of Cyprus near Cape Gréco lie the bathing resort of Ayía Nápa with the monastery from which it takes its name

itineraries lead in to the second part, in which features of tourist interest – towns and villages, areas of scenic beauty, archaeological sites – are described. The third part contains a variety of practical information. Both the sights and the practical information are listed in alphabetical order, separately for the two parts of the island.

The new Baedeker guides are noted for their concentration on essentials and their convenience of use. They contain numerous specially drawn plans and colour illustrations; and at the end of the book is a large map making it easy to locate the various places described in the "A to Z" section of the guide with the help of the co-ordinates given at the head of each entry.

Contents

Aphrodite's

Cyprus (Greek "Kypros"), first so called in antiquity on account of its then flourishing copper mines, appears in classical mythology as the island of Aphrodite, goddess of love and fertility. A wave-lapped rock, the famous Pétra tou Romioú, is said to mark the spot where the spume-born goddess rose from the sea. Not far away at Palaía Páphos (now Koúklia), are the remains of one of the largest temples of Aphrodite in the ancient world, to which in mythological prehistory devotees of the goddess flocked. Today the great attraction of this island where visitors receive a warm welcome, is the variety of leisure opportunities it provides. Anyone with cultural interests will find plentiful evidence of Cyprus' 9000 year history, much of it

Tróodos

Some of the most delightful scenery in Cyprus

spent under the hegemony of different foreign powers. The Ptolemies left the Tombs of the Kings cut into the rock at Páphos; the Romans bequeathed colourful mosaic pavements. In the Middle Ages the Knights of St John built the great castle at Kolóssi, which for a time was the headquarters of the Order and produced the celebrated Commandaria, one of the world's first branded wines.

Those for whom a good holiday means, first and foremost, the beach – pebble and sand beaches mainly, as, for example, at Ayía and Nápa – will not be alone in appreciating the island's unusually varied coastal scenery and its generally high standard of hotels with their wide range of facilities.

Rock of Aphrodite

Here, according to legend, the spume-born goddess of love rose from the waves

Famagusta/ Gazimağusa

View from the walls over the Old Town with its many churches

Island

Since the occupation of northern Cyprus by Turkish forces in 1974, and the ensuing partition of the island, holidaymakers have been slow to visit what today is the Turkish Republic of North Cyprus. It is only recently that tourism here has shown signs of hesitant recovery, chiefly in the idyllic little town of Kyrenia and in Famagusta, formerly the island's principal port.

Ramblers will relish the nature trails around Mt Ólympos, the highest peak in the Tróodos range where impassable mountainsides – like those in the vicinity of the mysterious Cedar Valley – once offered hermits the seclusion they sought, and where in the Middle Ages monasteries and Byzantine barn-roofed

churches were built. Unique to Cyprus, every single one of these small churches, their walls embellished with murals still for the most part well preserved, appears on UNESCO's list of world heritage sites.

Definitely not to be missed is a visit to Nicosia, the island's divided capital, a city with a distinctly oriental feel. In the Old Town, still encircled by its Venetian walls, Laiki Yitoniá ("the people's quarter"), where traffic is severely restricted, forms an oasis of peace. Nicosia is as typically Cypriot as the remotest mountain village. Here, in homely tavernas, you can drink good wine and sample delicious meze – a selection of 20 or so appetising starters illustrating the full variety of Cypriot cuisine, or enjoy folk music and dancing in one of the bouzoúki bars.

Commandaria
This sweet dessert wine can claim to be the world's first branded wine

Nicosia
A statue of President Makarios stands in front of the Archbishop's Palace in the southern part of the divided city

Facts and Figures

Note
Only the introductory section of this guide deals with the island as a whole. The greater part of the descriptive section (Sights from A to Z) is concerned with the Greek Cypriot Republic of Cyprus, which is internationally recognised as the legitimate authority over the whole island. The Turkish Republic of Northern Cyprus, unilaterally proclaimed in 1983 and recognised only by Turkey, is treated separately.

On February 16th 1995 it was agreed that the Cypriot capital Nicosia should officially be named "Lefkosia". Both names are used in this guide (see page 153).

General

Cyprus, the third largest Mediterranean island, lies between latitude 34°33' and 35°40' north and between longitude 32°17' and 34°36' east.

Situated in the eastern Mediterranean at the meeting-place of the continents of Europe, Asia and Africa, Cyprus lies 65km/40 miles off the coast of Turkey, 95km/59 miles from Syria, 173km/107 miles from Lebanon and 380km/236 miles from Egypt. The Greek island of Crete lies 553km/344 miles west of Cyprus.

Situation

With a total area of 9251sq.km/3571sq. miles, Cyprus is the third largest island in the Mediterranean, after Sicily (25,462sq.km/9831sq. miles) and Sardinia (24,090sq.km/9301sq. miles). Its greatest extent from west to east is 224km/139 miles and from north to south 96km/60 miles, and it has a total coastline of 780km/485 miles.

Area

As a result of its central position between East and West, at the focal point of many different interests, Cyprus has been since prehistoric times the scene of constant conflict between neighbouring powers. Successive periods of foreign rule have left their mark on the culture and mentality of the Cypriots, who in spite of it all have been able to preserve their own identity. It was only in 1960, after thousands of years of foreign domination, that the island achieved independence; and only fourteen years later, in 1974, Turkish troops invaded the northern part of the island, which they still occupy.

The Cyprus conflicts

Since 1974 some 38% of the island's area has been under Turkish occupation. The Turkish Republic of Northern Cyprus which was proclaimed in 1983 by its self-appointed President Rauf Denktash is internationally outlawed and recognised only by Turkey. The Greek Cypriot southern part of the island occupies 62% of its total area and forms the internationally recognised Republic of Cyprus, which in international law represents the whole island. The two parts of Cyprus are separated by a buffer zone, the "Green Line", established in 1974 and controlled by United Nations forces. It begins near Lefke in the north-west, cuts through Nicosia and ends to the south of Famagusta.

Division of the territory

◄ *Romantic coastal scenery on the Akámas peninsula*

Topography

Districts

The whole island is divided into the six districts of Nicosia, Limassol, Lárnaca, Páphos, Famagusta and Kyrenia – the last two of which have been separately administered since 1974.

Topography

Geological origin

Although in history and culture closely connected with Europe, Cyprus is geographically part of Asia. The two main ranges of hills, the Kyrenia (Pentadáktylos) range and the Tróodos Mountains, run parallel to the Taurus in Asia Minor.

In the Neolithic period, some 60 million years ago, an arm of the sea divided the island into two parts, corresponding broadly to the Kyrenia range in the north and the Tróodos massif in the south. In the Late Tertiary era earthquakes and a rise in the level of the sea-bed created the Mesaória plain, which lies between the two Early Tertiary ranges of hills.

Topographical variety

The characteristic outline of Cyprus, with the long and narrow Karpasía peninsula reaching north-east, was seen in antiquity as resembling a deerskin. This green Mediterranean island is also remarkable for the variety of its topography, with a series of sandy and shingly beaches, wide bays and rugged cliffs round the coasts, steeply scarped volcanic hills, forest-covered up to the highest peaks, upland regions with gently rounded hills and deep valleys, and fertile plains.

Five different landscape zones can be distinguished in Cyprus: the coastal regions, the ranges of hills (Kyrenia and Tróodos) which run parallel to them, the foothills of the Tróodos and the large central plain, the Mesaória, which lies between the two ranges of hills.

Coastal regions

The coastal regions show great variety of scenery. On the east coast are beautiful bays, the finest sandy beaches being at Famagusta and Ayía Nápa. On the south coast are the large towns of Lárnaca and Limassol and much tourist development carried out since 1974 which

Hills, Plains and Rivers

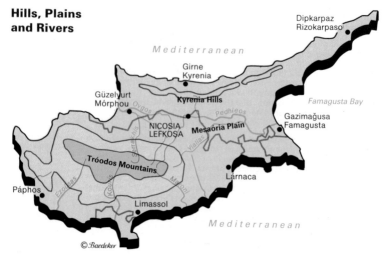

has reduced the natural charm of this coastal region. The north and west coasts have a varied pattern of scenery, long, lonely sandy beaches alternating with sheer cliffs, beautiful bays with rough and stony beaches.

The Kyrenia range in the north of the island – a rugged and sparsely wooded chain of hills 128km/80 miles long – consists of limestones, marbles, phyllites and serpentines. The highest point in the range, which extends eastward to the narrow Karpasía peninsula, is Kyparissóvouno (1024m/3360ft). The hills fall steeply down to the north coast.

Kyrenia and Pentadáktylos ranges

The Kyrenia Hills are also known as Pentadáktylos ("Five-Fingered") after the lower Pentadáktylos range (730m/2395ft), whose five peaks rise up like the fingers of a hand.

The volcanic Tróodos massif in south-western Cyprus, extending from west to east for a distance of 80km/50 miles and rising to 1951m/6401ft in Mt Ólympos (also known as Khionístra, the "Snow-Capped One"), occupies, including its foothills, almost a third of the island's area. Unlike the Kyrenia range, it is densely wooded up to its highest peaks. With its mild and agreeable climate and its refreshing coolness it is a popular recreation area in the hot summer months and offers skiing in winter.

Tróodos massif

The Mesaória plain lying between the two ranges of hills is an important agricultural region. It extends from Mórphou Bay in the north-west to Famagusta Bay in the east, and now lies mainly in the Turkish-occupied part of Cyprus. The plain consists of Late Tertiary sediments and fertile alluvial soils and is broken up by dry valleys and tabular hills.

Mesaória plain

The largest town in Cyprus is Nicosia (pop. 203,000), the island's capital, which lies in the Mesaória plain. It is now cut in two by the boundary between the Greek and Turkish parts of the island.

Towns

The rugged and sparsely wooded Kyrenia Hills

View from Stavrovouni over the Tróodos foothills to the coast

Second to Nicosia is Limassol (pop. 120,000), on the south coast, the largest port and tourist centre. To the east of Limassol, in a wide bay, is Lárnaca (pop. 60,000), which has increased in importance since 1974 following the construction of the new airport. Páphos (pop. 21,000), on the west coast, offers the attractions of its extensive ancient remains and in recent years has also developed into a popular seaside resort.

At the east end of the island is the town of Famagusta (Turkish: Gazimağusa), with a population of just under 25,000. Until 1974 it was Cyprus's largest port and principal tourist centre, but since the division of the island has declined in importance. On the Turkish-occupied north coast is the picturesque little port of Kyrenia (Turkish: Girne; pop. 7000), one of the most charming towns on the island.

Climate

Cyprus has a typical Mediterranean climate, with hot dry summers and mild wet winters. This seasonal variation results from the fact that in summer the subtropical zone of high pressure and aridity moves northward and influences weather conditions in the Mediterranean, while in summer the low-pressure zone of the temperate latitudes moves south over the Mediterranean.

Climatic regions

Climatic conditions in Cyprus are fairly uniform, with local variations resulting from:

● situation (on the coast or inland). On the coast, thanks to the moderating influence of the sea, temperature variations over the day and over the year are less than in the interior of the island, with its more continental climate. On hot summer days winds blowing off the sea bring a degree of coolness, a relief lacking in the interior.

● the alignment of the hills in relation to the prevailing winds. On the windward side of a range of hills the air masses rise and cool down, leading to the formation of clouds and in extreme cases to rain, while on the side exposed to wind the clouds break up and there is less rain.

● altitude. With increasing height temperatures fall by between 0.5°C/0.9°F and almost 1°C/1.8°F depending on season and the humidity of the air. Rainfall increases with height.

The climatic characteristics of different parts of Cyprus are shown in the climatic diagrams on page 14, based on data from six typical weather stations: Kyrenia for the north coast; Nicosia for the Mesaória plain in the interior of the island; Famagusta for the east coast; Limassol for the south coast; Páphos for the west coast; and Trikoukkia (1341m/4400ft) for the Tróodos Mountains.

Climatic diagrams

In the climatic diagrams the blue columns show annual rainfall in millimetres month by month in accordance with the blue scale on the right. Temperatures are shown in the orange band, the upper edge of which shows average maximum day temperatures and the lower edge average minimum night temperatures in accordance with the red scale on the right.

On the basis of these diagrams it is possible to estimate rainfall and temperatures for areas between the selected weather stations.

The highest levels of rainfall are in winter (December and January), with figures many times higher than in Central Europe. Phases influenced by areas of high pressure coming from the mainland of Asia, without rain, alternate with phases influenced by areas of low pressure, accompanied by rain. Frequently the centre of such areas of low pressure lies in the Cyprus area or in the Aegean. Altogether, however, there are only some ten or twelve days with rain in December and January. The other days are predominantly sunny. Nicosia has 170 hours of sunshine in each month, Famagusta 195 and 180. In the Tróodos Mountains there is heavier cloud cover, with 120 hours of sunshine in each month and 225mm/9in. of precipitation in January. Down to a height of 1000m/3300ft the precipitation are in the form of snow, and above 1500m/4900ft there are between 2 and 3 metres (6½ and 10 feet) of snow, often lasting until the end of April and offering good conditions for skiing.

Rainfall in winter

Temperatures in winter are mainly determined by situation (coastal or inland) and altitude. The lowest temperatures are in January and February. On the north and west coasts night temperatures rarely fall below 10°C/50°F, while in the plain around Nicosia, where temperature fluctuations over the day are greater, they fall well below that level. Water temperatures fall to 18–19°C/64–66°F in December and 16–17°C/61–63°F in January to April, reaching their lowest level in February and March.

Temperatures in winter

From February onwards monthly rainfall and the number of days with rain decline and temperatures increase. Levels of rainfall are shown in the climatic diagrams; the number of days with rain is about 9 in February, 5 in March and 3 in April, falling to zero in May/June. Water temperatures rise to 22°C/72°F by June, and to 23°C/73°F on the east and south coasts.

Climate in spring

Dry summers are characteristic of the Mediterranean climate. Between May and September the number of hours of sunshine per month is well

Rainfall in summer

13

Six typical weather stations in Cyprus

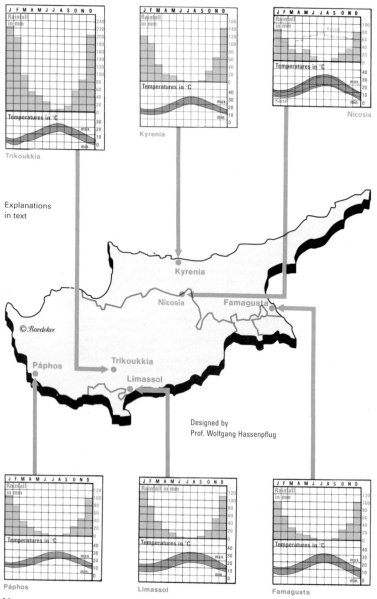

Trikoukkia

Kyrenia

Nicosia

Explanations in text

© Baedeker

Páphos

Trikoukkia

Limassol

Kyrenia

Nicosia

Famagusta

Designed by
Prof. Wolfgang Hassenpflug

Páphos

Limassol

Famagusta

over 300. In July Nicosia has 398 hours of sunshine, and the Tróodos Mountains have only seven hours less. From April to October evaporation is greater than such rainfall as there is. The drought increases from May to September, and many springs and watercourses dry up.

In July and August there is no rain anywhere in Cyprus except in the Tróodos Mountains, which average one rainy day (5mm/2in.). The clouds which give rise to such showers can be seen on most days in summer, particularly in the western hills. In some years June may not have a single rainy day. The rain returns, however, in September. In inland areas there may be dust-carrying winds and sudden showers which fill the dry valleys.

In July and August, and on the south and east coasts also in September, maximum day temperatures are consistently above 30°C/86°F. The highest summer temperatures are in the inland regions (at Nicosia in July and August fully 36°C/97°F). Since temperatures fall with increasing height, the southern slopes of the Tróodos range in particular, with the cool upper reaches of the valleys, are much favoured holiday areas. *(margin: Temperatures in summer)*

On the coasts the sea winds which blow throughout the day bring welcome coolness, though this reaches only a short distance inland. The currents of air flowing inland and upwards lead to the formation of clouds in the central Tróodos massif.

In summer the prevailing winds are northerly (the trade winds of the eastern Mediterranean), blowing steadily and often gustily, though in particular areas they may be diverted by hills.

More frequent in spring and autumn are sirocco winds from the south – hot and, when saturated with water vapour, oppressively sultry.

Water temperatures are about 26°C/79°F in August and September, on the east and south coasts 27°C/81°F in August.

Autumn is marked by slowly falling temperatures and an increase in monthly rainfall and the number of days with rain. October has three days with rain, November five. From September onwards it is warmer at night on the coast, particularly on the west and north coasts, than in the interior – a result of the slow fall in water temperatures (from 26°C/79°F in September to 21°C/70°F in November). *(margin: Climate in autumn)*

Flora and Fauna

Flora

Thanks to its mild and equable Mediterranean climate Cyprus has a rich variety of flora, with some 1900 different species of plants, including 100 endemic species found only on the island.

The flora of Cyprus is at its finest in March and April, when the island is covered by a many-coloured sea of blossom. In addition to various species of orchids there are tulips, gladioli, irises, wild poppies, great fields of intensely perfumed rape, blossoming fruit-trees and various decorative trees. *(margin: Spring)*

Since the watercourses soon dry up after the snow-melt and the brief rainy season in spring, Cyprus has a rather barren and dried-up air in summer; the plains of the interior and the coastal regions are burned up by the sun, and the golden-yellow colour of the grain gives place to various shades of brown. Only the blossoms of the oleanders give small touches of colour. In the hills, however, the coniferous and deciduous trees remain green. *(margin: Summer)*

With the first autumn rains Cyprus is transformed once again into a green and blooming island, with crocuses, narcissi, anemones, hyacinths and lilies. *(margin: Autumn)*

15

Flora and Fauna

Aloes

Mesembryanthemum

Forests

The felling of the island's great expanses of forest began in ancient times, when the sea powers of the eastern Mediterranean used the timber for the construction of their fleets. In addition to the felling which continued without control down the centuries further losses have resulted from grazing by goats, forest fires and Turkish incendiary bombs in 1974, reducing the forest cover of this once green Mediterranean island to barely 20%. Most of the forests are state-owned, mainly on the slopes of the Tróodos Mountains, where an intensive programme of re-afforestation has been under way since 1982. Measures to limit the danger of forest fires include the installation of forest telephones for emergency calls and the formation of special firefighting forces. Forest reserves and national parks such as the one at Kyrenia (Girne) also contribute to the protection of the island's forests.

Species of trees

Almost 90% of Cyprus's forests consist of Aleppo pines, which grow at lower altitudes. Above 1200m/3900ft the black pine, sometimes bizarrely shaped, is found. The native forest of the Tróodos range also includes cypresses, oaks and cedars, and in the foothills there are eucalyptus and olive-trees. Thanks to the island's mild climate apples, cherries, pears, almonds and walnuts can be grown up to a height of 1200m/3900ft. The annual show of cherry-blossom in the little town of Pedhoulás, to the north of Plátres, has given rise to a regular festival.

Vegetation in the plains

In the plains, in addition to the trees growing in the foothills of the main ranges, there are carob-trees, laurels, vines, citrus fruits and bananas. Grain and vegetables are grown in the Mesaória plain and in the coastal regions. Large areas of the island are covered with dark green macchia, a scrub of spiny bushes and shrubs.

Tróodos Mountains: black pines . . .   *. . . and Star of Bethlehem (May/June)*

Moufflon (wild sheep) – now a protected species

An adder: a reptile long superstitiously feared

Fauna

Moufflon

The fauna of Cyprus shows a much smaller range of species than its flora. Its best known animal, now a protected species, is the moufflon (Greek *agrinon*), a shy mountain sheep distinguished by the powerful curving horns of the male. These agile creatures, good climbers, live in small numbers in the Tróodos Mountains, but are rarely to be seen in the wild. The island's stock of moufflon, which numbered many thousands in ancient times, was decimated in the Middle Ages, when Cyprus was held by the French Lusignan dynasty, and more recently by British sportsmen. Nowadays visitors are likely to see them only in the moufflon enclosure at the Stavrós tis Psókas forestry station (north-west of Cedar Valley), at Platánia (near Kakopetriá) and in Limassol's small zoo.

A stylised moufflon is the emblem of Cyprus Airways.

Other animals

Accounts by medieval travellers refer to leopards, deer and wild asses, but these have long since been exterminated. Domestic animals such as donkeys, sheep, goats and cats, however, are to be seen all over Cyprus.

In the forests of Cyprus there are numerous small animals including hares, rabbits, foxes, squirrels and weasels. Reptiles include lizards, chameleons, turtles and two much dreaded poisonous snakes, the *koúfi* (green, with black spots) and the adder. When walking in the country, therefore, it is advisable to have stout footwear in case you happen to tread on a snake.

Birds

Cyprus's 300 species of birds include partridges, Cetti's warblers, wild pigeons and great tits. Birds of prey including falcons, vultures and imperial eagles are found in the hills. In marshy regions there are herons and snipe.

Cyprus is also a staging-point for large numbers of migrant birds on their journeys between three continents. Up to a thousand flamingos winter on the salt lakes of Lárnaca and Akrotíri; coming from the Caspian Sea, they spend the winter months until March in the mild climate of Cyprus.

National parks, national forest parks and nature reserves

The only national park of the Greek southern part of the island is the recently-established Athalasa Park. However, the Akámas peninsula and Stavrós tis Psókas at the western end of the island may shortly be assigned national park status. Meanwhile, some forest areas have been designated national forest parks and nature reserves for the protection of wildlife.

Population

Numbers and density

Of Cyprus's population of 722,800 (1994) 78% are Greek and 18% Turkish; the remaining 4% is made up of Armenian, Maronite, Latin and British minorities. The southern part of the island has a population of 556,000 (75 inhabitants to the sq. kilometre or 194 to the sq. mile), the Turkish-occupied northern part 160,000 (48 to the sq. kilometre or 124 to the sq. mile). These figures do not include 17,000 British troops stationed in the sovereign bases at Akrotíri and Dhekélia, 1300 United Nations soldiers, a few thousand refugees from Lebanon in the south and Turkish troops in the occupied northern part of the island (some 35,000 according to official Greek estimates).

The movement of refugees and the separation of the Greek and Turkish communities in 1974 led to over-population in the southern part of the island and under-population in the northern part – later made good by the bringing in of an estimated 70,000 Turks from mainland Turkey (Anatolia). Some 1600 Greeks who were unable to get out of the Turkish-occupied areas are still unaccounted for.

Population movements since 1974

Since the 1974 invasion the Turkish Cypriot population has steadily fallen, some 70,000 people having left the country because of the desperate economic situation.

In the Greek southern part of the island the influx of refugees made it necessary to establish refugee camps and organise other accommodation in great haste, and refugees from the occupied areas still enjoy special government assistance, including in some cases rent-free accommodation. Considerable numbers of Cypriots emigrated to the United States, Canada and Australia – mainly Turkish Cypriots who did not like the new political situation.

The large numbers of unemployed in the Greek part of the island in the first few years after partition were soon absorbed by the considerable investment in building projects and the gradually reviving tourist trade. Turkish refugees in the north found plenty of accommodation available in houses abandoned by Greeks who had fled to the south.

In spite of the separation of the two communities since 1974 there are still Greeks and Turks who have stayed in their old homes. Thus on the Karpasía peninsula in North Cyprus there are still some 550 Greeks (with another 220 on Kyrenia), mainly old, who are able with the agreement of the Turkish administration to visit their relatives in the southern part of the island. In the Greek part of the island, in the little frontier village of Pýla near Lárnaca, some 300 Turks live in peace with their Greek neighbours. The UN peace-keeping forces look after the interests of these minorities.

Greek/Turkish co-existence

The two official languages of Cyprus are Greek and Turkish; and since the British colonial period English has been the language of culture and commerce in both parts of the island, spoken fluently by most of the Greek and many of the Turkish Cypriots.

Language

Almost half the population live in the towns of Nicosia, Limassol, Lárnaca, Páphos, Famagusta and Kyrenia. The largest concentrations of population are in the Mesaória plain and in and around Limassol. The economic prosperity of the towns has led to an increasing flight from the land. This has not, however, endangered the old-established Cypriot family traditions. In spite of increasing urbanisation and the beginnings of female emancipation the male head of the family is still, among both Greeks and Turks, the focal point of the Cypriot sense of community.

Urbanisation

Religion

Orthodox Church

The religious allegiance of the Cypriot population matches their ethnic composition, with some 73% belonging to the Greek Orthodox faith.

Beginnings of Christianity

Religion

Orthodox priest

Young man in traditional costume

Cyprus can claim to be one of the world's oldest Christian countries, for the apostles Paul and Barnabas preached Christianity here as early as the year 46. It was only at the end of the 4th century, however, under Byzantine rule, that Christianity became firmly established on the island. The old pagan temples, destroyed in violent earthquakes, were replaced in the course of the century by Christian basilicas (for example at Sálamis and Páphos).

In the early years of Christianity the Orthodox church consisted of the five patriarchates of Rome, Jerusalem, Constantinople, Alexandria and Antioch. Cyprus belonged to the patriarchate of Antioch, but sought from an early stage to become independent of Antioch.

Autocephaly of the Cypriot church

In the year 477 Anthemios, Archbishop of Cyprus, saw in a vision the tomb of the apostle Barnabas, and duly discovered a tomb containing the saint's remains near Sálamis. The apostle was found to be holding in his hand a manuscript of the Gospel of St Matthew. This enabled the Cypriot church to prove that it was an apostolic foundation, and a synod held in 478 recognised the autocephaly (i.e. the independence, with the power to appoint its own head) of the Cypriot church. This first autocephalous church was followed by others – in the 7th century the Georgian church, in the 10th century the Bulgarian church, and thereafter the Russian, Serbian and Romanian churches. The Greek church became independent only in 1850.

The grant of autocephaly gave the Archbishop of Cyprus the right to wear purple robes on feast days, to sign documents in red ink and to carry a sceptre.

Development

The independent Cypriot church was little affected by the Great Schism of 1054, the split between the western and eastern churches.

The Mother of God with the Child: an icon from Troodhítissa Monastery ▶

Religion

In the Middle Ages Cyprus was ruled by a French noble family, the Lusignans, who declared the Roman Catholic faith to be the state religion, oppressed Orthodox believers and confiscated church property.

The Orthodox church recovered its ancient rights only under Ottoman rule. The Archbishop of Cyprus now became the official representative of the Cypriot people and gained increased political influence.

Between 1960 and 1977 Cyprus was the only state apart from the Vatican to be ruled by a prince of the church, Archbishop Makarios III.

Priests

In the Orthodox church the ordinary priests may be married provided that they have taken a wife before being ordained; they are, however, excluded from higher office in the church. Bishops, like monks, are celibate.

Islam

General

Some 22% of the population of Cyprus – living predominantly in the Turkish-occupied part of the island – are Muslims. The first Muslims came to the island when it was conquered by the Turkish Pasha Lala Mustafa in 1571.

The Muslims of Cyprus are Sunnites, who, unlike the Shiites, recognise the first four Caliphs and accept the authority, in addition to the Koran, of the Sunnah, a collection of Mohammed's sayings compiled in the 9th century.

Muslim duties

The five "pillars" of Islam laid down by Mohammed are the five duties of the Muslim: to believe in Allah as the one God and Mohammed as his Prophet, to pray five times daily, to give alms, to fast for forty days in Ramadan and to make the pilgrimage to Mecca if his health and his means permit.

The main source of the Muslim faith is the Koran, which consists of 115 suras (chapters). The consumption of pork, alcohol and drugs is prohibited to Muslims, as is gambling. The head of the Cypriot Muslim community is the Mufti, a man learned in Islamic law.

The mosque

The Muslim place of worship is the mosque, from the minaret of which the muezzin issues the call to prayer five times daily. Before entering the mosque believers must take off their shoes and perform a ritual purification. In Muslim belief water is Allah's highest gift to man, and accordingly in front of every mosque there is an ablutions fountain at which worshippers wash their face, hands, forearms and feet.

Inside the mosque is a mihrab (prayer niche) marking the direction of Mecca, and close to it is the minbar, the pulpit from which the imam leads the prayers.

Other Denominations

Armenian church

Armenian Christians from Eastern Anatolia and Cilicia came to Cyprus in successive waves of refugees from the 6th century onwards. There are now some 5000 Armenians on the island.

The head of the Armenian church, which looks back to St Gregory the Enlightener as the founder of Christianity in Armenia, is the Katholikos, whose seat is in the Armenian town of Etchmiadzin. The Armenians differ from the Roman Catholic and Orthodox churches in ascribing a divine, but not a human nature to Christ. The head of the Armenian community in Cyprus (now exclusively in the southern part of the island), which has its own schools and other organisations, is a bishop with his seat in Nicosia.

There are some 4000 Greek-speaking Maronites – a sect which originally came from Lebanon – on Cyprus, including small numbers in the Turkish-occupied north of the island. The Maronites maintain a close relationship with the Roman Catholic church and recognise the Pope as supreme head of the Church. The founder of the Maronite community was St Maro, who founded a monastery on the river Orontes in the 5th century. The first Maronites came to Cyprus in the 9th century, and in the Middle Ages there were 80,000 of them on the island. The head of the Maronite community in Cyprus is a bishop, whose church is in the Greek part of Nicosia, near the line of partition.

Maronite church

There are also small Roman Catholic and Anglican minorities with their own churches.

Others

Government and Society

The independent Republic of Cyprus was established in 1960. The Turkish intervention of 1974 led to the division of the island into the (Greek) Republic of Cyprus and the "Turkish Republic of Northern Cyprus", which is not recognised internationally and is still occupied by Turkish military forces. The Republic of Cyprus is recognised as the sole legitimate representative of the whole of Cyprus, although since 1974 it has, *de facto*, administered only the Greek-speaking southern part of the island.

South Cyprus

The Republic of Cyprus is a presidential democracy based on the Constitution of 1960. It is a non-aligned state, a member of the United Nations and of the Council of Europe. It is also associated with the (former British) Commonwealth and the European Union.

Government

The national flag of Cyprus, with a gold outline of the island on a white ground, symbolises its non-aligned status. The two crossed olive-branches below the island symbolise the striving for peace of the Cypriots, who have had from time immemorial to defend themselves against the expansionist urges of other peoples.

Flag

The coat of arms adopted in 1960 shows a white dove carrying a sprig of olive surrounded by an olive-branch, symbolising the desire for the peaceful co-existence of Cypriot Turks and Greeks.

Coat of arms

As its national anthem Cyprus adopted the Greek national anthem. The music was composed in 1828 by Nikolaos Mantzaros (1795–1872). The words (beginning "Se gnorízo apó tin kópsi tou spathioú", "I recognise you by the cut of your sword") come from the "Hymn to Freedom" by Dionysos Solomos (1798–1857), the first major Greek lyric poet of modern times.

National anthem

The President of the Republic of Cyprus (at present the conservative Glafkos Klerides, who succeeded the non-party Yeoryios Vasiliou in 1993) is directly elected by the population for a five-year term. He appoints and presides over the Cabinet, which consists of eleven ministers. The office of Vice-President is at present vacant, since under

Government

23

the 1960 constitution it must be held by a representative of the Turkish population.

Parliament

Since 1974 only 56 of the 80 seats in the House of Representatives have been occupied, since under the constitution 24 of them are reserved for representatives of the Turkish community. Representatives are elected every five years.

At present the following parties are represented in the House of Representatives:

DISY: the Democratic Assembly, a conservative party (Glafkos Klerides);

DIKO: the Democratic Party, a party of the centre (Spyros Kyprianou);

AKEL: the Communist Progressive Party (Dimitris Christofias); and

EDEK, the Democratic Union, a liberal socialist party (Vassos Lyssaridis).

Armed forces

All male citizens are liable for military service, which lasts 26 months. In 1986 the Greek Cypriot National Guard had a strength of 13,000, and in addition there were 3000 armed police officers. Since 1964 a UN peace-keeping force formed from troops of seven countries has been stationed on Cyprus. Originally numbering more than 6000, it has now been reduced to some 2000 men. The force (UNFICYP, United Nations Force in Cyprus), the members of which serve for six months at a time, controls the demarcation line between the two parts of the island (representing about 3% of the area of the country). Since the cost of stationing the peace-keeping forces on Cyprus is borne not by the UN but mainly by the countries concerned (Britain, Canada, Austria and Denmark), the gradual withdrawal of the blue-helmeted troops has begun.

There are also two British sovereign bases at Akrotíri and Dhekélia.

Town Hall, Nicosia

Social and Health Services

The social insurance system covers almost all employed persons and provides unemployment, health, pregnancy and accident insurance, old age and widows' pensions and disability insurance. It is financed mainly by contributions from employers and employed persons amounting to 15.5% of gross wages – 6% each from employers and employed persons and 3.5% from the state.

Social insurance

The social welfare service is concerned with the care of children, young people and families.

The health services have been considerably developed since 1986. In addition to municipal hospitals (general hospitals) in all the larger towns there are health centres in rural areas (all providing treatment free of charge) as well as private institutions, mostly specialist clinics, in which there are charges for treatment. The Mining Institute runs its own hospitals. Since there is no medical school in Cyprus all the island's doctors have been trained in other countries.

Hospitals

Education

There is an obligatory nine-year period of schooling. Six years in primary school (*dimotikon skholion*) are followed by three years of general education in a secondary school (*gymnasion*), after which pupils can go on to a "lyceum" (*lykion*) or vocational school. The lyceum provides specialist training, with both compulsory and optional subjects. After successful completion of a course at a vocational school, which 80% of all children take, pupils are entitled to go on to higher education.

Schools

In the last two years of primary school English is a compulsory subject.

The school system is controlled by the Ministry of Education. Schoolbooks and curricula come from Greece, but the system shows marked British influence.

There are the following specialised training establishments: hotel school, child care school, agricultural college, forestry college.

Vocational schools

25

Higher education
The foundation of a Pan-Cypriot university which had been under discussion for many years was for long frustrated by the division of the island, but at last a university on the British model, open equally to Greeks and Turks, was established at the end of 1992, headed by Nelly Tsouyopoulos (a philosopher, formerly a lecturer at Münster University). It has at present a teaching staff of 80 and 500 students; the largest faculty is arts (Greek, Turkish, sociology, education), followed by science and economics. Previously students had to go to universities in other countries. The most popular foreign universities are in Greece, Britain and increasingly in recent years Germany.

Cyprus has two teachers' training colleges and a college of technology with faculties of electrical engineering, building and graphic art.

Mass Media

Newspapers and periodicals
The 1960 constitution guarantees the freedom of the press, subject to possible restrictions in exceptional cases. Cyprus has eleven daily newspapers, ten in Greek and one in English, the "Cyprus Mail". The Greek dailies with the largest circulations are the "Philephtero", the "Apogevmatini" and the "Haravgi".

There are also eighteen weeklies, including the English-language "Cyprus Weekly", and nineteen magazines. "Cyprus Time Out", a tourist and shopping guide, is published monthly.

Radio and television
The Cyprus Broadcasting Corporation (CyBC), founded in 1952, transmits radio programmes in Greek, Turkish and English and also has two Greek and Turkish television channels. The directors of the CyBC are appointed by the government. British forces stationed in Cyprus have their own broadcasting system, the British Forces Broadcasting Service (BFBS), which is on the air daily throughout the 24 hours.

North Cyprus

Government

General
A year after the Turkish invasion of 1974 Rauf Denktash (Denktas), spokesman for the Turkish Cypriot community, declared the Turkish-occupied territories to be the Turkish Federal State of Cyprus. On November 15th 1983 he proclaimed the Turkish Republic of Northern Cyprus (Kuzey Kıbrıs Türk Cumhuriyeti, KKTC), and in 1985 amended the constitution introduced only ten years before. For postal purposes North Cyprus is part of the Turkish town of Mersin.

Flag
The Turkish Cypriot flag, following the model of the Turkish flag, has a red crescent and star between two red bands on a white ground.

Coat of arms
Like the Greek Cypriot arms, the Turkish Cypriot coat of arms has a white dove holding a sprig of olive in its beak, surrounded by an olive-branch, with the addition of a red crescent and star and the date 1983 (the year of foundation of the Turkish Republic of Northern Cyprus).

National anthem
The Turkish Republic of Northern Cyprus adopted the Turkish national anthem, "Istiklal Marşı" ("Independence March"). The tune was composed by Ali Rifat Çağatay, the

words by Lof Ersoy. The anthem begins "Korkma sönmez bu safak" ("Fear not, be not afraid").

The self-appointed and internationally not recognised President of the Turkish-occupied part of the island since 1976 has been Rauf Denktash, who has been re-elected every five years (most recently in 1990) with an overwhelming majority. He has power to call a general election, to impose martial law and to declare a state of emergency. The President appoints the Prime Minister (at present Derviş Eroğlu), and the President and Prime Minister together appoint the ten members of the Cabinet.

Government

The Parliament of North Cyprus, which met for the first time in 1985, is elected for a five-year term. The following four parties are at present represented in it:

Parliament

UBP: the Party of National Unity (conservative), founded by Rauf Denktash in 1975 (chairman Derviş Eroğlu);
CTP: the Turkish Republican Party, the main opposition party (left-wing; chairman Özker Özgür);
TKP: the Communal Liberation Party (centre left; chairman Ismail Bozkurt); and
YDP: the Party of Rebirth (liberal; chairman Colonel Aytaç Besesler).

The Kıbrıs Türk Işçi Sendikaları Federasyonu, a large trade union founded in 1954, has 15,000 members. Fifteen other trade unions are affiliated to it.

Trade union

Turkish Cypriots are subject to a two-year period of military service. In addition there are some 35,000 Turkish troops from mainland Turkey stationed in the northern part of the island. As in the Greek part of the island, there are UN peace-keeping forces watching over peace and security.

Armed forces

Social and Health Services

All employed persons are covered by social security, most of the insurance contributions being paid by employers. In the larger towns there are social service offices and kindergartens.

Health services fall far short of those in the Greek part of the island. There are two large government hospitals, two district hospitals and a psychiatric clinic, as well as national health centres and a number of private establishments. The doctors have all been trained abroad, mostly at British and Turkish universities.

Education

There is an obligatory nine-year period of schooling. In the primary school (six years) and secondary school (three years) education is free. Thereafter pupils can go on to three years of further education in a "lyceum", technical school or vocational school (nursing, midwifery, agriculture, hotel management, etc.).

Schools

In addition to a teachers' training college and a college of technology North Cyprus has two so-called "universities" – the Eastern Mediterranean University in Famagusta, founded in 1986, with faculties of engineering and electrical engineering, and a branch of the University of Anatolia, with departments of administration and economics. There

Higher education

View over the "Green Line" into North Nicosia

is also the University College of North Cyprus, an expensive private institution teaching administration and languages. Most students, however, go to foreign universities, mainly in Turkey, Britain and the United States.

Economy

From independence to partition	When Cyprus became independent in 1960 it was a mainly agricultural country, with just under 50% of the population working on the land. The economy, dependent on foreign trade, was backward, and the widespread unemployment led to mass emigration. In order to make good the country's major structural deficiencies – limited mineral and other natural resources, flight of capital – the government sought to promote entrepreneurial initiatives in a series of five-year plans. As a result the growth rate of the economy rose to 7% between 1960 and 1973 (1994: 3.7%). Agricultural production was doubled, there was a threefold increase in industrial production and tourism became the largest earner of foreign currency. Over half of the country's exports went to the countries of the European Union (mainly agricultural produce).
The Turkish invasion and its consequences	The Turkish invasion of northern Cyprus (38% of the island's area) in 1974 brought a previously flourishing economy to a standstill. The Turks now occupied the best agricultural areas – much of the Mesaória plain, the main wheat-, barley- and potato-growing area, which before partition produced almost 80% of the island's grain, and Mórphou Bay, still the principal area for the growing of citrus fruits and other fruit and vegetables.

Some 70% of the island's total economic potential was in the occupied territory: the principal tourist centres, Famagusta and Kyrenia, and most of the industrial installations. Famagusta, Cyprus's largest port, was now closed to the Greek Cypriots. In mid 1994 it was decided that goods from North Cyprus could only be imported into EU countries if they had export documents from the Republic of Cyprus. This amounts to a virtual economic embargo.

South Cyprus

The Republic of Cyprus made a rapid economic recovery after the Turkish invasion of 1974: so much so that it has been termed an "economic miracle".

The "economic miracle"

In the early years after partition the unemployment rate rose to 35% as a result of the huge influx of refugees, and war damage was estimated at something like a billion pounds sterling. By 1980, however, the economic situation had stabilised; by 1985 inflation had been brought down to 5.5% (falling still further to 3% in 1989); and by 1986 the unemployment rate was down to 3.5%. The Republic of Cyprus now enjoys a relatively high level of prosperity, and foreign currency earnings are rising steadily.

Financial support from the West made a major contribution to this recovery, and an additional boost was given to the economy when the war in Lebanon brought wealthy Lebanese businessmen and firms to Cyprus. Agricultural production was intensified; additional land was brought into cultivation and new factories processing agricultural produce were established. Foreign firms were attracted by tax concessions, and the establishment of new industries was promoted by government assistance. A new airport was built at Lárnaca and the port of Limassol was enlarged and developed to make up for the loss of Famagusta to the Turks.

Agriculture, Forestry and Fisheries

Just under 20% of the Greek Cypriot population work in agriculture, forestry and fisheries, compared with 25% in Greece. New agricultural centres have been created and the cultivation of agricultural produce has been intensified in the coastal plains between Lárnaca and Pólis. The main crops in these areas are groundnuts, bananas, almonds, olives, potatoes (with two harvests a year), vegetables, carob beans, tobacco and wine. The Tróodcs area produces abundant crops of apples, pears, cherries and almonds. Other crops such as sugar-cane (which has been grown in Cyprus since the Middle Ages), cotton and silk are now of only subordinate importance.

Agriculture

The most important crops are wine, vegetables, potatoes and olives. South Cyprus now has over 90% of the island's wine-growing areas, 80% of the area devoted to vegetables and 74% of the area producing olives and potatoes.

The principal exports are fruit, potatoes, vegetables, wine and tobacco. The main customers are the countries of the European Union, the former Soviet Union and the Arab countries.

The most important types of livestock are sheep and goats. There are something like 900,000 fat-tailed sheep in Cyprus, reared both for their meat and their wool. There are now practically no cattle as a result of the increasing conversion of pasturage to arable land. Poultry-farming is also of importance, and fowls and eggs are exported.

Stock-farming

In antiquity Cyprus was one of the most densely wooded countries in the Mediterranean area, but over the centuries the island's forests have been decimated by the felling of timber for the construction of ships

Forestry

29

Silkworm culture – an important element in the economy in medieval times

Orange tree

Lemons

and houses, mining, forest fires and over-grazing. Only about a fifth of the island's area is now covered by forests. The most important species are pines and cypresses. In 1984 some 80,000cu.m/105,000cu.yd of timber were felled, including 71,000cu.m/93,000cu.yd of softwood. Most of it was utilisable timber, only a third being used as firewood (which is now increasingly being imported in order to preserve the country's timber resources).

The fisheries of Cyprus are under-developed, since unfavourable environmental conditions and the intervention of man have hindered the growth of fish stocks. In 1983 the total catch was only 2058 tonnes (84% sea fish, 2% freshwater fish and 14% molluscs and crustaceans). Efforts are now being made to promote the freshwater fisheries by the development of trout and carp farms.

Fisheries

Mining, Water Supplies, Energy

Cyprus's mineral resources are now largely exhausted. The rich deposits of copper which were worked in ancient times are now recalled only by the island's name (*kypros* = "copper"). In the early years of the 20th century the British authorities tried to revive the copper-mining industry, but with little success; the last copper-mine closed down in 1980 after many years of uneconomic working.

Minerals

Until recently asbestos was mined by opencast methods at Amíandos, north-east of the hill town of Tróodos. Small quantities of chromium are still worked near Mt Ólympos. At Pólis, in north-western Cyprus, there is also some small-scale mining of sulphur, iron pyrites and iron ore. The various minerals are almost exclusively exported.

The supply of water has from time immemorial been one of the central problems of Cypriot agriculture. The difficulty is not a shortage of water but the uneven distribution of rain over the year. The loss of large areas of irrigated land in the Mesaória plain after the Turkish invasion still further aggravated the situation.

Water supply

The construction of reservoirs to store rainwater and snow-melt water in spring had begun before 1974, and the irrigation projects which they made possible have increased the yield of important agricultural products. The Páphos irrigation scheme, completed in 1983, provides irrigation for 5000 hectares (12,500 acres) of land in the south-western coastal region. The Vasilikos–Pendaskinos scheme, completed in 1987, with two dams at Léfkara and Kalavasós, has the capacity to irrigate 2200 hectares (5500 acres). One of the most important projects is the Southern Supply Scheme, work on which began in 1984. Under this scheme the water of three rivers will be held back by the Koúrris Dam and conveyed in a 110km/68 mile long pipeline to the towns on the coast, as well as irrigating 7200 hectares (18,000 acres) of arable land. The Akhna Dam will provide irrigation for the area around Ayía Nápa.

Irrigation projects

Since Cyprus has no rivers flowing throughout the year there is no possibility of generating hydro-electric power, and energy production therefore depends on the import of oil from the Middle Eastern countries. There is a large oil refinery near Lárnaca.

Energy

Cyprus has two power stations, run by the semi-state-owned Electricity Authority (established 1952), which also supplies power free to Turkish-occupied North Cyprus. The Moní station at Limassol has a capacity of 180 megawatts; the Dhekélia station near Lárnaca has a capacity of 84 megawatts in the old station and 120 megawatts in the new one.

A further source of power is solar energy, though this is used only in the private sector. Many households now get their supplies of hot water from solar heating installations.

Windmills at Ayía Nápa

Industry

General

Some 28% of the population work in the manufacturing industry, which since 1978 has overtaken agricultural production. In the 1960s only about 15% of the population were employed in industry: a figure which has been almost doubled since then, largely due to government measures to promote the development of industry. Increasing numbers of foreign firms have been attracted to Cyprus by tax concessions and relatively low wage levels; and since the great majority of firms in Cyprus are small and medium-sized government planning has made a useful contribution to the development of the country's economic life.

Industrial centres

Almost 50% of manufacturing firms are in and around Nicosia, and around 25% in the Limassol district. Nicosia is the centre for shoe manufacture, textiles, papermaking and chemical industries, Limassol for cement manufacture and the production of soft drinks. The main industries in the Páphos district are textiles and clothing.

Important branches of industry

The leading branch of industry, employing 30% of the industrial labour force, is textile production, which has been intensively promoted with the help of modern technology – though most of the raw materials have to be imported. The principal customers are Libya, Britain and Germany. In second place are the foodstuffs and tobacco industries, followed by building and civil engineering, which enjoyed a great boom after 1974, when large numbers of new dwellings had to be built for refugees.

Offshore companies

Since 1975 the Central Bank of Cyprus has issued more than 5500 licences for offshore companies (that is, businesses which operate and earn income outside Cyprus), and more than 700 such companies have been established in Cyprus. They include Western European, American and Arab companies in the fields of commerce, sales, shipping, banking, insurance and culture (press agencies). The government took this initiative after the partition of the island in order to prevent the emigration of highly qualified staff, of which there were above-average numbers in Cyprus.

Foreign companies were attracted by the offer of tax incentives, their net profit being taxed at the rate of only 4.25%. In addition foreign employees of offshore companies pay only half the normal rates of income tax and benefit from generous currency and customs regulations. Firms managed outside Cyprus pay no tax at all. The Central Bank guarantees complete confidentiality on the management and accounts of offshore firms, which has led to occasional criticisms that this facilitates the laundering of illicitly acquired money.

Thanks to its ideal geographical situation at the meeting-place of three continents and to its links with the Middle East, Eastern Europe and the European Union, Cyprus is on the way to becoming an important financial and commercial centre. The growth of this new branch of the economy is also promoted by the high educational level of the population and the country's modern telecommunications system.

Cyprus as a financial and commercial centre

Transport

South Cyprus has some 5000km/3100 miles of surfaced roads and 6000km/3700 miles of unsurfaced roads. The Turkish invasion of 1974 had a devastating effect on the island's road network. Since then important traffic arteries such as the Nicosia–Lárnaca and Nicosia–Astromerítis roads have had to be re-routed to avoid Turkish-occupied territory. Other important projects are the new Nicosia–Limassol and Nicosia–Lárnaca motorways; and a new stretch between Limassol and Páphos is under construction. There are still, however, considerable

Roads

A cruise ship in the eastern Mediterranean

33

numbers of dusty unsurfaced roads, particularly in the Tróodos Mountains, and drivers in these areas should allow plenty of time for their journeys.

Railways

There are no railways on the island.

Air services

Since the closing down of Nicosia's international airport in 1974 new international airports have been brought into operation at Lárnaca and Páphos (in 1983). Over thirty airlines now fly to Cyprus from Europe, Africa, the Middle East and the Gulf region. Increasing air traffic has forced the Government to agree to extend Lárnaca airport. A new terminal building is planned for completion in 2026 to tackle the problem.

Shipping

Soon after 1974 the ports of Lárnaca and Limassol were able to make good the loss of Famagusta. Thanks to Cyprus's increasing importance as an entrepôt for more than a hundred shipping lines sailing between three continents it now takes sixth place among the world's shipping nations. The transition from traditional methods of handling freight to the container system began in the late seventies, and the new container terminals now under construction in Limassol freeport are designed to handle the newest generation of cargo vessels. Lárnaca freeport has facilities for the overhaul and servicing of heavy equipment used in the oil industry of the Near and Middle East.

Cruises in the eastern Mediterranean are run by Louis Cruise Lines, 158 Roosevelt Avenue, Limassol.

Ferry services: see Practical Information, Map p. 311.

Tourism

A predominant position in the Cypriot economy is occupied by the services sector, in which some 40% of the working population are employed. From the early days of independence the government gave particular attention to the development of the tourist trade. In spite of the loss of 65% of the island's bed capacity in the Turkish-occupied towns of Famagusta and Kyrenia tourism quickly recovered and enjoyed a fresh period of prosperity only a few years after partition.

Tourist
infrastructure

New hotel developments mushroomed in the coastal towns of Limassol and Lárnaca, providing employment for the thousands of refugees. Just under a fifth of the employed population now work in the tourist trade, which accounts for some 40% of the country's total earnings of foreign currency. In 1994 2 million holidaymakers and business travellers visited Cyprus. The high standard of service provided is illustrated by the fact that 65% of visitors come back again.

A third of all visitors come from Britain, followed by Lebanese (14%), Scandinavians and Germans. Some 90% of visitors come for a seaside holiday, the remainder for the island's cultural attractions. The most popular destination for sun-lovers is Ayía Nápa, in the south-east of the country. The large tourist centres offer visitors not only beautiful beaches but large and comfortable hotels, discothèques, night clubs and bouzouki bars. Cyprus's season lasts throughout the year, for the mild winter months (when prices are particularly reasonable) attract many visitors.

Cyprus Tourism
Organisation
(CTO)

The body responsible for the promotion of tourism in Cyprus is the Cyprus Tourism Organisation (CTO), which runs ten tourist information offices throughout the country. The CTO fixes the categories and tariffs of hotels, and in 1989 imposed a ban on new hotel building in order to avoid further encroachment on the natural landscape. Increased attention has been given to the promotion of hotels in the higher price categories, the winter holiday trade and incentive and business tourism in order to avoid the development of mass tourism. Recently the rehabilitation of old Tróodos villages has been promoted by government subsidies in order to attract visitors away from the built-up coastal areas. The establishment of new guest houses and the preservation of village structures provide jobs and thus counteract the continuing flight from the land.

North Cyprus

After the Turkish intervention in 1974 the economic situation of North Cyprus was no less catastrophic than that of the southern part of the island. Although the north had the best agricultural land, the most interesting tourist centres and many industrial plants the departure of some 200,000 Greek Cypriots left it seriously under-populated.

General

In addition North Cyprus lacked the skilled workers needed in the factories and tourist facilities. In the years before the Turkish invasion the Turkish Cypriot population – mostly peasants, shopkeepers and craftsmen – had lived apart from the Greek population in their own enclaves and were thus frequently excluded from the country's prosperity and economic progress.

Lack of skilled workers

After the partition of the island some 70% of its economic potential was in Turkish hands, and the villages abandoned by Greek Cypriots were reoccupied by 70,000 peasants from Anatolia, whose educational level was far below that of the Turkish Cypriots.

Since Turkish-occupied North Cyprus was boycotted by nations throughout the world, international markets were closed to the new Turkish state. Its economy has still not recovered, and it could not survive without massive support from Turkey.

Economic boycott

Just under 40% of the population (compared with 35% in mainland Turkey) are employed in agriculture, and three-quarters of the country's area is under cultivation; but agriculture contributes only 20% of the gross domestic product.

Agriculture

The main agricultural crops are citrus fruits (Mórphou Bay), grain and potatoes (Mesaória plain) and tobacco (Karpasía peninsula). 72% of the island's total citrus fruit and tobacco growing areas are in North Cyprus. Vegetables, carob-nuts, fruit and walnuts are mainly grown for domestic consumption. Wine production (Pentadáktylos Hills and Karpasía peninsula) is of only minor importance.

Among the principal exports are citrus fruits, tobacco, vegetables and carob-nuts. The main customers are Turkey, Britain and Germany.

North Cyprus has limited water resources, with only a quarter of the island's springs. In recent years reservoirs have been constructed for the storage of water.

Water supply

Stock-farming brings in a third of the total revenue from agriculture. In addition to sheep and goats there are cattle and poultry. Products such as poultry, eggs and meat are exported.

Stock-farming

Some 18% of the total area of North Cyprus is covered by forest. Aleppo pines and cypresses grow in the Pentadáktylos range. Reafforestation began in 1976.

Forestry

Stocks of fish are low, and accordingly fisheries play a very minor role in the economy. Three-quarters of the fishermen still have small boats suitable only for inshore waters.

Fisheries

Sheep and goats – a common sight in North Cyprus

The harbour of Famagusta, until 1974 the busiest port on the island

Industry provides employment for 16% of the population. Most industrial firms are small, producing consumer goods and electrical appliances. An important branch of industry is textiles, centred in Nicosia. The soft drinks industry has developed in Mórphou Bay. In view of the surplus of housing and industrial accommodation in North Cyprus after partition the construction industry is of only limited importance in the economy.

Industry

The importance of mining also declined after 1974. The large mines at Karavostási/Gemikonağı (Morphoú Bay), which formerly yielded iron ore and pyrites, were closed down by the Cyprus Mines Corporation.

Mining

The only commercial port in North Cyprus – now mainly used by military traffic – is Famagusta. Before partition it was the only port with loading and discharging facilities, handling most of Cyprus's foreign trade.
  Ferry services: see Practical Information, Map p. 311.

Shipping

Tourism has begun to develop again in North Cyprus only in the last few years. The Cyprus Turkish Enterprise, founded in 1975, controls all hotels and private accommodation. After the division of the island North Cyprus was left with 65% of the island's hotel beds, but the development of the tourist trade was inhibited by lack of skilled staff and the international economic boycott. Nowadays 80% of visitors come from mainland Turkey, spending Turkish liras and bringing in no foreign currency. Second place is taken by British visitors, followed by Germans.

Tourism

History

Mythology

The island
of Aphrodite

Cyprus featured in ancient mythology as the island of Aphrodite. The celebrated Rock of Aphrodite, the Pétra tou Romioú, between Páphos and Limassol marks the spot where the goddess of love and fertility, foam-born (*aphros* = "foam"), is supposed to have risen out of the sea. The name Pétra tou Romioú literally means "Rock of the Roman" (the Byzantines, inheritors of the Eastern Roman Empire, referred to themselves as Romaioi, which came simply to mean Greeks).

Archaeological finds at Koúklia, near Páphos, show that this was the site of one of the largest shrines of Aphrodite in antiquity.

Hesiod's account
of the birth
of Aphrodite

The poet Hesiod gives an account in his "Theogony" (155–200) of the birth of Aphrodite off the coast of Cyprus. He tells us that Aphrodite was the daughter of Gaia (the Earth) and Uranos (the Sky), the primal Greek deities who emerged from Chaos (the Void). They had numerous children, the Cyclopes, the Hecatoncheires ("Hundred-Armed") and the Titans. Uranos exiled the Hecatoncheires and the Cyclopes to Tartaros (the Underworld), whereupon Gaia, angered, urged their son Kronos, one of the Titans, to take revenge on his father. Kronos hid in his parents' bedroom, cut off Uranos's testicles with a sickle and threw them into the sea. They were carried by currents to Cyprus, where Aphrodite then rose from the foam. In Hesiod's words:

"And even as he cut off the privy parts with the sickle and hurled them from the mainland into the foaming sea, even so were they borne over the sea for a long time, and from the immortal flesh a white foam arose round it, and therein a maiden grew. And first she came nigh unto holy Kythera, whence next she came to sea-girt Kypros. And she came forth as a fair goddess to be revered by men, and around her the grass grew under her tender feet. Her do gods and men call Aphrodite."
(After the translation by A. W. Mair)

*Aphrodite
(Archaeological
Museum, Nicosia)*

As goddess of beauty, of love, of fertility and of marriage Aphrodite was one of the most revered of the divinities of Olympus. She married the lame god Hephaistos, but did not remain faithful to him.

Oriental origin
of Aphrodite

When the Greeks came to Cyprus about 1000 B.C. they encountered the fertility cult of an Oriental mother goddess, reflecting a matriarchal society. The islanders worshipped the Babylonian love goddess Ishtar, who was identified with the Palestinian and Syrian goddess of fertility and war, Astarte. With the Hellenisation of the island this mother goddess was in turn identified with Aphrodite, the goddess of a patriarchal society.

According to Pausanias (2nd c. A.D.) the first Greek to set foot on the island was King Agapenor of Tegea in Arcadia, who landed in Cyprus on his way back from Troy and founded the first temple of Aphrodite at Páphos.

**Cypriot
legend**

Cypriot legend is closely bound up with the goddess of love, whose myth was blended with historical events.

According to one legend Pygmalion was king of the city state of Amáthous. Aphrodite had laid down a law that all women before being married must yield themselves to a stranger in the goddess's temple: a myth reflecting an old matriarchal tradition of temple prostitution, of which there is evidence in Cyprus. Since this law was not observed Aphrodite punished all women by giving them insatiable sexual desire. Horrified by this, Pygmalion withdrew into solitude and devoted himself to sculpture. He created a marble statue of Aphrodite, with which he then fell desperately in love. Aphrodite took pity on him and breathed life into the statue, creating Galatea, who bore Pygmalion a son called Paphos: hence the name of the town of Páphos.

Pygmalion

Paphos in turn lay with his sister Metharme and had a son named Kinyras, who according to Homer was the first priest-king of the temple of Aphrodite at Páphos.

Kinyras

Apollodoros (2nd c. B.C.) tells the story of Kinyras. His wife claimed to be fairer than Aphrodite, who took her revenge by causing Paphos's daughter Myrrha to form a violent passion for her father. One night, having made him drunk, she crept into his bed. When Paphos realised that he was the father of the child conceived by Myrrha he was about to kill her, but at the last moment Aphrodite transformed her into a myrtle-bush, from which nine months later Adonis was born.

The legends of Paphos, who married his own sister, and Kinyras, whose daughter bore him a son, Adonis, reflect the transition from a matriarchal to a patriarchal society. In a matriarchy royal authority was passed down from woman to woman, and a king could maintain that authority in his family only by marrying his sister or his daughter. The change from matrilinear to patrilinear succession also finds expression in the story of the birth of Aphrodite, born of the sperm of a male divinity.

Transition from a matriarchal to a patriarchal society

Chronology

Prehistory and Protohistory

The first traces of human occupation on Cyprus were found in Neolithic settlements of small round houses at Khirokitía, Sotíra and Kalavasós, dated to the 9th and 8th millennia B.C., in the early Neolithic period. Mainly nomadic hunters, with some sedentary farmers, the occupants came from the Syrian and Mesopotamian region and worshipped the mother goddesses Ishtar and Astarte. The most important object of trade was obsidian from Anatolia.

7000–3000 B.C.

In the Chalcolithic (Copper/Stone Age) copper begins to be worked for the manufacture of jewellery and implements. The existing village communities are fortified and new settlements are established, like Erími to the west of Limassol. An active trade develops with the Near East, Egypt and Phoenicia.

3000–2300 B.C.

In the Early Bronze Age copper is worked on an increasing scale and bronze begins to be produced. The copper-mining areas of Cyprus are densely populated.

The technique of making bronze from copper and tin is brought to Cyprus by immigrants from Anatolia. Evidence of this period is provided by finds at Alámbra (south of Nicosia) and Vounoús (near Bellapais).

2300–1900 B.C.

In the Middle Bronze Age Cyprus has trading contacts with Sicily and Crete: Bronze displaces copper. A large village settlement is established at Enkomi (near Famagusta). Copper and pottery are exported.

1900–1550 B.C.

Chronology

1550–1000 B.C.
The Cypro-Mycenaean syllabic script is evolved about 1500. The process of Hellenisation begins in the Late Bronze Age. From 1400 Mycenaean and Minoan traders visit the island. Around 1000 the Achaeans, fleeing from the advancing Dorians, seek a new home on Cyprus, bringing the patriarchal system. The working of copper brings prosperity to Cyprus. Foundation of the first urban centres at Enkomi, Kítion (Lárnaca), Márion (Pólis) and Tamassós.

1000–709 B.C.
On Cyprus as in the Aegean the Early Iron Age is a "Dark Age". The population declines, as does the working of copper. Iron becomes increasingly important. The first city-kingdoms come into being on the island. Phoenician traders, arriving about 800, establish a kingdom at Kítion, though their interest in Cyprus is purely commercial.

709–663 B.C.
The Assyrians conquer Cyprus. The city-kingdoms survive, but for the next forty years are obliged to pay tribute to Assyria.

663–560 B.C.
The city-kingdoms of Cyprus regain their independence.

560–525 B.C.
Cyprus under Egyptian rule.

525–333 B.C.
Persia gains control of the island, which is obliged to pay tribute. The city states, however, preserve their independence, prosper and enter into rivalry with one another.

499/498 B.C.
During the rebellion of the Ionian Greeks, led by King Onesilos of Sálamis, there is also resistance in Cyprus. Only the city-kingdom of Amáthous remains loyal to the Persians. The rebellion is crushed by the Persians with the help of their Phoenician allies.

478–477 B.C.
A Greek fleet commanded by Pausanias, a Spartan, liberates Cyprus from the Persians. A year later, however, the Persians regain control of the island.

450–449 B.C.
Cyprus is still involved in the conflict between the Greeks and the Persians. It has increasingly close cultural relations with Greece. Kimon of Athens attacks the Persians with a Greek fleet but dies of plague off the coast of Cyprus; the fleet then withdraws.

392–379 B.C.
Euagoras of Sálamis, one of the principal city-kingdoms on the island, conquers the other kingdoms and unifies Cyprus under his rule. Soon afterwards, however, he is defeated by the Persians.

333–331 B.C.
Alexander the Great defeats Darius III's Persian army at Issos in 333; Cyprus is granted independence in 331.

325–294 B.C.
After Alexander's death in 323 Cyprus is involved in the conflict between his successors, the Diadochoi. Ptolemy I and Antigonos fight for control of the Persian empire; both are anxious to secure Cyprus for the sake of its rich resources of copper and timber.
In 310 Zeno of Kítion founds his school of Stoic philosophy in the Stoa in Athens.

294 B.C.
Ptolemy I of Egypt becomes the new ruler of Cyprus. The city-kingdoms lose their political power, and Cyprus is ruled from Alexandria. The island is governed by a strategos (governor), with Páphos as capital. Much building activity.

from 168 B.C.
Rome becomes involved for the first time in the conflicts in the eastern Mediterranean and supports the Ptolemies in their military operations. In return Rome is promised possession of Cyprus.

Cyprus under Roman Rule (58 B.C.–A.D. 395)

Rome gains control of Cyprus. A Roman governor is appointed.	58 B.C.
Cicero is the Roman governor of Cyprus.	51/50 B.C.
After his victory over Pompey Caesar returns the island to Egypt. Cyprus is now ruled by Cleopatra.	47 B.C.
Augustus defeats Antony and Cleopatra in the battle of Actium, and Cyprus returns to Roman control.	31 B.C.
Much building activity; new temples and other buildings erected in Koúrion, Sálamis and other towns.	A.D. 1
The apostles Paul and Barnabas come to Cyprus on their first missionary journey and convert Sergius Paulus, the Roman proconsul.	A.D. 45/46
A large-scale Jewish rising, said to have resulted in over 200,000 dead. The Jews are expelled from Cyprus.	116
St Helen, mother of Constantine the Great, lands in Cyprus on her way back from the Holy Land with the True Cross and founds the monastery of Stavrovouní.	327
The island is devastated by violent earthquakes and famine. The town of Sálamis is rebuilt under the name of Constantia. Basilicas are erected at Páphos, Koúrion and Sálamis on the ruins of ancient buildings.	332–342
Division of the Roman Empire. For the next eight centuries Cyprus is part of the Byzantine Empire.	395

Cyprus under Byzantine Rule (395–1191)

After the finding of the remains of St Barnabas the church of Cyprus is granted autocephaly (independence).	478
Cyprus is ravaged by Arab raids. The first large Arab campaign is launched by Muawiyah in 647–649. During this campaign Hala Sultan, said to be a relative of Mohammed, dies and is commemorated by the Hala Sultan Tekke, a mosque built in her honour. For a time the island is obliged to pay tribute to the Arabs. Constantia is destroyed. The Byzantine Empire is weakened by the iconoclastic conflict between 726 and 843.	7th–10th c.
The Byzantine Emperor Nicephorus Phocas II finally liberates Cyprus from Arab rule.	965
A period of economic prosperity in the Byzantine Empire. Many monasteries are founded in Cyprus; some of them are still in existence (Chrysorroyiátissa, Makherás, St Neóphytos, Kýkko).	10th/11th c.
The fortresses of St Hilarion, Buffavento and Kantara in the Kyrenia Hills are built to provide protection against Arab raids.	
The Great Schism, the final split between the Eastern and Western churches, has both political and religious causes.	1054

Cyprus under the Lusignans (1192–1489)

Cyprus is ruled by the Byzantine general Isaac Comnenus. He breaks away from the Byzantine Empire and reigns in Cyprus *de facto* as an independent Emperor.	1185–91

A 17th-century map of Cyprus

1191	During the third Crusade Richard Coeur de Lion conquers Cyprus on his way to the Holy Land. He marries Berengaria of Navarre in Limassol. Before continuing on his way to the Holy Land he sells Cyprus to the Templars for 100,000 gold bezants.
1192–1489	After a rising against the Templars in 1192 Cyprus is sold to a French noble, Guy de Lusignan. Thereafter, for 300 years, Cyprus is a Frankish kingdom. Roman Catholicism is declared the state religion.
1228	The German Emperor Frederick II lands in Cyprus during the fifth Crusade and tries to seize control of the island. His troops occupy part of Cyprus.
1233	The Lusignans defeat the imperial forces.
1291	With the fall of Acre the last Christian stronghold in the Holy Land is lost. The Knights of St John withdraw to Cyprus (Kolóssi).
1359–69	The Frankish king Peter I is the most brilliant of the Lusignans. During his reign there is much building activity. On his initiative a crusade is launched against Alexandria.
1372–74	A conflict between the Genoese and the Venetians at Peter II's coronation ends in the predominance of Genoa in Cyprus. The Genoese

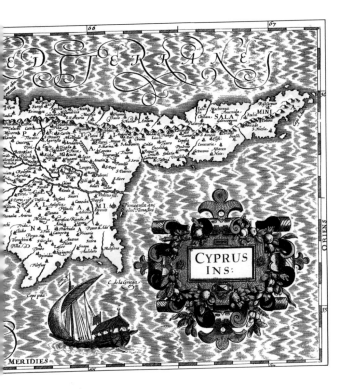

gain control of Famagusta, Páphos and Nicosia and take Peter prisoner; he regains his freedom only on payment of a ransom.

Peace treaty between Peter II and the Genoese; Famagusta remains in Genoese hands. 1374

Egyptian Mamelukes invade Cyprus. Battle of Khirokitía. King Janus is taken prisoner and carried off to Cairo, but is freed on payment of a ransom and an annual tribute. 1426

Constantinople falls to the Turks. 1453

Cyprus under Venetian Rule (1489–1571)

The widow of the last Lusignan king, Caterina Cornaro, hands over Cyprus to the Venetians, who appoint a governor to rule the island. The population is oppressed by high taxation. The Turks invade the Karpasía peninsula. 1489

Egypt falls to the Turks. Cyprus now has to pay its annual tribute to the Turks. 1517

The Turks destroy Limassol. In 1540 the Venetians sign a peace treaty with the Sultan. 1539–40

43

Chronology

<table>
<tr><td>from 1544</td><td>To meet the continuing threat from the Turks the Venetians begin to strengthen the defences of Famagusta, Nicosia and Kyrenia.</td></tr>
<tr><td>1562</td><td>Popular rising against the Venetians, provoked by high taxation and tribute payments. The rebellion is crushed and the ringleaders executed.</td></tr>
<tr><td>1566</td><td>Sultan Suleiman the Magnificent dies and is succeeded by Selim, who shows increased interest in Cyprus.</td></tr>
<tr><td>1570–71</td><td>Conquest of Cyprus by the Turks, led by Mustafa Pasha. The siege of Nicosia begins on July 25th, and after its conquest on November 9th Kyrenia also surrenders. The siege of Famagusta lasts ten months; it surrenders in 1571 and the Venetian commandant, Bragadino, is executed. Cyprus becomes a Turkish province.</td></tr>
</table>

Cyprus under Ottoman Rule (1571–1878)

<table>
<tr><td>1573</td><td>Venice surrenders all rights in the island to Turkey. Orthodox worship is again permitted. Economic and cultural decline. The population suffers from heavy taxation.</td></tr>
<tr><td>from 1660</td><td>The Archbishop of Cyprus is recognised by the Turks as the representative and spokesman of the Greek Cypriots.</td></tr>
<tr><td>1703</td><td>Cyprus becomes a fief of the Turkish Grand Vizier, who auctions it each year to the highest bidder. The tax burden on the population becomes steadily heavier. There are frequent popular risings.</td></tr>
<tr><td>1754</td><td>The Archbishop of Cyprus becomes Ethnarch: that is, leader of the Greek Cypriot community. The Dragoman (originally an interpreter) becomes the intermediary between the Sublime Porte and the Greeks and is also responsible for the collection of taxes.</td></tr>
<tr><td>1821</td><td>Beginning of the Greek war of independence on the mainland. As a deterrent to action by the Cypriots the Turkish governor, Küçük Mehmed, has Archbishop Kyprianos and his supporters executed in Nicosia.</td></tr>
<tr><td>mid-19th c.</td><td>The Turks establish a Council of State which includes the Archbishop and three Greek members as well as Turkish representatives.</td></tr>
</table>

British Colonial Rule (1878–1960)

<table>
<tr><td>1878</td><td>Under a secret agreement between Britain and Turkey the Sultan hands over the administration of Cyprus to Britain, subject to the payment of an annual rent of £92,799. In return Britain guarantees Turkey military protection against the advance of Russian troops in the Balkans. Britain is interested in Cyprus because of its convenient situation on the way to the Suez Canal, which had come into service in 1869 and opened up a new route to India.

The people of Cyprus look forward to an improvement in their political and economic situation under a Christian power with a parliamentary system of government. The return of the Ionian Islands, a British colony, to Greece in 1864 encourages Cypriot confidence in Britain as a power friendly to Greece.

Britain appoints a High Commissioner, with supreme judicial authority, to govern the island. A Cypriot parliament of six British, nine Greek and three Turkish members is established. The health services and the legal system are reformed and the tax system altered in favour of the taxpayers. But Britain shows no sign of being prepared to hand over Cyprus to Greece. This leads to unrest among the Greek population,</td></tr>
</table>

and the call for Enosis (union with Greece) becomes increasingly insistent. Archbishop Sophronios comes out in favour of Enosis and travels to Britain with a delegation to press for it.

When Turkey enters the First World War on the side of Germany Britain annexes Cyprus, and the Turkish inhabitants of the island (who represent some 25% of the population) are declared to be British citizens. 1914

Britain seeks to induce Greece to enter the war on the side of the Allies, offering in return the union of Cyprus with Greece. Because of its military weakness Greece decides not to enter the war. The British offer to return Cyprus to Greece is not thereafter repeated. 1916

Turkey recognises the British annexation of Cyprus, which becomes a Crown Colony. 1925

The British authorities repress widespread riots by supporters of the Enosis movement. Political associations are forbidden, press censorship introduced and the election of an Archbishop prohibited. 1931

Cyprus enters the Second World War on the side of the Allies, which leads to an improvement in the political climate on the island. Britain introduces new measures of democratisation. In 1943 local government elections are again permitted. 1940

Makarios III becomes Archbishop. He raises the question of Enosis (union with Greece) to the international plane and brings it before the United Nations. In a referendum organised by the Orthodox church 96% of Cypriots vote for Enosis. Britain still resists the idea. 1950

Makarios visits the United States, Britain and France, but makes no progress towards achieving Enosis. 1952–53

Britain again rejects the idea of Enosis. Makarios publicly declares his support for it in Troodhitissa monastery. 1954

General Grivas and his EOKA (Epanastatiki Organosis Kypriakou Agonos), an underground movement fighting for Enosis, enters the struggle against British rule, carrying out bomb attacks on leading British figures and institutions. 1955

Makarios and his principal associates are exiled to the Seychelles. 1956
  The Turks step up their opposition to Enosis. As a counterpart to EOKA they found TMT, an organisation for the defence of the rights of the Turkish minority on Cyprus. TMT advocates the division of the island according to ethnic groups.

Makarios returns from exile. Conversations begin on the granting of independence to Cyprus. 1956

Independence (since 1960)

Cyprus becomes an independent Republic, with Archbishop Makarios as President and the Turkish Cypriot leader Fazıl Küçük as Vice-President. The new Cypriot Parliament has 35 Greek and 15 Turkish members. Under the agreed constitution the Vice-President has a right of veto – a provision which was one of the factors in the failure of the young republic. Greece, Turkey and Britain guarantee the sovereignty of Cyprus, which becomes a member of the Commonwealth, the United Nations and the Council of Europe.
  Britain retains two sovereign military bases. The movement for Enosis continues. 1960

A constitutional crisis leads to disturbances. General Grivas founds EOKA/B, a radical right-wing organisation. There are violent clashes 1963

President Makarios driving through Nicosia

between Greeks and Turks. The Turkish representatives leave the government.

The United Nations send a peace-keeping force of over 6000 men to Cyprus. The Turkish population withdraw into Turkish enclaves. Violence between the two population groups continues. — 1964

A military junta led by Yeoryios Papadopoulos seizes power in Greece. Makarios no longer advocates Enosis, and his violent criticism of the Greek junta leads to increasing tension with Greece. He also alienates the United States with his neutralist, pro-Soviet policy. — 1967

After a number of unsuccessful attempts on Makarios's life in the earlier months of the year he is overthrown on July 15th. The Presidential Palace is bombed, but Makarios escapes to Páphos and from there to Britain. Nikos Sampson, a former EOKA fighter noted for his anti-Turkish views, assumes power. — July 15th 1974

Turkish forces land on the north coast of Cyprus and within ten days occupy Kyrenia, part of Nicosia and a strip of land between the two towns. By mid August a third of the island is in Turkish hands. Turkey claims to have intervened for the protection of the Turkish minority. By its intervention it has achieved its objective of separating the population of the island on an ethnic basis. — July 20th 1974

The Greek military junta, which was involved in the failed coup against Makarios, is compelled to resign. In Cyprus there is a panic movement of refugees: some 200,000 Greek Cypriots flee from Turkish-occupied North Cyprus into the southern part of the island, while 45,000 Turks flee from the south into the north. — July 24th 1974

◀ *Monumental statue of Archbishop Makarios III*

47

Cyprus Divided

December 8th 1974	Makarios returns from Britain to Cyprus. He remains President of the Republic, and continues to press for the abolition of the frontier between the two parts of the island, now controlled by UN troops.
June 20th 1975	Rauf Denktash proclaims the "Turkish Federal State of Cyprus", with himself as President. The new state is not recognised by the international community.
1977	Death of Makarios. He is succeeded by Spyros Kyprianou as President and by Chrysostomos as Archbishop.
1983	Rauf Denktash is elected President of the "Turkish Republic of North Cyprus", which is recognised only by Turkey.
1988	Yeoryios Vassiliou becomes President of the Republic of Cyprus and initiates further peace negotiations with Denktash.
1989	Discussions between President Vassiliou and Rauf Denktash under the chairmanship of UN Secretary-General Pérez de Cuellar produce no concrete results.
1990	Further discussions in New York presided over by Pérez de Cuellar also fail to make any progress. The problem is discussed at a summit meeting between the Presidents of the United States and the former Soviet Union. In July the Republic of Cyprus applies for full membership of the European Community. In October the Republic celebrates its 30th anniversary.
1991	The Gulf War has catastrophic effects on the economy of Cyprus, with a steep fall in the number of visitors. A general election is held in the Republic of Cyprus in May. In August Greece and Turkey declare themselves ready to take part in a conference on Cyprus under UN chairmanship.
1992	The first university in Cyprus is opened in Nicosia (South). Under the aegis of Boutros-Ghali, UN Secretary-General, an agreement is reached on a considerable reduction in the Turkish-occupied area, under which the Turks would give up Famagusta and Mórphou and 34 villages near Nicosia. Once again, however, the negotiations collapse.
1993	In a parliamentary election in March the opposition candidate, Glafkos Klerides, leader of the Democratic Assembly (DISY), is elected President.
1994	Measures aimed at restoring confidence are proposed by the UN, of which the most important are the reopening of Nicosia Airport (in the occupied sector) and the return of the former Greek resort of Varosha to the Greek south. Goods from North Cyprus can be imported into the EU only if accompanied by Republic of Cyprus export papers (July).
1995	In April Rauf Denktash, who has held office all this time, is re-elected to the presidency in North Cyprus.
1996	Negotiations on the Republic of Cyprus's entry to the EU are expected to begin.

Cyprus Divided

Island in crisis	Cyprus's geographical situation in the eastern Mediterranean has determined the course of its history from the first settlement of the island 9000 years ago down to the present day. Since the last war Cyprus has been of great strategic importance to NATO, serving as a

large static "aircraft carrier". When the island became independent in 1960 Turkey, Greece and Britain, as guarantor powers, retained the right to intervene if the status of the new republic should be threatened. Britain also had the right, under the London agreement, to maintain two sovereign air and naval bases at Dhekélia and Akrotíri.

The origins of the Cyprus crisis go back to the Ottoman conquest in 1571, when the Turkish general, Lala Mustafa Pasha, settled soldiers of the Ottoman army and peasants from Anatolia on the island. The three hundred years of Turkish rule, however, left undiminished the power of the Orthodox church, which maintained traditions inherited from Byzantine times. From 1754 to 1821, under Ottoman rule, the Archbishop of Cyprus, as Ethnarch, represented the interests of the Greek ethnic group, which made up four-fifths of the total population of the island.

Origins of the conflict

The establishment of an independent state of Greece in 1830 raised for the first time the question of Enosis: that is, the union of all Greek-speaking territories – among them Cyprus – with the Greek motherland.

Enosis

Britain promised the Ottoman Empire military protection against the Russian thrust in the Balkans, and in return the Turks ceded Cyprus to Britain in 1878. In 1925 the island became a British Crown Colony. After the first violent clashes between Greek Cypriot supporters of Enosis and the British colonial authorities in 1931 Britain encouraged the idea of Turkish claims on Cyprus, since it had no interest in an independent Cyprus which would have threatened its essential base on the route to the Suez Canal.

Escalation of the conflict

During the campaign of violence mounted against the British from 1955 onwards by the Greek-Cypriot independence movement EOKA led by Giorgios Grivas, Britain supported the Turkish underground organisation TMT (founded to protect the Turkish minority in Cyprus), and agreed in 1959 to grant Cyprus independence only under international pressure.

Under the 1960 constitution President Makarios had a Turkish Cypriot Vice-President with an unlimited right of veto. The disproportionate representation of Turks in the Cypriot Parliament was resented by the Greeks, and in 1963/64 there were further violent conflicts between the two population groups, which were settled by the stationing in Cyprus of the United Nations peace-keeping force.

In 1974 the Greek military junta led by Dimitrios Ioannides, with the help of Cypriot fanatics, sought to overthrow Archbishop Makarios, who was concerned to maintain the independence and unity of Cyprus, and bring about union with Greece by violent means. Turkey, claiming to act under its rights as a guarantor power, sent in troops (under the code name Operation Attila) to protect the Turkish Cypriot population against possible attacks by Greek extremists. According to official Greek statements almost 200,000 Greeks were expelled from the Turkish-occupied areas, and some 1600 are still recorded as missing. At the same time the Turkish Cypriots who had hitherto been living in separate enclaves, were called on by the Turks to move into the northern part of the island.

1974 – fateful year

Since a third of the population of the Republic of Cyprus consists of refugees from the north the partition of the island is unlikely in future to be acceptable to Greek Cypriots.

The 180km/112 mile long demarcation zone, often several kilometres wide, is guarded by the Greek Cypriot National Guard, Turkish troops and the United Nations peace-keeping force. The "Green Line" (or "Attila Line") – so called because in 1953 a British colonial official drew

Demarcation zone

a partition line on a plan of Nicosia with a green pencil – cannot be crossed by Greek Cypriots. Foreign visitors are allowed through on foot at the crossing-point by the former Ledra Palace Hotel for a day visit.

Proposed
solutions

Since 1974 attitudes have hardened. In spite of repeated attempts by representatives of the two ethnic groups, with United Nations mediation, to establish a dialogue no progress was made. After Yeoryios Vassiliou became President of the Republic of Cyprus in 1988 further attempts were made to break the deadlock. So far, however, discussions on the proposals put forward by the United Nations to bring the two parts of the island together either in a federal state on the Swiss model or in a loose confederation have produced no results. Glafkos Klerides, elected President in 1993, rejected the plan in part.

The Greek Cypriot
position

In the event of the reunion of the two parts of the island the flourishing Greek south would have to share its recently won prosperity with the economically backward north. The main demands of the Greek Cypriots are the withdrawal of all foreign troops, freedom of movement for all Cypriots, freedom of settlement for all those expelled from their homes and an unlimited right of ownership (involving the return of abandoned houses and businesses to their original owners).

The Turkish
Cypriot
position

In the event of reunion the Turkish Cypriots are apprehensive about the revival of the idea of Enosis, since the Greeks are superior to them not only in numbers but also in economic strength. They are in two minds about the relationship with mainland Turkey. On the one hand they want a close link with Turkey and regard the stationing of Turkish troops in Cyprus as a protection against Greek preponderance; on the other hand they are concerned about the burden of the Turkish military presence.

According to official Greek estimates the Turkish Cypriot leader Rauf Denktash has brought in some 70,000 mainland Turks from Anatolia in order to make good the loss of population from northern Cyprus. Most of Denktash's political support, indeed, comes from the mainland Turks. Many Turkish Cypriots are unhappy about their new neighbours, since they regard themselves as better educated, more cosmopolitan and more law-abiding than their Anatolian fellow-citizens. They are also concerned that the large numbers of incomers will swamp the Turkish Cypriot community, the character of which is gradually being changed by the Anatolians. Resentment at the loss of their cultural identity has led tens of thousands of Turkish Cypriots to emigrate since 1974.

The Turkish
position

In spite of the high cost of maintaining troops in Cyprus and providing financial help for the Turkish Republic of Northern Cyprus, which economically is wholly dependent on Turkey, the Turkish government has shown no signs of being ready to yield any ground.

The success of Turkey's application for full membership of the European Union will depend in part at least on the solution of the problem of Cyprus.

Famous People

This section contains brief biographies, in alphabetical order, of notable people belonging to Cyprus or connected with it.

Alexander was born in Pella (north-western Greece), the son of King Philip II of Macedon and his wife Olympias, daughter of King Neoptolemos. From 342 to 340 B.C. his tutor was the great Greek philosopher Aristotle. He distinguished himself at an early age in the battle of Chaironeia in 338 B.C., and two years later, after his father's murder, made good his claim to the throne after eliminating his rivals. After being appointed general-in-chief of the Confederacy of Corinth he led campaigns against the Thracians and Illyrians and repressed a rebellion by Thebes (335 B.C.). Then, as supreme commander of the Greek forces, he set out in 334 B.C. with an army of 35,000 men on a "pan-Hellenic campaign of vengeance" against the Persians. Thrusting through the Taurus Mountains into Cilicia, he defeated Darius III in November 333 in the cavalry battle of Issos (north of present-day Iskenderun, Turkey). His victory over the Persians brought the end of Persian rule in Cyprus, and in 332 the Cypriot city-kingdoms took part in the campaign which led to the capture of Tyre and thereafter continued to support Alexander. The victory at Issos opened up the road to Egypt, where Alexander founded the city of Alexandria and consulted the oracle of Zeus Amun in the Siwa oasis, which confirmed his divine descent and claim to royal power.

From Egypt Alexander led his army on to Babylonia and after decisively defeating Darius at Gaugamela in the plain of Mosul (now in Iraq) in 331 B.C. pushed on to Persia and finally India (327–325 B.C.) in a campaign which took him to the river Hyphasis (Beas; now in the northern Indian state of the Punjab), where his exhausted army compelled him to turn back. After marching down the Indus valley part of the Greek army took ship down the Persian Gulf, while Alexander himself, with the rest of the army, followed a gruelling route through the Gedrosian desert and returned by way of Persia to Babylon, where Alexander died while planning a campaign against Arabia.

Alexander's declared – and in some respects partly realised – policy of unifying and consolidating his newly established empire, made up of so many heterogeneous elements, was finally doomed to failure, and his death was followed by conflicts between his successors, the Diadochoi.

Rauf Raşit Denktaş (Denktash), self-appointed President of the Turkish Republic of Northern Cyprus, was born in Páphos, the son of a judge. After studying law in London he became a solicitor in Nicosia and from the outset fought strenuously for the rights of the Turks in Cyprus. He was a close associate of Fazıl Küçük, first Vice-President of the newly established republic and leader of the Turkish Cypriots, and from 1958 to 1960 was chairman of various Turkish Cypriot institutions.

After Cyprus became independent in 1960 there were violent clashes between Turkish and Greek nationalists. An inflammatory speech by Denktash to the United Nations in New York led to a ban on his entry into Cyprus. In 1963 Denktash and other Turkish representatives withdrew from the government, but during the troubles of the 1960s he remained leader of the Turkish Cypriots. In 1968 he headed the Turkish delegation in negotiations with Archbishop Makarios and advocated the partition of Cyprus into separate Greek and Turkish areas. In 1973 he succeeded Fazıl Küçük as Vice-President of the Republic of Cyprus.

After the Turkish invasion in 1975 Denktash was elected "President" of the Turkish Cypriot part of the island, and in 1983 he proclaimed the

Alexander the Great (356–323 B.C.)

Rauf Raşit Denktaş (b. 1924)

Famous People

Alexander the Great

Rauf Denktash

Lawrence Durrell

"Turkish Republic of Northern Cyprus", a state recognised only by Turkey. After various unsuccessful attempts to solve the problem of Cyprus Denktash declared in 1989 that he was ready to consider a federal Turkish–Greek state. So far, however, no progress has been made in achieving this.

Lawrence Durrell
(1912–90)

The Anglo-Irish poet, novelist and dramatist Lawrence Durrell was born at Jullundur in northern India, at the foot of the Himalayas, and went to school in Darjeeling and in Britain. Thereafter he spent many years travelling in Athens, Corfu, Egypt and Cyprus. While in Paris he became a close friend of Henry Miller. From 1941 onwards he was a press attaché in Cairo, Alexandria, Rhodes and Belgrade. From 1953 to 1956 he lived in Cyprus, first as a teacher in the Pancyprian Gymnasium in Nicosia and then as press attaché in the diplomatic service. He now bought a house in Bellapais. His book "Bitter Lemons" was based on his experiences in Cyprus against the background of the struggle for independence which was then developing. Durrell's last years were spent in Nîmes (southern France).

Durrell's works included novels, essays, travel impressions, satirical sketches, lyric poetry and verse dramas, but his main preoccupation was with man's quest for an identity. One of his finest works is the "Alexandria Quartet", in which, in a series of changing perspectives and periods influenced by the theory of relativity, he demonstrates the variety of human truths.

Euagoras I
(c. 435–373 B.C.)

Euagoras was one of the outstanding rulers of ancient Cyprus. He was a scion of the Teucrian dynasty which for generations had been kings of Sálamis. In the 5th century B.C., however, the Teucrians were expelled by the Phoenicians, who were allied with the Persians, and in 415 Euagoras fled to Soli in Cilicia. In 411 he returned and overthrew Abdemon, a Phoenician who had been appointed king of Sálamis. In 394 B.C. he took part in a campaign, together with the Persians and Athenians, against the Spartans, which ended in a victory at Knidos. Thereafter Euagoras embarked on a campaign of expansion, securing the submission of other city-kingdoms on Cyprus in 392 and conquering Tyre (Lebanon). In 382 the Persians sent a fleet against Sálamis, and a treaty was concluded under which Euagoras remained king of Sálamis until 374/373 B.C. but was compelled to pay tribute to Persia. Soon afterwards, however, he fell victim to an intrigue at his own court.

Yeoryios Grivas
(1898–1974)

Yeoryios (George) Grivas was born in Tríkomo/Iskele, near Famagusta. He attended the Cadet School in Athens and in 1919 was granted Greek nationality. In 1920–22 he fought in the Greek–Turkish War as an infantry officer. In 1928 he was promoted to staff officer and entered the French Military Academy in Paris. Returning to Greece, he joined the teaching staff of the Officers' School in Salonica and then the Military Academy in Athens. In 1940 he was appointed to the operational staff of the Greek army and became Chief of Staff. During the Italian and German occupation of Greece he founded an underground organisation known simply as X.

In 1951 Grivas, then a colonel, retired and returned to Cyprus, where he founded EOKA, an underground organisation which began to operate against the British occupying forces in 1955. Under the cover-name of Dighenis he organised a partisan war aimed at securing Enosis (union with Greece). EOKA now became the main driving force in the struggle against British rule. Grivas's objective of securing Enosis, however, was frustrated by the establishment of an independent Republic of Cyprus in 1960. He returned to Greece, where he was promoted to general and awarded high decorations. In 1961 he published the first part of his memoirs.

In the late sixties Grivas, who in the fifties had fought for Enosis along with Makarios, turned against him, disappointed by his new anti-Enosis policy, and from 1970 began to work for his overthrow. In 1971 he founded EOKA/B, which organised demonstrations and bomb attacks with the aim of securing Enosis. He died in January 1974 and was buried in a friend's garden in Limassol.

Namík Kemal was one of the great Turkish popular poets. The son of an aristocratic family in Tekirdağ in European Turkey, in 1857 he became an official in Istanbul. A fierce opponent of the despotic Sultans from an early age, he published strongly critical articles in newspapers and periodicals and in 1867 fled to Paris and from there to London, where he ran an anti-government newspaper. He returned to Turkey in 1870, but after the performance of his play "Vatan yahud Silistre" ("Home or Silistria") had led to riots he was exiled to Cyprus. From 1873 to 1876 he was confined in Famagusta prison, which occupied a wing of the Palazzo del Provveditore. He is commemorated by a bust erected in 1953 opposite the Palazzo, in front of the Lala Mustafa Mosque (formerly St Nicholas's Cathedral). After his release he left Cyprus and went to Paris, where he founded the Young Turks party in 1876. He died of tuberculosis on Chios.

By awakening the spirit of Ottoman patriotism Namık Kemal's works prepared the way for Atatürk's revolution.

Namık Kemal (1840–88)

Kimon of Athens, son of Miltiades, victor over the Persians in the battle of Marathon (490 B.C.), was one of Athens' leading statesmen, a conservative aristocrat belonging to the Athenian feudal nobility. He gained a great reputation with his military successes, particularly against the Persians. In 468 he launched a great campaign in Cyprus but failed to recapture it from the Persians. Between 469 and 466, however, he won a double victory over the Persians on the river Eurymedon. Well disposed towards the Spartans, he was overthrown in 461 by the democratic and anti-Spartan party in Athens and was exiled from Attica for ten years. In 450 B.C. he distinguished himself as a general in the Athenian fleet sent to reconquer Cyprus from the Persians. Landing at Márion (now Pólis), he took Sálamis, but during the siege of Kítion (Lárnaca) died of plague. The Greek army thereupon abandoned the siege and left Cyprus, which remained under Persian sovereignty.

Kimon of Athens (c. 510–c. 449 B.C.)

Spyros Kyprianou, ex-President of the Republic of Cyprus, was born in Limassol. After studying economics and law in Britain he became in 1950 a close associate of Archbishop Makarios, promoting and defending his policy in Britain and Greece and at the United Nations. From 1960 to 1972, as foreign minister of the Republic of Cyprus, he pursued a policy of neutrality. Thereafter he founded the Democratic Front

Spyros Kyprianou (b. 1932)

Yeoryios Grivas

Archbishop Makarios III

Zeno of Kítion

(later the Democratic Party), which won an election in 1976, when Kyprianou became Speaker of the Cypriot Parliament. In 1977 he was elected President of the Republic. In spite of repeated conflicts with Parliament he remained in power, surviving a vote of no confidence moved in 1985. He rejected a proposal by Rauf Denktash to form a federation of two separate Cypriot states. In 1985 he took part in discussions with Denktash in New York under the chairmanship of UN Secretary-General Pérez de Cuéllar, but these made no progress. In 1988 Kyprianou was replaced as President by Yeoryios Vassiliou.

Hadjigeorgákis
Kornésios
(1779–1809)

Hadjigeorgákis Kornésios was the son of a wealthy Christian cloth merchant. He received an excellent education, learned Turkish at an early age and took an active part in the intellectual life of Cyprus. In 1779 the Sultan appointed him "Dragoman of the Seraglio" for Cyprus.

The Dragoman was a paid official responsible for acting as an intermediary between the Sultan and his Christian subjects and also for the collection of taxes. Hadjigeorgákis held the post for thirty years. All public and private business passed through his hands. As Dragoman he acquired great possessions, but his wealth and his role as tax-collector made him many enemies. In 1804 the oppressive burden of taxation and a period of famine led to rioting by Turkish Cypriots, in the course of which the Dragoman's house was looted. The Dragoman himself had already gone to seek help from the Sultan, who sent an army to Cyprus to crush the rising. Hadjigeorgákis spent the last years of his life in Istanbul, where he became involved in intrigues at the Sultan's court and was executed in 1809.

Archbishop
Makarios III
(1913–77)

Archbishop Makarios was one of the outstanding personalities of modern times in Cyprus. As Archbishop and as President of the Republic of Cyprus he played a major part in determining the destinies of the island over many years.

Makarios was born Michalis Christodoulou Mouskos in Páno Panayiá, near Páphos. After the death of his mother he entered Kýkko monastery as a novice at the age of thirteen. Three years later the monastery arranged for him to attend the Pancyprian Gymnasium in Nicosia. In 1938 he was ordained as a deacon. With the help of a scholarship from Kýkko monastery he went to Athens to study theology. He was ordained as a priest in 1946, taking the name of Makarios, and then went to Boston for two years' study with a bursary from the World Council of Churches. In 1948 he became Bishop of Kítion and in 1950 Archbishop of Cyprus.

Makarios supported the Greek Cypriots in their desire for union with Greece, and repeatedly raised the problem of Cyprus in the United Nations, in the United States and in Greece. When all efforts to achieve a peaceful solution failed he supported General Grivas's underground activities. As a result he was exiled to the Seychelles in March 1956. In 1957 he returned to Cyprus, and in 1960 he agreed to the proposals for Cypriot independence and became President of the new Republic of Cyprus.

In the late sixties, when Makarios increasingly turned away from the idea of union with Greece, his relations with the Greek military junta deteriorated. In 1974 the Greek government was involved in a coup d'état by the National Guard and EOKA/B against Makarios, who managed to flee to Páphos and from there to London. After the failure of the coup he returned to Cyprus and remained President of the Republic until his death in August 1977.

Yeoryios (George) Vassiliou, until March 1993 the President of the Republic of Cyprus, was born in Famagusta, the son of a doctor who was one of the founding members of the communist party AKEL. After studying economics in Genoa, Vienna and Budapest he specialised in marketing and market research in London. In 1962, after his return to Cyprus, he founded the largest market research business in the Third World, with offices in eleven countries. Although without any political experience and with no party allegiance but with the support of the communist AKEL and the socialist party EDEK, he won a surprising victory over Spyros Kyprianou and the conservative candidate Glafkos Klerides in the Presidential election of 1988. In line with his undertaking during the election campaign to make a fresh start in seeking a solution to the problem of Cyprus, he initiated negotiations with the leader of the Turkish Cypriots, Rauf Denktash, meeting him for the first time in 1988 in the buffer zone occupied by the UN peace-keeping force and discussing the possible establishment of a federation of two largely independent states. So far, however, the discussions have led to no concrete results.

Yeoryios Vassiliou (b. 1931)

Zeno, founder of the Stoic school of philosophy, was born in Kítion (Lárnaca) to a family of Phoenician origin. At the age of 22 he went to Athens and became a disciple of the Cynic philosopher Krates of Thebes. About 300 B.C. he began to teach in the Stoa Poikile, the Painted Hall (with paintings by Polygnotos), in the agora of Athens, from which the Stoic school took its name.

Zeno of Kítion (Zeno the Younger; c. 333–262 B.C.)

Stoicism was a complete philosophical system, consisting of logic (including grammar, rhetoric and dialectic), physics and ethics. In the Stoic view the Cosmos is governed by reason and rigid determinism. Accordingly ethics is based on the maxims of reason, which alone leads to perception and to good fortune. Virtues like courage, self-control, humanity and justice help the wise man to achieve harmony with himself and with nature. But since each man bears reason within himself there can in principle be only one law, one right and one state. Zeno conceived a universal state in which men could live in peace with one another and with equal rights.

Zeno developed his philosophy in a time of change in Greece. The city states were beginning to fall apart and men were in a state of uncertainty. Against this social background it is easy to understand the wide appeal of Zeno's philosophy, which looks forward to a happy state independent of external circumstances – a happiness which men can find within themselves, unaffected by government or politics.

Zeno died by his own hand about 262 B.C.

Art and Culture

Art and Architecture

Neolithic
(7000–3000 B.C.)

The oldest traces of human life on Cyprus date from the Neolithic period: for example the settlement at Khirokitía of the 6th millennium B.C. Under the earth floors of the semi-underground circular dwellings the dead were buried in a tightly contracted foetal position, perhaps in the expectation of later rebirth. The inhabitants of this village community were farmers, and on the evidence of bones found on the site had domesticated wild sheep and goats. Needles and pointed implements made from shells point to the beginnings of spinning and weaving.

Towards the end of the Neolithic period the first pottery vessels appear alongside domestic utensils and implements made from stone and bone. With the help of a comb-like instrument made from shell or bone the pottery was decorated with incised ornament (combed ornament). The vessels, mostly gourd-shaped, were covered with a reddish-brown glaze. Necklaces of carnelian beads and obsidian blades are evidence of trading contacts with Asia Minor and Syria. Violin-shaped stone idols also begin to appear.

Chalcolithic
(3000–2300 B.C.)

In the Chalcolithic period Cyprus has trading contacts with Asia Minor and the Levant. Settlements are established at Erími, Lápithos, Kythréa and other sites. The round dwellings of the Neolithic period increasingly give place to rectangular houses. The dead are now buried outside the village.

Different types of pottery are now produced. The predominant type is Erími ware (Red-on-White ware), named after the principal site where it was found. Decoration is mainly linear and geometric. Cross-shaped idols in steatite or clay are increasingly common. They now show female sexual characteristics, pointing to the cult of a mother goddess, predecessor of Aphrodite. Jewellery and implements of beaten copper are thought still to be imports.

Towards the end of the Chalcolithic period occasional alabaster vases begin to appear, showing Egyptian influence. The pottery shows great variety of form, with geometric and plant ornament. Red and black polished ware with incised decoration is now predominant.

Bronze Age
(2300–1050 B.C.)

In the Early Bronze Age settlements are established at Vounoús, Politikó, Tamassós and other sites. Copper-mining provides the raw material for metal weapons and domestic requisites and jewellery of copper and silver. The villages are now increasingly fortified, and the dead are buried in dromos tombs outside the settlement.

The Red Polished ware of this period has incised decoration in the form of wavy lines, bands of zigzags or circles.

Middle Bronze Age

In the Middle Bronze Age the technique of bronze production is brought to Cyprus by Anatolian merchants. Red Polished ware is produced in a great range of forms; the rims and handles of jars are decorated with animal protomes (the upper parts of animals' bodies). Pottery models of cult ceremonies are now found, for example a walled shrine from Vounoús (Archaeological Museum, Nicosia). There are also models of scenes from everyday life such as ploughing and baking bread.

The range of pottery forms is extended by the production of composite vessels, combining several different types. Narrow-necked vases appear for the first time, trading relations with Egypt and Palestine having brought new wares including oils and luxury ointments to Cyprus. Towards the end of the Middle Bronze Age Red Polished ware begins to give place to White Painted ware and Black Slip ware.

Also characteristic of this period are flat-bodied "plank idols" in red pottery with incised decoration and necklaces formed from imported beads of glass paste or faience.

The Late Bronze Age is a period of trading contacts with Minoans, Mycenaeans and Achaeans. Settlements such as Énkomi, Kítion and Márion are established as a result of the increasing importance of copper-working. The most important house type in this period is the megaron house with an antechamber. Settlements are now laid out on a regular plan. The dead are buried in chamber tombs with a long dromos (entrance passage) and several tomb chambers. Gold jewellery now appears, often made from beaten gold foil and decorated with spiral ornament or animal motifs. Mycenaean influence can be detected in the forms of the jewellery.

Mycenaean influence also appears in the White Slip and Black Slip ware, which, like the Zeus Crater in the Archaeological Museum in Nicosia, is decorated with mythological scenes and representations of cult ceremonies.

Late Bronze Age

The extraordinary variety of pottery forms in the Late Bronze Age includes full-bodied craters (wide-mouthed jars for mixing water and wine), small decorative vases, jars imitating metal (at this period still very costly) and bird-headed mother figures holding a child. Carved ivories with Oriental motifs like griffins or lions reflect the close links between Aegean and Oriental cultures. Representations of the Egyptian god Bes become increasingly common. A valuable and magnificently decorated rhyton from Kítion (Archaeological Museum, Nicosia) shows that vases were now much more than utility objects. Bronze statuettes such as the horned god from Énkomi (Archaeological Museum, Nicosia) point to an active metalworking industry in the final stages of the Bronze Age.

In the 16th century B.C. the first forms of writing appear in Cyprus. The Cypro-Minoan syllabic script shows close affinities with the Minoan Linear A script. The hundred or so characters of the syllabary have not yet been deciphered. Inscribed on everyday objects, they no doubt indicated the contents of a vessel or the name of the owner.

Cypro-Minoan syllabic script

After the coming of the Achaeans, bringing with them their beliefs and cults, the Hellenisation of the island begins.

In Cyprus as in Greece a certain cultural stagnation can be observed at the beginning of the Geometric period. A fresh cultural flowering occurs only from the 10th century onwards, influenced by the island's close connections with Phoenicia. Phoenician traders introduce the technique of iron-working and found the first Phoenician city, Kítion. The Achaeans build a number of towns – Koúrion, Márion, Sóloi, etc. Tombs now have a long narrow dromos with a pointed roof.

Geometric period (1050–725 B.C.)

In pottery the predominant types are Red Slip ware and Black-on-Red ware. The decoration consists of both geometric patterns and pictorial scenes. The neck and rim of vases are now also decorated. Occasional gold, silver and bronze dishes are found.

Assyrian, Egyptian and Persian influences now make themselves felt. City-kingdoms like Sálamis and Amathoús flourish. Richly furnished tombs at Sálamis and Tamassós bear witness to a period of cultural flowering. The grave goods show Oriental influence, while the architecture of the tombs comes from Greece. The dead are no longer buried in a tightly contracted position but lie on their backs in stone sarcophagi. Stelae begin to appear as grave-markers.

Archaic period (725–475 B.C.)

Archaic wine-jar

A "royal" tomb, Néa Páphos

In view of the lack of marble on Cyprus large sculpture is mainly in limestone. The dress and hair styles of the statues show Oriental influence. At Ayía Iríni more than 2000 terracotta figures were found, including many small figures of bulls – indicating that the old mother goddess had been displaced by male fertility symbols. In spite of the Assyrian and Egyptian influences Cypriot sculpture shows affinities with the Archaic sculpture of mainland Greece in its intense concern with the human body.

The powerful influence of the city-kingdoms leads to the formation of local styles and the emergence of distinctive artistic personalities. Bichrome vases decorated with flower and plant motifs now appear. The Orientalising style, which had come to the fore in mainland Greece at the end of the Geometric period, begins to establish itself in Cyprus. The "free-field" style also develops. Polychrome decoration with figures of animals and fabulous beasts is found principally on bulbous vases. The rich painted decoration spreads freely over the vessels with no frames to confine it, and the painting of the figures is more concerned with decorative effect than with anatomical accuracy.

Towards the end of the Archaic period black-figured vases imported from Greece begin to appear.
Egyptian glassware, faience and scarabs are common during the period of Egyptian rule.

Classical period
(475–325 B.C.)

The Classical period is also the period of the conflict with Persia, but even under Persian rule Cyprus establishes increasingly close cultural relations with Greece. The magnificent palace at Vouní (5th c. B.C.) shows a mingling of Oriental and Greek elements.

Imports of Attic black-figured and red-figured vases increase, but vase-painting in Cyprus itself also follows Greek styles. In the reign of King Euagoras of Sálamis Greek artists and scholars come to the island.

From the middle of the 5th century Cypriot sculpture shows Ionian and Attic influences. Fine bronze sculpture is produced, for example the figure of a cow from Vouní (Archaeological Museum, Nicosia).

After the death of Alexander the Great Cyprus is held by Ptolemy I of Egypt. The city-kingdoms are dissolved and the island is ruled from Alexandria. At Páphos large peristyle tombs with a colonnaded inner courtyard are built, showing Egyptian influence; the architectural decoration, however, is still Greek. The island's close political and cultural links with Egypt do not displace Greek cultural influence. Increasing prosperity and the desire for show lead to the building of new temples at Páphos and Sálamis.

Hellenistic period (325–58 B.C.)

Pottery continues to be imported from Greece or to be modelled on Greek products. The so-called "Hadra vases" – mass-produced ware in their country of origin – are imported from Egypt. Valuable pieces of small sculpture reflect the island's prosperity. One of the few surviving marble statues, the Aphrodite of Sóloi, can be seen in the Archaeological Museum in Nicosia. Glassware begins to be produced in Cyprus, and pressed glass is used in the manufacture of honey-coloured and sea-green drinking glasses.

As a Roman province Cyprus continues Hellenistic traditions. Towns such as Páphos, Sálamis and Sóloi grow in size and are embellished with Roman temples. After a great earthquake in the 4th century many towns are rebuilt. Theatres, gymnasia and palaestras are erected. Under the Ptolemies the peristyle house comes to Cyprus. The peristyle, a colonnaded courtyard, has frequently a colourful mosaic pavement (fine examples found at Páphos and Koúrion), an ornamental pool and flowerbeds.

Roman period (58 B.C.– A.D. 395)

Sálamis now becomes the cultural centre of Cyprus. Public buildings and private houses are decorated with sculpture, strongly influenced by Roman models. There are portraits and statues of Emperors, leading citizens, gods and heroes (e.g. the statue of the Emperor Septimius Severus from Kythréa, now in the Archaeological Museum, Nicosia).

The pottery consists mostly of undecorated ware for everyday use, showing Syrian and Cilician influence. Terra sigillata, a red ware with moulded decoration bearing the potter's stamp (sigilla), becomes popular in Cyprus.

In the 2nd century A.D. the scale of glass production increases. Undecorated glass for everyday use is manufactured on the island, but glassware is also imported from Syria.

Byzantine Period (A.D. 330–1191)

When Constantinople became capital of the Roman Empire in 330 this multi-national state faced the difficulties involved in seeking to create a unified Roman nation. An effective means to this end was Christianity, which was granted toleration in Constantine the Great's Edict of Milan in 313 and was made the state religion by Theodosius the Great at the end of the 4th century. Thereafter there was much building activity.

General

Byzantine Church Types

The first Christian basilicas in Cyprus were built at Koúrion, Páphos, Amathoús and Sálamis in the 4th century, some three hundred years after Paul and Barnabas's missionary work on the island. This type of

Early Christian basilica

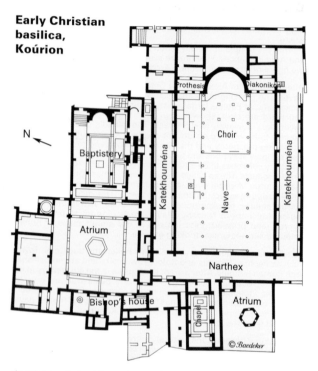

Early Christian basilica, Koúrion

Prothesis

Diakonikon

Choir

Baptistery

Katekhouména

Nave

Katekhouména

Atrium

Narthex

Bishop's house

Chapel

Atrium

© Baedeker

N

church was derived from the secular basilicas of the Roman world which served as market halls and law courts. It had a central aisle (nave) with its own windows which was higher than the lateral aisles and separated from them by columns or pillars.

The basilicas found on Cyprus are long buildings of three to five aisles with one or more apses at the east end. Behind the altar, on a higher level, is the bishop's throne (*kathedra*). The apse and the area containing the altar form the sanctuary (*bema*), which only the officiating clergy can enter. It is separated from the body of the church (*naos*) by a low screen, the *templon*.

On either side of the sanctuary there are usually two small rooms, the diakonikon or sacristy to the right and the prothesis, in which the eucharist is prepared, to the left. In addition to the lateral aisles some churches have outer aisles (*katekhouména*), separated from the church itself, which are occupied by catechumens (members of the congregation who have not yet been baptised). At the west end of the church is a kind of antechamber, the narthex, and beyond it the atrium, with a fountain (*kántharos*) for ablutions. The baptismal font is in the baptistery, outside the church.

The interior of the church is decorated with mosaics and wall paintings.

Church of Ayía Paraskeví   Yeroskípos

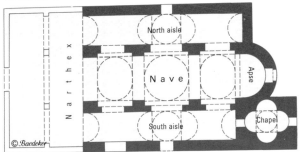

In the 9th and 10th centuries the basilican type of church increasingly gives place throughout the Byzantine Empire to the domed cruciform type, a church on a centralised plan of the same type as Hagia Sophia in Istanbul. The immediate prototype of the Cypriot churches is the basilica of St John at Ephesus, a hybrid of the basilican and the centralised plan. There are usually three domes over the nave and two more over the arms of the cross (Peristeróna, Yeroskípos, St Barnabas's Monastery). The sanctuary has one or more apses.

Domed cruciform church

The sanctuary is separated from the main part of the church by the templon, a marble screen. In the 13th century this develops into the iconostasis, a tall wooden screen bearing tiers of icons.

A type of church peculiar to Cyprus is the barn-roofed church, a long, single-aisled church which is particularly favoured in the Tróodos Mountains. These medieval churches in the upland regions were given saddle roofs in the Crusader period; if the church had a dome this was covered by a tiled saddle roof. With its deep overhanging eaves the roof, borne on a supporting wall, provides protection from snow and rain. The ambulatory between the church and the supporting wall provides constant ventilation and thus helps to conserve the walls with their rich decoration of paintings.

Barn-roofed church

Church of Panayía tou Arákou   Lagoudherá

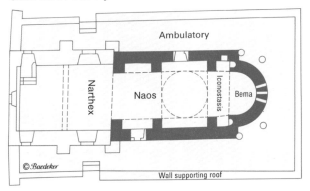

Byzantine Wall Paintings

Byzantine churches are usually decorated with magnificent frescos, which were painted on the fresh, wet plaster (Italian *al fresco*). The pigments thus penetrate into the plaster ground, which acts as a binding medium and makes the painting more durable.

The veneration of images is based on the belief that the likeness of God or of a saint is a representation of the archetypical conception of God or the saint; and in order to approach as closely as possible to the archetype the form of representation must be fixed and unchanging. The flat linear composition of the iconography disregards normal principles of scale and spatial relationship and sets the figures in a false perspective.

Wall paintings also served as a kind of "poor man's Bible" for those who could not read the Biblical story; they depicted Biblical events and parables and thus symbolised the teachings of the Church.

The Byzantine religious art of Cyprus can be divided into Early, Middle, Late and Post-Byzantine periods. It incorporates Hellenistic, Roman, Syrian and Oriental (Persian) elements.

Early Byzantine period

In the Early Byzantine period (6th–8th c.) the wall paintings depict only scenes from the life of Christ. The style is lively and expressive.

Iconoclasm

The iconoclastic conflict between 726 and 843 turned on the meaning and veneration of sacred images. The iconoclasts ("destroyers of images") opposed any pictorial representation of Christ or any other sacred persons, citing the third commandment: "Thou shalt not make unto thee any graven image, or any likeness of any thing that is in heaven above . . ." This view was influenced by religions like Judaism and Islam which were also hostile to images.

Those who believed in the power of images – mainly monks and the ordinary people – saw Christ, who took on human form, as an image of

Wall painting in the church of Ayia Paraskeví, Yeroskípos

God and thus as a justification for the representation of other sacred persons and saints. It was also believed that Luke the Evangelist had himself painted the first likeness of Mary, the Mother of God.

A historical basis for the veneration of images was also seen in the existence of the Mandílion and the Keramídion, explained by the story in apocryphal writings that the king of Edessa in Syria sent a painter to Christ to paint his likeness. Christ did not agree to the painting of his portrait, but pressed his face into a cloth, which he gave to the painter. The cloth, now imprinted with the likeness of Christ's face, was then hung on the city gate of Edessa, where it left an impression on a tile. In the 9th century the Holy Cloth (Mandílion) and Holy Tile (Keramídion) were taken to Constantinople, where they were the subject of great veneration.

Mandílion, Keramídion

The iconoclastic controversy ended in victory for the supporters of images, and the view of St John of Damascus that images should be regarded only as intermediaries between man and the divine became orthodox doctrine.

The Middle Byzantine period (870–1204) followed the period of iconoclasm, after which the theological content and form of representation of images were precisely defined. The decoration of churches with wall paintings now followed an established iconographic programme. The paintings depicted figures in a rigidly frontal position, and perspectives were based on relative importance, the principal figures being shown larger than the subsidiary ones. The paintings covered a wide range of scenes of theological significance. The paintings of the "Macedonian Renaissance" (9th–11th c.), which developed after the end of the iconoclastic controversy in the reign of the Emperor Basil I, are distinguished by delicate draughtsmanship and the elongated representation of the figures. Under the Comnene dynasty (1081–1185) there was a return to Hellenistic models, with gently flowing movement, elaborately folded draperies and delicate chiaroscuro effects.

Middle Byzantine period

The oldest surviving wall paintings in Cyprus are in the church of Ayios Nikólaos tis Stéyis at Kakopetriá (11th c.).

In the Late Byzantine period (1204–1453), also known as the Palaeologue period after the Palaeologue imperial dynasty, the paintings are full of contrasts, tensions and richly contrasting colours. During the period of Frankish rule western elements are incorporated in the traditional style.

Late Byzantine period

The post-Byzantine period (15th–19th c.), which begins with the conquest of Constantinople by the Turks in 1453, is characterised by a profusion of figures, the representation of subsidiary persons and genre scenes, the introduction of central perspective and the painting of detailed backgrounds.

Post-Byzantine period

After the end of the iconoclastic period the arrangement of paintings in a church is determined by a strict canon. The painters' artistic intentions do not count: what is important is the theological message of the paintings.

Iconographic programme

The paintings are arranged in accordance with a horizontal and a vertical hierarchy. There may be minor variations in content and style, usually attributable to the donors of the paintings.

The horizontal hierarchy begins in the sanctuary (*bema*), which is regarded as the point of contact between heaven and earth. In the apse is the Mother of God with the Infant Christ, and below this are the Communion of the Apostles, symbolising the Last Supper, and the fathers of the Church, representing the timelessness of the Church. In the body of the church (naos) are scenes from the legends of saints, the

Horizontal hierarchy

life of the Virgin and the life of Christ, based on the twelve great festivals of the Orthodox church (the Annunciation, the Nativity of Christ, the Presentation in the Temple, the Baptism, the Transfiguration, the Raising of Lazarus, the Entry into Jerusalem, the Crucifixion, the Descent into Hades, the Ascension, Pentecost and the Dormition of the Mother of God).

At the west end of the church, over the doorway or in the narthex, is the Last Judgment.

The vertical hierarchy begins in the dome, which represents heaven, with the figure of Christ Pantokrator (Ruler of All), surrounded by angels. In the pendentives are prophets or the four Evangelists, forming a transition to the earthly sphere, in which are scenes from the life of the Virgin or of Christ. In the lowest register are saints and representatives of the ecclesiastical and secular hierarchies.

Vertical hierarchy

In a sociological interpretation the rigid iconographic programme can be seen as representing the unshakeable order of the Byzantine Empire, in which the Emperor was supreme head of the Church as well as of the state.

Icon-Painting

Like the wall paintings, icons also serve for the instruction of the worshippers. An icon (Greek *eikon*, "image") is a likeness of Christ, the Mother of God or a saint. During the iconoclastic controversy of the 8th and 9th centuries countless icons were destroyed by the iconoclasts. Others were hidden away, and their rediscovery in later times led to the foundation of monasteries (Makherás, Kýkko).

Icon-painting, like wall painting, was subject to strict rules. Painters' handbooks laid down not only the subjects but also the technique and the treatment. The representation, frequently on a gold ground, was flat and without central perspective. The emphasis was on the theological message: the background was left blank, since otherwise it might divert attention from the main figure. The flat, two-dimensional effect of the icon was deliberate, not the result of any lack of artistic skill.

Frankish and Venetian Art (1191–1571)

The conquest of Cyprus by Richard Coeur de Lion in 1191 brought in western influences. Thereafter the island was ruled by a French noble family, the Lusignans, who initiated an active building programme. Masons were brought in from the West and palaces and churches were built by the king, the bishops and wealthy citizens. The first large Gothic cathedrals were erected in Nicosia and Famagusta (St Sophia, St Nicholas). In the Pentadáktylos Hills the castles of St Hilarion, Buffavento and Kantara were built to protect the island from foreign attacks.

Cypriot Gothic

Cypriot Gothic lacks the lightness and upward movement of French Gothic. Heavy, squat forms predominate. The long nave and lateral aisles often have flat roofs rather than the saddle roofs usual in France, and the interiors of the churches are bare in comparison with the sumptuous decoration of French churches. They lack galleries and triforia; there are no chapels round the choir and no transepts. Most churches have a choir with three apses at the east end; usually there is no ambulatory round the choir (though the cathedral of St Sophia in Nicosia is an exception).

◀ *An elongated figure of St Peter in the Comnene style (Laghouderá)*

The barn-roofed church of the Panayía tou Arákou, Laghouderá

Barn-roofed churches

The little churches in the hills have a special type of "barn roof". The churches, usually barrel-vaulted or domed, have an additional steeply pitched roof with deep overhanging eaves which provides protection from rain and snow.

Pottery

The predominant type of medieval pottery – mainly dishes and drinking vessels – is brownish-green, with rich and imaginative sgraffito decoration.

Ottoman Art (1571–1878)

After the conquest of Cyprus the Turks converted abandoned Catholic churches into mosques. The cathedral of St Sophia in Nicosia became the Selimiye Mosque, St Nicholas's Church in Famagusta the Lala Mustafa Pasha Mosque. Minarets were built on the stumps of church towers, and the Gothic decoration of the interiors was removed. The new mosques that were now built were in classical Ottoman style, with a square ground-plan and a dome.

Mosques

The mosque was not only the Muslim house of God and a meeting-place for prayer and the Friday sermon: it was also used as a place for teaching, for legal proceedings and for political meetings.

The layout of the mosque was originally derived from the plan of an Arab dwelling-house, out of which developed the courtyard mosque on the model of Medina (e.g. the Omayyad mosque in Damascus). The large inner courtyard (sahn) with the fountain for ritual ablutions is surrounded by galleries (riwaks) and a long multi-aisled prayer hall facing in the direction of Mecca. Also oriented towards Mecca are the mihrab (prayer niche) and the minbar, the high pulpit for the Friday sermon. From the Omayyad period (666–750) onwards the minaret

Cathedral of St Sophia, now the Selimiye Mosque

from which the muezzin issued the five daily calls to prayer became an essential element in the structure of the mosque.

In the 11th century a new element stemming from the palace architecture of the pre-Islamic period, the iwan – a barrel-vaulted hall open on one side and preceded by a courtyard – was introduced. From the 12th century the mosque may have four iwans axially related to one another. The iwans were frequently used as medreses (theological schools).

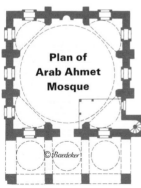

Plan of
Arab Ahmet
Mosque

© Baedeker

Domed mosques

The domed mosque, modelled on domed Byzantine churches, developed in the Ottoman Empire from the 13th century onwards. The type of the square domed building on a centralised plan (e.g. the Suleimaniye Mosque in Istanbul) now became established. Most of the mosques built in Cyprus followed this pattern, for example the Hala Sultan Tekke near Lárnaca and the Arab Ahmet Mosque in Nicosia.

Rectangular mosques

In the 19th century the rectangular type of mosque without a dome, entered through a columned narthex, came to Cyprus. Examples of this type are found in Lefke and Nicosia (Sarayönü Mosque).

Secular buildings   In addition to mosques numbers of secular buildings were also erected in the Ottoman period, such as the two hans (caravanserais) in Nicosia and various bath-houses, including the Büyük Hamam with its domed hot bath in the Turkish-occupied part of Nicosia (still open to the public). Other examples of Ottoman architecture are a library, a fountain and a number of dwelling-houses in the Turkish part of Nicosia and the aqueduct at Lárnaca.

Glossary of Technical Terms (Art, History, Religion and Mythology)

Abacus   The upper part of the capital of a Doric column, a square slab above the echinus. See diagram, page 71.

Acropolis   The highest part of a Greek city, usually its religious centre.

Agorá   The market-place of a Greek city, the main centre of public life; the equivalent of the Roman forum.

Ayía, Ayios   Holy; (prefixed to a name) Saint.

Amphitheatre   An oval arena surrounded by tiers of seating.

Anástasis   Christ's Descent into Hades: the usual representation of the Resurrection in the Eastern church.

Apocrypha   Biblical writings not recognised by the Western church as canonical.

Archaic art   Greek art of the 7th and 6th centuries B.C.

Architrave   A horizontal stone lintel resting on the columns of a temple.

Archivolt   The under surface of an arch.

Asklepieion   Sanctuary of Asklepios, the Greek god of healing.

Atrium   An open courtyard in the centre of a Roman house; the forecourt of an early Christian basilica.

Basilica   A type of church with three or more aisles in which the central aisle (nave) is higher than the lateral aisles and has its own windows.

Bema   The sanctuary of a Byzantine church.

Blacherniótissa   A representation of the Mother of God standing in the attitude of prayer, without the Child.

Bothros   A pit for offerings.

Caldarium   The hot room of a Roman bath-house.

Capital   The moulded or carved top of a column or pillar, supporting the entablature. See diagram, page 71.

Cavea   The auditorium of a Roman theatre (Greek *koilon*).

Cella   The inner chamber of a temple, the holy of holies.

Chalcolithic   A period transitional between the Stone and Bronze Ages (on Cyprus 3000–2300 B.C.).

Cippus   A monumental stone or pillar.

A projecting bracket supporting a cornice, etc.	**Console**
See Orders	**Corinthian order**
A large open bowl or jar for mixing wine.	**Crater**
The three-stepped platform of a temple. See diagram, page 71.	**Crepidoma**
In Byzantine painting, a representation of Christ between the Virgin and St John interceding for mankind.	**Deesis**
A room on the south side of the sanctuary in an Orthodox church; sacristy.	**Diakonikon**
See Orders	**Doric order**
The corridor or passage leading to a tomb (on Cyprus frequently stepped).	**Dromos**
A convex moulding under the abacus of a Doric capital. See diagram, page 71.	**Echinus**
An ancient method of painting in which wax colours were fused to the surface.	**Encaustic**
Hermitage.	**Enkleistra**
The superstructure carried by columns.	**Entablature**
The Roman market-place and place of assembly; the equivalent of the Greek agorá.	**Forum**

Temple of Apollo, Koúrion (reconstructed)

Doric Order

Ionic Order

Corinthian Order

© Baedeker

Doric Order:

a Acroterion
b Sima (with lion's-head water-spouts)
c Geison
d Tympanon
e Guttae
f Triglyphs
g Metopes
h Regulae
i Architrave (plain)
k Abacus
l Echinus
m Shaft, with sharp-edged fluting
n Stylobate
o Crepidoma

Ionic Order:

a Sima
b Geison
c Tympanon
d Frieze (zophoros)
e Architrave (three-stepped)
f Capital (with volutes)
g Shaft, with 24 flutings separated by ridges
h Attic base (with double torus and trochilus)
i Stylobate
k Crepidoma

Corinthian Order:

a Geison
b Dentils
c Frieze
d Architrave
e Capital
f Shaft of column
g Base
h Crepidoma

The Classical Orders

A decorative band above the architrave of a temple; in the Doric order made up of metopes and triglyphs, in the Ionic order plain or with continuous carved decoration. See diagram, page 71.	**Frieze**
The cold room in a Roman bath-house.	**Frigidarium**
Greek art between 1050 and 700 B.C.	**Geometric art**
Turkish bath.	**Hammam**

◀ *Corinthian columns in the Gymnasium, Sálamis*

Glossary of Technical Terms (Art, History, Religion and Mythology)

Han A Turkish caravanserai or hostelry.

Hellenistic art Greek art between 330 and 30 B.C.

Hippodrome An elliptical course for chariot races.

Hodigitria A type of representation of the Mother of God as "She who shows the Way", with the Child on her left arm.

Hypocaust An under-floor heating system in Roman houses and baths.

Hypogeum An underground vault, especially one used for burials.

Iconoclasm A movement in the Eastern church 8th and 9th centuries opposed to the veneration of images.

Iconostasis A screen in a Byzantine church between the sanctuary and the main part of the church, bearing tiers of icons.

Impluvium A basin for collecting rainwater in the atrium of a Roman house.

Ionic order See Orders

Kantharos A fountain in the forecourt of an early Christian basilica.

Katekhoumenon A room for catechumens (unbaptised members of the congregation) in an early Christian basilica.

Keramidion The Holy Tile: see above, Byzantine Wall Paintings.

Koimisis The Dormition ("Falling Asleep") or Death of the Mother of God; the equivalent in the Eastern church of the Assumption of the Virgin.

Kore Maiden; statue of a girl.

Kouros Statue of a naked youth, characteristic of the Archaic period.

Mandilion The Holy Cloth: see above, Byzantine Wall Paintings

Metope A rectangular panel between the triglyphs in the frieze of a Doric temple, either plain or with relief decoration. See diagram, page 71.

Mihrab The prayer niche in a mosque, indicating the direction of Mecca.

Minaret The tower of a mosque, from which the muezzin issues the call to prayer.

Minbar The high pulpit in a mosque.

Muezzin The official in a mosque who calls the faithful to prayer.

Naos The enclosed chamber of a temple (the Greek equivalent of the Roman *cella*).

Narthex A rectangular entrance hall preceding the nave of a church, occupied by the unbaptised (*catechumens*) during services.

Nestorians Adherents of a heresy attributed to Patriarch Nestorius of Constantinople which was condemned by the Church in the 5th century.

Nymphaeum A Roman fountain-house with a façade like that of a temple.

Odeion A hall (usually roofed) for musical performances, etc.

A circular or semicircular area between the stage and auditorium of a Greek theatre in which the chorus danced. — **Orchestra**

The different styles of classical architecture, characterised by the type of columns and entablature. — **Orders**
1. Doric order: column without a base; shaft with (usually 20) sharp-edged flutings; capital consisting of echinus and abacus; entablature with frieze of metopes.
2. Ionic order: column standing on base; 20 flutings separated by ridges; capital with spiral volutes; architrave made up of three sections, each projecting over the one below; frieze continuous, without triglyphs.
3. Corinthian order: column base and shaft as in Ionic order; capital consisting of two rows of acanthus leaves.
The composite capital developed in Roman times, with a combination of Ionic and Corinthian elements.

A courtyard surrounded by colonnades, a training school for physical exercises. — **Palaestra**

"All Holy": the Mother of God, the Virgin. — **Panayía**

Christ as the "Ruler of All". — **Pantokrator**

The rooms to left and right of the sanctuary in an Orthodox church, the diakonikon and prothesis. — **Pastophoria**

A colonnade surrounding a courtyard. — **Peristyle**

A large storage jar. — **Pithos**

A colonnade, usually in front of a building. — **Portico**

Gateway. — **Propylon**

(Temple) with columned portico in front. — **Prostyle**

A room on the north side of the sanctuary in an Orthodox church in which liturgical utensils and vestments are kept. — **Prothesis**

A figure used as decoration on a vase, etc. — **Protome**

A cylindrical vase. — **Pyxis**

A drinking vessel, often in the form of an animal's head. — **Rhyton**

A room in a monastery for the writing or copying of manuscripts. — **Scriptorium**

A type of ceramic or mural decoration in which the top layer of glaze, plaster, etc., is incised with a design to reveal parts of the ground. — **Sgraffito**

The stage building of a Greek theatre. — **Skene**

1. An ancient measure of length (600 feet). — **Stadion**
2. A running track 600 feet long.
3. A stadium, with a running track and embankments or benches for spectators.

An upright stone slab (often a tombstone), usually with an inscription and frequently with relief carving. — **Stele**

A portico; a hall with columns along the front. — **Stoa**

Cyprus's Threatened Cultural Heritage

Stylobate	The uppermost step of a temple platform. See diagram, page 71.
Sudatorium	The "sweat-bath" in a Roman bath-house.
Tekke	The Muslim equivalent of a monastery.
Temenos	A sacred precinct bounded by a wall.
Tholos	A circular building, rotunda.
Triglyph	A projecting member, with two vertical channels, between the metopes of the Doric order. See diagram, page 71.
Volute	The spiral scroll of an Ionic capital. See diagram, page 71.

Cyprus's Threatened Cultural Heritage

The looting of Greek Orthodox churches, excavation sites and museums in the Turkish-occupied part of Cyprus was not the first threat to Cypriot culture. The destruction began with the Ottoman conquest in 1571.

Ottoman rule

In the 16th century the Ottoman rulers of Cyprus, who in general were tolerant of Christianity in their empire, converted the Gothic churches built during the Lusignan and Venetian periods into mosques, complete with minarets. The Cathedral of St Sophia in Nicosia became the Selimiye Mosque, St Nicholas's Cathedral in Famagusta the Lala Mustafa Pasha Mosque.

19th century

With the increasing interest in antiquities in the 19th century the export of excavation finds began. Thus the former American consul in Cyprus, Luigi Palma di Cesnola, assembled a private collection of antiquities which was displayed in the newly founded Metropolitan Museum of Art in New York in 1872.

North Cyprus since 1974

After the invasion by Turkish troops in 1974 the occupying forces began systematically to obliterate all traces of Greek settlement; the Greek language, Greek philosophers and Greek books were now banned. Apart from the historic archaeological sites of Sóloi, Vouní, Énkomi and Sálamis all Greek place-names were replaced by Turkish names.

The gravest loss, and one which is irreparable, is the indiscriminate destruction of material from Greek churches, some of which has found its way on to the international art market. Hardly a single Orthodox chapel has been left unscathed, and many Greek cemeteries have been desecrated. Churches have fallen into disrepair, been used for housing sheep or goats or converted into mosques. The crosses on the roofs of churches have been torn down, the ropes for ringing the bells cut off. The monastery of St John Chrysostom at Koutsovéndis, below Buffavento Castle, is now a military post, since it affords wide views extending as far as Nicosia and the Tróodos Mountains. Cycles of frescos of incalculable value have been torn off the walls by "persons unknown"; icons, altars and liturgical utensils have disappeared.

One notorious instance was the sale in New York of a cycle of frescos, broken up into innumerable parts, from the former church of St Thermionaros, Famagusta. Six of the 6th century mosaics which disappeared from the church of Panayía Kanakariá, Lythrángomi – among the finest examples of early Christian art in the territory of the former Byzantine Empire – were rediscovered in 1989 and recovered by the

The ravaged church of the Panayía Kanakariá, Lythrángomi

Republic of Cyprus. They can now be seen in the Icon Museum in Nicosia. Only two other churches with valuable mosaics survived the iconoclastic conflict unscathed, thanks to the three hundred years of Arab rule in the turmoil of the 8th/9th centuries: the Panayía Kerá at Livádia (North Cyprus; looted by the Turks) and the Panayía Angelók-tistos at Kíti (in the Greek Republic of Cyprus).

Folk Art and Traditions

Religious Festivals

Cypriot popular culture still holds to the old traditions. Thus Easter, the principal Orthodox church festival, has from time immemorial been celebrated in country areas with particular ceremony. The fast begins 50 days before Easter. In the week before Easter houses are white-washed and spring cleaned, the *flaoúna,* a special Easter cheese pastry, is baked and on the Thursday eggs are dyed red. On Good Friday the epitaphion, a reproduction of Christ's shroud, is laid out under a portable canopy which is decorated by young girls with flowers and fine fabrics. The icons in the churches are covered with black cloths, and after the evening service the epitaphion is carried about the village.

    On Easter Saturday the church is decked with flowers and the black cloths are removed from the icons. At 11 o'clock at night the con-gregation, carrying candles, gather for the Easter night service; then at midnight the priest comes out from behind the iconostasis and pro-nounces the words "Christos anesti" ("Christ has risen") and lights the first candle. Outside the church a large bonfire is lit and a doll sym-bolising Judas is burned. Then the children announce the glad news of

Easter

Christ's resurrection with noisy fire-crackers. People then go home and eat the traditional Easter soup (*maryeiritsa*) made from lambs' entrails. On Easter Day families eat the Easter lamb.

Since the Orthodox Easter is determined according to the Julian calendar and that of other Christian churches by the Gregorian calendar the two coincide only every three years.

Kurban Bayramı (Feast of the Sacrifice)

Kurban Bayramı, the four-day Feast of the Sacrifice, is the highest Islamic festival, celebrating God's goodness to and care for his people. The origin of this custom goes back to the Old Testament story of Abraham's sacrifice: God calls on Abraham to sacrifice his only son, Isaac, but while he is preparing to do so God intervenes again and through an angel tells him to sacrifice a lamb instead of his son. This Islamic reference to an Old Testament story, which may at first sight seem surprising, reflects the common origin of the two religions in Arab territory.

At Kurban Bayramı families eat a roast sheep in accordance with a religious rite, and what is left over is given to the poor, the sick or some social welfare institution. Well-to-do families, after praying in the mosque, give presents of money to charitable institutions and poor families.

Circumcision ceremony

One of the most important events in the life of male Muslims is the circumcision ceremony, which symbolises a boy's admission to the Islamic community. The reasons for the continuation of this tradition are religious, social, hygienic and sexual. About two weeks before the ceremony invitations are sent out to relations and acquaintances. Then, just before the actual ceremony, the boy is taken round the village in special garb with a red scarf, to the accompaniment of music and dancing. The circumcision itself is performed by an "official" circumciser (*sünnetçi*). After the ceremony the boy is put to bed in a specially made nightshirt, and the celebrations continue round him. He has now been accepted into the community of men.

Folk Art

Arts and crafts

In spite of changing cultural influences Cypriot folk art has preserved its own distinctive character. Traditional crafts are still practised in many villages. The Folk Museums of Nicosia, Yeroskípos and Páphos offer visitors an informative view of the island's characteristic arts and crafts. In Nicosia, Lárnaca, Limassol and Páphos there are government-run handicraft centres which give demonstrations of a great variety of crafts and have showrooms for the sale of the products. The object of these centres is to preserve and promote the island's native arts and crafts, the raw materials for which (wood, clay, cotton, linen, silk) are all found locally.

Symbols as decorative elements

The elements used in the decoration of wooden chests and stands, in embroidery and in pottery decoration originally had symbolic and indeed magical significance in the everyday life of Cypriot people; they gave expression to their view of the world and their religious beliefs. For example cypresses (as in the catacombs in Rome) and cedars were symbols of death, while a rosette symbolised the sun, and thus life. Wavy lines represented eternity, birds announced coming events and a snake meant temptation.

Woodcarving

Woodcarving was formerly an important craft in Cyprus, as is demonstrated by the sumptuous carved iconostases in Cypriot churches. The chapterhouse of Ómodhos monastery has a magnificent carved cedarwood ceiling. Everyday household objects were made of walnut or

Greek costumes

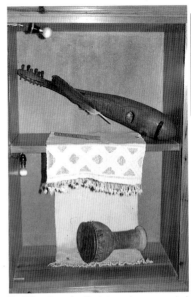

Traditional musical instruments

pinewood. In villages such as Moutoullás wooden troughs and bread-boards are still made in traditional style, and carved chests and presses remain part of the equipment of every Cypriot bride.

Old traditions of textile manufacture are carried on in the production of woven cloths of the highest quality in geometric patterns.

Textiles

In Lápithos and Karavás the culture of silkworms provides the raw material for beautiful silk fabrics. Silkworm culture was brought to Cyprus by the Crusaders.

The village of Léfkara is famed for its embroidery and lace. The craft of hemstitch embroidery (*lefkarítika*), which dates back to Venetian times, is still handed down from mother to daughter.

The little village of Phití (Páphos district) is noted for its brightly patterned woven fabrics (*phithkiótika*).

Pottery has been an important Cypriot craft since ancient times and is today produced manually in traditional style at Phiní, Kórnos and Lápithos. In the villages of Kórnos and Phiní the potters are mainly women. Phiní is noted for its large wine jars, still made on the ancient model.

Pottery

In the Páphos area and in the village of Liopétri flat baskets with brightly coloured geometric patterns are made in traditional fashion. The materials used are reeds and palm fronds.

Basketwork

Even during the period of Ottoman rule the tradition of icon-painting was maintained, and the craft has been preserved in its authentic form down to the present day. The nuns in the convent of Ayios Minás (Léfkara) make a contribution to the cost of running the convent with their icon-painting. The Chrysorroyiátissa and Ayios Alemános monasteries are also famed for their icon-painting.

Icon-painting

Folk Art and Traditions

Metalwork

The origins of metalworking on Cyprus can be traced back to the first finds of copper in the Chalcolithic period. Traditional goldsmiths' and silversmiths' work is mainly produced nowadays in Léfkara, Limassol and Nicosia. The Orthodox churches of Cyprus have fine silver lamps and richly decorated metal candlesticks.

Costumes

Cypriots now wear ordinary European dress, and traditional costumes are seen only in folk performances, on major festivals and occasionally in villages.

The traditional women's dress consists of a cotton or silk under-garment and baggy trousers, over which is worn a cotton dress (*sayia*), in colours and patterns which vary from village to village. The dress is drawn in by a diagonally folded square of cloth by way of belt. On their head the village women wear a head-scarf (*mantíla*). The dress in towns is different, usually consisting of a long skirt, a short low-necked bodice over a white blouse, a short jacket and a fez.

The men's costume consists of baggy black trousers (*vraka*) reaching down to the knee and held up by a woven belt (*sostra*) – still common in the villages – with a white shirt, an embroidered waistcoat and high black boots.

Folk dances

Cypriot folk dances are generally similar to Greek dances. Men and women dance separately. Two types of dance can be distinguished – the measured tread of the syrtós dances and the vigorous movements of the pidik dances. The syrtáki, the best known Greek dance, is also performed in Cyprus.

One typical Cypriot dance is the potíri, which is performed in every bouzoúki taverna. Great skill is required for this as the dancer balances anything up to twenty glasses on his head.

The potíri *dance*

A lively Cypriot dance

78

In the syrtós antikristós men and women dance opposite one another. The men's steps show agility, strength and courage; the women's movements are restrained and graceful.

In the zeibékkiko dance the women balance water-jars on their heads and are courted by the men. At first they are coy, but later show themselves ready to flirt with the men.

The drépani is danced by men carrying scythes, in a simulation of harvesting wheat.

The Nikolís dance tells the story of Nikolís, a great lady's man, who is made fun of by his friends. They stick a newspaper in his belt and try to set light to it, while Nikolís eludes them by his skill and agility.

The soústa is a round dance for both sexes in which each performer in turn must dance solo in the centre of the ring.

Folk music

As early as the 10th century wandering minstrels such as the ballad-singers of Europe were travelling round Cyprus and passing on the latest news in their songs. These *poietárides,* who came from the villages of south-eastern Cyprus, have continued to influence Cypriot poetry down to our own times.

The folk music of the present day takes as its themes both historical events and topics of current interest. The singer is accompanied by the bouzoúki (an instrument resembling a lute), the sandoúri (a kind of dulcimer), the violin and the flute.

The folk music of the Turkish Cypriots comes from the little villages of Anatolia but is accompanied by instruments similar to those which accompany the Greek singers – the bozuk (a stringed instrument) and the kaval (flute). Western influences began to arrive in the 19th century.

Literature

Ancient Greek poetry

The Cypriots have maintained since ancient times that Cyprus was the home of Greece's great epic poet Homer. Euklos, a Cypriot poet of the 8th/7th century B.C., claims that Homer was born in Sálamis and concludes from this that Cyprus was the cradle of Greek literature. An ancient epic poem which is preserved only in fragments, the "Kypria", is attributed either to Homer or to the Cypriot poet Stasinos (8th/7th c.); it deals with events preceding those described in the "Iliad". The Cypriot king Kinyras, who according to Homer was the first priest-king of Páphos, is said to have been a great lyric poet.

Folk poetry

From the medieval period onwards folk poems were written on historical themes and love poems in the Cypriot dialect. In the 19th century folk poetry took on a new lease of life in Cyprus. Vassilis Mikhailides and Dimitris Lipertis wrote in Cypriot dialect.

Greek Cypriot literature

Modern Cypriot literature is closely associated with the literature of mainland Greece, and the Cypriot dialect has given place to modern Greek. The best known representative of modern Cypriot writing is Costas Mondis, who after serving as director of the Cyprus Tourism Organisation founded Cyprus's first professional theatre, the Lyriko. The most important contemporary prose writer is Ikonomides Iannis Stavrinos.

Turkish Cypriot literature

Turkish Cypriots have had a number of notable writers, including Aziz Ibrahim and Yasin Mehmet. The poems of Yasin Nese have been set to music as nursery rhymes.

Quotations

Homeric Hymn I will sing of Aphrodite, the stately one, the fair one, the golden-crowned one: sea-girt Cyprus and its walled cities are her sole domain.

6th Homeric Hymn (date uncertain but after Homer)

Herodotus
Greek historian
(490–425 B.C.) Onesilus, being now king of Sálamis, sought to bring about a revolt of the whole of Cyprus. All were prevailed on except the Amathusians, who refused to listen to him; whereupon Onesilus sate down before Amathûs and laid siege to it . . .

Tidings came to Onesilus, the Sálaminian, who was still besieging Amathûs, that a certain Artybius, a Persian, was looked for to arrive in Cyprus with a great Persian armament. So Onesilus, when the news reached him, sent off heralds to all parts of Ionia and besought the Ionians to give him aid. After brief deliberation these last in full force passed over into the island; and the Persians about the same time crossed in their ships from Cilicia and proceeded by land to attack Sálamis; while the Phoenicians, with the fleet, sailed round the promontory which goes by the name of the Keys of Cyprus . . .

. . . By sea the Ionians, who that day fought as they have never done either before or since, defeated the Phoenicians, the Samians especially distinguishing themselves. Meanwhile the combat had begun on land, and the two armies were engaged in a sharp struggle, when thus it fell out in the matter of the generals. Artybius, astride upon his horse, charged down upon Onesilus, who, as he had agreed with his shield-bearer, aimed his blow at the rider; the horse reared and placed his fore feet upon the shield of Onesilus, when the Carian cut at him with a reaping-hook and severed the two legs from the body. The horse fell upon the spot, and Artybius, the Persian general, with him.

From Book V of Herodotus's "History" (translation by George Rawlinson, 1858)

Pomponius Mela
Roman
geographer
(1st C. A.D.) Cyprus, with a range of hills running along it in a straight line from east to west, lies almost in the middle of the gulf which extends farthest towards the coast of Asia, in the angle between Cilicia and the Syrias. It is so large that it once included nine kingdoms and now has a series of towns, the most famous of which are Sálamis, Páphos and Old Páphos – the place where the natives believe that Venus rose from the sea.

From "De Chronographia", II,102.

Strabo
Greek geographer
(63 B.C.–
1st C. A.D.) Such is the situation of the island. In excellence it falls behind none of the islands, for it has good wine and good oil and grows all the corn it needs. The copper-mines of Tamassós are highly productive, yielding also sulphate of copper and verdigris, both useful in the production of medicines. Eratosthenes tells us that in ancient times the land was densely covered with forest, so that the land could not be cultivated for the abundance of trees. The mines here were of some service, since the trees were felled for the smelting of copper and silver; and ship-building also made a contribution when men ventured over the sea with large fleets.

From "Geographica", vols 8–10

Opposite Tyre is the island of Qubrus, which is said to be twelve days' journey round. It is full of populous cities and offers the Muslims many advantages in their trade; for there are great quantities of merchandise, goods and raw materials produced there.

Muqadassi
Arab writer
(10th c.)

From his "Description of Syria", written in 985

The island is extremely fertile and produces excellent wine. It lies near the Cyclades but is not one of them. Its length is four days' journey, its breadth more than two. It has high mountains. There is one archbishop, who has three suffragans. These are Latins; but the Greeks, over whom throughout this land the Latins have dominion, have thirteen bishops, of whom one is an archbishop. They all obey the Franks and pay tribute like slaves. Whence you can see that the Franks are lords of this land, whom the Greeks and Armenians obey as serfs. They are rude in all their habits, and shabby in their dress, sacrificing chiefly to their lusts. We shall ascribe this to the wine of the country, which provokes to luxury, or rather to those who drink it. It is for this reason that Venus was said to be worshipped in Cyprus ... For the wines of this island are so thick and rich that they are sometimes specially prepared to be eaten like honey with bread. Cyprus rears many wild asses and rams, stags and hinds; but it has no lions, bears or wolves, or other dangerous beasts.

Wilbrand
von Oldenburg
German pilgrim
(13th c.)

From the journal of a pilgimage in 1211, first published in 1653

Cipres is a good yle and a great, and there are many good cities, and there is an Archbishoppe at Nichosy, and foure other Bishops in the lande. And at Famagost is one of the best havens on the sea that is in the worlde, and there are christen men and Sarasins and men of all nations. In Cipres is the hill of the holy crosse, and there is the crosse of the good thefe Dismas, as I sayd before, and some wene that there is halfe of the crosse of our lord, but it is not so, and they do wrong that make men to believe so. In Cipres lieth S Simeon, of whome the men of the countrey make a great solempnitie, and in the Castell of Amours lyeth the body of Saint Hillarion, and men kepe it worshipfully, and beside Famagost was sainct Barnarde [Barnabas] borne.

Sir John
Mandeville
English writer
(14th c.)

From "The Voiage and Travayle of Syr John Maundeville Knight" (a compilation based on earlier travellers' accounts)

Cyprus, a noble island situated in the Carpathian Sea, in the middle of the greatest bay of Asia, lying from east to west in a right line between Cilicia and Syria, the most considerable and famous island in the world, anciently abounding with riches, too much addicted to luxury and for that reason consecrated to Venus, is very large and formerly had the wealth and title of a kingdom. This island is called Cethim in the Holy Scripture; it is very fruitful of corn, abounding with silkworms, silks, oil, sugar and wine. Here are very beautiful hills, most pleasant and delightful valleys, always resounding with the melodious singing of birds. Here are warm suns, shady groves, dewy herbs, green grass and soft downy meadows to lie down and rest upon. Yet notwithstanding all this fruitfulness and pleasantness neither its cities nor villages are much frequented, but it is inhabited only by a few people that live in cottages, as if it was barren and a desert place. It has no cities but Nicosia and Famagusta, the former famous for its size and for the ruling power of the governor residing there, the latter remarkable

Martin von
Baumgarten
German pilgrim
(16th c.)

for its harbour and fortifications. All the inhabitants of Cyprus are slaves to the Venetians, being obliged to pay to the state a third part of all their increase or income . . . The poor people are so flayed and pillaged that they hardly have wherewithal to keep body and soul together.

From the account of a pilgrimage to the Holy Land in 1508, first published in 1594

John Locke
English pilgrim
(16th c.)

The second of October we returned to Arnacho (Lárnaca), where we rested untill the sixth day. This towne is a pretie village, there are thereby toward the sea divers monuments, that that there hath bene great overthrow of buildings, for to this day there is no yere when they finde not, digging under ground, either coines, caves, and sepulchres of antiquities, as we walking, did see many, so that in effect, all alongst the seacoast, throughout the whole Island, there is much ruine and overthrow of buildings; for, as they say, it was disinhabited sixe and thirtie yeres before Saint Helens time for lacke of water. And since that time it hath bene ruinated and overthrowen by Richard the first of that name, king of England, which he did in revenge of his sisters ravagement comming to Jerusalem, the which inforcement was done to her by the king of Famagusta.
   The sixt day we rid to Nicosia, which is from Arnacho seven Cyprus miles, which are one and twentie Italian miles. This is the ancientest citie of the Island and is walled about, but it is not strong neither of walles nor of situation. It is by report three Cyprus miles about, it is not thoroughly inhabited, but hath many great gardens in it, and also very many Date trees, and plentie of Pomegranates and other fruites. There dwell all the Gentilitie of the Island, and there hath every Cavallier and Conte of the Island an habitation . . . The streetes of the citie are not paived, which maketh it, with the quantitie of the gardens, to seeme but a rurall habitation. But there be many faire buildings in the Citie, there be also monasteries both of Frank and Greekes.

An account of a visit to Cyprus in 1553, included in Hakluyt's "Principal Navigations . . ."

Count Nestor
Martinengo
Venetian officer
(16th c.)

On the next morning at daybreak the town was attacked on all sides. This assault lasted six hours, but the losses on our side were small, for the Turks fought with less vigour than usual. They continually presented us with great problems on the seaward side, firing from their galleys at every attack and covering every part of the town that they could reach with their cannon. This onslaught was once again beaten off, but the town was now in a desperate situation, for there remained only seven casks of powder. Our leaders decided, therefore, to surrender on honourable conditions.

From a "Report to the Doge". In 1570–71 Martinengo defended the fortress of Famagusta for eleven months against Lala Mustafa's Turkish forces.

Giovanni Mariti
Italian merchant
(18th c,)

The town and fortress of Cerines (Kyrenia) are some twenty miles from Nicosia. The town has no great number of inhabitants. The schismatic Greeks who make up the Christian population of the island have a church there, the seat of a bishop, and the Turks have a mosque. Government business is administered by a commissioner and a judge. The inhabitants cultivate the land round the town, which brings them a good subsistence, for with its many springs this is one of the most fertile areas in Cyprus, yielding wheat, barley, silk, cotton, oil and carobs, of which last whole cargoes are sent every year to Alexandria.

From "Journeys in the Island of Cyprus, Syria and Palestine" (1769). Mariti was secretary of the British consulate in Cyprus from 1760 to 1767.

I felt no little surprise on landing to observe a handsome English coach – a vehicle which I had not seen for many years. I was still more surprised when a European came up to me and invited me to take up my quarters with the British consul here, Mr Turner. I was received by the secretary of the consulate, called Mariti, later well known and indeed famous for his "Viaggi per l'Isola di Cipro". According to my observations Lárnaca lies in latitude 34°35' north. About half the inhabitants are Mohammedans, who have two magnificent mosques for their religious practices. The Franciscans and Capuchins have four churches, which are most diligently attended by the eastern Christians in communion with the Roman church. The climate of Lárnaca was formerly most unhealthy, and innumerable inhabitants were carried off by a malignant fever. The cause of this was the bad drinking water. Things are now different thanks to Bekir Pasha, who had a water conduit constructed from the village of Arpera to Lárnaca and Saline and the surrounding swamps filled in.

Carsten Niebuhr
Frisian surveyor
(18th c.)

From "Discoveries in the East: A Journey to Arabia and Other Countries in 1761–67". Niebuhr, a member of a Danish expedition to Yemen, visited Cyprus in 1766 on the way home.

The population of Levkosia amounts to some 20,000: it cannot be exactly determined, since no account is taken of women in the census. The majority of the inhabitants are Turks, although the Greeks are almost equal in numbers . . .

   The Turkish spoken on Cyprus is particularly pure: it is said to be the best after the Turkish spoken in Constantinople. Cypriot Greek, on the other hand, is more like a dialect, containing many words from Italian . . . and also numbers of expressions from Turkish. Turkish is universally spoken in Levkosia: we found very few men who did not have some command of it, and many who spoke only Turkish; indeed most of the Greek women are also well acquainted with it. In this connection a very common custom must be mentioned: neither Greeks nor Turks say "No", but merely jerk their head up a little, for that is their manner of expressing negation.

Archduke Ludwig
Salvator
of Austria
(19th c.)

From "Levkosia, Capital of Cyprus" (1873)

I shall never forget the first impression I had of the town of Larnaca, my future official residence, while the vessel was slowly steaming towards her anchorage. The day was cloudy, and the sea very rough. The anchor was cast at a mile or so from the shore, there being no harbour, only an open bay. The town from that distance looked like the very picture of desolation; no sign of life, no vegetation anywhere visible, except a few solitary palm trees, with their long leaves drooping, as if in sign of mourning. I admit that my first thought was to remain on board, and not to land on such a forlorn-looking island . . . A large lighter, called by the natives "Mahòna", flying the American colours, soon approached our steamer. The craft contained about twenty persons; some armed with antiquated pistols, others with yatagans, and all carrying silver-headed batons six feet in length. All had the red "fez", a common headdress of both the Mussulman and Christian natives of the island.

Luigi Palma
di Cesnola
US consul
in Cyprus
(19th c.)

From "Cyprus: its Ancient Cities, Tombs and Temples" (1877). Cesnola was American consul in Cyprus from 1865 to 1876. With his private

Quotations

collection of Cypriot antiquities he founded the Metropolitan Museum of Art in New York in 1872.

Nikos Kazantzakis
Greek writer
(1882–1957)

Cyprus is the true home of Aphrodite. Never have I seen an island with such a feminine character; never have I breathed an air so full of dangerous, most sweet temptations. I feel slightly dazed, sleepy and well content, and towards evening, when the sun goes down and the wind blows in from the sea, and to right and left the sailing cutters begin to pitch and toss and the children with their bunches of jasmine flock on to the quay, my heart looses its girdle and yields itself up like Pandemos Aphrodite. What elsewhere you sense only in moments of enchantment you sense here all the time; you feel the fragrance of jasmine slowly permeating your being.

From "Descriptions of Palestine and Cyprus"

Yeoryios Seferis
Greek writer
Nobel Prizewinner
(1900–71)

What is Platres? And this island, who knows it?
I have lived my life, have become aware of names never heard before,
new lands, new madnesses of men or gods.
My fate, all astir between the last sword-stroke of an Ajax and another Sálamis,
has brought me here, to this arching coast.
The moon rose out of the sea like Aphrodite, covering the constellation of the Archer, and now moves questingly towards the heart of the Scorpion,
transforming them all.
Where is truth?
I too was an archer in the war;
my fate was that of a man who missed his target.

From the poem "Helena"

Lawrence Durrell
English writer
(1912–90)

Bellapais:
The full magnificence of the Abbey's position is not clear until one enters the inner cloister, through a superb gate decorated with marble coats of arms, and walks to the very edge of the high bluff on which it stands, the refectory windows framing the plain below with its flowering groves and curling palm-trees . . . We simply walked in quiet, bemused friendship among those slender chipped traceries and tall-shanked columns, among the armorial shields of forgotten knights and the blazing orange-trees, until we came into the shadow of the great refectory with its high roofs where the swallows were building . . .

I have one firm hold over my neighbours. I know more about Greece than they do. I am regarded with awe and respect because I have actually lived "over there", among those paragons of democratic virtue. Their idea of Greece is of Paradise on earth – a paradise without defect. And I have lived there, have Greek friends . . . Now if I wish to bring pressure to bear upon my neighbour I simply say to him: "My dear fellow, no Greek would do that, charge that, think that, etc. You astonish me." And this phrase acts like a charm, for everyone is jealous of the good character of Greeks and tries to be as like them as possible.

From "Bitter Lemons" (1957)

Johannes Gaitanides
German-Greek writer
(1909–88)

Those who are familiar with Greece are in a constant state of astonishment on Cyprus: they must be prepared for a drastic change in their ideas. Whether you are dealing with a private person or with an official, you cannot now rely on the normal Greek unpunctuality. In the vocabulary of the Cypriot the eternal putting off to "avrio", to tomorrow, is unknown. He keeps his word, although he does not lightly give it . . .

You will have the same experience in houses and in hotels. Like the streets, they are cleaner, and their technical equipment preserves the visitor from the constant struggle against the malice of *things*. The locks of doors and catches of windows perform their function in a wholly trouble-free fashion, without constantly falling into their constituent parts; taps abstain from their nerve-shattering and sleep-destroying habit of constantly dripping; and the plug-hole in the wash-basin respects the law of gravity which in Greece it likes so perseveringly to disregard. The list could be further extended: shops close punctually at 7, and for quietness on the day of rest Cyprus can compete with the British Sunday.

From "Aegean Trio: Crete, Rhodes, Cyprus" (1969)

"Cyprus"

Costas Mondi
Cypriot writer
(b. 1914)

What bound these hills so closely together?
Where were these hills so skilfully fashioned?
This sea, this sky,
how did they achieve their form
so that we can compare all others with them,
take only them as an example?

As the seas flow eastward into one another – Adriatic, Ionian, Aegean – and Europe merges with Asia, the past leaves itself visibly on the landscape. The soil of the Levant is eroded to its shore-line where forests were felled for ancient fleets, and villages remain on inland hilltops where they were driven by pirates. These half Asiatic lands, dazzled into harshness, elicit awe and a strange excitement. Their beauty is of contour and light. The olive, the rock, an arc of blue – their effect is made with magic economy, amd to them a man is always, inexplicably, returning, as if their very starkness were a lure.

Colin Thubron
English writer
(20th c.)

A March evening brought back this hard affection, on a Cyprus hillside where no colour intimated spring. Below me the land lay in calm. Half the ridges were eroded to glittering bones, and the tracks showed white and permanent in its valleys . . .

The village of Kouklia, as we walked through it, seemed almost asleep. But it was an optimistic community, in which Greek and Turk still lived together. The Turkish quarter, as always, was poorer than the Greek, but its poverty was of a clean, rural kind, and the whole village, as Giorgos had said, was knit with the stones of Aphrodite's temple. The streets, bounded by houses pleasantly shabby, with tile roofs, converged on a tiny square where a church and the coffee-shops were. On the outskirts they petered into tracks, and the courtyards were littered with ploughs, cattle troughs beaten out of petrol cans, turkeys, bread ovens and a hundred improvised odds and ends. Donkeys stood patiently in this dowdy surrealism, and the women, dressed in head-scarves and dour European clothes, stooped over their washing to show thick stockings pulled unalluringly above the knee.

From "Journey into Cyprus" (1975). Colin Thubron spent four months on the island in 1972, before partition, and describes his book as "the record of a country which will not return".

"The Refugee Children"

Yasin Nese
Turkish-Cypriot
writer
(b. 1959)

On the flight
from north to south
a Cypriot boy
had

85

left his mouth-organ behind,
had left his mouth-organ
behind;
and now he wants to play the finest tunes on it.
On the flight
from south to north
a Cypriot boy
had
left his almond-tree behind,
had left his almond-tree
behind;
and now he wants constantly to weep.
"Let me give you back your mouth-organ,
and bring back my almond-tree in exchange."
But the children cannot
climb the high wall;
the children cannot walk
through the churned-up fields.

Cypriot
proverbs

Friday's laughter is Saturday's weeping.
Nothing spreads faster than gossip and a forest fire.
Work is hard; no work is harder.
You cannot strike sparks from last year's ashes.
The son of the priest is the grandson of the devil.
If you have a tree you also have shade.
Always buy your shoes in your own country, even if they have been
   mended.
When there is a war you do not hide your sword.
Walls have ears and palings have eyes.
Our wealth is our people.

Suggested Routes

The following routes – all day trips – are intended merely as suggestions to guide visitors in planning a visit to Cyprus, leaving them free to select and vary the routes in accordance with their particular interests and preferences. Except where otherwise indicated, all the routes are on asphalt roads.

The suggested routes take in all the main tourist sights in Cyprus; but not all the places of interest described in this guide lie directly on the routes, and to see some of them it will be necessary to make detours from the main route.

The suggested routes can be followed on the map enclosed with this guide, which will help with detailed planning.

Since the "Green Line" between North and South Cyprus can be crossed only in Nicosia, the suggested routes are described separately for the two parts of the island. Visitors taking a day trip from the Greek part of the island into the Turkish-occupied north must be back by 6pm at latest. It is advisable, therefore, to make Nicosia the base for trips into North Cyprus. North and South Cyprus

In these routes the names of places which are the subject of a separate entry in the A to Z part of the guide are given in **bold** type.

The distances given in brackets at the head of each route are approximate figures for the main route, taking no account of detours or alternatives.

South Cyprus

1: Nicosia to Asínou and Kakopetriá and back (140km/85 miles)

Leave **Nicosia** on the road which runs west to **Peristeróna** (28km/ 17 miles) with the important five-domed church of SS Hilarion and Barnabas. From there continue on the main road into the **Tróodos Mountains** and then, 4km/2½ miles beyond Astromerítis, take a narrow road on the left which leads south to Nikitári and Asínou. After passing the little barn-roofed church of Vizakiá it comes to Nikitári. Ask in the kafeníon for the local priest (papas), who has the key of the church of **Asínou** (4km/2½ miles from the village), with its magnificently restored frescos of the 12th and 14th centuries. Route

From Nikitári return to the main road by way of Páno Koutraphás and turn left. 18km/11 miles beyond the junction is **Galáta**, which once had seven churches. Particularly worth seeing are two adjoining barn-roofed churches, the Panayía tis Podíthou, with unusually well preserved frescos, and the church of the Archangel Michael.

Beyond Galáta is **Kakopetriá**, the old part of which is protected as a national monument (restaurants and coffee-houses). 5km/3 miles south-west is the church of Ayios Nikólaos tis Stéyis, St Nicholas of the Roof.

The return to Nicosia is on the main road. From the road, which runs close to the border with North Cyprus, guard posts can be seen on the hills.

2: Nicosia to Tamassós and Makherás and back (70km/45 miles)

Leave Nicosia on the road which runs south-west to Palekhóri. At Káto Dhefterá, in a rock face to the right of the road, is the cave church of the Panayía Chrysospiliótissa, which is well worth a visit. Main route

From Káto Dhefterá the road goes south to Péra, near which can be found the site of ancient **Tamassós**, with tombs and the remains of temples dating from the 7th century B.C. 1.5km/1 mile west of Péra, in the village of Politikó, stands the convent of Ayios Iraklidhios (St Heraclidius).

From Péra a road runs south by way of Kambiá and Kapédhes to the monastery of **Makherás** (16km/10 miles), picturesquely situated in the foothills (800m/2600ft) of the Tróodos Mountains. The monastery was founded in the 12th century after the discovery of a legendary icon of the Mother of God.

The return to Nicosia is either on the same route as on the outward journey or on a road west via Lazaniá to Goúrri (partly unsurfaced) to rejoin the main road from Palekhóri to Nicosia.

From Lazaniá it is worth making a short detour (unsurfaced road) to the village of **Phikárdhou**. Recently restored, it displays typical 18th-century village architecture. | Detour

3: Nicosia to Limassol (140km/85 miles)

Leave Nicosia either on the ordinary road or on the motorway to Limassol. In 17km/10½ miles there is an exit from the motorway to the village of Perakhório, with a small church containing 12th century frescos. From Perakhório the motorway continues south to the exit for **Stavrovoúni**. Commandingly situated on its hill, the monastery of Stavrovoúni, the oldest and strictest (women not admitted) in Cyprus, can be seen from a long way away. In clear weather there is a magnificent view from the summit of the hill, extending over terraced slopes to the coast. 14km/8½ miles farther down the motorway a road goes off to **Léfkara**, famed for its hand-made lace and embroidery. From Léfkara the road continues south-west by way of Vávla to **Khirokitía**, where excavations have brought to light the remains of one of the oldest Neolithic settlements on the island. From here the motorway continues to **Limassol**, Cyprus's second largest town. Shortly before reaching the town it is well worth while making a detour to the remains of Amathoús, one of the city-kingdoms of ancient Cyprus. | Route

4: Lárnaca via Ayía Nápa to Dherínia and back (110km/70 miles)

From **Lárnaca**, the point of arrival for most visitors flying to Cyprus, the coast road runs east to **Ayía Nápa** (37km/23 miles), a former fishing village which is now the most popular seaside resort on the island. From the beach of fine golden sand can be seen, 8km/5 miles away, Cape Gréco, the imposing crag which rises out of the sea at the south-easterly tip of Cyprus. The coast road continues to the hotel town of Protarás and Paralímni, passing innumerable windmills, which draw up water to irrigate the extensive fields of grain and vegetables. From Dherínia, near the border with Turkish-occupied territory, there is a view of the ghost town of Varósha, only a few kilometres away. It was the hotel district of **Famagusta** before the Turkish invasion in 1974. | Main route

The return route to Lárnaca is by way of Sotíra and Liopétri, famed for its basketwork.

If the round trip is done from Ayía Nápa the distance is 55km/34 miles. | Alternative

◀ *Pétra tou Romioú, the mythical birthplace of Aphrodite*

5: Lárnaca to Pyrgá, Khirokitía and Kíti and back (140km/85 miles)

Main route	Leave **Lárnaca** on the motorway to Limassol and at Kalókhorio turn off into a road on the right which runs via Ayía Anna to the village of **Pyrgá** (21km/13 miles), with the historic old Royal Chapel. From here the route continues south on the old Nicosia–Limassol road. A detour can be made on a steep hill road (10km/6 miles) to the monastery of **Stavrovoúni** (see Route 3). In another 14km/8½ miles take a road on the right to **Léfkara**, famed for its hand-made lace and embroidery. From Léfkara the route continues by way of Vávla to **Khirokitía**, the oldest settlement on Cyprus. Then back to the motorway, and in a few kilometres take the exit for Lárnaca. In 4km/2½ miles take a road on the right signposted to Menoyía, which runs through beautiful scenery via Alaminós and Mazotós to **Kíti** (short stretch of unsurfaced road), with the church of the Panayía Angelóktistos and its magnificent 6th century mosaic. From Kíti it is a short distance to the Salt Lake of Lárnaca, on the shores of which is the **Hala Sultan Tekke**, attractively situated amid palms and cypresses. Just beyond this is Lárnaca.
Alternative Lárnaca to Limassol	Leave Lárnaca on the road signposted to the airport, Hala Sultan Tekke and Kíti; then back to the main Limassol road, from which detours can be made to Léfkara, Khirokitía and, shortly before reaching Limassol, the site of ancient Amathoús. Distance about 110km/70 miles.

6: Limassol to Plátres and Ólympos and back (130km/80 miles)

Main route	From **Limassol** take the bypass to the Tróodos/Ypsonas exit, from which a road leads 40km/25 miles north through beautiful scenery to the hill resort of Páno Plátres in the **Tróodos Mountains** with its inviting tavernas and coffee-houses. 7km/4½ miles higher up is Tróodos, the highest village on the island, well equipped with hotels and tavernas and pleasantly cool in the hot summer months, a good base for walks and climbs in the hills (see A to Z, Tróodos Mountains). From here take the road to Pródhromos and turn off into a side road on the left which leads to the highest peak in the Tróodos massif, Mount Ólympos (1951m/6401ft). From here there are magnificent views of the whole mountain range, extending in clear weather as far as the coast. On the way back a detour can be made to the legendary monastery of Troodhítissa, a place of pilgrimage for childless couples. Soon after Páno Plátres take the road to Ómodhos, with another interesting monastery. From Ómodhos the route continues through extensive vineyards by way of Kissoúsa, Ayios Amvrósios and Káto Kivídhes to join the coast road. On the way back to Limassol a visit to the medieval castle of **Kolóssi**, once held by the Knights of St John, is recommended.
Alternative Limassol to Asínou and back	Follow the road into the Tróodos Mountains, described above, as far as **Kakopetriá**, with its picturesque old town and the church of Ayios Nikólaos tis Stéyis (fine frescos). Farther north is **Galáta** with its barn-roofed churches. 4km/2½ miles beyond this take a road on the right, signposted to Nikitári, which leads to the early medieval church of **Asínou** with its fine Byzantine wall paintings. Distance about 180km/110 miles.

7: Limassol to Kolóssi and Koúrion and back (36km/22 miles)

Main route	This route takes in the most interesting sights around Limassol. Leave **Limassol** by way of Archbishop Makarios Avenue or Franklin Roosevelt Street, on the road to Páphos. The road runs through large

plantations of citrus fruits and comes in 10km/6 miles to **Kolóssi**, with the medieval castle of the Knights of St John.

6km/4 miles beyond this, on a plateau to the left of the road, are the excavated remains of ancient **Koúrion**.

A few kilometres farther west on the Páphos road are the remains of the ancient sanctuary of Apollo.

On the way back the interesting Koúrion Museum in Episkopí can be visited. There is a good beach for bathers and sunbathers at Koúrion.

From Limassol take the road to Kolóssi and Koúrion, and from there continue on the coast road, passing Pétra tou Romioú, the legendary rock marking the spot where Aphrodite emerged from the foam. A few kilometres farther west is **Koúklia**, with the most important shrine of Aphrodite in the ancient world. Beyond this are **Yeroskípos**, with the domed church of Ayía Paraskeví, and **Páphos**, with its many interesting ancient remains. Distance about 70km/45 miles.

Alternative
Limassol to
Páphos

8: Round Trip from Páno Plátres through the Tróodos Range
(100km/60 miles)

Leave Páno Plátres on the road to Tróodos and from there continue on the Nicosia road, passing **Kakopetriá** and **Galáta**. At Káto Koutraphás take a road on the right to Nikitári and ask for the priest (papas), who takes visitors to the church of **Asínou**, outside the little town.

On the way back it is worth making a detour to Vizakiá, which has a small barn-roofed church. Then back to the Tróodos–Nicosia road, which leads to Kakopetriá.

Galáta and Kakopetriá have interesting barn-roofed churches with wall paintings. From Kakopetriá the road returns to Páno Plátres.

Main route

This route passes through beautiful scenery; the roads are narrow, with many bends.

From Páno Plátres take the road running up to Tróodos and from there continue on the road to Kakopetriá, turning off in 7km/4½ miles onto the road to Kyperoúnda and Khandriá. From here the road continues to **Lagoudherá**, a finely situated old mountain village with a notable monastic church. Then back to Khandriá, passing vineyards and fruit orchards, and from there via Polystipos to **Platanistása**, where the custodian of the barn-roofed church of Stavrós tou Ayiasmáti can be picked up. From Platanistása a narrow road runs via Alona and Askás to Palekhóri (fine wall paintings); then back to Khandriá and Páno Plátres.

Alternative
Into the
eastern Tróodos

From Limassol take the main road into the Tróodos range by way of Káto Amíandos. Distance about 180km/110 miles.

Starting from
Limassol

9: Páphos to the Akámas Peninsula and back (110km/70 miles)

Leave **Páphos** on the Pólis road (Tombs of the Kings Street), which runs past the Tombs of the Kings and comes to Emba, with an interesting little church. 10km/6 miles from Páphos, on higher ground, is **St Neó-phytos Monastery** (16th c.), with the 12th century cave hermitage (Enkleistra) of Neóphytos.

From here return to Emba and follow the coast road (rewarding detour to picturesque Coral Bay) to Péyia and the basilicas of Ayios Yeóryios. Near the basilicas is an attractive taverna from which there are fine views of the little port of Péyia and the coast. From here a detour can be made to Lara Bay (beautiful beach; protected area for turtles), on the unsurfaced road to the Akámas peninsula.

Route

From Péyia the route continues via Káthikas and Droúsha to **Pólis**, on a beautiful road with fine views of the vineyards, the sea and the Tróodos Mountains. The quiet little town of Pólis, unlike other coastal towns, has remained unspoiled by tourism; it has no large hotels and is patronised mainly by backpackers. From here the route continues by way of the little port of Lakhí to the "Baths of Aphrodite" (6km/4 miles), amid rocky coastal scenery. There is an attractive walk along the promontory to the Fontana Amorosa, Aphrodite's Fountain of Love. Then return to Páphos on the main road.

10: Walks in the Tróodos Mountains

See Sights from A to Z in South Cyprus, Tróodos Mountains

North Cyprus

1: Nicosia to Kyrenia and back (70km/45 miles)

From **Nicosia** a new road cuts through the Pentadáktylos Hills to the north coast. 20km/12½ miles from Nicosia, just beyond a pass, take a road on the left which runs through a military area to **St Hilarion**, the best preserved castle in the Kyrenia Hills. From the hill on which it stands there are fine views of the idyllically situated little town of Kyrenia and the surrounding hills. After visiting Kyrenia, until 1974 a flourishing tourist resort, with a picturesque harbour and castle, take the road signposted to **Bellapais** (6km/4 miles south-east), where many British people still have houses. Bellapais Abbey is the finest Gothic monastic ruin in the Mediterranean area. From here a narrow road leads west to join the main road back to Nicosia.

Alternatives
From Famagusta

Leave Famagusta on the Nicosia road and at Trakhóni/Demirhan turn right into a road which runs north to Kyrenia. Distance about 180km/110 miles.

From Kyrenia

The round trip from Kyrenia to St Hilarion Castle and Bellapais Abbey is about 30km/20 miles.

2: Nicosia to Famagusta and Sálamis and back (120km/75 miles)

Main route

From Nicosia take the expressway which runs east to the port of **Famagusta** (61km/38 miles), with its old town surrounded by Venetian walls. From here the coast road runs 8km/5 miles north to the world-famed excavations of ancient **Sálamis**, once the most powerful of the city-kingdoms of Cyprus. A few kilometres west of the necropolis of Sálamis, the largest cemetery area on the island, is the abandoned monastery of St Barnabas, which is well worth a visit. Before returning to Nicosia on the more northerly of the two main roads from Famagusta a visit should be made to the site of ancient Enkomi, near Tuzla.

Alternatives
From Famagusta

Kantara Castle in the Pentadáktylos Hills. Distance about 90km/55 miles.

From Kyrenia

From Kyrenia take the coast road running east, which in 10km/6 miles turns south through the Pentadáktylos Hills to join the more northerly Nikosia–Famagusta road at Trakhóni/Demirhan. Then as described above. Distance about 150km/95 miles.

3: Nicosia to Mórphou, Sóloi and Vouní and back (120km/75 miles)

Take the road which goes west from Nicosia and at Skylloúra/Yılmaz-   Main route
köy turn into a road on the left to Philiá/Serhadköy. (An alternative
route is to continue on the main road to Mýrtou/Çamlıbel and from
there take a road on the left to Mórphou). The road runs south-west via
Káto Kopiá/Zümrütköy to the little town of **Mórphou**, with the abandoned church of St Mamas and an interesting small museum. 12km/7½
miles west on the coast road is Karavostási/Gemikonağı. Above the
village is the site of ancient **Sóloi**, with a restored Roman theatre and
the remains of an early Christian basilica. From here a road ascends,
with many bends, to the palace of **Vouní** (5km/3 miles), on a hill
(250m/820ft) from which in clear weather the view reaches to the coast
of Turkey. The return to Nicosia is by way of Mórphou and then on the
new expressway.

Leave **Kyrenia** on the coast road to the west, which in 8km/5 miles   **Alternative**
passes the Peace Monument, commemorating the Turkish landings in   From Kyrenia
1974. At Mýrtou/Çamlıbel turn right into the road to Mórphou/Güze-
lyurt. Then as described above. Distance about 120km/75 miles.

4: Tour of the Karpasía Peninsula from Famagusta (230km/145 miles)

Leave **Famagusta** on the road which leads north past the remains of   Route
ancient **Sálamis** to Tríkomo/Iskele. From here there is an attractive
detour (30km/20 miles there and back) to **Kantara** Castle on a winding
road which runs up into the Pentadáktylos Hills, passing endless olive-
groves and lonely hill villages. The romantic ruins of Kantara Castle
(signposted) lie on the summit of a hill, overgrown by grass and trees.
From here there is a superb view of the long, narrow Karpasía peninsula with its cliff-fringed coast and idyllic little bays.
   From Tríkomo/Iskele the route continues on the coast road (recently
improved) and then turns inland by way of Livádhia/Sazlıköy to Lyth-
rángomi/Boltaslı. It then continues via Ayía Triás to the largest place on
the peninsula, Rizokárpaso/Dipkarpaz (30km/20 miles). From here
there is an attractive detour to Cape Andréas, with beautiful bathing
beaches. On the way back there is another possible detour from Rizo-
kárpaso/Dipkarpaz to the church of Ayios Phílon and the ancient site of
Aphéndrika. Then back to Famagusta on the main road.

Sights from A to Z: South Cyprus

Ασίνου
Altitude: 450m/1475ft

Half way between Nicosia and Tróodos a road goes off on the left to the village of Nikitári, 4km/2½ miles south of which is the isolated barn-roofed church of Asínou, with magnificent wall paintings; the key is held by the village priest in Nikitári. On Sundays and public holidays this is a very popular resort with the people of Cyprus.

Until the medieval period there was a little town called Asínou here, thought to have been founded in the 11th century B.C. by settlers from the ancient city of Asine in the Argolid (Peloponnese).

Situation and characteristics

★★ Church of the Panayía Phorviótissa

The church, built in the early 12th century, belonged to the monastery of Phorvia, which existed until the 16th century. The name Phorvia comes from the euphorbias (spurges) which are common in this area. After the destruction of the monastery the name was transferred to the church.

The church is single-aisled, with an apse at the east end and barrel vaulting under the barn roof. The narthex, added at the end of the 12th century, has apse-like projections at each end. While the church itself is built of undressed stone with lime mortar, the narthex has walls of carefully dressed ashlar.

An inscription under the painting of SS Constantine and Helen records that the church was built and the walls painted at the expense of Nikephoros Magistros in 1105/06. The Byzantine title of *magistros* was borne by a high official or judge.

The narthex was built on at the end of the 12th century. Under the painting of St George is another inscription giving the donor's name as Nikephoros, "owner of a racing stable". A third inscription over the doorway of the narthex gives the date 1333, with Theophilos as donor; at that time the paintings in the church and narthex were renewed.

A painting of the early 14th century over the south doorway of the church shows Nikephoros Magistros presenting the church to the Mother of God. It can be seen that the church originally had no narthex but already had a saddle roof.

Inscriptions and portrait of donor

The wall paintings have been excellently restored in clear colours by the Dumbarton Oaks Institute of Harvard University. Two main phases can be distinguished, the early 12th century and the 14th century.

Wall paintings

The paintings of this period, which date from about 1105/06, are in the sanctuary and the western part of the naos.

In the conch of the apse, in accordance with Byzantine tradition, is the Mother of God as Theotokos ("God-Bearer"), with arms raised in prayer, flanked by the Archangels Michael and Gabriel (over-painted in 14th century). Under her is the Communion of the Apostles (a reference to the Last Supper), in which Christ gives bread and wine to the apostles, with Judas turning his back on Christ and taking the bread out of his mouth. In the lowest register are six Fathers of the Church, symbolising the timelessness

Early 12th c.

◀ *The ancient theatre of Koúrion (reconstructed)*

The church of Asínou, with beautifully restored wall paintings

of the Church. In niches flanking the apse are the Birth of the Virgin and the Presentation of the Virgin in the Temple.

The west bay of the church, separated from the central bay by rectangular piers, also has 12th century paintings. In the vaulting is the Descent of the Holy Ghost (Pentecost). On the south wall is the Raising of Lazarus. Below the painting of Constantine and Helen (who were canonised by the Eastern church) are other Orthodox saints.

On the west wall are the Entry into Jerusalem, the Last Supper and the Dormition of the Mother of God (Koimisis). On the north wall, below the Washing of the Feet, are the 40 Martyrs of Sebaste, frozen to death on an ice-covered lake.

14th c.

The rest of the church has 14th century paintings. On the vaulting above the south doorway are the Nativity of Christ, the Presentation in the Temple, the Baptism and the Transfiguration. On the opposite side are the Betrayal (Judas's Kiss), the Bearing of the Cross, the Crucifixion and the Entombment. In the lowest register are various Orthodox saints. On the piers between the central and west bays are Peter and Paul, the Princes of the Apostles.

In the narthex are St George, St Mamas on his lion and St Anastasia. In the dome is Christ Pantokrator surrounded by angels. Below him are scenes from the Last Judgment.

Surroundings of Asínou

Vizakiá

6km/4 miles north of Asínou on the road to Nicosia is the little village church of Vizakiá (key in house next to church), with 16th century wall paintings which are of interest for their naïve but impressive style. The paintings, which date from the Venetian period and show clear western influence, depict scenes from the life of Christ.

On the south wall are the Annunciation, the Nativity, the Presentation in the Temple, the Baptism and the Raising of Lazarus. The central painting on the west wall is the Crucifixion; the soldier who is piercing Christ's side with his spear is dressed in the style of a Venetian noble. Below this are the Washing of the Feet, the Last Supper, the Betrayal and the Descent from the Cross.

An example of the naïve and very lively narrative style of the paintings is the Last Supper, in which the disciples are holding forks. In the representation of the Betrayal the soldiers have Venetian swords.

Ayía Nápa   F 11/12

Αγία Νάπα
Altitude: sea level
Population: 2000

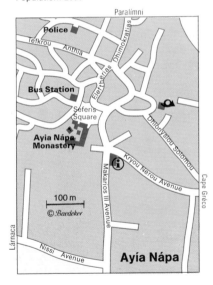

The popular seaside resort of Ayía Nápa lies 40km/25 miles east of Lárnaca in a bay bounded on the south-east by Cape Gréco and on the west by Cape Pýla. Beyond the "Green Line" between the Greek and the Turkish-occupied parts of the island is the former hotel town of Varósha, now a ghost town (see Sights in North Cyprus, Famagusta).

Ayía Nápa, formerly a small fishing village, takes its name from the monastery of Ayía Nápa, the town's principal tourist sight. It lies in one of the most fertile agricultural areas on the island (fruit and vegetables). The area is also known Kokkino-khoria ("red villages") on account of its reddish-brown soil.

Situation and characteristics

After the Turkish invasion of 1974, which left the Famagusta hotel district of Varósha in Turkish hands, Ayía Nápa developed in a very short time into the most popular seaside resort in southern Cyprus. Numerous new hotel complexes mushroomed, and the town now has more than 10,000 beds available for visitors. With its beautiful sandy beaches – a rarity on the island – its varied coastal scenery and its facilities for all kinds of water sports it offers everything the holidaymaker can wish for. The tourist infrastructure – tavernas, bars, souvenir shops, discothèques and other entertainment facilities, cater for every holiday need. Only the harbour with its old tavernas still recalls the former fishing village.

★The resort

★ Monastery of Ayía Nápa

Situation and
characteristics

In the centre of the town, on Makarios III Avenue, is the monastery of Ayía Nápa, now an œcumenical conference centre for the World Council of Churches.

The monastery is dated by an inscription to the year 1530, during the period of Venetian rule. According to legend the church was built on the spot where a hunter found the legendary icon of the Mother of God in a grotto. Situated in a densely wooded area, the monastery was dedicated to Our Lady of the Forests, Ayía Nápa. The present buildings date mainly from the Venetian period; the bell-tower is modern.

In the centre of the monastery courtyard, in a domed fountain-house, can be seen an octagonal fountain basin decorated with garlands and Cupids, and with the heads of a man and a woman, presumed to be the founders of the monastery. Round the courtyard are the conventual buildings, with arcades of pointed arches – a feature characteristic of Crusader Gothic. Facing the south entrance is a two-storey gatehouse with Renaissance-style windows. In the church steps lead down to the cave church below, the grotto in which the icon of the Mother of God is said to have been found.

Church tower

In front of the monastery can be found a centuries-old mulberry fig-tree (*Ficus sycomorus*), a tree of North African origin which is thought to have been planted during the period of Lusignan rule. The fruit is edible.

Surroundings of Ayía Nápa

Cape Gréco

8km/5 miles east of Ayía Nápa is Cape Gréco, the south-easterly tip of the island. Many ships are believed to have been wrecked on this rugged crag rising sheer out of the sea. At the tip of the cape is a radar station. There is good walking along the cliff-fringed coast.

Fountain, Ayía Nápa Monastery

Cape Gréco, the south-easterly tip of Cyprus

Paralímni and Protarás have developed in recent years into popular holiday resorts. Between the two villages is the "Valley of Windmills". The windmills draw up the water needed for the irrigation of the fields of potatoes and other vegetables.

Paralímni, Protarás

From a viewing terrace in the village of Dherínia, which lies just inside the border with North Cyprus, there is a view over the "Green Line" of Famagusta and the abandoned and dilapidated hotels of Varósha.

Dherínia

The village of Liopétri, a little way inland, is famed for its basketwork. The octagonal-domed village church of Ayios Andrónikos dates from the 15th century.

Liopétri

14km/8½ miles west of Ayía Nápa is the harbour of Potamós, with small tavernas which serve excellent fish. It is reached on a road which runs down to the coast from Xylophágou.

Xylophágou, Potamós

The British Sovereign Base of Dhekélia lies to the west of Ayía Nápa.

Dhekélia

Chrysorroyiátissa Monastery   F 3

Μονή Χρυσορρωγιατίσσης
Altitude: 850m/2790ft

From the Páphos–Pólis road, just before Stroumbí, the road to Polémi goes off on the right and climbs through the Tróodos Mountains to the Chrysorroyiátissa Monastery (40km/25 miles), the present buildings of which date from the 18th and 20th centuries. From here there are fine views of the gently sloping vineyards in the surrounding area.

Situation and characteristics

99

Chrysorroyiátissa Monastery

Foundation legends

The origins of the monastery go back to 1152, when, in a cave near Yeroskípos, a monk named Ignatius is said to have salvaged an icon, unscathed, from a blazing fire.

An alternative story is that during the iconoclastic controversy of the 8th and 9th centuries a woman threw the icon into the sea at Constantinople, from where it was carried by the sea to Cyprus and washed ashore. There it was found by a fisherman, who hid it in a cave. Later a monastery was founded to house the icon, which was believed to have been painted by Luke the Evangelist, and dedicated to Our Lady of the Hill of the Golden Pomegranate.

History

During the period of Turkish rule the monastery was impoverished and fell into ruin, until in the 18th century the Bishop of Páphos built a new monastery. When the abbot supported the Greek struggle for independence in 1821 the Turkish authorities sent troops who destroyed much of the monastery.

Church

In the church, which is surrounded by a two-storey range of cells, is the wonderworking icon of the Mother of God, which is credited with the power of healing the sick and protecting criminals. Every year on August 15th (by the Julian calendar) the feast of the Dormition of the Mother of God is celebrated with great splendour. The carved iconostasis dates from the 18th century. The church has a fine silver-plated cross, discovered by a local shepherd in 1970.

Winery

In the cellars visitors can see the monastery's own wine-making establishment with its huge oak casks. Excellent wine (see Practical Information: South Cyprus, Wine) is made here by traditional methods, using Cypriot types of grape which were not attacked by phylloxera (Xynisteri white grapes and Ophthalmo, Mavron and Maratheftiko red grapes).

Vineyards round the monastery

Chrysorroyiátissa Monastery

Surroundings of Chrysorroyiátissa

3km/2 miles south stands the Ayía Moní, a small daughter house of Chrysorroyiátissa which is no longer occupied by monks and is used as a guest house. The monastery is said to have been built in the 4th century on the site of an ancient temple of Hera. Stones from ancient buildings are incorporated in the structure of the monastery, which was renovated in the 17th and 19th centuries.

Ayía Moní

3km/2 miles north of Chrysorroyiátissa lies the village of Páno Panayiá (alt. 2625ft). Here, in 1913, the future Archbishop and President Makarios was born in a house (now a museum) which had just two rooms where the family lived, ate and slept, with a stall to the rear for the livestock. Photographs illustrate Makarios's life, while the simple domestic equipment shows how modestly the future archbishop's family lived.

Páno Panayiá

Galáta

E/F 5

Γαλάτα
Altitude: 600–620m/1970–2035ft

55km/34 miles south-west of Nicosia on the main road to Tróodos, in the valley of the river Karyótis, is the hill village of Galáta. Like nearby Kakopetriá (see entry), it is a popular holiday resort during the hot months of the year. Of Galáta's churches, originally seven in number, four remain, the most notable are the churches of the Panayía tis Podíthou and the Archangel Michael, to the north of the village, while the other two, the Church of Áyios Sozómenos stands in the middle of the old village, and the smaller Church of Ayía Paraskevi lies on the old Galáta to Kakopetriá road. The keys of the churches can be obtained from the village priest (on the road to the Panayía tis Podíthou, opposite the Gymnasium).

Situation and characteristics

★Church of the Panayía tis Podíthou

The church of the Mother of God Eleousa (the Compassionate), originally belonging to the monastery of the Panayía tis Podíthou, was built in the early 16th century. It has a saddle roof supported on a wall surrounding the church. Thanks to the circulation of air in the "ambulatory" thus formed round the church the wall paintings are unusually well preserved. See Art and Architecture, Byzantine Wall Paintings.

General

The paintings show the influence of the Italian Renaissance, which reached Cyprus towards the end of the 15th century. The strictly prescribed Byzantine style of painting is relaxed in the sharply individualised representation of the figures.

An inscription on the west front of the church gives the date of building as 1502, and there are portraits of the donors, a French nobleman named Demetre de Coron and his wife Helen. The donor, an old man, is shown presenting a model of the church to the Mother of God. To the left of this scene are the figures of other donors.

Inscription; portraits of donors

In the apse is a painting of the Mother of God enthroned holding the Child, flanked by two angels. The style of the painting is reminiscent of the paintings in Kalopanayiótis Monastery (see entry). Below this is the Communion of the Apostles, in which the handsome, classically formed faces of the disciples show clear western influence. On the east gable Moses is depicted receiving the Tables of the Law and seeing the burning bush. On the north and south walls of the sanctuary (bema) are scenes from the story of Joachim and Anne. On the west wall of the church is a dynamic representation of the Crucifixion, with a use of perspective which is the clearest indication of the influence of the Italian Renaissance.

Wall paintings

The church of the Panayía Podíthou, Galáta

★Church of the Archangel Michael

Situation and characteristics

100m/110yd south of the Panayía tis Podíthou stands the church of the Panayía Theotókos (the "God-Bearer"), previously a family chapel. Some years ago it was given a new saddle roof in order to prevent any further deterioration of the wall paintings.

Portraits of donors

An inscription over the north doorway gives the date of foundation as 1514. There are portraits of the donors of the church, Stefano Zacharia and his wife, and the donors of the paintings, Polos Zacharia, his wife Madelena and their children. These last are below the representation of the Deesis – Christ enthroned with the Mother of God and St John, who are interceding for mankind. Madelena is holding a rosary, which suggests that she was a Roman Catholic. The daughter kneeling behind her is holding an open book with the verses of the Acathist Hymn, an Orthodox hymn to the Mother of God – indicating that the children were brought up in the Orthodox faith. The lion in the family coat of arms prompts the speculation that Madelena belonged to the Lusignan family, kings of Cyprus, and had married a Venetian. The name of the painter is given as Symeon Axentes, who was also responsible for the paintings in the church of Ayios Sozómenos (below).

Wall paintings

The wall paintings inside the church show western influence. On the south wall is a cycle of New Testament scenes, beginning with the Annunciation and continuing with the Nativity, the Presentation in the Temple, the Raising of Lazarus, the Entry into Jerusalem, the Transfiguration and the Last Supper.

On the west wall are the Bearing of the Cross, the Crucifixion and the Descent from the Cross. Next to these are the Washing of the Feet, Christ on the Mount of Olives, the Betrayal, Christ before Annas and Caiaphas, Christ before Pilate and Peter's Denial. On the north wall are the Mocking of Christ, the Flagellation, the Lamentation, the Resurrection, Christ with

Mary Magdalene and the Descent into Hades. After these are scenes from the life of the Virgin. In the sanctuary are the Ascension, the Descent of the Holy Ghost (Pentecost), the Hospitality of Abraham and the Sacrifice of Isaac.

Church of Ayios Sozómenos

Above the old road from Galáta to Kako-petriá, to the right of the new church, is the church of Ayios Sozómenos (key held by the village priest), which has a fine cycle of wall paintings (not yet restored). An inscription over the west doorway records that the church was built by thirteen inhabitants of the village and that the donor of the paintings was one Ioannis.

Situation and characteristics

Along the upper part of the walls are New Testament scenes, beginning over the south doorway with the Annunciation. On the lower half of the walls are various saints, notable among them St Mamas and St George. The figure of St George has an inscription naming the donor of the paintings and the painter, Symeon. Under this painting are scenes from the life of St George, and adjoining these are scenes from the life of the Virgin. On the north wall are military saints.

Wall paintings

The outer walls of the church also have paintings. On the north wall are the Last Judgment and the seven Oecumenical Councils, including the Triumph of Orthodoxy. The representations of the Councils show the Emperor in the middle, flanked by prelates, with the condemned heretics crouching in front of them.

Hala Sultan Tekke

F 9

Τεκκεξ Χαλα Σούλταν
Altitude: sea level

On the road from Lárnaca to the airport, beyond the Salt Lake, can be seen, surrounded by palms, cypresses and lemon-trees, the burial mosque of Hala Sultan ("Honoured Mother"), foster-mother or aunt of the Prophet Mohammed, or according to another version of the legend the aunt of one of Mohammed's close associates. Soon after the turning for the airport a road branches off on the right to the Tekke (a kind of Muslim equivalent of a monastery), the fourth most important Islamic place of pilgrimage, after the Kaaba in Mecca, the tomb of the Prophet in Medina and al Aksha in Jerusalem.

Situation and ★importance

Hala Sultan, whose Arabic name was Umm Haram, was the wife of the governor of Palestine and came to Cyprus in 647 in the Sultan's suite during the victorious advance of the Muslim forces, but while in Cyprus in 649 was killed by falling from her mule. Thereafter, during the period of Turkish rule, Turkish ships sailing past her tomb dipped their flags in her honour.

The present mosque was built by Seyyit Emir Effendi, the Turkish governor of Cyprus, in 1816.

History

In the gardens in front of the mosque is the usual ablutions fountain. The mosque itself, in the classical manner of mosque architecture (see Art and Culture, Ottoman Art), has a square ground-plan and a domed roof. The

The mosque

Hala Sultan Tekke

A glimpse of the gardens

dome is borne on four pillars with relief decoration, on which are inscriptions with the names of the Caliphs. The sparse furnishings of the mosque, which is whitewashed and has mats and carpets on the floor, consist of the mihrab (prayer niche) marking the direction of Mecca and the minbar (pulpit).

The tomb

Beside the mihrab is a doorway leading to the tomb chamber. The tomb is screened by curtains, but with the aid of a pocket torch it is possible to see, above the sarcophagus, a large stone on two timber supports. According to the legend the stone flew from Mecca to Cyprus on the day Umm Haram died and hovered over her tomb.

An alternative legend has it that on the day before Umm Haram's death three stones sailed over the sea from Jerusalem; and according to still another version the stone was transported from Sinai by angels.

In a side room are the sarcophagi of important Muslim figures, including the grandmother of King Hussein of Jordan.

Surroundings of the Hala Sultan Tekke

Excavations

500m/550yd west on the unsurfaced road which passes the Hala Sultan Tekke is the fenced excavation site of a Late Bronze Age settlement on which work is still in progress. The excavators have brought to light a large town of about the same size as Kítion, laid out on a rectangular plan, the name of which is unknown. The grave goods found in tombs included artistic articles in gold, silver and faience. The most interesting find was a bath of dressed stone, similar to Minoan baths on Crete. Objects recovered in the excavations are displayed in the Turkish fort in Lárnaca.

Salt Lake

The Salt Lake of Lárnaca has an area of some 5sq.km/2sq. miles and a circumference of 11.5km/7 miles. Between November and March this is the haunt of flamingos from the Caspian Sea and other migrant birds. The existence of the Salt Lake is explained by a popular legend. It is said that Lazarus one day passed a large vineyard in which the vines were heavy with grapes and, being hungry and thirsty, asked the woman who owned it for a few grapes. She refused to give him any, saying that all her grapes were dried up: whereupon Lazarus cursed the vineyard and it turned into a salt lake.

The extraction of salt from the lake began in ancient times, and from the Middle Ages until the beginning of the 20th century salt was an important export, sold in large quantities to Europe and neighbouring countries. Accordingly during the period of Lusignan rule Lárnaca was known as Salines. Since the lake lies some 2.5cm/1in. below sea level it is thought to be fed by sea-water seeping through the dunes. Additional water had to be brought in from the sea in pipelines.

Salt extraction

During the rain-free months of August and September, when the lake is covered with a layer of salt 3cm/1¼in. thick, the salt was extracted with the aid of donkeys and small tractors and piled up in great mounds on the shores of the lake. Since 1992, however, owing to increasing air pollution from nearby Lárnaca airport, salt is no longer extracted here or from the larger salt lake of Akrotíri.

Kakopetriá F 5

Κακοπετριά
Altitude: 670m/2177ft

60km/37 miles south-west of Nicosia and 15km/9 miles north of the little town of Tróodos in the Tróodos Mountains (see entry) is Kakopetriá ("bad stones"), now a popular holiday resort whose hotels, tavernas and coffee-houses attract large numbers of Cypriots, particularly from Nicosia. It lies near the neighbouring village of Galáta (see entry) in the beautiful and fertile Karyótis valley with its large plantations of poplars, apple-trees and walnut-trees. Kakopetriá is an important apple-growing centre famed for its preserved fruit (glykó).

Situation and characteristics

The old centre of the village, built on a ridge above the river, is now a statutorily protected national monument, and the houses, mostly dating from the 18th and 19th centuries, have been restored with the help of state grants. They are built of sun-dried brick – with a plaster facing – on stone foundations. The other main sight is the saddle-roofed church of Ayios Nikólaos, 5km/3 miles south-west of the village.

Sights

★★ Church of Ayios Nikólaos tis Stéyis

To reach the church (open: Tues.–Sat. 9am–4pm, Sun. 11am–4pm) leave the village on the Tróodos road and turn right into a narrow road sign-posted to the church.

Situation and characteristics

The church of Ayios Nikólaos tis Stéyis (St Nicholas of the Roof), on a site which now belongs to the Archbishop of Cyprus, is attached to a holiday home for schoolchildren. It was originally the church of a monastery founded in the 9th century of which no trace survives.

As the name "of the Roof" indicates, this is one of the characteristic Cypriot barn-roofed churches (see Art and Culture, Byzantine Church Types). The original domed cruciform church of the 11th century was given an additional saddle roof and a narthex was built on to the west end in the 12th century.

The wall paintings (well restored) were the work of six centuries, from the early 11th century – among the earliest wall paintings in Cyprus – to the 17th century.

Wall paintings

Church of St Nicholas "of the Roof"

11th century	The paintings at the west end of the naos date from the early 11th century. On the north side are the Transfiguration and the Raising of Lazarus, on the south side the Entry into Jerusalem. The fragments of the Dormition of the Mother of God also date from this period. In the bema other 11th century paintings were discovered under 14th century paintings, including the Mother of God flanked by angels, the Ascension and the Descent of the Holy Ghost (Pentecost). The paintings are in the style characteristic of the art of Constantinople at that period.
12th century	On the south-west wall of the church are paintings of the early 12th century, including a scene from the life of the Virgin and the Forty Martyrs of Sebaste. Near the bema is St Nicholas with a small figure of the donor, a work of outstanding quality. In the narthex is a representation of the Last Judgment. Like the frescos in the church at Asínou (see entry), these paintings belong to the Middle Byzantine period.
14th century	Other paintings were added during the period of Lusignan rule. The Crucifixion and the Resurrection on the north side of the church date from the early 14th century. In the dome is Christ Pantokrator, and in the south arm of the church are the Nativity, the Presentation in the Temple and the Annunciation. The Nativity is depicted in an unusual form – probably reflecting Oriental influence – with the Mother of God sitting up rather than in the usual reclining position, in the type of the Galaktotrophoúsa (suckling the Child).

Church of the Panayía Theotókos

Situation and importance	On the outskirts of Kakopetriá, on the right of the old road to Galáta (near the BP filling station), stands the modest little 16th century barn-roofed church of the Panayía Theotókos (key in the house next the filling station). The church is built of sun-dried brick on a stone foundation.

The Forty Martyrs of Sebaste

About half of the original wall paintings have been preserved. Over the entrance is a painting of the donors, who are named as Leontius and his wife Lucretia, with an inscription giving the date of construction as 1520. The names of the donors and their dress show that Leontius was a Greek and his wife a Venetian. In the foreground is another man in a black tunic, probably the donor of the wall paintings.

Portraits of donors

On the north wall are the Entombment, the Holy Women at the Tomb, the Resurrection, the Descent of the Holy Ghost (Pentecost) and the Dormition of the Mother of God. In the Dormition, note the small figure of the Jew Jephonias who according to an apocryphal gospel tried to touch the bier and had his hands cut off by an angel.

In the bema are the Sacrifice of Isaac, the Hospitality of Abraham, the Ascension and figures of prophets. The Hospitality of Abraham (entertaining the three angels unawares) is seen in the Orthodox church as a symbol of the Trinity. On the conch of the apse is the Mother of God with arms raised in prayer, in the type known as Blacherniótissa, flanked by the Archangels Michael and Gabriel. Below this are the Communion of the Apostles and six fathers of the Church.

Wall paintings

Kalopanayiótis   F 4

Καλοπαναγιώτης
Altitude: 720m/2360ft

In the Marathása valley on the northern slopes of the Tróodos Mountains, 20km/12½ miles from the village of Tróodos, is the hill village of Kalopanayiótis, famed for its sulphur springs.

Situation and characteristics

Near the springs is a complex of three churches (keys obtainable from the village priest) which belonged to the former monastery of Ayios Ioannis

Lampadistís (St John Lampadistes). The churches have wall paintings of
different periods.

★ Monastery of Ayios Ioannis Lampadistís

General

The three churches are covered by a common roof. The most southerly of
the three, an 11th century domed cruciform church, is dedicated to St
Heraclidius. The second church, dedicated to St John Lampadistes, was
rebuilt in the 18th century. The two churches have a common narthex of the
15th century at the west end. On the north side is a small 15th century
chapel known as the Latin Chapel.

**Church of
St Heraclidius**

The church of St Heraclidius has wall paintings of the early 13th and the
early 15th centuries. Heraclidius was appointed by Paul to be the first
bishop of Tamassós (see entry). He is buried in the monastery of St Heraclidius at
Tamassós (see entry).

**13th century
wall paintings**

The paintings in the dome and the west and south arms of the church date
from the 13th century. The paintings, in a reversion to an earlier Comnene
style, show Oriental influence.

In the dome is Christ Pantokrator, surrounded by angels and prophets. In
the pendentives are the four Evangelists. In the western arm of the church
are the Entry into Jerusalem, the Raising of Lazarus, the Sacrifice of Isaac
and the Crucifixion. The Entry into Jerusalem is a painting of particular
quality; an unusual but realistic feature is that the children cutting palm
branches are wearing black leather gloves. Unusual too is the placing of the
Sacrifice of Isaac (normally found in the bema) on the west wall. On the
vaulting of the south arm of the church is the Ascension.

**15th century
wall paintings**

The second series of paintings – in a Late Byzantine style of a very individual character – dates from the early 15th century. Over thirty New
Testament scenes are depicted on the remaining vaults of the church.

Monastery of St John Lampadistes

Courtyard of the monastery of St John Lampadistes

The cycle of scenes from the life of Christ begins on the east wall above the altar with the Annunciation and continues with the Nativity, the Adoration of the Kings, the Presentation in the Temple, Christ dispatching his disciples to fetch the colt, the Entry into Jerusalem, Mary, sister of Lazarus, meeting Christ on his way to Bethany and the Raising of Lazarus.

In the northern vault are Christ before Annas and Caiaphas, Christ before Pilate, the Mocking, the Bearing of the Cross and, in the lunette, the Dormition of the Mother of God.

In the south-west of the naos are another representation of Christ before Annas and Caiaphas, various healing miracles by Christ, the appearance of Christ after his Resurrection and Doubting Thomas.

On the other walls are the Entombment, the Descent into Hades (Anástasis), the Tree of Jesse and various saints. In the conch of the apse is the Mother of God Blacherniótissa, standing between the Archangels Michael and Gabriel with her hands raised in prayer.

Church of St John Lampadistes

The barrel-vaulted church of St John Lampadistes was built in the early 18th century, probably succeeding an earlier church of the 15th century. The skull of this local saint is preserved in a silver casket above his tomb. According to his legend St John Lampadistes lived in a village in the Tróodos in the 11th century. He was engaged to be married, but renounced matrimony in favour of the monastic life, whereupon his bride's parents caused him by enchantments to go blind. Heraclidius died at the age of 22 and was buried in the monastery which bears his name; but his grave remained unknown until an epileptic was cured by accidentally touching it. In the 12th century a church was built in his honour, and thousands of people came in pilgrimage to seek healing at his tomb. His feast day is October 4th.

Narthex

In the 15th century the great numbers of pilgrims necessitated the construction of the narthex which serves the two churches. The walls are covered with paintings of that period, on themes related to the hopes of the pilgrims (healing miracles, Christ's appearances after the Resurrection). Until quite recently sick people used to bring their bedding and lodge in the narthex. An inscription over the south entrance records that the paintings were the work of a painter from Constantinople – no doubt a refugee who had come to Cyprus after the fall of Constantinople in 1453.

Wall paintings	At the south end of the east wall is a representation of the Last Judgment, with four figures of donors. Above the doorway in the south wall are the Three Youths in the Fiery Furnace and Daniel in the Lions' Den. On the upper part of the east wall is Christ with the woman of Samaria, followed by a series of his miracles of healing, beginning with the healing of the paralytic at the pool of Bethesda and continuing with the healing of the man with dropsy, in which Christ is shown touching the man's swollen belly, and the healing of the man born blind. The middle zone shows Mary Magdalene telling Peter and John about the empty tomb and the two disciples at the tomb, seeing for themselves. Beyond this are Mary Magdalene at the empty tomb, her encounter with Christ ("Touch me not"), Doubting Thomas and the Miraculous Draught of Fishes.
Latin Chapel	The paintings in the Latin Chapel, which date from the 15th and 16th centuries, show a mingling of Italian and Byzantine elements. The iconographic programme still follows the Byzantine scheme, but the artist's conception of space, his use of perspective and the physical form of his figures point to his training in Italy.
Acathist Hymn	The main theme of the paintings is the Acathist Hymn, the famous Orthodox hymn in honour of the Virgin, which was sung standing (*akáthistos*). The hymn, based on apocryphal narratives of the Nativity, consists of 24 verses, each beginning with one of the 24 letters of the Greek alphabet. The cycle of scenes begins on the south wall with the Annunciation and ends on the north wall with the Mother of God enthroned, holding out her hand to two Popes – a clear indication of western influence.

In the apse, in accordance with the Byzantine canon, is the Mother of God with the Child. On the left-hand wall Moses is depicted receiving the Tables of the Law, on the right-hand wall Moses seeing the burning bush. In the lunette of the apse is the Hospitality of Abraham.

Surroundings of Kalopanayiótis

Moutoullás

Situation and characteristics	2km/1¼ mile south of Kalopanayiótis is the hill village of Moutoullás (alt. 760m/2495ft), whose clear spring water is bottled and sold all over Cyprus. The village also produces large quantities of a Cypriot speciality, *soutzoúko*, strings of almonds soaked in grape juice. The pears grown here are particularly esteemed. Moutoullás is also noted for its traditional craft of making *vournes* (troughs for kneading dough and washing clothes) and *sanides* (bread-boards with round cavities for shaping loaves) from pine trunks.

At the far end of the village is a little barn-roofed church.

Church of Panayía tou Moutoullá	The little church of the Panayía tou Moutoullá (key from the adjacent house) was built in 1280 and is believed to be the oldest surviving saddle-roofed church in Cyprus. The wall paintings are dated to the same year in an inscription on the north wall of the bema. Below the inscription are the figures of the donors, John and his wife Irene.

The paintings follow the usual Byzantine iconographic programme, with figures of saints in the lower zone and scenes from the life of Christ in the upper zone.

In the conch of the apse is the Mother of God Blacherniótissa, with six fathers of the Church in the lower register. On the south wall are the

Nativity and the Presentation in the Temple (the latter dating from the 15th century); on the west wall the Raising of Lazarus, the Entry into Jerusalem and the Crucifixion; and on the north wall the Descent into Hades (Anástasis) and the Dormition of the Mother of God. On the outside of the north wall is the Last Judgment (15th c.).

Pedhoulás

Situated 8km/5 miles south of Kalopanayiótis at an altitude of 1100m/3610ft above the beautiful Marathása valley, Pedhoulás is a popular summer resort with small hotels and tavernas. It is famed for its cherry-blossom, and hosts of visitors are attracted to the village in spring when its 100,000 cherry-trees are in flower.

Also of interest is the church of the Archangel Michael with its 15th century wall paintings.

Situation and characteristics

This little saddle-roofed church can be found in the lower part of the village (key in the house to the right of the church. An inscription over the north doorway names the donor as Basileos and gives the date of construction as 1474. Above the inscription the donor, accompanied by his family, is shown presenting the church to the Archangel Michael. The women's dresses have embroidery of a type similar to that made in Léfkara today. The painting is in a rather rustic style. Western influence is evident in the dress of the soldiers in the Betrayal scene.

Church of the Archangel Michael

On the iconostasis are the arms of the Lusignan family, suggesting that the site for the church was donated by the Lusignan rulers of Cyprus.

In accordance with Byzantine practice, the paintings in the naos are in two zones, with figures of saints in the lower zone and New Testament scenes in the upper one.

Wall paintings

The cycle begins on the south wall with the Birth of the Virgin and continues with the Presentation of the Virgin, the Annunciation, the Nativity of Christ, the Presentation in the Temple, the Baptism, the Entry into Jerusalem and the Betrayal. In the pediment of the west wall is the Crucifixion, badly defaced by rain water. On the north wall are the Lamentation, the Descent into Hades and the Dormition of the Mother of God. In the conch of the apse is the Mother of God Blacherniótissa, standing with her hands raised in prayer, with six fathers of the Church below. In the vaulting is the Ascension, on the north wall the Sacrifice of Isaac.

Khirokitía

G 7/8

Χοιροκοιτία
Altitude: 100–200m/330–660ft

Half way between Lárnaca and Limassol, 7km/4½ miles from the coast, just off the motorway (junction 14), is the site of Khirokitía (open: daily 7.30am–5.30pm, in summer to 7.30pm). Dating from 6800 B.C., this is the oldest settlement on the island and its most important Neolithic site (see Art and Architecture).

Situation and characteristics

In the Neolithic period men began to give up their nomadic life as hunters and gatherers and to change to a sedentary life, farming and domesticating wild animals (as evidenced by finds of the bones of sheep and goats). The first settlers on Cyprus came from Syria and Cilicia and established themselves in the well watered foothills of the mountains. Other Neolithic settlements have been identified at Kalavasós/Tenta near Khirokitía, Pétra tou Limniti on the north coast and Sotíra, near Koúrion.

Neolithic settlements

Neolithic houses, Khirokitía

★Excavations

Excavation of the site began in 1936 under the direction of Porphyrios Dikaios, and the work is being continued by French archaeologists. The water supply of the settlement was provided by the river Maroni, at the foot of the south-facing slope on which it was built.

Thóloi

On both sides of a wall running up the steep hill from the river are a series of round houses (*thóloi*) similar to those of the Thessalian Sesklo culture (near Vólos in mainland Greece). The largest of the houses have an external

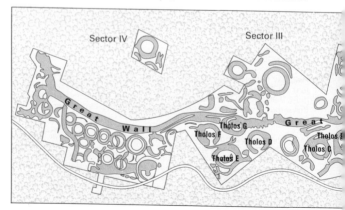

diameter of some 10m/33ft and an internal diameter of 5m/16½ft and could accommodate two or three people. The smaller houses, with a diameter of only 2–3m/6½–10ft, could accommodate only a single individual, or may have been animal stalls or store-rooms. Families presumably occupied several houses, forming a kind of homestead.

The beehive-shaped houses stood on 50cm/40in. thick foundations of river boulders (still preserved), on which was erected a superstructure of sun-dried brick. Some of the houses had pillar-like supports in the middle, presumably bearing an upper storey. The floor was of beaten earth. The only furnishings were a stone bench, tables and a hearth.

Neolithic man buried the dead under the floors of their houses. Several generations might be buried in the same house, and up to 26 skeletons were found in some houses. The dead were buried in a crouching position, lying on their sides. Since Neolithic man seems to have believed in a life after death, the bodies were covered with heavy stones to prevent them returning.

Burials

Among the commonest grave goods were food jars, offering dishes, jewellery, tools and weapons – further evidence of a belief in an afterlife. The graves of women were more richly furnished than those of men; the grave goods included necklaces of carnelian beads and obsidian knives. The average age of the dead was 33–35.

A great wall 2m/6½ft wide and 3m/10ft high runs between the houses, following a winding course from the river up the slope of the hill and down again to the river at the other end. The first excavators took this to be the "main street" of the village, but recent investigations have shown that it was originally a defensive wall. When new settlers came to the village in the 4th millennium B.C. further tholoi were built outside the wall and a new defensive wall was later constructed.

The wall

The wall thus yields evidence of two phases of settlement, a phase beginning in the 6th millennium B.C. in which pottery was unknown and, after an unexplained hiatus of 1500 years, a new culture in the 4th millennium B.C. using comb-decorated pottery. No material of a later period has been found, and it is not known why Khirokitía was not occupied after the 4th millennium B.C.

Surroundings of Khirokitía

8km/5 miles west of Khirokitía on the road from Lárnaca, just before Kalavasós, an unsurfaced road goes off on the left to the Neolithic site of Kalava-

Kalavasós

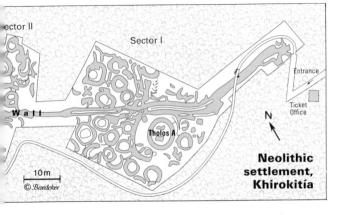

Sector II

Sector I

Entrance

Ticket Office

Wall

Tholos A

N

10m

© Baedeker

Neolithic settlement, Khirokitía

sós/Tenta. Here too were found round houses with skeletons under the floors. The most interesting find was a completely preserved child's skeleton of the 7th millennium B.C. Excavation of the site is continuing.

A few hundred metres nearer the motorway is the Bronze Age site of Kalavasós/Ayios Dhimitrios, which shows longer continuity of settlement than Khirokitía. On this site was found a rectangular structure of unknown function built round a central courtyard with an area of 10sq.m/110sq.ft. A few metres away were two chamber tombs with rich grave goods, including fine gold jewellery, of the 14th century B.C.

Lèfkara   See entry

Kíti   F 9

Κίτι
Altitude: 50m/165ft

Situation and characteristics

11km/7 miles south-west of Lárnaca on the road running past the airport and Hala Sultan Tekke is the village of Kíti, which takes its name from ancient Kítion (now Lárnaca). The inhabitants of the ancient port moved inland in the 7th century, presumably for safety from Arab raids, and settled in this area, as is shown by the fragments of late antique masonry, Corinthian capitals and remains of architraves built into the old walls of the settlement. The church of the Panayía Angelóktistos is notable for an early Christian apse mosaic (6th c.) which is unique in Cyprus (see Art and Culture, Cyprus's Threatened Cultural Heritage).

★ Church of the Panayía Angelóktistos

The present church of the Panayía Angelóktistos ("built by angels") contains elements from different periods. The apse at the east end with its mosaic decoration dates from the original 6th century building. The church was rebuilt as a domed cruciform church in the 11th century after its destruction in Arab raids; then in the 12th century the extension on the north side was built, and in the 13th century the annexe on the south side which now serves as a narthex was added; and finally in the 20th century the west end was extended. Below the bell-tower are the arms of the Gibelin family who built the south annexe as a private chapel. The groined vaulting in the interior points to the Frankish origin of the donors. On the west wall of the chapel is the gravestone of Simone, wife of Renier de Gibelet. Open: Mon.–Sat. 8am–4pm, Sun. 9am–midday and 2–4pm.

★ Mosaic

In the apse of the church can be seen a 6th century mosaic of the Mother of God of the Hodigitría type ("She who shows the Way") with the Child on her left arm, flanked by the Archangels Michael and Gabriel. The mosaic is the only surviving pre-iconoclastic example of the Hodigitría type. An inscription above the Mother of God refers to her as Hagia Maria. The mosaic is notable for the lively representation of the archangels and the lifelike figure of the Child. Round the mosaic is a frieze of animal figures – parrots, ducks and stags – between acanthus leaves.

Terebinth tree

Outside the church is a 300-year-old terebinth (Pistacia terebinthus), with fragrant branches and edible fruits. An aromatic substance resembling turpentine is made from its bark.

Surroundings of Kíti

Tersephánou

2km/1¼ miles north-east of Kíti, near the dam on the river Tremithos (turn right just beyond the bridge), stands the little church of Ayios Yeóryios of

Church of the Panayía Angelóktistos

Arpera (key in the farmhouse beside the church). This 18th century church of St George preserves remains of wall paintings. There is a fine portrait of the donor, the Greek Dragoman (see History, Chronology) Christophakis. On the iconostasis is an icon of the dog-headed St Christopher (who according to his legend was a man-eating creature with a dog's head before his conversion to the Christian faith).

Kolóssi Castle   G 5

Κολόσσι
Altitude: sea level

10km/6 miles west of Limassol on a road flanked by cypresses lies the village of Kolóssi, with the massive castle of the Knights of St John (open: daily 7.30am–5pm, in summer to 7pm). The castle lies in an intensively cultivated area, with large plantations of citrus fruits established in 1933 by a co-operative of Cypriot and Israeli agricultural specialists. In this area too are grown the vines – originally planted by the Knights – which produce Commandaria, a sweet dessert wine named after the commandery of the Order of St John (see Practical Information, South: Wine).
Situation and characteristics

Commandaria

★The Castle

Around 1210 the Frankish king Hugo I presented a fertile territory around Kolóssi to the Knights of St John. The castle which they built in this area was held for a time by the Templars; but even after the Knights of St John transferred their main base from Cyprus to Rhodes between 1291 and 1310 Kolóssi remained a commandery of their order. The fertile soil of the region
History

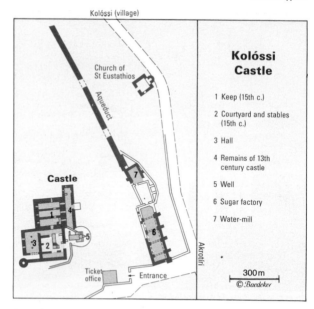

Church of St Eustathios

Kolóssi (village)

Aqueduct

Castle

Akrotiri

Ticket office

Entrance

Kolóssi Castle

1 Keep (15th c.)

2 Courtyard and stables (15th c.)

3 Hall

4 Remains of 13th century castle

5 Well

6 Sugar factory

7 Water-mill

300 m

© Baedeker

produced large yields of wheat, grapes for wine (Commandaria), cotton, oil and cane sugar.

In 1373 the Genoese attacked the castle but were repelled. In the mid 15th century Grand Commander Louis de Magnac began the renovation of the castle, then much dilapidated, which gave it its present form.

Keep

Of the castle built in the mid 15th century only the high keep, 16m/52ft square, remains intact. On the east side of the outer wall, at first floor level, can be seen four coats of arms – in the middle the arms of the Lusignan kingdoms of Jerusalem, Cyprus and Armenia, below this the arms of Louis de Magnac and to right and left the arms of Grand Masters Jean de Lastic and Jacques de Milli.

First floor

The keep is entered on a modern drawbridge leading to the first floor. Over the entrance is an elaborately decorated machicolation. In one of the two rooms on the first floor, which were presumably the kitchen and living quarters (with store-rooms and cisterns on the ground floor), is a fireplace. To the left of the entrance can be seen a painting of the Crucifixion, with the arms of Louis de Magnac.

Second floor

A spiral staircase leads up to the second floor, with the Commander's state apartments. Large cavities for beams in the upper part of the walls show that there was originally an intermediate timber floor, no doubt with sleeping accommodation. On the fireplaces are the arms of Louis de Magnac. From the battlemented roof platform there are fine views over the vineyards to Limassol.

13th century castle

East of the keep is a semicircular structure with a well, a relic of an earlier 13th century castle. To the south of the keep are the remains of stables.

The Knights of St John

The Order of the Knights of St John or Knights Hospitallers, the oldest of the Crusading orders, has survived in altered form into our own day. It was founded in the 11th century, when a pilgrim hospice dedicated to St John the Baptist was established in Jerusalem. After its recognition by the Pope in 1113 the Order began to found daughter houses along the pilgrim roads. Originally a charitable order, it soon developed into a military order of chivalry which fought against the infidel in the Holy Land. To distinguish themselves from the Templars, who wore a white habit with a red cross, the Knights of St John wore a black habit with a white cross.

After the fall of Acre in 1291 the Knights of St John were obliged, like the other Crusading orders, to leave this last Christian stronghold in the Holy Land. Their headquarters were moved to Cyprus and remained there for nineteen years before being transferred to Rhodes. The head of the Order was the Grand Master, who while on Rhodes was also ruler of a secular state.

After withstanding a six months' siege on Rhodes the Knights were compelled in 1522 to surrender to overwhelmingly superior Turkish forces and moved to Malta, which had been granted to the Order by the Emperor Charles V. There they successfully defended the island against a siege by Sultan Suleiman the Magnificent in 1565.

Thereafter the Order increasingly devoted itself to caring for the sick. At the Reformation it split into two – the Protestant Order of St John and the Catholic order of the Knights of Malta. During the French Revolution the Order was expelled from Malta and its property confiscated. Its headquarters were then moved to St Petersburg, where Tsar Paul I illegitimately declared himself Grand Master. After Paul's death the Order moved to Catania in Sicily, then to Ferrara and finally to Rome, where it still has its headquarters. After reorganisation in the 19th century the Order was usually known as the Order of the Knights of Malta.

The Order has national associations in many countries, including Britain. There is also in Britain a Grand Priory of the Order of St John which is independent of the Roman Catholic Order.

To the east of the castle are the remains of an old sugar factory, consisting of a rectangular barrel-vaulted main building and other structures, probably a watermill, to the north. The necessary water supply was provided by an aqueduct. (On sugar manufacture see Koúklia/Palaía Páphos.)

Sugar factory

Near the aqueduct is a tipa tree (*Machaerium tipu*, a member of the Papilionaceae family, originally from North America) over 150 years old. Named after its razor-sharp seed-pods (Greek *makhaira*, "knife"), it stands 27m/90ft high.

Machaeron tree

100m/110yd north of the castle is the little Byzantine church of Ayios Efstáthios (key in house next door). Eustathius, one of the great military saints and martyrs of the Orthodox church, was a Roman officer in the reign of Trajan (1st/2nd c. A.D.) who according to his legend was converted to the Christian faith when he encountered a stag bearing a white cross between its antlers.

Ayios Efstáthios

This domed cruciform church with a semicircular apse at the east end, built in the 12th century and restored in the 15th, was presumably the church of the Knights of St John. There are scanty remains of a painting of

Kolóssi Castle

Remains of sugar factory

Stone of Aphrodite, Koúklia

St Eustathius in full armour mounted on a horse, and in the dome is Christ
Pantokrator with the four Evangelists below him.

Koúklia/Palaía Páphos   G 3

Κούκλια Παλαία Πάφος
Altitude: 100m/330ft

Some 15km/9 miles south-east of Páphos is the old village of Koúklia,   Situation and
whose inhabitants live mainly by growing and processing groundnuts. It   characteristics
takes its name from the Frankish castle of Covocle. This was the site of Old
Páphos (Palaía Páphos), with the most celebrated shrine of Aphrodite in the
ancient Greek world, the Sanctuary of Aphrodite (open: daily 7.30am–5pm,
in summer to 7pm). Excavations have also brought to light remains of
temples of the Bronze Age and Roman period. Outside the village are the
scanty remains of a mound built by the Persians during a siege of the town
in the 5th century B.C.

The castle of Covocle (Manor House), built by the Lusignans to protect their
sugar-cane plantations, now houses a small museum displaying finds from
the surrounding area. Below the castle are remains of a medieval sugar
factory.

★Sanctuary of Aphrodite

Palaía Páphos (Old Páphos) began to be so called in the 4th century B.C. to
distinguish it from Néa Páphos (New Páphos), the new foundation on the
coast. The importance of Palaía Páphos was based on its status as the
religious centre of Cyprus, only a short distance from Pétra tou Romioú,
where Aphrodite was believed to have risen from the sea-foam (see Surroundings of Koúklia, also History, Mythology).

According to the Greek traveller Pausanias (2nd c. A.D.) the shrine of   **History**
Aphrodite was founded by Agapenor, king of Tegea in Arcadia, who landed
here during his return from Troy. According to another account the temple
was founded by the legendary priest-king Kinyras, son of Páphos.
   There is evidence of a settlement on the site in the 15th century B.C.
During the Hellenisation of Cyprus, in the 12th century B.C., Achaean settlers established themselves in Páphos, where they encountered a cult of
Ishtar/Astarte, who was worshipped in the form of a conical black stone. In
the course of centuries this Great Mother (Magna Mater) developed into
the Greek goddess Aphrodite.

There are remains of a temple and tombs of the Late Bronze Age. The
earliest king of Páphos known to us by name was Eteandros, who is
recorded as having paid tribute to the Persians in the 7th century B.C. The
kings of Páphos were both political and religious heads of their state. In 499
B.C. Páphos joined the Ionian rising against the Persians, but was compelled to surrender when the city was besieged in the following year.

The heyday of Páphos was in the Archaic and Classical periods. Nikokles,
the last independent priest-king of Páphos, moved his capital to the coast,
founding Néa Páphos at the end of the 4th century. When, soon afterwards,
the city-kingdoms of Cyprus were incorporated in the Ptolemaic empire the
kings of Palaía Páphos became chief priests of Aphrodite. Néa Páphos took
over the political and economic role of Palaía Páphos, whose importance
now depended solely on the sanctuary of Aphrodite.
   In Roman times the shrine continued to draw pilgrims from all over the
Roman world, among them the Emperor Titus.

Palaía Páphos continued to flourish into the 4th century A.D., but the spread
of Christianity led to the decline of the cult of Aphrodite. In Byzantine times

Massive stone blocks in the sanctuary of Aphrodite

Palaía Páphos was an insignificant village. In the 13th century the Franks built the castle of Covocle near the ancient shrine to protect their sugarcane plantations. Later it was taken over by the Turks.

Cult of Aphrodite

Every spring the great festival of Aphrodite, the Aphrodisiae, was celebrated in Palaía Páphos. Pilgrims came from all over the ancient world to take part in a great procession through the Sacred Gardens to Palaía Páphos, and young trees were planted in front of the temple of Aphrodite as votive offerings to the goddess.

The celebration of the mysteries lasted several days. The votaries began by taking a ritual bath in the sea in honour of the goddess, and offerings (not involving the effusion of blood) were made to her. This was followed by various contests between the worshippers. The Aphrodisiae also incorporated the cult of Adonis, Aphrodite's handsome lover. The culmination of the ceremonies was the Sacred Marriage of the priest-king with the goddess in the form of a priestess. The sacred stone was anointed with oil and offerings of incense were made to Aphrodite.

Temple prostitution

An important element in the cult of Aphrodite was temple prostitution, a practice described by Herodotus (5th c. B.C.). Before their marriage all brides were required to give themselves to a stranger near the temple precinct. "When a woman has come here she may not return home until a stranger has thrown gold into her lap and has lain with her outside the sanctuary" (Herodotus I,119). This custom was presumably a rite of initiation for men and the virginity of the woman an offering to Aphrodite. It was also an important source of income for the temple.

In Roman times there was said to be an oracle here. The shrine was also a place of sanctuary for those pursued by their enemies.

The sanctuary

Two complexes of buildings (open: daily 7.30am–5pm, in summer to 7pm), one dating from the Bronze Age and the other from the Roman period, are

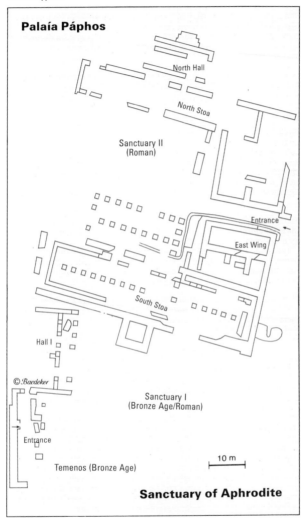

Palaía Páphos

North Hall

North Stoa

Sanctuary II
(Roman)

Entrance

East Wing

South Stoa

Hall I

© *Baedeker*

Sanctuary I
(Bronze Age/Roman)

Entrance

10 m

Temenos (Bronze Age)

Sanctuary of Aphrodite

all that remains of a sanctuary which was frequented from the 13th century B.C. to the 4th century A.D.

At the south end of the site, aligned from north to south, is the earlier sanctuary, which dates from the Late Bronze Age. There are only a few remains of the cyclopean wall round the sacred precinct which enclosed the temple containing the goddess's sacred cult stone. Within the precinct were a small chamber and a basin for ritual ablutions, and no doubt also an altar and various votive offerings. The function of the round holes in the cyclopean walls is not known.

Earlier sanctuary

121

Later sanctuary	The sanctuary of the Roman period, covering an area 79m/260ft by 67m/220ft, is thought to have been built after an earthquake in the 1st century A.D. At the north end were two colonnaded porticoes enclosing a courtyard. Roman coins depict the large black sacred stone under a tripartite canopy.
Roman peristyle house	40m/45yd west of the sanctuary, on the far side of the road, are the remains of a Roman peristyle house, presumably the dwelling of the priestesses.

Other Sights

Manor House (Château de Covocle)	The inner courtyard of the Manor House or what used to be known as Château de Covocle, built in the 13th century as the headquarters of the sugar industry, is entered under a large gate-tower. The sugar-cane plantations were a royal domain which was a major source of revenue in the 15th and 16th centuries. The castle still preserves Frankish structures on the south and east sides, notably the large hall with Gothic buttresses below the Museum. The rest of the castle was rebuilt and restored in the Turkish period.
Museum	The Museum is housed in the upper range of buildings. In the first room is the black cult stone of Aphrodite; other exhibits include a large Bronze Age jar and a small Iron Age bath. The second room contains material ranging in date from the Chalcolithic period to the Middle Ages. Of particular interest are ivories of the Bronze Age, fragments of sculpture of the archaic period and a reconstruction of the Persian siege mound at Palaía Páphos.
Katholiki Church	To the east of the later sanctuary of Aphrodite is the little Katholiki Church, which at the beginning of the 20th century still bore the name of the Panayía Aphrodítissa. It is thought to have been built in the 12th century and altered in the 14th. It originally belonged to a monastery, and it is still surrounded by the half-ruined precinct wall of the monastery, with pointed arches. The courtyard round the church was used as a cemetery. The cruciform church had a barrel-vaulted roof, with a dome over the crossing. Only a few 15th century paintings have survived. In the dome is Christ Pantokrator surrounded by angels, and on the west wall is an interesting representation of the Last Judgment in which the rivers Euphrates and Tigris are represented by masks from whose mouths water is flowing.
Sugar refinery	The remains of medieval foundations point to the existence of a sugar refinery built by the Lusignans on the site of the ancient sanctuary. Part of the water supply system can still be identified. In a vaulted underground chamber was the mill wheel, turned by animal power, which crushed the sugar-cane. The fibre was then crushed for a second time in a watermill, driven by water from a mill-race with a narrow end which directed a powerful jet of water against the horizontal wheel. Thereafter the juice was boiled several times in large copper boilers and then fed into funnel-shaped vessels with a hole at the bottom through which dripped the residual liquid from the sugar crystallising in the vessel.
North-east gate and town walls	600m/660yd from Koúklia on the road signposted to Arkhimandríta is an enclosed site on the right of the road containing the remains of the town walls of Palaía Páphos and its fortified north-east gate, prominently situated on Marcello Hill above the town. The wall was built of sun-dried brick – the usual technique of the period – about 700 B.C., but in later periods was given an additional stone facing. By the end of the 6th century B.C. it was 6.30m/20ft thick.
Siege mound	Of particular interest is the siege mound built by the Persians in 498, when they took the city. They began by filling in part of the 10m/33ft wide ditch round the city with tree trunks, earth and stones, and then built up a mound

against the town walls on which they could set up their timber siege tower and so gain entry to the city. The defenders dug mines under the mound, supporting the roofs of their tunnels on timber props, which they then set on fire, so that the mound fell in. Despite all their efforts, however, they were unable to hold out against the Persians and soon afterwards were forced to surrender.

Some of the tunnels can still be seen. In them were found small niches with oil lamps of the Archaic period which gave light to the diggers. The excavators removed the Persian siege mound, which was found to contain numerous fragments of sculpture, columns and inscriptions.

Surroundings of Koúklia

7km/4½ miles from Koúklia and 21km/13 miles south-east of Páphos, just off the west coast of Cyprus, is Pétra tou Romioú, the stone marking the spot where Aphrodite was believed to have emerged from the sea (see History, Mythology). The name means Stone of the Roman, for the Greeks of the Byzantine (East Roman) Empire were still described as Romans (*Romaioi*).

★Pétra tou Romioú

7km/4½ miles from Pétra tou Romioú on the expressway to Limassol, at the turn-off for Pissoúri, a road goes off on the left to Alékhtora. Just before the village a dusty unsurfaced road crosses a bridge and runs between vineyards and olive-groves. In the 1st century this was the main east–west Roman road between Koúrion and Páphos, used throughout the Middle Ages and into modern times, when it was remade by the British authorities. The Roman paving can still be seen at Yermános.

Roman road to Páphos

A few kilometres along the road lies the picturesque abandoned hamlet of Lakko Franko (not shown on maps), which during the Frankish period

Lakko Franko

Pétra tou Romioú, where Aphrodite rose from the foam

Bizarre rock formations east of Koúklia

(13th/14th c.) was a feudal stronghold of some importance. There are also the ruins of an old village han (caravanserai) of the Turkish period. Better preserved is the fine old farmhouse and steading.

Yermános

From here the road leads west, climbing to the hill of Yermános (1km/ ½ mile), on which a late 19th century German amateur archaeologist, Max Ohnefalsch-Richter, discovered ancient tombs and a Hellenistic shrine of Aphrodite. Some traces of his excavations can be seen.

Asprokremnos

On the road to Páphos, soon after the turn-off for the airport, a road goes off to the huge Asprokremnos dam, recently completed.

Koúrion   G 5

Κούριον
Altitude: 70–80m/230–260ft

Situation and
★★ importance

Some 16km/10 miles west of Limassol, on a crag rising high above the sea, are the excavations of the ancient city of Koúrion (Latin Curium; open: 7.30am–5pm, in summer to 7.30pm), an extensive site with a theatre, handsome villas and a basilica dating from Hellenistic, Roman and early Christian times. The first investigation of the site was carried out by the American consul, Luigi Palma di Cesnola, in 1873. Systematic excavation began in 1933 and is still continuing. An area to the east destroyed by violent earthquakes during the 4th century A.D., including an imposing Nymphaeum dedicated to water nymphs, is currently under excavation. To the west are the remains of a sanctuary of Apollo and a Roman stadium.

Stone pithos in the Palaestra, with the Temple of Apollo in the background ▶

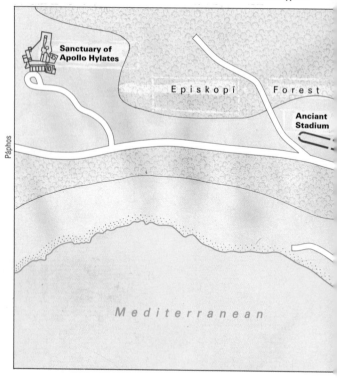

History

Foundation

The Koúrion area has been continuously occupied since Neolithic times (finds at Sotíra). According to a legend reported by Herodotus in the 5th century B.C. Koúrion was founded by warriors from Argos in the Peloponnese on their way back from the Trojan War. Finds from the immediate vicinity of Koúrion show that there was an Achaean settlement here in the 12th century B.C.

City-kingdom

There was a sanctuary of Apollo near the city from the 8th century B.C. In the 7th century Koúrion is mentioned as one of the city-kingdoms which paid tribute to the Persians. During the rebellion of the Greek cities against Persian rule in the 5th century B.C. under the leadership of Onésilos of Sálamis, the king of Koúrion, Stásanor, went over to the Persian side during the battle of Sálamis and contributed to their victory. Under Ptolemaic and Roman rule Koúrion was a place of considerable consequence. New temples, theatres and sporting facilities were now built. In the 4th century the town was ravaged by violent earthquakes and razed to the ground.

Episcopal see

At this period Christianity had already come to Koúrion, and in the following century it was firmly established, and the town, partly rebuilt, became the see of a bishop. Arab raids in the 7th century led to the transfer of the episcopal see to Episkopí (from *epískopos*, "bishop"). Under Frankish rule Koúrion passed into the hands of the Cornaro family. The area was then famed for its sugar plantations, which gave place in the 16th century to fields of cotton.

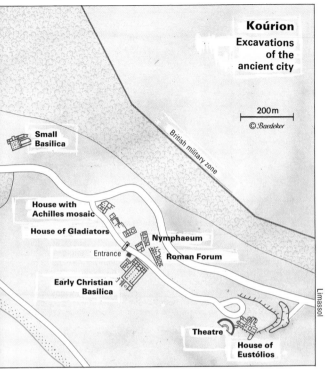

Koúrion

Excavations of the ancient city

200 m

© Baedeker

British military zone

Small Basilica

House with Achilles mosaic

House of Gladiators

Nymphaeum

Entrance

Roman Forum

Early Christian Basilica

Theatre

House of Eustólios

Limassol

Sights

Entering the site of ancient Koúrion at the foot of the hill, we come first to the theatre, at the southern tip of the hill. It was excavated by American archaeologists, who in 1961 rebuilt part of the structure (which had suffered severe destruction). In summer performances of ancient plays are given in the theatre. The theatre was built in the 2nd century A.D. on the site of an earlier Hellenistic theatre of the 2nd century B.C. – a rather smaller building which had a circular orchestra and a cavea with an area of 180sq.m/215sq.yd.

The semicircular orchestra of the present theatre is surrounded by a semicircular cavea which could accommodate 3500 spectators. The stage wall originally stood as high as the top of the cavea. A vaulted corridor to the rear of the theatre gave access by way of five passages to the tiers of seating. Over the top rows was a colonnade. At the beginning of the 3rd century the lowest tiers of seating were removed and replaced by a metal barrier – suggesting that the arena was used for the fights with wild beasts which were so popular in that period. The earthquakes of the 4th century left the theatre a heap of ruins.

Immediately adjoining the theatre is a peristyle house of the early Christian period (4th/5th c.), with its own baths, which later were probably given over to public use. In the entrance hall at the west end of the house is a mosaic with the welcoming inscription "Enter . . . Good fortune to the house". This

Theatre

House of Eustólios

127

Theatre and House of Eustólios

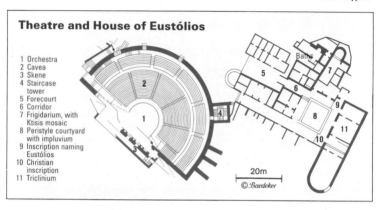

1 Orchestra
2 Cavea
3 Skene
4 Staircase
  tower
5 Forecourt
6 Corridor
7 Frigidarium, with
  Ktisis mosaic
8 Peristyle courtyard
  with impluvium
9 Inscription naming
  Eustólios
10 Christian
  inscription
11 Triclinium

20m

© Baedeker

leads into an inner courtyard surrounded by columns, in the centre of which is an impluvium (water basin).

To the left, higher up, is the bath-house. The large central room, probably the frigidarium, is decorated with mosaics (with a representation of the Ktisis, the personification of the creative spirit, holding a measure of the Roman foot). To the west is the hypocaust which provided heating for the baths, to the north a semicircular basin.

From here we enter the peristyle round the courtyard with its mosaics. A fragmentary inscription names Eustólios as the builder of this "cool, sheltered retreat". Another inscription in front of a mosaic with Christian

Mosaic of Ktisis in the House of Eustólios

animal motifs says: "In place of great stones and solid iron, gleaming bronze and diamonds this house is girt by the much venerated symbols of Christ." There are also two representations of the fish which was a common symbol of Christ in early Christian times.

Following the tarred road north, we pass on the right an area which is at present being excavated. A large stoa with monolithic columns and Corinthian capitals probably belonged to the Roman forum. Excavation has also revealed the walls of Hellenistic buildings of unknown function. Adjoining the stoa on the east is a Roman building, presumably a dwelling-house. A nymphaeum of the 1st century A.D. probably served as a reservoir for the town's water supply; it is still under excavation.

Acropolis

The most recent excavations in the acropolis area have brought to light remains of the city which was destroyed in the earthquakes of the 4th century and have thrown fresh light on the way of life of the citizens of ancient Koúrion. Since the catastrophe occurred in the early morning most people were at home. In the Koúrion Archaeological Museum at Episkopí (see Limassol, Surroundings) can be seen the skeletons of a young family buried in the ruins of their home.

The House of the Gladiators, an atrium house belonging to a wealthy patrician family of the 3rd century A.D., takes its name from the mosaics of fights between gladiators in the inner courtyard. The mosaic to the north depicts two fully armed gladiators with blunted swords engaged in a practice bout, giving their names as Margareitis and Ellinikos. The second mosaic shows a heavily armed gladiator named Lytras with a curved dagger advancing on his opponent (mosaic damaged), while between them an unarmed figure named Dareios wearing a white toga, probably a referee, appears to be trying to calm them.

House of the Gladiators

Near the Páphos motorway are the remains of a Roman building of the 4th century A.D., with a courtyard flanked on both sides by rooms and a portico containing a mosaic of Achilles.
   In the ancient myth Achilles was sent by his mother Thetis to the court of King Lykomedes of Skyros to be brought up among his daughters. By this means Thetis sought to prevent her son being killed at Troy as had been destined by fate. But since Troy could be captured only with the help of Achilles the wily Odysseus had recourse to a stratagem. He appeared before the king of Skyros laden with gifts, among which were weapons; then he caused the war trumpet to be blown, whereupon Achilles seized the weapons and thus revealed his presence. This is the moment depicted in the mosaic.

Achilles mosaic

In the adjoining building is a richly ornamented mosaic pavement preserving fragments of a scene depicting Ganymede being carried off by Zeus in the guise of an eagle.

Ganymede mosaic

Opposite the Roman forum is an early Christian basilica which bears witness to the re-occupation of Koúrion after the great earthquakes of the 4th century. The well preserved foundations of the church show that it was a three-aisled basilica 55m/180ft long by 37m/120ft wide with a semicircular apse flanked by two pastophoria. Over the altar was a canopy borne on four columns, the foundations of which can still be seen. Between the sanctuary and the naos was a screen, the position of which is marked by cavities in the floor. Flanking the lateral aisles were *katekhouména*, long corridors with benches for the catechumens, the unbaptised members of the congregation, who were confined to these areas and the narthex. At the west end of the church was an atrium with a hexagonal fountain for ablutions. To the north of this was the bishop's house.

Early Christian basilica

On the north side of the basilica was the baptistery, which, like the church, had three aisles and was preceded by a narthex and an atrium with a

Baptistery

Ruins of the early Christian basilica

Mosaic of the Gladiators

fountain for ablutions. The large font on the east side was designed for the adult baptisms by immersion which were then normal. To left and right were two rooms in which those about to be baptised were undressed and anointed.

Surroundings of Koúrion

1km/½ mile west of the Koúrion excavations on the road to Páphos can be found a stadium of the 2nd century A.D., in which the city of Koúrion continued until the 5th century to stage contests – races between eight to ten runners, discus-throwing, ball games – in honour of military victories or on the occasion of Christian festivals. The name stadium was derived from a Greek measure of length normally equivalent to 192m/630ft but in Koúrion only to 186m/610ft. The stadium, the foundations of which survive, was a U-shaped structure 229m/750ft long by 24m/70ft across, with seven tiers of seating, which could accommodate 7000 spectators, and three entrances. At the east end traces of the starting line can be distinguished.

Stadium

150m/165yd east of the stadium are the foundations of a three-aisled basilica of the late 5th century with a narthex and an atrium containing a fountain for ablutions. On the north side is a small chapel.

Small basilica

★Sanctuary of Apollo Hylátes

2km/1¼ miles farther along the Páphos road is the shrine of Apollo Hylátes (open: daily 7.30am–5pm, in summer to 7pm). Here Apollo was worshipped as the protector of the forest (Hylátes) and of animals – which were numerous in this area in antiquity. In its present form the sanctuary dates from Roman times, but excavation has revealed remains of an earlier sanctuary of the 6th century B.C.

The sacred precinct was entered by two doorways – to the west the Páphos Gate and to the east the Koúrion Gate, which is the present entrance.

Outside the sacred precinct, in front of the Koúrion Gate, is a palaestra of the 1st century A.D., the scene of wrestling contests and ball games. The large sand-floored courtyard is surrounded by colonnades, with seven rooms to the rear in which the athletes changed, oiled themselves and washed. At the north-east corner of the courtyard is a large stone pithos which contained water for the refreshment of the athletes.

Palaestra

Also outside the sacred precinct, in a bath-house of the time of Trajan, can be seen the hypocaust which provided under-floor heating for the baths.

Baths

The sacred precinct is entered through the Koúrion Gate. To the left stands the large South Building, with five similar rectangular rooms opening off a long Doric stoa (portico) in which pilgrims to the shrine presumably rested and set up their votive offerings. Each room is surrounded on three sides by a raised Doric colonnade. An inscription over one of the doors records that two of the rooms were built by the Emperor Trajan in A.D. 101. Facing the South Building is the North-West Building, with a similar function, which consists of two long rooms surrounded by raised Doric colonnades.

Sanctuary

From the courtyard in front of the South Building a long paved Sacred Way runs north past lodgings for priests and the temple treasury to the temple of Apollo. A stone altar of the Archaic period (7th c. B.C.) is the oldest feature in the sanctuary.

Sacred Way

The temple of Apollo Hylátes of the 1st century A.D. (reconstructed) was built on the foundations of an earlier temple of the late classical or Hellenistic period. A broad flight of steps leads up to this prostyle temple, standing on a podium preceded by four columns with Nabataean capitals.

Temple of Apollo

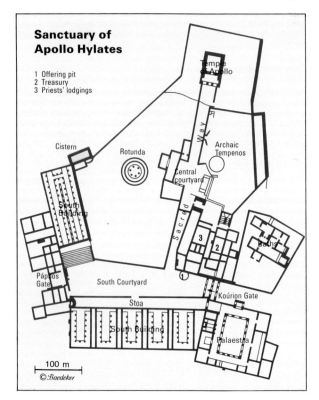

Sanctuary of Apollo Hylates

1 Offering pit
2 Treasury
3 Priests' lodgings

Cistern

Rotunda

Temple of Apollo

Way

Archaic Tempenos

Central courtyard

South Building

Sacred

3
2
1

baths

Páphos Gate

South Courtyard

Stoa

Koúrion Gate

South Building

Palaestra

100 m

© Baedeker

Rotunda

One of the oldest parts of the sanctuary is the rotunda of the Archaic period (6th c. B.C.), a circular temple surrounded by a gravel path, round which passed processions in honour of Apollo, lord of the forests. Seven cavities in the rock were once occupied by trees, which played a central part in the ritual of worship.

Offering pit

At the south end of the Sacred Way is a small semicircular pit (*bothros*) in which over hundreds of years the priests deposited offerings to Apollo which must not be destroyed. The oldest material found here dated from the 5th century B.C.

Episkopí

See Limassol, Surroundings

Kolóssi

See entry

Kýkko Monastery   F 4

Μονή Κύκκου
Altitude: 1140m/3740ft

30km/19 miles north-west of the little town of Tróodos, in a lonely mountain setting, stands the monastery of Kýkko, which is famed throughout the Orthodox world. Its name seems to be derived from the *koukous* (ebony) trees which used to grow here. The wealthiest and most powerful monastery in Cyprus, it owes its great reputation to its possession of an icon of the Mother of God which is believed to have been painted by Luke the Evangelist.

Kýkko formerly owned property in Asia Minor and Russia, and it still has large possessions in Cyprus, including numerous farms, which are administered centrally from Nicosia. The monastery (open: daily) runs various social institutions such as hospitals, schools and museums and wields considerable political influence on the island. It is a scene of great activity on Sundays and public holidays (religious fairs take place on 15th August and 8th September) and on the occasion of christenings and marriages, and is well equipped to cater for large numbers of people, with its long ranges of guest rooms, its large restaurants and its snack bars.

Situation and
★ importance

Archbishop Makarios III spent several years as a novice in Kýkko, and later built a chapel on the hill at Throni 3km/1¾ miles west of the monastery, near which he is now buried. Two soldiers form a guard of honour at his tomb day and night. During Cyprus's struggle for independence in the 1950s Kýkko Monastery supported the underground movement EOKA, and the hiding-place of the EOKA leader General Grivas was only some 2km/1¼ miles from the monastery.

Tomb of
Archbishop
Makarios

The monastery was founded at the end of the 11th century by a hermit monk named Isaias. According to legend the Byzantine governor of Cyprus, Manuel Voutoumetes, intruded on Isaias's solitude when he lost his way while hunting in the Tróodos Mountains. When Isaias refused to show him the way the governor kicked him; but when he got home he fell gravely ill and, pricked by conscience, begged Isaias to forgive him and

Foundation
legend

Kýkko Monastery, the wealthiest and most powerful in Cyprus

cure him of his illness. At the behest of the Mother of God, who appeared to him in a dream, Isaias healed the governor and in recompense received from the Emperor in Constantinople the icon of the Mother of God painted by Luke the Evangelist.

Sights

The present buildings of the monastery date only from the 19th and 20th centuries, since the older buildings were repeatedly destroyed by fire. As a result the mosaics and wall paintings in the church and monastic buildings show all the colour and skill of Orthodox painting but lack the patina of age.

Icon of the
Mother of God

The monastery's greatest treasure is the precious icon of the Mother of God, which is covered by a silver gilt plate and preserved in a special shrine. The icon, which is believed to have been painted by Luke in the Virgin's lifetime and is therefore regarded by the Orthodox church as the authentic portrait of the Mother of God, has been the model for innumerable later icons. It is credited with the power of bringing rain.

Near the icon is a black bronze arm, the presence of which is explained by a local legend. It is said that a negro impiously tried to light a cigarette at the oil lamp in front of the icon, whereupon the Mother of God caused his arm to wither and turn into metal.

Also of interest is the "sword" of a swordfish, presented by a seaman who was saved from drowning by the intervention of the Mother of God.

Surroundings of Kýkko Monastery

★Cedar Valley

18km/11 miles west of Kýkko on an unsurfaced road with many bends is Cedar Valley (alt. 1100m/3610ft), a secluded valley on the southern slopes of Mt Trípylos (1408m/4620ft). A labyrinthine track, little used, ascends through an unspoiled tract of country which has a mysterious and almost eerie aspect. The impression of a primeval forest is not belied by the facts,

The rugged slopes of Cedar Valley

for the cedars which grow here, some 40,000 in number, belong to a species unique to Cyprus (*Cedrus brevifolia*) which is believed to have covered the whole island in ancient times, when it was much used in the construction of ships and houses.

Very occasionally to be seen in Cedar Valley and the forests to the north is the moufflon, a species of wild sheep which is in danger of extinction (see Facts and Figures, Flora and Fauna).

The road continues through forests of cedar, pine, cypress and oak to the lonely forestry station of Stavrós tis Psókas (alt. 800m/2600ft), surrounded by volcanic peaks which are used as fire-watching points and afford magnificent panoramic views of the forests of Páphos.

Stavrós tis Psókas

Features of particular interest here are the small Forestry Museum, the tree nursery and especially the moufflon enclosure, where visitors can see these shy mountain creatures. The forestry station also offers accommodation and a simple restaurant.

Lagoudherá

F 5/6

Λαγουδερά
Altitude: 1000m/3300ft

The remote mountain village of Lagoudherá lies 25km/15 miles east of the little town of Tróodos and 65km/40 miles north of Limassol. Above the village is a modest little barn-roofed church which originally belonged to a monastery (key from the village priest, who lives in the former monastic buildings next to the church).

Situation and characteristics

★★Church of the Panayía tou Arákou (Arakiótissa)

As at Asínou (see entry), the designation of the Mother of God is taken from a plant, in this case from *arakás,* the pea. This single-aisled church built at the end of the 12th century has a dome which was later covered by a saddle roof borne on supporting walls. The west end of the church, which has no paintings, was also a later addition.

The surviving wall paintings are among the finest in Cyprus, and since being restored in 1973 are resplendent in glowing colour. An inscription dates them to 1192: that is, immediately after the conquest of Cyprus by the Crusaders in 1191. Dating from the Middle Byzantine period (see Art and Culture, Byzantine Wall Paintings), the paintings were probably the work of artists from Constantinople; they are in the classical style of the Comnene period and are of powerful dynamic effect, the elongated figures being depicted with great expressive force.

Wall paintings

On the north wall of the church, below a representation of the Holy Tile (Keramídion), is an inscription naming the donor as a man named Leon.

In the conch of the apse is the Mother of God enthroned with the Child on her lap, attended by the Archangels Michael and Gabriel. Below this are seven busts of Cypriot prelates and eight fathers of the Church. On the side walls of the bema are two stylite saints, the solitary ascetics who sought solitude on the top of a pillar. In the vaulting is a representation of the Ascension.

In the dome of the church is Christ Pantokrator, surrounded by angels. Between the windows in the drum of the dome are Old Testament prophets. On the western pendentives are the four Evangelists, on the eastern pendentives the Annunciation.

In a lunette on the north wall of the church, below the dome, is the Presentation of the Virgin in the Temple. According to an apocryphal

St Anthony

Church of the Panayía tou Arákou

Wall painting of the Nativity

gospel Mary was taken by her parents to serve God in the Temple in fulfilment of a vow, accompanied by seven virgins of the house of Judah. Below this scene are a figure of St Nicholas, the Keramídion (Holy Tile) and the Presentation of Jesus in the Temple, which depicts the aged priest Simeon with the Child on his arm and John the Baptist pointing upward.

In the vaulting of the naos are the Descent into Hades (Anástasis) and, below this, the Baptism of Christ. On the south wall, in a niche below the dome, are the Dormition of the Mother of God and below this the slender figure of the Panayía tou Arákou with the Child on her arm, flanked by an over-lifesize figure of the Archangel Michael. Opposite the Descent into Hades is a particularly fine representation of the Nativity. In the lower zone are figures of saints.

Lárnaca/Lárnax   F 9

Λάρναξ
Altitude: sea level. Population: 54,000

Lárnaca (Greek Lárnax, "sarcophagus"), Cyprus's third largest town, lies in a wide bay in the south-east of the island on the site of ancient Kítion. During the period of Turkish rule it was an important trading town. Foreign consuls were stationed in Lárnaca, and it grew to become the island's second largest town. In the early 20th century it declined into a provincial town of little consequence.

Situation and
★ importance

Lárnaca's rise began after the Turkish invasion of 1974, when the island's principal port, Famagusta, fell to the Turks. This gave a great boost to Lárnaca, which became Cyprus's second largest export port and now handles almost all the oil imports from the Middle East.

Post-1974
boom

On the northern outskirts of Lárnaca various industries have been established, in particular an oil refinery, and a number of Western European firms have factories in this area. The division of the island has given Lárnaca an increased share in international trade, and it has become an important traffic junction. It now also has a modern marina with moorings for over 200 boats.

After the closing down of Nicosia airport in 1974 a new international airport was established at Lárnaca, which is now the point of arrival for most foreign visitors (though there is also an airport at Páphos: see entry). Bathing beaches have been built up with imported sand, and hotels, restaurants and bars have proliferated.

Airport

With the great influx of refugees in 1974 the population of Lárnaca grew to more than double its previous size. New housing schemes were built in great haste, and these developments still set the pattern in the outer districts of the town. There was a further influx of population after the outbreak of civil war in Lebanon, which brought thousands of Lebanese refugees to Lárnaca and Limassol.

Population

The townscape of Lárnaca is marked on the one hand by the neo-classical buildings of the colonial period along the harbour front and on the other by the old part of the town with its narrow lanes and Turkish mosques. The best area for shopping and souvenirs is the old quarter, where jewellery and leather goods can be bought at very reasonable prices. Along the harbour front are a series of excellent restaurants.

★ The town

On Whit Monday country people from the surrounding area flock into Lárnaca for the Kataklysmós festival, which commemorates Noah's preservation from the Flood and is a thanksgiving to Our Lady of the Sea. People spray each other with water in order to cleanse themselves from their sins.

Whitsun festival

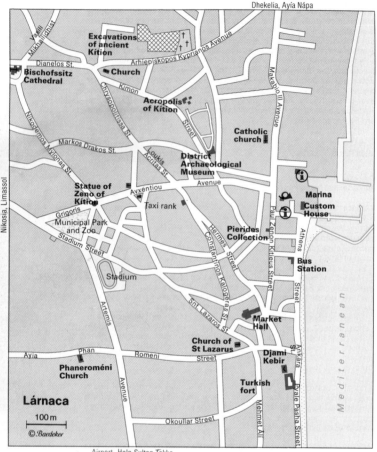

Dhekelia, Ayía Nápa

Vasíli Mikhaílidst.

Excavations of ancient Kítion

Dianelos St.

Arhiepískopos Kyprianos Avenue

Bischofssitz Cathedral

Church

Kimon

Chrysopolitissa St.

Nikoláenos Myronas St.

Markos Drakos St.

Acropolis of Kítion

Loúkis Akrítas St.

Street

Catholic church

Makabio III Avenue

District Archaeological Museum

Avenue

Statue of Zeno of Kítion

Avxentíou

Grigóris

Municipal Park and Zoo

Stadium Street

Taxi rank

Hermes Street

Constantínos Kalogéras St.

Pierides Collection

Paul Zenon Kitieus Street

Athens Street

Marina

Custom House

Bus Station

Stadium

Artemis

Snt Lazaros St.

Market Hall

Ankara Street

Pyale Pasha Street

M e d i t e r r a n e a n

Ayía

Phan

Romeni Street

Church of St Lazarus

Djami Kebir

Phaneroméni Church

Avenue

Turkish fort

Mehmet Ali

Lárnaca

100 m

© Baedeker

Okoullar Street

Nikosia, Limassol

Airport, Hala Sultan Tekke

In these Christian ceremonies there are reminiscences of ancient water festivals in honour of Aphrodite, who had risen from the waves and was regarded as the patron goddess of the sea.

History

Ancient Kítion

The earliest settlement on the site of Lárnaca for which there is evidence dates back to the Early Bronze Age. In ancient times the town was known as Kítion; in the Old Testament it is called Chittim or Kittim. In the 14th and 13th centuries B.C. there must have been large copper-working establishments and a harbour for exporting the copper. At the end of the 13th century the area was settled by Achaeans driven out of mainland Greece by Doric incomers. In the 11th century B.C. the town was ravaged by an earthquake. Around 800 B.C. the abandoned site was reoccupied by Phoenicians, who remained there until 312 B.C., rebuilding the old temples and founding a sanctuary of Astarte. Lárnaca now became one of the leading city-kingdoms on the island. An alliance with Persia saved it from the conquest suffered by other city-kingdoms.

The famous philosopher Zeno of Kítion, founder of the Stoic school of philosophy in Athens, was born in the town in 336 B.C. (see Famous People).

Legend has it that Christianity was brought to Lárnaca by St Lazarus, whom Christ had raised from the dead. The Jews put Lazarus and his sisters into a boat without either sails or a rudder which was miraculously carried to Lárnaca, and Lazarus became the first bishop of the town. During the period of Lusignan rule the town was known as Salines, after the nearby salt-pans. The port was much used by Crusaders and pilgrims. Under the Turks Lárnaca became the diplomatic centre of the island.

Christianisation

It is not known when the town began to be called Lárnaca, but from the 17th century onwards the name was well established. It is thought to be derived from the Greek word *lárnax* ("sarcophagus") because of the many sarcophagi found in ancient Lárnaca.

The name Lárnaca

Sights

The Turkish fort (open: Mon.–Fri. 8am–5pm) in Ankara Street, the seafront promenade, was built in 1625 on the walls of an earlier Venetian fort. A two-storey gatehouse leads into the inner courtyard, surrounded by four ranges of buildings. To the right of the entrance is a staircase leading to the upper floor, on which is the District Medieval Museum displaying finds from ancient Kítion and a Late Bronze Age settlement near Hala Sultan Tekke, together with photographs documenting the course of the excavations. To the left of the gatehouse is the sea wall of the fort. An open hall here contains ancient anchors from Kítion. Steps lead up to the wall-walk, from which there are fine views of the sea and the harbour. During the Turkish period passing ships were greeted by a cannon-shot from here. Under British rule the fort was used as a prison, and later as a store for finds from ancient Kítion; today part of the fort operates as the Lárnaca Municipal Cultural Centre.

Turkish fort

The mosque opposite the fort, the Djami Kebir, is dated by an inscription to 1835/36. The ablutions fountain is 18th century. The mosque is still used by Arab visitors to Cyprus.

Mosque

From the fort, Lazaros Street leads to the church of St Lazarus (open: daily), a multi-domed church built in the 10th century on the spot where a sarcophagus bearing the name Lazarus was found in A.D. 890. This was believed to be the tomb of St Lazarus, first bishop of Kítion. The relics of the saint were taken to Constantinople, but in 1204 were stolen by the Crusaders and carried off to Marseilles. They are now in the church of Saint-Lazare in Autun (Burgundy).

★Ayios Lázaros

After the building of the church the tomb of St Lazarus attracted large numbers of pilgrims. In the Middle Ages the church was served by Benedictines and later by Armenians. It was taken over by the Turks but in 1589 was sold back to the Christian community. Thereafter it was used both by Orthodox and Catholic worshippers. In the 19th century the domes collapsed and were rebuilt. The bell-tower and the loggia on the south side of the church also date from the 19th century.

The church, three-aisled, is over 30m/100ft long and 20m/65ft wide, with three domes over the nave. Corinthian capitals from ancient Kítion are built into the pillars at the crossing. The iconostasis, one of the finest in Cyprus, dates from the 18th century. On a pillar near the south doorway is a 17th century icon of the Raising of Lazarus which eight days before Easter is paraded through the streets of Lárnaca. To the right of the iconostasis are steps leading down to the saint's empty sarcophagus.

There is a new museum next to the church with valuable old icons.

Museum

Pierides Museum

Chalcolithic terracotta figure

From here Phaneroméni Street leads west to the new church of Ayía Phaneroméni. In front of it, set into the ground, can be seen a pre-Hellenistic chamber tomb which in Christian times was converted into a small church. The low, barrel-vaulted interior contains a number of icons. The icon of Ayía Phaneroméni ("Revelation") is credited locally with the power to heal serious diseases.

Phaneroméni Church

In Zenon Kitieus Street is the little Pierides Museum (open: Mon.–Sat. 9am–1pm), with an interesting collection of finds dating from the Chalcolithic period to the Middle Ages. The museum occupies a house which belonged to the diplomat and merchant Dhimitrios Pierides (b. 1811), who was a great art collector and saved much archaeological material from being exported from Cyprus. Later generations of the family shared his interest in archaeology and added to the collection, which now contains valuable antiquities from many different periods.

★Pierides Museum

The first room on the left displays material of the Chalcolithic era, the Bronze Age and the Geometric and Archaic periods. In addition to numerous idols the most notable items are the examples of Bronze Age pottery. Particularly interesting (in the case in the centre of the room) is a terracotta figure from Soúskiou (Chalcolithic, 4th millennium B.C.) representing a naked man sitting on a chair with his hands to his ears and his mouth wide open. Two holes, one in his head and the other in his penis, suggest that it may have been a rhyton (libation vessel). In the same case is a pyxis in the form of a sarcophagus (Geometric period).

The next room contains pottery of the Geometric and Archaic periods. Among the finest items are the beautifully decorated vases in the "free field" style.

In the third room are black-figured and red-figured vases and terracotta figures.

◀ *Church of St Lazarus*

The last room shows glass from many different periods and medieval pottery with sgraffito decoration.

Lárnaca District Archaeological Museum

The Lárnaca District Archaeological Museum in Lord Byron Street (open: Mon.–Wed. and Fri. 7.30am–2.30pm, Thur. also 3–6pm) has a collection of material ranging in date from the Neolithic period to the Middle Ages. The most notable items in the room to the right are the Neolithic objects from Khirokitía and Kalavasós, together with Bronze Age metal implements, pottery from Kítion and Arsos and Mycenaean and Bronze Age pottery. Of particular interest is a vessel made up of seven smaller vases. The second room contains sculpture, torsos and funerary stelae of different periods and an Egyptian sarcophagus of the 7th century B.C.

From here Kimon Street runs north-west to the excavations of ancient Kítion, passing on the right the remains of the ancient acropolis.

Ancient Kítion

Kimon Street joins Archbishop Kyprianos Avenue, to the north of which are the excavations which have brought to light the scanty remains of ancient Kítion (open: Mon.–Fri. 7.30am–2.30pm). The city lay in the wide sheltered Bay of Lárnaca, with a harbour which was partly natural and partly man-made. It was bounded on the south by the Salt Lake of Lárnaca, and salt-working was an important source of revenue from its earliest times. The section of the site known as Area II contains the city's sacred precinct, which was enclosed by a wall. The excavations have shown that there was a sanctuary here in the 2nd millennium B.C., probably in the form of a sacred garden containing plants and two small shrines, each with a court-yard at the east end and a chamber containing an altar at the west end.

At the end of the 13th century B.C. this first sanctuary was destroyed, and about 1200 was replaced by a new one, which incorporated the old sacred

Excavations of ancient Kítion

South Cyprus

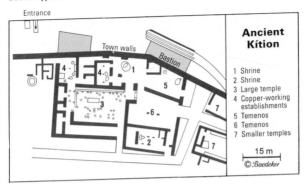

Ancient Kítion

1 Shrine
2 Shrine
3 Large temple
4 Copper-working establishments
5 Temenos
6 Temenos
7 Smaller temples

15 m
© Baedeker

garden. Most of the remains date from this period. The sacred precinct now covered an area 33.60m/110ft by 22m/72ft, with a large temple on the west side.

From the large temple an opening in the walls led to the copper-working establishments immediately north of the sacred precinct – pointing to the close association between the religious cult and copper. In the workshop area, which was open to the sky, were wells and smelting furnaces.

Copper-working establishments

On the south side of the sacred precinct one of the two earlier temples was rebuilt. At the east end were built smaller temples, in which a hoard of ivories, including a figure of the Egyptian god Bes, was found.

Other temples

In the 9th century B.C. Kítion was occupied by the Phoenicians, who did much building in the sacred precinct and altered the large western temple. In the 7th century the temple was divided into three aisles. Finally in 312 B.C. the whole area was destroyed by fire.

Surroundings of Lárnaca

On the road to Limassol an aqueduct (Kamares means "the arches"), built by the Turkish governor in 1745, brought water to Lárnaca from the river Trémithos, 10km/6 miles south-west. The aqueduct remained in use until 1939.

Kamares (Aqueduct)

7km/4½ miles north-east of Lárnaca lies the village of Kelliá, which was established in the medieval period and burned down by the Mamelukes in 1425. On a low hill is the church of Ayios Antónios (key in coffee-house), which incorporates work of different periods between the 11th and 15th centuries. Nothing remains of an earlier church of the 9th century. The church has wall paintings dating from the early 11th to the 13th century, which are thus among the earliest paintings on the island. Particularly fine is a representation of the Sacrifice of Isaac on the south-western pillar, in a style similar to the paintings in Ayios Nikólaos tis Stéyis at Kakopetriá (see entry).

Kelliá
Church of
Ayios Antónios

From the coast road east of Lárnaca a side road runs north-east to the little village of Pýla. United Nations troops are on duty in the village square, which has a Greek taverna on one side and a Turkish coffee-house on the other. Pýla lies on the "Green Line", the buffer zone between the Greek and Turkish parts of the island, and is the only place in the Republic of Cyprus where Greeks and Turks live together. Of the 1000 or so inhabitants of the

Pýla

village some 300 are Turks. Although the two communities live peaceably together they each have their own mayor and their own school. The Turkish inhabitants have freedom of movement both in the Republic of Cyprus and in the Turkish part of the island, but the Greek villagers cannot enter Turkish territory.

Hala Sultan Tekke	See entry
Kíti	See entry
Stavrovoúni	See entry

Léfkara   F 7/8

Λέυκαρα
Altitude: 600–650m/1970–2130ft

Situation and ★ townscape

The picturesque village of Páno Léfkara (Upper Léfkara), part of which is now protected as a historic monument, lies in the southern foothills of the Tróodos range between Limassol and Lárnaca, 18km/11 miles north of the Neolithic settlement of Khirokitía. It is a pretty little place with its houses in traditional style, its red tiled roofs white walls (originally light blue). The elaborately decorated wooden balconies and oriels on the upper floors give welcome shade during the warmer months of the year.

★ Léfkara lace/ Léfkaritika

The village is mainly famed, however, for its traditional lace (known as "Léfkaritika") and embroidery, the making of which can be traced back to Venetian times. In those days this cool hill village was a favourite summer

Léfkara lace

retreat for noble Venetian ladies, who spent their time working hemstitch embroidery; and their example was imitated by the local women who worked in their households. It is said that Leonardo da Vinci came here in 1481 to buy an altar-cloth for Milan Cathedral. There are now numerous souvenir shops selling Léfkara lace and also the gold and silver jewellery which is made here by hand following ancient models.

Surroundings of Léfkara

8km/5 miles south-west of Léfkara in Kato Léfkara stands the Convent of Ayios Minás, one of the few nunneries in Cyprus. Originally founded in 1670, it had remained empty for many years before being recently re-occupied. The nuns maintain the convent largely by the sale of the icons which are painted here, supplemented by the sale of honey also produced here.

Convent of
Ayios Minás

The church (1754) has a beautiful 18th century carved iconostasis. The principal icon depicts Ayios Minás (St Menas), a military saint who served in the Roman army in Phrygia (Asia Minor), became a convert to the Christian faith and was martyred in the reign of Diocletian (end of 3rd century A.D.).

Limassol/Lemesós

G/H 6

Λεμεσός
Altitude: sea level
Population: 121,000

Limassol (Greek Lemesós; recently the official name), Cyprus's second largest city and since the partition of the island in 1974 its principal port (see Facts and Figures, Economy and Transport), lies on the south coast, to the east of the Akrotíri peninsula. Following the loss of Famagusta (see Sights in North Cyprus, Famagusta) Limassol developed into the island's principal trading port and a rising commercial and industrial town. On the western outskirts of the town are a range of industrial installations. The large Keo, Etko, Sodap and Loel wineries have made Limassol the centre of the island's wine trade. In addition to table wines sherry, brandy, liqueurs and ouzo are produced here. The Keo winery makes a local brand of beer.

Situation and
★importance

After the partition of the island the population of Limassol increased rapidly as a result of the influx of refugees. Tourism now developed into a major source of revenue and created new jobs. Something like a third of all visitors to Cyprus now spend their holiday in Limassol, which has taken over the role of Varósha, the hotel district of Famagusta. Along the coast to the east of the town are a range of high-rise hotels, and the seafront road is lined with restaurants, bars and shops.

★Holiday resort

After the outbreak of civil war in Lebanon many Lebanese fled to Limassol and established businesses and banks there. These Arab immigrants have left their mark on the street scene, and many shops and bars draw attention to their wares in Arabic. Limassol now consists of two very different parts, the hotel district to the east and the old town to the west. The old town has preserved an Oriental air, with small craftsmen's shops huddled round the market square. Since in the past Limassol had many Turkish inhabitants it has preserved a number of mosques and a Turkish bath-house. The old town is a good shopping area, in which leather goods and gold and silver jewellery can be found at reasonable prices.

The town

Limassol also offers a varied night life, with discothèques and night clubs as well as numerous bars and restaurants.

In summer Limassol offers the attractions of various festivals – flower and fruit festivals as well as cultural events. In spring there is a large and

Festivals

145

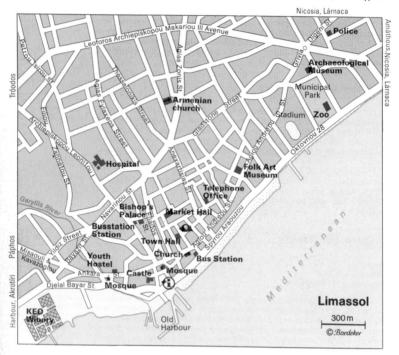

Limassol

300 m

© Baedeker

colourful Carnival parade. Other major occasions are the International Arts
Festival in June/July and the Wine Festival in September.

History

Limassol was a place of no particular consequence until the time of the
Crusaders. In ancient times there are references to various place-names
like Nemesos and Theodosia, but the scanty remains that have survived
from pre-Christian times suggest that there was only a small and insignificant settlement on the site, overshadowed by the two important
city-kingdoms of Koúrion to the west and Amáthous to the east. In Byzantine times the town seems to have been the see of a bishop, with a fort to
the west of the present Castle.

Richard
Coeur de Lion

In 1191 Richard Coeur de Lion landed in Amathoús, to the east of Limassol,
and destroyed the town. After freeing his betrothed bride, Berengaria of
Navarre, from her confinement by Isaac Comnenus, self-appointed ruler of
Cyprus, he conquered the whole island and, according to the local tradition, was married to Berengaria in St George's Chapel in Limassol Castle.
He then continued on his crusade to the Holy Land, after handing over
control of the island to the Templars, who now moved the headquarters of
their order to Limassol Castle.

Later history

After the destruction of ancient Amathoús Limassol began hesitantly to
develop, though suffering many setbacks in later centuries. In the 14th
century it was ravaged by a severe flood; in 1330 it was sacked by the
Genoese; and in the 15th century it was raided by the Mamelukes. It
suffered further devastation during the Turkish conquest in 1570. Until the

Street scene in Limassol

beginning of British rule in 1878 and the establishment of a military base on the Akrotíri peninsula Limassol was an unimportant provincial town; thereafter, however, the port was developed and the town improved and embellished.

Sights

Limassol Castle (open: daily 7.30am–5pm; in summer to 7pm) stands at the west end of the seafront promenade. Limassol's only historic building, it reflects the town's eventful history.

★ Castle

The Castle occupies the site of an earlier Byzantine fort. Soon after Richard Coeur de Lion's marriage to Berengaria in the castle in 1191 he handed it over to the Templars. When the Order of the Temple was dissolved by the Pope in the 14th century the castle passed into the hands of the Lusignan kings of Cyprus and later to the Knights of St John, whose headquarters were in Kolóssi Castle.

On the west side of the castle is a square Gothic hall, built by the Knights of St John, which was used as a church. From here a spiral staircase leads up to the roof. St George's Chapel was later converted into a prison. The Venetians strengthened the castle, but were unable to hold out against the Turkish attack. The tower at the entrance to the castle was built by the Turks. During the period of British rule the castle was used as a prison.

Cyprus Medieval Museum

The castle now houses the Cyprus Medieval Museum, with a collection which includes part of a hoard of silver found at Lamboúsa and a variety of medieval antiquities – architectural fragments, gravestones of the 14th and 16th centuries, copper domestic articles, arms and armour. There is a collection of coins ranging in date from Byzantine times to the Turkish

Limassol Castle

period, and pottery of the 13th to 19th centuries. In front of the castle is a reconstruction of a Byzantine oil-press.

Reptile House

At the entrance to the Old Harbour, at the end of the promenade, is the Reptile House (open: daily 9am–7pm), with an unusual collection of boas, pythons, cobras, adders, rattlesnakes, lizards and crocodiles. Visitors are allowed, if they wish, to handle the creatures under the supervision of the owner.

Folk Art Museum

In Ayios Andreas Street is the little Folk Art Museum (open: Mon.–Sat. 8.30am–1pm and 3–5pm; closed Tues. and Thur. afternoon and Sun.), which illustrates the folk art of the 19th and early 20th centuries. The exhibits in its seven rooms include embroidery and other types of needle-work, traditional costumes, weaving looms and spinning wheels, beds and presses, and an elaborate bride's headdress in wax.

District Archaeological Museum

Near the Municipal Gardens in Lord Byron Street is the District Archaeological Museum (open: daily 7.30am–5pm, Thur. to 6pm), with a wide range of exhibits from the Neolithic period to the Middle Ages. In the courtyard are mosaics from Alássa, including a fine representation of Aphrodite bathing.

Of particular interest is the Chalcolithic material from Erími (the Erími culture) and Sotíra in the first room, including needles, arrowheads and stone axes. There is also a collection of pottery ranging in date from the Bronze Age to the Roman period.

The second room is mainly devoted to finds from Amathoús, including small sculpture of the Archaic and Roman periods, bronze objects of various dates, seals and jewellery.

The third room contains sculpture and sarcophagi. Among the items from Amathoús are a large statue of the Egyptian god Bes (2nd/3rd c. A.D.), a huge capital with a female head and a sarcophagus with a recumbent figure on the lid. Other exhibits include Hellenistic sculpture from Koúrion and a small statue of the god Bes (5th c.).

Also in the Municipal Gardens is a small zoo, including some moufflon, the rare wild sheep which is now a protected species. In a side street opening off Ayios Andreas Street is a Turkish bath-house which is still in use. On the western outskirts of the town is the Keo winery, which can be visited.

Other sights

Surroundings of Limassol

To the west of Limassol extends the Akrotíri peninsula, which culminates in Cape Gáta, the most southerly point on Cyprus. This is one of the British Sovereign Bases, and much of the area is closed to the public. The vegetation is rich and luxuriant, with extensive plantations of citrus fruits and vineyards. The citrus plantations were laid out in 1933 by the Cyprus Palestine Plantation Society, a co-operative organisation of Cypriot and Israeli agricultural experts.

Akrotíri peninsula

The Salt Lake of Akrotíri is no longer used for the extraction of salt. It is possible to drive along its shores for some 8km/5 miles to a point just beyond the village of Akrotíri where the road is closed by a barrier manned by British troops.

See entry

Kolóssi

14km/8½ miles west of Limassol on the road to Páphos is Erími, one of the most important Chalcolithic sites on Cyprus. The excavations lie to the south of the village, but the scanty remains are likely to be of interest only to specialists. Pottery from the site can be seen in the archaeological museums of Limassol and Nicosia.

Erími

1.5km/1 mile west of Erími is Episkopí (a name derived from Greek *episko-pos,* "bishop"), to the north of which is the Episkopí Cantonment, a large residential area for the families of the British forces, with British-style houses, schools, sports facilities, a shopping centre and a hospital.

Episkopí

It is worth looking into Episkopí, however, for the sake of the small Koúrion Archaeological Museum (open: Mon.–Fri. 8am–2pm, Sat. 8am–1pm), which occupies a small house opposite the church. The museum displays finds from Koúrion and the surrounding area – sculpture, inscriptions, coins, pottery – bearing witness to human settlement in this area from the Neolithic period to early Christian times.

Koúrion Archaeological Museum

The most remarkable exhibit is the group of skeletons of a young family killed in an earthquake in the 4th century which buried the town in mounds of debris. Since the earthquake occurred in the early morning most of the inhabitants were at home; and the attitudes of these skeletons, discovered some years ago, show that the family were huddled together on a bed, with the man trying to protect his wife and children from the catastrophe.

See entry

Koúrion

Just beyond Erími a road goes off on the right to Tróodos. From this road, soon after Kandoú, a minor road on the left leads north-west to Sotíra (8km/5 miles from Erími), where excavations on the hill of Teppes have brought to light one of the oldest settlements on the island.

Sotíra

A short way outside Sotíra it is worth visiting the church Ayios Georgios where many icons, including a 15th c. Virgin and Child, are on display in a museum.

Amathoús

8km/5 miles east of Limassol on the coast road to Lárnaca with its innumerable holiday hotels, just beyond the Amathus Beach Hotel, the remains of the town walls of the ancient city-kingdom of Amathoús (Latin Amathus;

Excavations of ancient Amathoús

alt. 0–150m/0–490ft) can be seen on the right. To the left of the road are the remains of the lower town, part of which, including dwelling-houses as well as the harbour, has been swallowed up by the sea. Only slight remains of the upper town – the acropolis, with the city's temples – have so far been discovered.

Foundation legends

The origins of this powerful city-kingdom are the subject of various myths. One legend makes Amathusa, mother of King Kinyras, the foundress of the city. According to Plutarch (1st/2nd c. A.D.) Theseus put Ariadne, then highly pregnant, ashore here because of a storm which was raging at sea but was then driven away by the storm. Discovering on his return that she had died in childbirth, he founded a shrine in her honour. A third version has it that Pygmalion was the founder and first king of the city. It is known, at any rate, that Eteo-Cypriot (i.e. non-Greek) cults were practised in Amathoús, which was notorious in ancient times for its human sacrifices and temple prostitution (see Koúklia, Cult of Aphrodite).

History

Human settlement in this area is thought to have begun in the Iron Age. With its numerous copper-mines Amathoús, like Kition, prospered as a centre of the copper trade, and the proud, independent city began at an early stage to mint its own coins. In the conflict between the Greeks and the Persians Amathoús frequently changed sides, and in the 5th century it was the only city-kingdom on Cyprus not to rebel against Persian rule.

In the 4th century, however, Amathoús sent ships to support Alexander the Great against the Persians. The city continued to flourish in Roman and early Christian times, but its decline began with the Arab raids of the 7th and 8th centuries. The city was finally destroyed by Richard Coeur de Lion in 1191 (see Limassol, History). Looting by tomb-robbers and the use of stone from ancient buildings in the construction of the Suez Canal did further damage to the ancient remains.

Excavations by French and Cypriot archaeologists since 1980 have brought to light scanty remains of the acropolis on the hill, where there once stood a Late Hellenistic temple of Aphrodite. So far the foundations of the temple and part of a pediment have been found. At the foot of the hill is the agora, which is much better preserved. Tombs dating from the 7th–2nd centuries B.C. have also been discovered.

The remains

Convent of Ayios Yeóryios Alemános

15km/9½ miles east of Limassol (leave on the old road to the east and just after the Moni power station take a road on the left) is the convent of Ayios Yeóryios Alemános, lying amid vineyards and fruit orchards in a valley running down to the sea.

The convent, which is little visited by tourists, was originally founded in the 12th century and is occupied by nuns who besides their religious duties are mainly engaged in icon painting and flower and herb cultivation. After the partition of the island in 1974 the convent offered a home to the last of the three famous icon-painters from the monastery of St Barnabas, near Famagusta.

Louvarás

F/G 6

Λουβαράς

The little village of Louvarás lies in the Tróodos Mountains 22km/14 miles north of Limassol.

Situation

Church of St Mamas

Louvarás is notable only for the saddle-roofed church of St Mamas (key in the house immediately in front of the church). Built in 1455, it has well preserved wall paintings of 1495; the narthex is a later addition. It is dedicated to St Mamas, a saint much venerated in Cyprus (see Sights in North Cyprus, Mórphou).

An inscription over the west doorway gives the dates of construction and painting of the church. To left and right of the inscription are the kneeling figures of the donors, Constantine (the building) and John (the paintings), accompanied by their wives. The paintings were the work of Philip Goul, who was also responsible for the paintings in the church of the Stavrós tou Ayiasmáti at Platanistása.

Portraits of donors

The paintings are arranged in three zones: various saints in the lowest zone and 27 New Testament scenes in the two upper zones.

Wall paintings

The narrative begins on the south wall of the church with the Nativity of Christ and continues with the Presentation in the Temple, the Baptism, the Transfiguration, the Raising of Lazarus, the Entry into Jerusalem, the Holy Women at the empty tomb, the healing of the paralytic at the Pool of Bethesda, Christ preaching to the Jews, Christ and the woman of Samaria, the healing of the man born blind and the healing of Peter's mother-in-law.

Naos

On the west wall, under the Crucifixion, are the Last Supper, the Washing of the Feet, the Betrayal, Christ before Annas and Caiaphas, Christ casting out devils, the foundation inscription and the Descent from the Cross.

On the west wall are Pilate washing his hands, the Mocking, the Bearing of the Cross, the Descent of the Holy Ghost (Pentecost), the Descent into Hades (Anástasis), the Ascension and the Dormition of the Mother of God.

151

Bema In the conch of the apse is the Mother of God Blacherniótissa, standing with her arms raised in prayer between the Archangels Michael and Gabriel. Below this are six fathers of the Church. On the north wall is the Sacrifice of Isaac, on the south wall the Hospitality of Abraham.

Makherás Monastery F 7

Μονή Μαχαίρα
Altitude: 800m/2625ft

Situation Makherás Monastery lies 36km/23 miles south of Nicosia in the eastern foot-hills of the Tróodos range. It is reached on a road which runs south-west from Nicosia, passing the site of ancient Tamassós (see entry). The last few kilometres are on a hill road which climbs, with many bends, to the monas-tery, picturesquely situated at the foot of Mt Makherás (1423m/4669ft).

Foundation As was the case with other monasteries in Cyprus, the foundation of Makherás followed the discovery of a wonderworking icon in the 12th century. During the iconoclastic controversy of the 8th and 9th centuries (see Art and Culture, Byzantine Wall Paintings) many icons were hidden to save them from destruction by the iconoclasts, and their rediscovery in the Middle Ages led to the foundation of monasteries.

The monastery was rebuilt in the 19th century after a devastating fire.

Legends According to the foundation legend two 12th century hermits, Ignatios and Neóphytos, discovered an icon of the Mother of God in a cave under the present monastery, together with a mysterious knife (*makhaíra*) which later gave the monastery its name. Thereupon the Byzantine Emperor Manuel Comnenus gave the two hermits land and money for the founda-tion of a monastery.

Makherás Monastery, in the foothills of the Tróodos range

In the early 14th century Alice d'Ibelin, wife of King Hugo IV of the Lusignan dynasty, is said to have forced her way into the monastery church, which women were forbidden to enter: whereupon the Mother of God punished her by striking her dumb.

Also in the 14th century King James I and his family sought refuge in Makherás to escape from the plague which was then raging.

On the large iconostasis of the church is the much venerated icon of the Mother of God, almost entirely concealed under a silver cover. It is credited with the power to heal wounds and bring rain. Miraculously, it survived the fire which destroyed the monastery in the 19th century.

Icon of the Mother of God

In a small room in the monastery are displayed photographs and mementoes of Grigóris Afxentíou, Grivas's second-in-command in the EOKA movement, who died near here. During the uprising he sought refuge in the monastery, but his presence was betrayed by a local peasant. He then withdrew to a cave below the monastery, where he was burned to death in March 1957 in an attack by British forces.

Afxentíou Memorial

Below the monastery is a memorial to Afxentíou, now a national hero. From here there is an attractive footpath (14km/8½ miles) to Politikó.

Nicosia/Lefkosía   D/E 7/8

Λευκοσία
Altitude: 165m/540ft
Population: 203,000

Nicosia (Greek Lefkosía, Turkish Lefkoşa, now officially Lefkosía), the largest city in Cyprus, lies in the wide Mesaória plain, within easy reach of Limassol and Lárnaca by motorway. Since the Turkish invasion in 1974 the demarcation line between Greek and Turkish-occupied Cyprus runs through the centre of the city, which is the capital both of the Republic of Cyprus and Turkish-occupied North Cyprus (see History, Cyprus Divided).

Situation and ★★ importance

In contrast to the Greek part of the city, which has continued to grow and now has a population of about 165,000, the population of the Turkish part has stagnated at approximately 45,000 (see Sights of North Cyprus, Nicosia/Lefkoşa).

Nicosia is the seat of the government, foreign embassies, all national organisations and the country's leading businesses. In order to avoid the economic stagnation with which the city was threatened after the closing down of Nicosia's international airport in 1974 a motorway was built between Nicosia and Limassol (see entry), providing the essential link with the largest exporting port in Cyprus.

Along Hermes Street, once the heart of the old town, runs the Green Line, at some points only a few metres wide, between the two parts of Cyprus. It is so called because a line of separation was drawn on a map with a green pencil in the 1960s, when there were already secret plans for a possible division of Cyprus. Although the frontier is marked only by sandbags, barbed wire and old oil drums, it is nevertheless impenetrable. In the buffer zone between the two territories, in which everything must remain unchanged, there are constant motorised and foot patrols by the United Nations peace-keeping force, which also mans guard posts to maintain peace and order in the border area.

Green Line

The only crossing point between the two sides is at the Ledra Palace Hotel, once one of Cyprus's most renowned hotels. Only Armenians and Maronites can cross the frontier without restriction. Visitors to the Republic of

Frontier crossing: Ledra Palace Hotel

Cyprus can get a visa for a day trip (8am–6pm) into Turkish-occupied North Cyprus (though this is frowned on by the government); but visitors to North Cyprus cannot cross the frontier in the reverse direction, since the Greek Cypriot authorities regard entry into the Turkish "pseudo-state" as illegal. By the same token Greek Cypriots are not allowed to enter North Cyprus; exceptions are made only in cases of particular hardship (e.g. a family funeral) through the intermediary of the UN peace-keeping force. The frontier is also closed to Turkish Cypriots wishing to enter South Cyprus (see Practical Information for South Cyprus, Frontier Crossing).

★ Old Town

The Old Town of Nicosia is still enclosed within the star-shaped circuit of its Venetian walls. Here visitors will encounter the authentic life of Cyprus: the blaring of car horns in narrow labyrinthine streets, the insistent clamour of Greek folk music, people dozing outside their open front doors in a summer temperature of 40°C/104°F in the shade – the relaxed and undemanding Mediterranean way of life, combined with an unconcerned tolerance of a noise level which for visitors from more northerly latitudes may be harder to bear.

An oasis of peace is the Laïkí Yitoniá ("People's Neighbourhood") quarter of the town, in which traffic is restricted. This district, now an essential item in the programme of any sightseeing tour of the city, has been under renovation in recent years under a comprehensive slum clearance and redevelopment plan, and new houses have been built in traditional style, so that the area now gives a very fair impression of Nicosia as it used to be. The city's principal shopping streets are Ledra Street and Onaságoras Street.

New Town

While in the evening the Old Town empties – many houses are unoccupied and the tourists return to their hotels on the coast – the newer parts of the town continue to hum with activity; for in contrast to the Turkish part of the city, where life seems to have stood still, the Greek part has acquired new

Workshop in the Old Town   *Gardens in the old moat*

A Venetian bastion

and modern suburbs with blocks of flats, banks, hotels, shops and entertainment quarters.

Thanks to the city's situation in the Mesaória plain there are no natural boundaries to its expansion, and many new businesses have been established within the Nicosia conurbation.

After the removal of the tented camps in which Greek Cypriots from the Turkish-occupied territories were originally housed new accommodation was provided with remarkable speed in settlements on the outskirts of the city in which many refugees still live rent-free.

There are two tours of Nicosia organised by the Nicosia Municipality. A **Nicosia Tours** walking tour of the Old Town takes place each Thursday at 10am. Also, a tour of Kaimakli, one of Nicosia's oldest suburbs, takes place each Monday at 10am. The latter includes a bus ride along Kaimakli's demarcation line, passing the old railway station and flour mill, followed by time walking in Kaimakli. Each tour is free, lasts two hours, and starts from the Cyprus Tourist Information office in Laïkí Yitoniá (east of Elefthería Square).

Although the Mesaória plain was occupied by man as early as the Neolithic **History** period the first traces of settlement within the area of Nicosia date only from the Bronze Age. Nicosia first appears in the records in the 7th century B.C., when it is mentioned in Assyrian documents, under its then name of Ledra, as one of the ten city-kingdoms paying tribute to Assyria. In the 6th century the little town of Ledra was incorporated in the powerful city-kingdom of Sálamis.

In the 3rd century B.C. Leukos, son of the Egyptian ruler Ptolemy Soter I, founded a city which he called Leukosía on the site of the older settlement of Ledra. In later centuries the town was frequently ravaged by earthquakes. In Roman times Leukosía was a place of little importance, since the Romans preferred the coastal towns.

155

From Byzantine to Frankish rule	The town gained in importance in the 4th century A.D., under Byzantine rule, when it became the see of a bishop. During the Arab raids in the 7th century many inhabitants of the coastal towns sought refuge in Lefkosía. In the 10th century, after the expulsion of the Arabs, the town flourished. During a rebellion against the Templars (who had bought Cyprus from Richard Coeur de Lion for 100,000 gold bezants) in 1192 the Latin name Nicosia was used for the first time.

The town enjoyed its greatest period of prosperity from the end of the 12th century under Frankish rule (the Lusignan dynasty). It became capital of the kingdom of Cyprus and the see of a Roman Catholic archbishop. In the medieval period it had more than 250 churches as well as a royal palace and splendid aristocratic mansions.

From Venetian to British rule	When the Venetians gained control of Cyprus at the end of the 15th century they developed Nicosia still further. In the 16th century, anticipating attack from the Turks, they built new town walls which enclosed a smaller area than the old walls but were much stronger. The construction of the walls involved the demolition of considerable areas of the town.

In 1570 Nicosia was taken by the Turks after a seven-week siege and became the seat of the Turkish governor. During the period of British colonial rule (1878–1960) it remained the official residence of the governor (and later of the high commissioner) and gradually developed to its present size and importance.

★ The Venetian Walls

Construction	The walls, built in 1567–70 to the design of the Venetian military engineer Giuliano Savorgnano, have a total length of just under 4.5km/2¾ miles. They enclose a circular area, with eleven bastions (bearing the names of leading Venetian families) forming a star-shaped pattern. To provide better

Famagusta Gate (Municipal Culture Centre), Nicosia

protection against Turkish attack the walls were thicker than the previous walls, with a receding slope from the ground upwards, and were surrounded by a moat. In order to give a clear field of fire all buildings outside the walls were razed to the ground, involving the destruction of the royal palace, the burial chapel of the Lusignan dynasty and a Dominican monastery.

In September 1570, however, after a seven weeks' siege, Turkish troops under Mustafa Pasha broke through the walls and captured the town, at the cost of 20,000 lives.

There were originally three gates in the walls: the Porta Domenica (now the Páphos Gate) on the west side, the Porta Giuliana (Famagusta Gate) on the east and the Porta del Provveditore (Kyrenia Gate) on the north.

Town gates

There are now numerous breaches in the walls to allow the passage of traffic. The moat has been drained and is occupied by parks and gardens, sports grounds and play areas. At the Famagusta Gate is an open-air theatre, frequently used for concerts and other events.

Moat

The best preserved of the old gates, the Famagusta Gate (open: Mon.–Sat. 10am–1pm and 4–7pm), originally known as the Porta Guliana after the Christian name of its architect, stands in Nikiphoros Phokas Avenue. 45m/150ft long, it was the main entrance to the town, to which all the principal streets led. Well restored, it now houses the Municipal Cultural Centre, which is used for exhibitions, lectures, etc.

Famagusta Gate

Sights in Southern Nicosia

Old Town

All the main features of interest in Nicosia lie within the walls. From Elefthería (Freedom) Square on the south side of the Old Town the main shopping and business street, Ledra Street, runs north to end, like many other streets, at the boundary with the Turkish-occupied northern half of the town. To the right, just inside the walls, is the Laïkí Yitoniá ("People's Neighbourhood") quarter, now cleaned up and rehabilitated, with typical old restaurants, souvenir shops and bookshops.

Ledra Street
Laïkí Yitoniá

In Hippocrates Street, in the Laïkí Yitoniá quarter, is the Leventis Municipal Museum, Cyprus's first historical museum, opened in 1989 (open: Tues.–Sun. 10am–4.30pm). Jointly financed by the Leventis Foundation and the city, it occupies a three-storey 19th century merchant's house in Neo-Classical style. The ground and first floors illustrate the history of Nicosia with the help of photographs, pictures, coins, clothing and a variety of other exhibits. The displays are arranged in chronological order, from the earliest archaeological finds by way of Byzantine, Frankish and Venetian times, Turkish and British colonial rule, to Nicosia as capital of the Republic of Cyprus. On the second floor are rooms for special exhibitions, a reading room and administrative offices.

Leventis Municipal
Museum

From Elefthería Square Onaságoras Street runs north-east to the Phaneroméni Church ("Church of the Revelation"; open: daily 6am–noon and 3–5.30pm, and for services), the largest church in Nicosia, built in 1872 during the period of Turkish rule. Notable features of the interior are the figure of God the Father in a triangular halo (the symbol of the Trinity), the magnificent iconostasis and the large crystal chandeliers.

Phaneroméni
Church

In the gardens outside the church is a mausoleum containing the remains of Archbishop Kyprianos and other bishops executed by the Turkish governor in 1821 as a deterrent to the movement for Greek independence.

In a building attached to the church is the Phaneroméni Library, which contains the oldest icons in Cyprus.

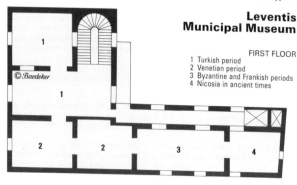

Leventis Municipal Museum

FIRST FLOOR

1 Turkish period
2 Venetian period
3 Byzantine and Frankish periods
4 Nicosia in ancient times

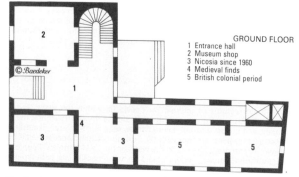

GROUND FLOOR

1 Entrance hall
2 Museum shop
3 Nicosia since 1960
4 Medieval finds
5 British colonial period

Tripiótis Church

North of the Laïkí Yitoniá quarter in Solon Street, once a prosperous residential area, stands the Tripiótis Church, dedicated to the Archangel Michael, which was built in 1690 on the site of an earlier church of the 15th/16th century. Over the west doorway are architectural fragments from the older church – eight marble trefoils, with pediments and pinnacles. Even older is a fragment of a frieze over the south doorway depicting a man between vine-leaves surrounded by other human figures and birds. The church has a fine iconostasis (17th/18th c.), with icons in gold and silver covers, signs that it was once a "society" church.

Ömeriye Mosque

From the south-east side of the walled town Ares Street leads to the Ömeriye Mosque. Now run by Syrians, it is the only mosque in the Greek part of Nicosia which is still used for Muslim worship. It was built on the ruins of a 14th century Augustinian monastery which was destroyed by Turkish gunfire in 1570. The Augustinian house was one of three major monasteries in the old town, the others being the Dominican and Franciscan friaries.

The Gothic buttresses of the original church can still be seen in the interior of the mosque, and a small vaulted room on the north side, now used as a prayer hall for women, has a beautiful Gothic rose window. From the minaret there are fine panoramic views over the town to the Kyrenia Hills. Opposite the mosque are the Ömeriye Baths, which are still in use.

South Cyprus

On the Podokataro Bastion, to the south-east of the walled town, is the large Freedom (Elefthería) Monument, erected in 1960 after the end of British colonial rule, which symbolises the liberation of the people of Cyprus. Two EOKA fighters are shown raising the iron grille at the gate of a prison, from which men, women, children and priests are emerging. The monument is crowned by a huge figure personifying Freedom.

Freedom
Monument

From the Freedom Monument Koraes Street leads to the Archbishop's Palace, St John's Cathedral, the Byzanatine Museum and Art Galleries and the Folk Art Museum.

The neo-Byzantine Archbishop's Palace was built by Archbishop Makarios III between 1956 and 1961. Completed just after Cyprus achieved independence, this magnificent building demonstrates the power and wealth of the Orthodox church. The palace is open to the public only on special occasions. The old archiepiscopal palace next to it now houses the Folk Museum. The monumental bronze statue of Makarios III in front of the palace was erected by Archbishop Chrysostomos in 1987.

★Archbishop's
Palace

St John's Cathedral (Ayios Ioánnis; open: Mon.–Fri. 9am–noon and 2–4pm, Sat. 9am–noon) was built in 1662, during the period of Turkish rule. It is of modest size, since the Ottoman authorities would not allow the building of a large church. The ringing of church bells was also prohibited, and the addition of a bell-tower was permitted only in 1858.

★St John's
Cathedral

The cathedral succeeded an earlier building belonging to a 15th century Benedictine monastery (later taken over by Orthodox monks), which itself was the successor to a still older church dedicated by the Knights of St John to their patron John the Baptist. The Lusignan king Peter I was buried in the earlier church. Built into the outer walls of the church on the south and west sides are various architectural fragments and a coat of arms of the Lusignan period.

The church has been since 1730 the cathedral of the Archbishops of Cyprus, who have been consecrated here since the end of the 18th century.

The church is single-aisled, with a barrel-vaulted roof. The most striking feature of the interior is the magnificent iconostasis, of carved wood covered with gold leaf, with icons of the 18th and 19th centuries. Below the 18th century pulpit is an icon of St John the Evangelist, the oldest in the church, painted by Theodóros Poullákis in the 17th century. On the archbishop's throne to the right of the iconostasis is an icon of St Barnabas. On another throne is the double-headed eagle which is the emblem of the Orthodox church, and in the floor is another large double-headed eagle on which the archbishop stands during his consecration.

The wall paintings in the church are post-Byzantine (18th c.). In the centre of the vaulting is Christ Pantokrator, surrounded by angels, prophets and apostles. On the south and north walls are New Testament scenes, from the Annunciation to the Crucifixion. Over the south doorway is the Last Judgment, with the Tree of Jesse to one side.

Wall paintings

On the north wall are the Mandílion, the Crucifixion and the scenes from the Passion cycle which usually follow it, the Descent into Hades (Anástasis) and the Ascension. Opposite the Tree of Jesse is a representation of the Creation. At the west end of the church are paintings of Christ's miracles. The most interesting paintings are on the south wall, to the right of the archbishop's throne. They depict the finding of the remains of St Barnabas and their recognition by the Byzantine Emperor. This was the event that won autocephaly (independence) for the church of Cyprus (see Facts and Figures, Religion).

The Icon Museum (Byzantine Museum), opened in 1982, occupies the right-hand wing of the Archbishop's Palace, next the Archbishop Makarios III Cultural Foundation (open: Oct. 1st–Apr. 30th, Mon.–Fri. 9am–1pm and 2–5pm, Sat. 9am–1pm; May 1st–Sept. 30th Mon.–Fri. 9.15am–1pm and 2–5.30pm, Sat. 9am–1pm).

★Icon Museum

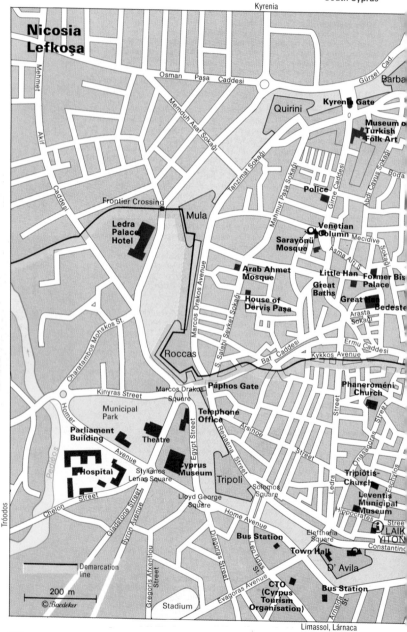

Nicosia
Lefkoşa

Kyrenia

Osman Paşa Caddesi

Mehmet

Akif

Memduh Asal Sokağı

Gürsel Cad.

Barba

Quirini

Kyrenia Gate

Museum o
Turkish
Folk Art

Boda

Caddesi

Abdi Çavuş Sokağı

Tanzimat Sokağı

Mahmut Paşa Sokağı

Girne Caddesi

Police

Frontier Crossing

Mula

Ledra
Palace
Hotel

Venetian
Column

Sarayönü
Mosque

Mecidive

Asma Altı

Sokağı

Arab Ahmet
Mosque

Little Han

Former Bis
Palace

Marcos Drakos Avenue

S. Salahi Şevket Sokağı

Great
Baths

House of
Derviş Paşa

Great M

Bedeste

Arasta
Sokağı

Roccas

Ermu Caddesi

Kyrenia

Baf Caddesi

Kykkos Avenue

Charalambos Monskos St.

Kinyras Street

Marcos Drakos
Square

Páphos Gate

Phaneroméni
Church

Homer

Pedieos

Municipal
Park

Telephone
Office

Street

Street

Parliament
Building

Theatre

Egypt Street

Arsinoe

Street

Onasagoras Street

Eschylos

Street

Renaria Street

Avenue

Cyprus
Museum

Tripoli

Solomos
Square

Ledra

Hippocrates

Tripiótis-
Church

Stylianos
Lenas Square

Hospital

Tróodos

Chelon Street

Gladstone Street

Byron Avenue

Lloyd George
Square

Home Avenue

Leventis
Municipal
Museum

Stree

LAIK
YITON

Gregoris Afxentiou
Street

Bus Station

St. Lechroas

Diagoras Street

Eleftheria
Square

Constantino

Town Hall

D' Avila

Demarcation
line

200 m

© Baedeker

Stadium

Evagoras Avenue

CTO
(Cyprus
Tourism
Organisation)

Bus Station

Amalda St.

Limassol, Lárnaca

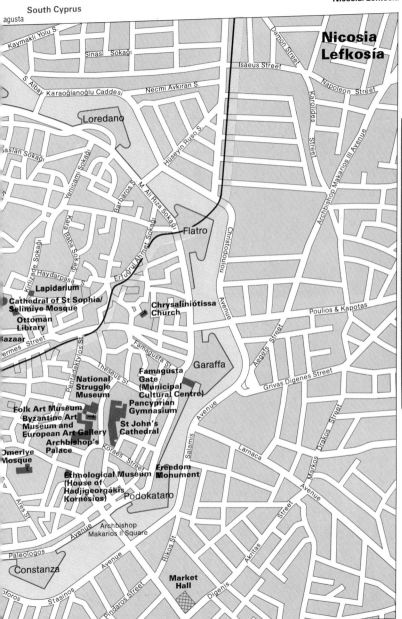

South Cyprus

Nicosia
Lefkosía

agusta

Kaymakli Yolu S.

Sinasi Sokağı

Isaeus Street

Damion Street

Napoleon Street

S. Albay Karaoğlanoğlu Caddesi

Necmi Avkiran S.

Karolides Street

Loredano

Saslan Sokağı

Yenicami Sokağı

Hüseyin Ruso S.

Archbishop Makarios III Avenue

Barbaros S.

M. Ali Rıza Sokağı

Flatro

Christodoulou Avenue

Kara Baha Sokağı

Erfuğrul Ahmet Sokağı

Kırlızade Sokağı

Haydarpaşa S.

Poulios & Kapotas

Lapidarium

**Cathedral of St Sophia/
Selimiye Mosque**

**Chrysaliniótissa
Church**

**Ottoman
Library**

Bazaar

ermes Street

Pentadaktylos St.

Famagusta St.

Garaffa

Aegeis Street

Theseus St.

**Famagusta
Gate
(Municipal
Cultural Centre)**

Grivas Digenes Street

**National
Struggle
Museum**

**Pancyprian
Gymnasium**

Salamis Avenue

Drakos Street

Folk Art Museum

**Byzantine Art
Museum and
European Art Gallery**

**St John's
Cathedral**

**Archbishop's
Palace**

Koraes Street

Larnaca

**Omeriye
Mosque**

Markos Avenue

Ares St.

**Ethnological Museum
(House of
Hadjigeorgákis
Kornésios)**

**Freedom
Monument**

Podokataro

Street

Akritas

Paleologos

Archbishop
Makarios II Square

Constanza

Avenue

Rikos St.

Pindaros Street

Digenis

foros

Stasinos

**Market
Hall**

161

Tripiótis Church　　　　　　　　　　　　　*Freedom Monument*

This valuable collection of some 150 icons ranging in date from the 9th to the 18th century, the finest in Cyprus, brings together icons from churches all over the island. There were undoubtedly many other old icons in Cyprus, but most of them fell victim to the iconoclasts, to the Turks or to fires.

The mosaics which disappeared from the Kanakariá church in Turkish-occupied Cyprus and were recently recovered by the Republic of Cyprus (see Art and Culture, Cyprus's Threatened Cultural Heritage). Six of the lost mosaics are now on display here in an exhibition of the Evangelists Matthew and John.

Well-known icons

One of the oldest icons in the collection is an encaustic icon of the Mother of God, hung near the entrance. The icon of SS Cosmas and Damian dates from the 10th century. Opposite the entrance is an icon of St John from the church of Asínou which dates from the 12th century, the heyday of icon-painting. An icon showing early western influence is a 13th century Mother of God, painted for Dominican monks, with Latin inscriptions in the marginal scenes.

The Ottoman conquest of Cyprus in 1571 led to a marked decline in the craft of icon-painting.

At the end of the main hall in a small room (reconstructed) can be seen 15th century wall paintings from the church of Ayios Nikólaos tis Stéyis (see Kakopetriá).

European Art Gallery

The first floor of the Museum houses the European Art Gallery (same hours), with European paintings (mainly religious themes) of the 17th century Spanish, Dutch and Flemish schools and French pictures of the 17th and 18th centuries. On the second floor is a collection of prints and drawings illustrating ancient architecture and 19th century Greek history.

Archbishop's Palace

Opposite the Archbishop's Palace stands the Neo-Classical Pancyprian Gymnasium, the oldest gymnasium (grammar school) in Cyprus, with the best school library. In the 1950s this was a hotbed of support for the Enosis movement. In his book "Bitter Lemons" Lawrence Durrell (see Famous People), who taught for a time in the school, describes the beginnings of the Cypriot rising against British colonial rule. The most notable pupil of the Pancyprian Gymnasium was Archbishop Makarios III.

Other sights
Pancyprian Gymnasium

The Folk Art Museum (open: Mon.–Wed. and Fri. 8.30am–1pm and 2–4pm; Tues. and Thur. 8.30am–1pm, and 2–5pm; Sat. 8.30am–1pm) occupies the ground floor of a 15th century Gothic building which originally belonged to a Benedictine monastery and from 1730 was the Archbishop's palace. The museum was established in 1950 by the Society of Cypriot Studies, but had no suitable premises until 1961, when the Archbishop moved to his new palace. In the Museum's twelve rooms, which still preserve some Frankish architectural features, are displayed Cypriot costumes, jewellery, woven fabrics, embroidery, everyday objects and old carved chests. A notable feature is the cloister of the former monastery, surrounded by monks' cells. Room 11 is furnished in traditional Cypriot style, with a painting of a wedding scene by the naïve Cypriot painter Michalis Kashialos.

Folk Art Museum

Between the Folk Art Museum and St John's Cathedral is a bust of Archbishop Sophronios, head of the Church of Cyprus from 1865 to 1900 and a leader of the resistance to British colonial rule. Another marble bust is of Archbishop Kyprianos, who was executed by the Turks in 1821.

In a side wing of the old Archbishop's palace, next to the Folk Art Museum, is the National Struggle Museum (open: Mon.–Sat. 8am–2pm and 3–5pm), established in 1961, which documents the activities of EOKA, the underground organisation which from 1955 to 1959 fought for Enosis, the union of Cyprus with Greece (see History, Cyprus Divided). In addition to photographs, press cuttings, books and other publications the exhibits include

National Struggle Museum

Makarios Cultural Foundation and Byzantine Art Museum and European Art Gallery

weapons, models of home-made bombs, a gallows on which Greek rebels were executed and (in the garden) the car used by General Grivas, the EOKA leader.

In another room are thirty volumes containing the signatures of all the Greek Cypriots who voted for Enosis in a referendum held by the Orthodox church in January 1950.

Chrysaliniótissa Church

Going along Ayios Ioánnis Street as far as Theseus Street and then turning into Antigonos Street, we come into one of the fine old quarters of Nicosia. In Chrysaliniótissa Street is the church of the Panayía Chrysaliniótissa, Our Lady of the Golden Flax (*chrysós* = "golden", *linón* = "flax, linen"); the key can be obtained from the house to the right of the church. The church takes its name from an 11th century icon painted on linen depicting the Mother of God with a golden hand and wearing a golden crown. The church was built in the 15th century but incorporates fragments from an earlier church of the 11th/12th century.

The church, roofed with two domes over the nave, has a fine 17th century iconostasis. In a side room are displayed icons and old Bibles of the 16th and 18th centuries.

Taht el-Kale Mosque

Chrysaliniótissa Street and Ymitou Street lead to the little Taht el-Kale Mosque, in the charming quarter of that name, now being cleaned up and rehabilitated. The mosque, which has been renovated, is no longer used.

★ House of Hadjigeorgákis Kornésios

Near the new Archbishop's Palace, in Patriarch Gregorios Street, is the House of Dragoman Hadjigeorgákis Kornésios (see Famous People), a handsome mansion in traditional 18th century style (open: Mon.–Sat. 7.30am–2pm). In the 18th century the Dragoman was an official whose function was to act as an interpreter and intermediary between the Archbishop of Cyprus and the Sultan in Istanbul and whose salary was paid by the Sublime Porte. The Archbishop, as representative of the Greek

House of Dragoman Hadjigeorgákis Kornésios (Ethnological Museum)

community, was responsible for the collection of taxes but delegated his responsibility to the Dragoman, who had the privilege of direct access to the Sultan.

Over the doorway of this three-storey stone-built house is a marble relief of the Lion of St Mark, a relic of the period of Venetian rule. The use of stone in building a house was unusual in 18th century Cyprus, since stone was expensive, and most houses were built of sun-dried brick. Above the lion is a closed wooden balcony, with narrow openings through which the ladies of the household could watch what was happening in the street without themselves being seen. The house is built around three sides of an arcaded courtyard, in which is a small Turkish bath-house. The ground floor was occupied by domestic offices, with a wooden staircase leading to the first floor, on which were the living quarters and state apartments. The rooms are now furnished in period style.

New Town

In the newer districts of the town outside the Venetian walls are govern-   Sights
ment departments, foreign consulates, office blocks and banks. The princi-
pal streets in this part of the town are Evagoras Avenue and Archbishop Makarios III Avenue, with modern shops, restaurants and bars (with or without music). At the end of Demetrios Severis Avenue is the Presidential Palace. In Ayiou Prokopiou Street is the handsome 19th century mansion (church with fine wall paintings) from which Kýkko Monastery administers its extensive properties. In Athalassa Avenue (no. 186) is the Cyprus Handicraft Centre (open: Mon.–Fri. 7.30am–2.30pm, Thur. also 3–6pm), where visitors can watch local craftsmen at work and buy their products. At the corner of Stassinos Avenue and Crete Street is the State Gallery of Contemporary Art (open: Mon.–Fri. 10am–5pm, Sat. 10am–1pm) with paintings

and sculpture by 20th century Cypriot artists (currently closed for renovation).

★★Archaeological Museum

The principal sight in the newer part of Nicosia, however, is the famous Archaeological Museum (Cyprus Museum) opposite the Municipal Theatre and the Parliament Building (open: Mon.–Sat. 9am–5pm, Sun. 10am–1pm, closed on official public holidays).

The museum, exclusively devoted to Cypriot material from the Neolithic period to Byzantine times, gives a comprehensive picture of the cultural history of the island. It was founded in 1882 and moved into its present Neo-Classical premises, built in memory of Queen Victoria, in 1909. There are currently plans to move the museum to a larger building. Attached to the museum is an archaeological library.

In this section we give a brief account of the exhibits displayed in the museum's 14 rooms. On the technical terms used, see the section on Art and Culture (see Facts and Figures).

Room 1

Neolithic and Chalcolithic
Neolithic material from Khirokitía: violin-shaped stone (andesite) idols, carnelian necklaces, early comb-decorated pottery. Chalcolithic cross-shaped idols of steatite, Red-on-White ware.

Room 2

Bronze Age terracotta figures
The terracotta models of shrines and of various domestic activities are among the most important exhibits in the museum. An Early Bronze Age model from Vounoús depicts a religious ceremony in which a priest and a mother and child participate; opposite the entrance to the shrine are three bull-headed creatures, and the ceremony is secretly watched by a man looking over the wall. Red Polished ware of the Early Bronze Age is represented in a variety of attractive forms.

Cyprus Museum

1 Neolithic, Chalcolithic
2 Bronze Age
3 Bronze Age, Classical period
4 Archaic period
5 Archaic sculpture
6 Statue of Septimius Severus
7 Bronzes, gold and silver
8 Reconstructions of tombs
9 Funerary stelae
10 Cypro-Minoan syllabic script
11 Finds from the Tombs of the Kings, Sálamis
12 Copper-working and bronze manufacture
13 Statues from Sálamis
14 Terracotta figures

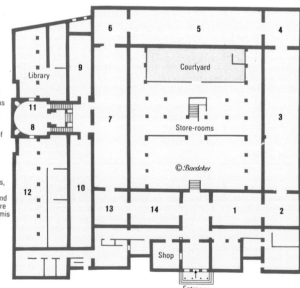

South Cyprus

Late Bronze Age and Classical period
Bronze Age pottery: Red-on-Black ware, Black Slip ware, White Slip w...
Mycenaean vases, pointing to trading links with the western Aegean...
most important vase, the Zeus Crater (14th c. B.C.), depicts a scene from th...
Iliad (according to M. P. Nilsson): Zeus holding the scales of fate before
the Greeks set out in their chariots for the battle.

Notable items in the free-standing cases include a faience rhyton of the
Late Bronze Age and Attic red-figured and black-figured vases. At the far
end of the room, to the right, are some fine vases of the Archaic period in
the "free field" style; particularly notable are vases decorated with a bull
and lotus flower and a bird holding a fish in its bill.

Room 4

Shrine of Ayía Iríni (Archaic period)
A large selection of the 2000 terracotta figures found in this shrine. Most of
the figures are armed; some are on carts drawn by oxen.

Room 5

Large sculpture of the Archaic period
Since there was no marble on Cyprus, most of the sculpture is in limestone.
The exhibits include votive offerings ranging in date from the Archaic
period to Hellenistic times, showing Syrian, Egyptian and Greek influence.
Note particularly the female head (3rd c. B.C.) from the sanctuary of Aphrodite at Arsos, the head of a Kore from Idálion (5th c. B.C.) and a small figure
of Zeus hurling a thunderbolt (c. 500 B.C.). The Aphrodite of Sóloi (1st c. B.C.)
is one of the most famous items in the museum.

Room 6

An over-lifesize bronze statue of the Emperor Septimius Severus from
Kythréa is an example of the self-glorification of the Roman Emperors.

Room 7

Bronze, gold and silver objects
The first part of the room is mainly devoted to bronze articles – weapons,
coins, seals and small statuettes. Among the most interesting items are the
bronze cow from Vouní (5th c. B.C.) and the horned god from Énkomi

Bronze statue of Septimius Severus

Figures of Heracles from Sálamis

Cyprus Museum (Archaeological Museum)

(12th c. B.C.). At the far end of the room is gold and silver jewellery, including a gold sceptre from a tomb at Koúrion (11th c. B.C.) and a silver dish from Énkomi (14th c. B.C.).

Reconstructions of tombs   Room 8
Steps lead down to a lower floor, with reconstructions of tombs (including grave goods) ranging in date from the Neolithic period to the 5th century B.C.

Funerary stelae, etc.   Room 9
Stelae, cippi, urns and sarcophagi, illustrating different burial rites. One stele depicting a woman holding a bird in her hand has an inscription in Cypro-Minoan syllabic script giving her name.

Cypro-Minoan syllabic script   Room 10
Tablets from various periods in different scripts illustrate the writing skills of the peoples of antiquity. The most important item is a tablet of the 16th century B.C. written in the Cypro-Minoan syllabic script, which has not yet been deciphered.

Finds from the Tombs of the Kings at Sálamis   Room 11
(see Sights in North Cyprus, Sálamis)
Particularly notable are the grave goods from the magnificent Tomb 79 (8th/7th c. B.C.). A large bronze cauldron with griffin protomes on an iron tripod, bronze accessories from chariots and harness bear witness to the dead man's wealth. The grave furniture included an ivory chair and bed.

Copper-working and bronze manufacture   Room 12
Exhibits relating to the mining of copper and the production of bronze reflect the importance of these metals in ancient times. Geological maps

◀ *The Aphrodite of Sóloi, one of the chief treasures of the Cyprus Museum*

Pottery model of a Bronze Age shrine

show the location of the main sources of metal ores. The reproduction of a copper-mine and the explanation of the smelting process illustrate ancient technologies of mining and processing copper.

Room 13   Statues from the Gymnasium, Sálamis
Statues of the Hellenistic and Roman periods, including Apollo with his lyre and figures (2nd c. A.D.) of Heracles, Nemesis and Hera.

Room 14   Terracotta figures
A bird-headed divinity, plank idols and figures of bulls (Bronze Age); statuettes of divinities and scenes from everyday life, including a birth (Geometric to Classical periods).

Sights in Northern Nicosia

See page 237

Surroundings of Nicosia

Pérakhorio   18km/11 miles south of Nicosia, to the left of the motorway to Limassol, lies the village of Pérakhorio, with the little church of the Holy Apostles on a mound (160m/525ft) south-west of the village (key obtainable at No. 12 in the street leading to the church).

Church of the
Holy Apostles   This little single-aisled domed church has wall paintings dating from the second half of the 15th century. The paintings are in poor condition, since the paint was not always applied when the plaster was still wet and the colours therefore did not bind properly into the surface. The peeling off of the paint has revealed the lines sketched out to guide the painter.

The dome has the usual figure of Christ Pantokrator surrounded by angels. In the apse is the Communion of the Apostles, a frequent theme in the Eastern church which was later taken up by the Protestants. Above this is the Mother of God flanked by Peter and Paul. In the nave is a vivid painting of the Ascension.

4km/2½ miles north-east of Pérakhorio is the village of Dháli. On the road which bypasses the village is a signpost to the site of ancient Idálion, on two hills to the south of the village.

Dháli

Idálion, in ancient times one of the most important of the city-kingdoms of Cyprus, was founded before the coming of the Achaeans, and was continuously inhabited into classical times. In the 5th century B.C. it was conquered by the Phoenicians, whose stronghold of Kítion was only a short distance away.

Idálion

Idálion worshipped Aphrodite and her lover Adonis, who according to the myth was killed here by a boar sent by Ares. Excavations by Swedish and American archaeologists brought to light a number of tombs and remains of the town's massive walls (5th c. B.C.), which stood 6m/20ft high. Few finds of any value were made, since the site had been plundered by tomb robbers, including the American consul Palma di Cesnola, in the latter part of the 19th century.

On the outskirts of Dháli, on the road to Potamiá, is the little single-aisled church of Ayios Demetriános (key from the neighbouring house). Of its wall paintings there survive only an inscription with the date 1317 and portraits of the donor, Michael Katzouroubis, and his wife presenting a model of the church to Christ.

Church of Ayios Demetriános

4km/2½ miles south-west of Pérakhorio, at Alámbra, are the scanty remains of a large Bronze Age settlement. Finds of metal showed that this was once a copper-working centre.

Alámbra

5km/3 miles south-west of Nicosia on the road to Páno Dheftérá can be found the Arkhángelos Monastery (key kept by the custodian, who lives at No. 4 in the range of cells). The monastery, now abandoned, dates from the 17th century and was dedicated to the Archangel Michael. In the narthex of the 12th century church is the tomb of the founder, Nikiphoros. The iconostasis dates from the 17th century, when the monastery became a dependency of Kýkko Monastery. The monastery now houses the Kýkko Monastery Research Centre.

Arkhángelos Monastery

14km/8½ miles south-west of Nicosia, just before Káto Dheftérá, is a cave church hewn from the rock face which dates back to early Christian times; unfortunately its painted interior is badly damaged. It is dedicated to the Panayía Chrysospiliótissa (Our Lady of the Golden Cave), whose rain-bringing power is celebrated on August 15th, the feast of the Dormition of the Mother of God.

Káto Dheftérá

See entry

Tamassós

See Tamassós

Monastery of St Heraclidius

See entry

Makherás Monastery

Páphos

G 2

Πάφος
Altitude: 0–150m/0–490ft. Population: 23,000

Páphos, a town of great historical and artistic interest, lies on the south-west coast of Cyprus. The favourable natural conditions for the construction of a harbour led to the foundation of Néa Páphos (New Páphos) on the

Situation and characteristics

site of present-day Káto Páphos (Lower Páphos). The rise of Néa Páphos began with the decline of Palaía Páphos (Old Páphos), 15km/9 miles south-east near Koúklia (see entry) – though the shrine of Aphrodite at Old Páphos continued to attract pilgrims.

Káto Páphos

An old Turkish fort guards the picturesque harbour, now occupied only by yachts and fishing boats. The seafront is lined with fish restaurants and souvenir shops and in summer is crowded with visitors.

Immediately adjoining the harbour are the archaeological sites and the hotel district – a relatively quiet and peaceful area, without the high-rise hotels which have defaced Ayía Nápa, Lárnaca and Limassol. The normal population is about 2000, but during the holiday season this is multiplied many times. The building boom in Káto Páphos, once an idyllic fishing village, began with the opening in 1984 of the international airport, 12km/7½ miles south-east.

Ktíma

2km/1¼ miles inland, on a projecting spur of rock, is a very different part of the town, the district known as Ktíma (the word means a country estate: in Frankish times this was a royal domain), with a busy shopping quarter, the town market, banks, schools and public buildings. Most of the population of Páphos – Cyprus's smallest district capital – live here. Near the Djami Kebir (Great Mosque) is the old Turkish quarter, now abandoned.

For many centuries Páphos was a remote and unimportant little provincial town, and it was only after the partition of the island in 1974 that it was linked with the rest of Greek Cyprus by good roads and developed into the economic, cultural and administrative centre of a region, the most thinly populated district in the Republic of Cyprus, which depends mainly on agriculture for its subsistence, with great plantations of bananas, citrus fruits and vines.

History
Foundation

According to the ancient myth the city of Páphos and the shrine of Aphrodite at Palaia Páphos were founded by King Agapenor of Tegea in Arcadia

Evening light in Páphos harbour

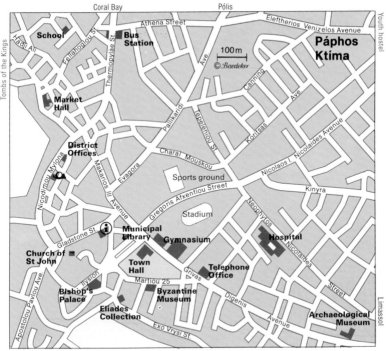

Tombs of the Kings, Káto Páphos

when he was cast ashore on Cyprus by a storm on his way back from Troy. Material of the Chalcolithic period found at Lemba, Yialia and Souskia, however, show that the first settlements in the area were established as early as the 3rd millennium B.C. In later centuries these were overshadowed by the powerful city of Palaía Páphos, which drew hosts of pilgrims to its shrine of Aphrodite, the largest in the ancient world.

There is historical evidence for the foundation of Néa Páphos in the 4th century B.C., when the last priest-king of Palaía Páphos, Nikokles, moved his capital there.

Néa Páphos became a place of some consequence, however, only in the 2nd century B.C., under Ptolemaic rule. The town took over the leading role hitherto held by Sálamis and became capital of the whole island, thanks to its excellent coastal situation within easy reach of Alexandria and to the huge forests in its hinterland which provided supplies of timber for shipbuilding.

Ptolemaic rule

The prosperity of the town in Ptolemaic times is attested by the Tombs of the Kings – tombs not of kings but of wealthy citizens of Páphos.

Under the Romans Néa Páphos became the residence of the Roman pro-consul and enjoyed its period of greatest prosperity. After an earthquake in the 1st century B.C. the town was rebuilt by Augustus in splendid style. Evidence of this prosperity is provided by a series of splendid mansions,

Roman rule

173

named by the archaeologists after their mosaics the Houses of Dionysus, Aion, Theseus and Orpheus. The Romans gave the "sacred capital of all Cypriot cities" the name of Augusta Claudia Flavia.

Christianisation

In A.D. 46 Paul and Barnabas came to Cyprus on one of their missionary journeys and converted the Roman proconsul, Sergius Paulus, to the Christian faith. After the end of the persecutions of Christians Páphos became the see of a bishop, with one of the largest basilicas on the island.

Arab raids

In the 4th century A.D. the town was destroyed by earthquakes but was not rebuilt, since Sálamis now became capital of Cyprus. The resultant decline of Néa Páphos was accelerated by Arab raids in the 7th and 8th centuries.

Later history

Under the Lusignans Páphos recovered some of its former importance and became the see of a Roman Catholic bishop. Earthquakes and piratical raids, however, soon led to its abandonment and the foundation of the new town of Ktíma on a higher inland site.

During the period of Turkish rule Páphos was a place of no importance, since towns such as Nicosia and Famagusta lay nearer Turkey.

Sights in Ktíma

District
Archaeological
Museum

Visitors coming from Limassol and entering Ktíma on Grivas Dighenis Avenue pass on the right a series of Neo-Classical buildings dating from the period of British colonial rule – three gymnasia (grammar schools), the Town Hall and the Municipal Library. One of the few modern buildings in Páphos is the District Archaeological Museum at the near end of Grivas Dighenis Avenue (open: Mon.–Fri. 7.30am–1.30pm and 3–5pm, Sat. and Sun. 7.30am–1pm).

The Museum's four rooms display in chronological order finds from Páphos and the surrounding area ranging in date from the Neolithic period

District Archaeological Museum

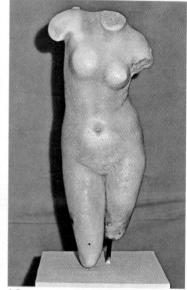

A Roman torso of Aphrodite

to the Middle Ages. Rooms I and II are mainly devoted to small objects and pottery. The Neolithic period is represented by implements and idols, the Bronze Age by Red Polished and White Slip ware. The black-figured and red-figured pottery of the Archaic and Classical periods points to contacts with Greece. There are also sculpture, funerary reliefs and sarcophagi of the Archaic period. The Hellenistic and Roman periods are represented by votive figures and glassware. A particularly notable item is a Roman torso of Aphrodite which was found in a badly damaged condition on the sea bed off Páphos.

The most interesting of the museum's exhibits are the pottery "hot water bottles" in the form of arms and legs which were applied to the appropriate part of the body in the treatment of patients suffering from rheumatism.

Room III displays Hellenistic and Roman domestic pottery from the House of Dionysus.

Room IV is devoted to Byzantine and medieval material. Of particular interest is a Renaissance baldachin supported by four angels (Venetian work), found during the excavation of the Frankish church in the Chrysopolítissa complex.

At 1 Exo Vrysi Street is the private collection of George Eliades, an ethnographical museum housed in a late 19th century stone-built mansion (open: daily; in winter 9am–1pm and 3–5pm; in summer 9am–1pm and 4–7pm). ★Ethnological Museum

The founder and owner of the museum, George Eliades, who still lives in the house, began to assemble his collection in 1939 and opened it to the public in 1958. The house has preserved its original architecture and to some extent the original furnishings (on the lower floor), giving an excellent impression of the Cypriot way of life. On the site of the house were found rock-cut tombs of the 3rd/2nd millennium B.C. similar in style to the Tombs of the Kings.

An old kitchen in the Eliades Museum

The material in the collection ranges in date from ancient times to the 20th century. On the lower floor are everyday objects including furniture, domestic equipment, weaving looms, agricultural implements, pottery, traditional costumes, needlework, wooden chests and an oil-press. On the upper floor are carved shelves and chests, metalwork and silver.

Byzantine Museum	The Byzantine Museum, situated in Ioanou Andrea Street, has a collection of icons of the 12th–18th centuries (open: in winter Mon.–Fri. 9am–1pm and 2–5pm, in summer daily 9am–12.30pm and 4–7pm).

Sights in Káto Páphos

★★ Roman villas

Between the lighthouse and the harbour are the excavated remains of a number of Roman villas with fine mosaic pavements (open: June 1st to August 31st, 7.30am–7.30pm; September 1st to May 31st, 7.30am–7pm). Like other places in Cyprus, Néa Páphos was devastated by earthquakes in the 4th century A.D. Most of the houses were destroyed and thereafter were abandoned. In 1962 a peasant's plough uncovered the foundations and mosaics of a Roman house built on the remains of an earlier Hellenistic building of the 4th/3rd century B.C. (evidence of its date being provided by the discovery of a hoard of 2000 silver tetradrachms of the Ptolemaic period). Since Dionysus featured several times in the mosaics the house became known as the House of Dionysus. Subsequently the remains of other houses in what was evidently an exclusive residential district were discovered nearby, including the governor's palace (the House of Theseus), the House of Aion and the House of Orpheus.

Mosaic-working technique

The technique of mosaic-working which was practised throughout the ancient world involved extensive preparatory work. After the ground had

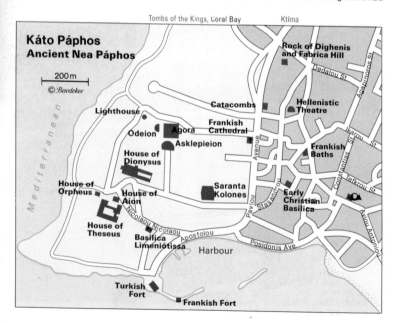

Personification of Winter

been levelled and beaten hard several layers of bottoming were laid down
and sealed with mortar – first rough stones, then gravel and sherds of
pottery. Over this was spread a layer of fine mortar into which small cubes
of stone (tesserae) were set to form the mosaic. To ensure the durability of
the mosaic it was then scoured with marble dust, sand and lime. The
tesserae, usually measuring about 1 centimetre each way, were mostly of
coloured stones, with which Cyprus was well supplied; glass tesserae were
used only for certain colours (light orange, yellow, green and blue).

The mosaic pictures were not original creations but were based on
designs contained in pattern books.

★★ House of Dionysus

The House of Dionysus, evidently the residence of a prosperous citizen of
Páphos, dates from the late 2nd century A.D. and covers an area of some
2000sq.m/21,500sq.ft, including 556sq.m/6000sq.ft of mosaic pavements.
It is a typical Roman atrium house, built around a colonnaded inner courtyard (atrium) with an impluvium, a basin for collecting rainwater. Opening
off the atrium are living rooms, bedrooms and domestic offices. While the
main living and reception rooms have mosaic pavements, the bedrooms
on the east and north sides of the atrium have plain pebble floors and the
domestic offices have floors of beaten earth.

The following description takes account only of the rooms with the finest
mosaics.

To the left of the entrance is the oldest mosaic in the villa, the only one to   Scylla mosaic
survive from the earlier Hellenistic house. It depicts the sea monster Scylla
whom Odysseus and his companions encountered in the Straits of Mesina.
In contrast to the Roman mosaics, this fine mosaic is composed of plain
black and white pebbles.

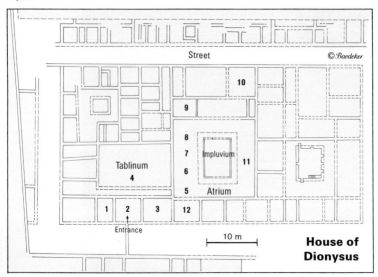

House of Dionysus

MOSAICS

1 Scylla	5 Pyramus and Thisbe	9 Phaedra and Hippolytus
2 Narcissus	6 Dionysus and Icarius	10 Zeus and Ganymede
3 Four Seasons	7 Amymone and Poseidon	11 Hunting scenes
4 Triumph of Dionysus	8 Apollo and Daphne	12 Peacock

Narcissus mosaic

Next to this is a mosaic of Narcissus, the youth who fell in love with his own likeness as a punishment for his rejection of the beautiful nymph Echo. When he began to waste away for love of himself Aphrodite took pity on him and turned him into the flower which bears his name.

Four Seasons

The mosaics with personifications of Earth and the four Seasons are enclosed in frames consisting of tesserae creating an effect of perspective. The inclusion of a formula of greeting suggests that this was probably the entrance hall of the villa.

The largest and most important room in the house, the tablinum, served as a reception room and dining room. The mosaic depicting the triumph of Dionysus shows the god in a carriage drawn by panthers accompanied by his retinue of Satyrs, Silenuses, the god Pan and musicians.

In the centre of the tablinum is a large scene depicting the grape harvest, with peasants cutting the fruit amid vine tendrils, birds and hares.

Pyramus and Thisbe

Around the atrium ran a colonnade paved with a series of mosaics. The first scene depicts the story of Pyramus and Thisbe. The parents of the young lovers opposed their marriage, so they had to meet secretly in a wood. One day when Thisbe went to their meeting-place she found a panther there, with blood dripping from its jaws, and fled. Then Pyramus arrived and, seeing the panther with Thisbe's kerchief in its mouth, thought that it had killed her and threw himself on his sword. Thisbe then killed herself to be with him.

Dionysus and Icarius

The next mosaic depicts the first wine-drinkers. Dionysus, having been a guest of King Icarius of Attica, showed his gratitude by teaching the king

Triumph of Dionysus

how to grow vines and make wine. In the mosaic Dionysus is depicted on the left drinking wine with the nymph Acme. In the centre of the scene Icarius, delighted with his new skill, offers the drink to two shepherds, the first wine-drinkers. They become drunk and, thinking that Icarius is poisoning them, kill him.

The beautiful Amymone, one of the fifty daughters of King Danaus, is looking for a spring when she encounters a satyr who tries to ravish her. She is saved by Poseidon, who falls in love with her, presents her with the spring of Lerna and has a son by her, the hero Nauplius. Between Amymone and Poseidon is Eros.

Amymone and Poseidon

The last mosaic on the west side of the atrium depicts the unconsummated love of Apollo for the nymph Daphne. Daphne is shown fleeing from Apollo to her father, the river god Peneius. Zeus takes pity on her and turns her into a laurel bush (*daphne* in Greek) to save her from Apollo. The mosaic shows her legs already turning into the stem of a laurel.

Apollo and Daphne

One of the finest of the mosaics tells the story of Phaedra and Hippolytus. Phaedra, the second wife of Theseus, falls in love with her stepson Hippolytus; but Hippolytus, shown standing on the left of the scene, is wholly devoted to the service of Artemis and to the hunt and rejects her advances. Thereupon Phaedra, her pride wounded, accuses Hippolytus of trying to rape her. Theseus calls on his father Poseidon to punish Hippolytus with death. Poseidon sends a wild bull which frightens the horses drawing Hippolytus's chariot, who drag him to his death. Phaedra then kills herself.

Phaedra and Hippolytus

On the north side of the house is a small mosaic of Zeus and Ganymede. Zeus falls in love with the handsome youth Ganymede and, taking on the form of an eagle, carries him off to Olympus, where he becomes the cup-bearer of the gods.

Zeus and Ganymede

Along the north, east and south sides of the atrium are a series of hunting scenes. Among the animals depicted are moufflon, which must have been a favourite species of game in Roman times.

Hunting scenes

★House of Aion

The House of Aion lies opposite the entrance to the much larger House of Theseus, the Roman governor's palace. The mosaics in this villa, named after the god Aion, who appears in a mosaic in the principal room, were discovered by Polish archaeologists in 1983. The latest mosaics in Páphos, dated to the 4th century A.D., they were probably created after the earthquakes which devastated the town in 332 and 342.

In the entrance hall are five large mosaic panels depicting scenes from Greek mythology in the so-called "beautiful style", in which the shading of the colours produces a vigorous plastic effect.

Leda and the swan

The first panel (upper left) tells the story of Leda and the swan. In the centre of the scene is Leda, the beautiful queen of Sparta, accompanied by female attendants and personifications of Lacedaemon and the river Eurotas. Zeus is seen approaching her in the form of a swan. From their union are born the twins Castor and Pollux and Helen.

Dionysus and Tropheus

In the second panel (upper right) the boy Dionysus is shown sitting in the lap of Hermes, the messenger of the gods, identified by the small wings on his forehead and feet. Dionysus is being handed over to the care of Tropheus, a Silenus who is to be his protector, and the nymphs who are already preparing the boy's bath.

Cassiopeia and the Nereids

The large central panel depicts the beauty contest between Cassiopeia and the Nereids, which is won by Cassiopeia. She is shown being crowned by Crisis, the personification of Justice, on the left, with Helios, Zeus and Athena looking on. In the centre of the scene is Aion, god of Time, the judge of the contest. To the right are the Nereids, riding away on a Centaur and a Triton (personifications of the sea).

Apollo and Marsyas

The fourth mosaic (lower left) depicts the fate of the satyr Marsyas, who had dared to challenge Apollo to a musical contest. The contest is won by Apollo, who is depicted on the right of the scene with his lyre. As punishment for his presumption Marsyas is flayed alive. Two of Apollo's attendants (Scythians) are shown holding Marsyas by the hair.

★ House of Theseus

The excavation of the House of Theseus, which dates from the 2nd/3rd century A.D., was begun by Polish archaeologists in 1965. Since it is the largest of the villas (five times the size of the House of Dionysus) it is thought to have been the palace of the Roman governor. Covering a total

Apollo and Marsyas

area of almost 9500sq.m/102,000sq.ft, it consists of four ranges of build-ings round a large inner courtyard in the tradition of Hellenistic peristyle houses, with rooms for ritual purposes, living and sleeping accommoda-tion and baths (which could be used by the citizens of the town as well as the occupants of the palace). The villa, which was occupied until the 7th century, was richly decorated with wall paintings, marble statues and more than 1400sq.m/15,000sq.ft of mosaic pavements. The mosaics are mostly in geometric designs but include two scenes from Greek mythology.

The first mosaic in the House of Theseus, dating from the 3rd century, is in a semicircular apse at the end of the southern colonnade. Circular in form, it depicts the fight between Theseus and the Minotaur in the Cretan Laby-rinth. Theseus has just killed the Minotaur, which lies dead at his feet on the right. To the left of Theseus crouches the bearded god of the Labyrinth. Looking on are two female figures: above, to the right, the personification of Crete, wearing a mural crown, and to the left Ariadne, who gave Theseus the thread which would enable him to find his way out of the Labyrinth. The border of the mosaic with its geometric ornament is also an allusion to the Labyrinth.

Theseus mosaic

A wooden gangway leads to the principal room of the villa, with a mosaic depicting the first bath of the new-born Achilles. His divine mother Thetis, seeking to frustrate the prophecy that he will be killed at Troy, dips her son in the waters of the Styx in order to render him invulnerable; but the heel by which she holds him is not immersed in the water, and this is destined to be the cause of his death. On the right of the scene are the three Fates – Clotho, Lachesis and Atropos – as a reminder that he cannot escape his destiny. Also in the scene are two midwives and Achilles' father Peleus, seated on a throne with his wand of office.

Achilles mosaic

The Achilles Mosaic: Thetis, Peleus and the three Fates

House of Orpheus

Mosaics

To the west of the House of Theseus is another small villa excavated in 1984, named the House of Orpheus after a large mosaic (4m/13ft by 5m/16ft) depicting Orpheus seated on a rock with his lyre and surrounded by the animals of the forest who have been attracted by his playing.

Another mosaic – originally discovered by a British soldier in 1942 and covered up again – shows Heracles fighting the Nemean lion.

The third mosaic depicts an Amazon holding a double axe, with her horse.

These three mosaics, dating from the 2nd/3rd century A.D., are similar in style to those in the House of Dionysus. Excavations are still in progress, but the mosaics are to be put on show to the public shortly.

Other Sights in Káto Páphos

Between the House of Dionysus and the lighthouse are the Asklepieion, the Agora and the Odeion of the 2nd century A.D. (open: daily until sunset). The lighthouse stands on the ancient acropolis of Páphos.

Agora

To the right are the remains of the Agora, the old market square and place of assembly, an area 95m/310ft square surrounded by colonnades. On the east side is a three-stepped stylobate. Here were found granite columns with marble Corinthian capitals.

Odeion

Opposite the Agora is the Odeion, which was almost completely destroyed in the earthquakes of the 4th century and has now been largely reconstructed since it was uncovered in 1972–73. It originally had 25 tiers of seating and could accommodate an audience of 3000. An odeion (odeum) was a hall for concerts and lectures; like a theatre, it consisted of a semi-circular orchestra, a cavea and a stage, but unlike a theatre was usually roofed. Today it serves its original purpose as in summer months it is a venue for ancient Greek drama and musical performances.

Asklepieion

To the left of the Odeion are the remains of an Asklepieion, a shrine of the healing god Asklepios. It was in three parts, with rooms for sleeping (which was part of the therapy) and for treatment. The Asklepieion was linked with the Odeion by a long passage.

Some 300m/330yd north are remains of the Hellenistic town walls.

Saranta Kolones

To the east of the Roman villas are the ruins of a medieval castle known as Saranta Kolones ("Forty Columns"), after the forty columns of Roman origin used in its construction. The castle was built by the Byzantines about 1100 to protect the coastal region and later was taken over by the Franks. It was destroyed in an earthquake in 1222 and thereafter was used as a quarry of building stone.

The castle, almost exactly square in plan, was surrounded by two circuits of walls, which can be clearly distinguished when it is approached from the west. The outer walls were reinforced by eight bastions of different types, while the inner circuit had four rectangular towers at the corners. The entrance was in the central bastion on the east side. The castle chapel was probably over the barbican at the entrance to the inner stronghold. In the inner courtyard were stables, in which can be seen feeding troughs formed from Roman columns.

On the north side of the castle are the remains of a mill worked by animal power. Within the large piers supporting the upper floor were latrines. A staircase led to the upper floor.

Early Christian basilica

To the east of the castle of Saranta Kolones, beyond Apostle Paul Avenue, is a large excavation site. To the right are the remains of one of the largest early Christian basilicas in Cyprus. Built in the 4th century, it was 50m/165ft long by 38m/125ft wide and originally was seven-aisled, with a double apse. In the 6th century it was rebuilt as a five-aisled basilica with a central apse. At the west end the atrium, ablutions fountain and narthex can still be distinguished. Remains of mosaic pavements indicate that the church was richly decorated. When the Crusaders captured Cyprus the basilica was already in ruins.

Close by, in the street to the left, are the remains of a Frankish church of the late 13th century, dedicated to St Francis. Three aisles can be distinguished, with the remains of twin columns and Gothic pointed arches. In the 16th century the church was renovated and decorated with Renaissance sculpture, some of which can be seen in the District Archaeological Museum. After the church fell into ruin at the end of the 16th century the present church of the Ayía Chrysopolítissa was built on the site.

Frankish church

To the west of the Frankish church is a much worn column at which the apostle Paul is said to have been scourged during his visit to Páphos. The New Testament account (Acts 13,1–13) tells how before converting the Roman proconsul, Sergius Paulus, Paul was involved in a dispute with a sorcerer named Bar-jesus, whom he struck with blindness. According to the local tradition Paul was tied to a column and given 39 lashes for preaching Christianity in Páphos. Paul punished the Jewish mayor of the town by making him blind: whereupon the Roman governor, impressed by Paul's power, became a Christian. The column is still visited by numbers of pilgrims.

Paul's Column

In Minoos Street, to the north of Paul's Column, is a Frankish bath-house which was roofed with a number of domes during the Turkish period. The medieval masonry still stands 3m/10ft high.

Frankish baths

On the west side of the harbour is a massive Turkish fort (open: September 1st to May 31st, Mon.–Fri. 7.30am–2pm; June 1st to August 31st, Mon.– Sat. 7.30am–1.30pm). It stands at the point where the ancient town walls ended, at the head of a breakwater. At the end of the breakwater are the slight remains of a small Frankish fort. The remains of another ancient breakwater can be seen under the water.

Turkish harbour fort

The large fort, originally built as a Byzantine fort to protect the harbour, was rebuilt by the Lusignans during the 13th century. In the latter part of the 16th century the Venetians abandoned the fort and neglected the walls, thereafter concentrating on the defence of Famagusta and Nicosia. In 1592 the Turks rebuilt it, as an inscription records. During the British occupation it was used as a salt store. In the centre of the fort is the square keep of the Lusignan fort.

From the harbour Nikolaou Street runs north-west towards the House of Dionysus. Half way along this street, on the left, are the remains of the church of the Panayía Limeniótissa (Our Lady of the Harbour), which was built in the early 5th century and almost completely destroyed by the Arabs in the 7th. Arabic inscriptions on the columns, however, show that the building continued in use. In the 10th century a new church was built on the ruins, but this was destroyed in an earthquake in the 12th century. The early Christian church was three-aisled, with an apse at the east end and a narthex and atrium at the west end.

Basilica of Panayía Limeniótissa

At the north end of Apostle Paul Avenue, on the road to Ktíma, is Fabrica Hill, so called because the stone-masons had their workshop here. The remains of wedge-holes show that the hill was used as a quarry – though probably not before Roman times, since Hellenistic tombs were found here. The remains of a Hellenistic theatre are at present being excavated.

Fabrica Hill, Rock of Dighenis

This was the scene of a legendary conflict between the Byzantine hero Dighenis and Queen Regaena. The queen had promised to yield to him if he brought her water from the Pentadáktylos Hills; but when she broke her promise Dighenis, enraged, flung a gigantic block of stone at her palace.

Turkish fort, Páphos harbour

Regaena responded by throwing a spindle at him. The legend has it that Fabrica Hill is the rock thrown by Dighenis and a granite column found here the queen's spindle.

Catacombs of
Ayía Solomoní

Near Fabrica Hill are a group of catacombs in which the early Christians sought refuge. Here, where the cave church of Ayía Solomoní now stands, there was once a Jewish synagogue. Solomoní, mother of the seven Maccabee brothers, was killed with them during the persecution of Jews in the reign of Antiochus IV (2nd c.). She is now revered as a martyr and is credited with the power of curing diseases of the eyes. The poorly preserved paintings in the church date from the 12th century. From the inner courtyard a flight of steps leads up to a spring which is believed to have a healing effect on eye conditions.

On the other side of the street, in the direction of the harbour, can be seen the surviving south-west corner of a Frankish cathedral of the 13th century.

★★Tombs of the Kings

2.5km/1½ miles north of Páphos, reached by way of Tombs of the Kings Street, is one of the most interesting sights in Cyprus, the necropolis of ancient Néa Páphos, known as the Tombs of the Kings (open: daily 7.30am–5pm in winter, 7.30am–7pm in summer). The tombs date from the 4th century B.C., when Cyprus was held by the Ptolemies and governed from Alexandria. Since there were then no kings in Cyprus "Tombs of the Kings" is a misnomer. The tombs in fact belonged to the wealthier citizens of Páphos, and give a vivid impression of the town's prosperity under the Ptolemies.

The tombs were used continuously from the 4th century B.C. to the 3rd century A.D. Thereafter they provided a refuge for the early Christians in times of persecution, and during the Middle Ages some of them were

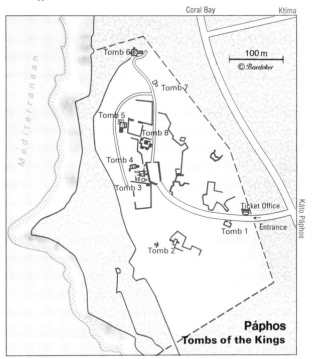

Páphos
Tombs of the Kings

converted into houses or were used as prisons. Few grave goods were found by the excavators of the tombs, since they had been systematically pillaged over the centuries, particularly in the 19th century.

The architecture of these peristyle tombs, modelled on the houses of the Ptolemaic period, is particularly striking. Although the idea of constructing underground house-tombs came from Egypt, the architectural details are purely Greek. Opening off a colonnaded inner courtyard (atrium) are the individual tomb chambers, the walls of which were plastered and decorated with stucco ornament or paintings. In all the larger tombs were wells. The tomb chambers lead to the small burial recesses (*loculi*). Architraves with a frieze of triglyphs and metopes are borne on Doric columns.

Peristyle tombs

Immediately at the entrance to the site is an above-ground chamber tomb with traces of paintings on the walls. It contains two small loculi for children and five larger ones for adults.

Tomb 1

Tomb 2 was altered in Roman times, when the original stepped dromos was closed and a new entrance opened up on the south side. Two altars were set up on the north side.

Tomb 2

Tomb 3, which is entered by a stepped dromos, has a large atrium with a Doric colonnade.
   Immediately adjoining this tomb are a number of simple shaft graves surrounded by a wall. These family tombs are thought to date from the Hellenistic period.

Tomb 3

Rock-cut peristyle tomb, Néa Páphos

Tomb 5	Tomb 5 is one of the largest of the tombs, with a dromos over 7m/23ft long and 2.80m/9ft wide. The atrium was surrounded by a colonnade of tall and massive columns, with a well in the centre and the principal tomb chamber on the south side. Built into the tomb was a medieval potter's kiln with a ventilation system. Pottery found here and incised crosses on the walls show that the tomb was in use for one purpose or another from Hellenistic times into the Middle Ages.
Tomb 8	Tomb 8 has no peristyle atrium. The tomb chambers are hewn out of a large block of stone which stands in a rectangular courtyard.

Surroundings of Páphos

Emba	5km/3 miles north of Ktíma, off the road to Pólis, lies the village of Emba, in the centre of which is the 12th century church of the Panayía Chryseleoúsa (Our Lady Blessed with Gold). Originally cruciform, it was later converted into a three-aisled church with two domes and a narthex. Of its 15th century wall paintings only fragments survive. The 16th century iconostasis has a number of interesting icons, notably one of Christ Antiphonítis (1536) and 16th century icons of the Mother of God and John the Baptist. A local shopkeeper holds the key.
St Neóphytos Monastery	See entry
Coral Bay	Coral Bay, 10km/6 miles north of Páphos, has one of the most popular sandy bays within reach of the town. A few years ago there were only a few restaurants and small hotels here, but since the lifting of the ban on new building the bay has suffered the same fate as other coastal resorts and two large new hotels are under construction.

At the nearby village of Máa are the remains of cyclopean walls belonging to a fortified Bronze Age settlement of about 1200 B.C.

18km/11 miles north-west of Páphos, at Péyia, can be found the basilica complex of Ayios Yeóryios, on which excavations are still in progress. The remains date from the 6th century, when this seems to have been an important episcopal see. In Roman times there was a town here below Cape Drepanum. The foundations of a large three-aisled basilica with three apses, a narthex and an atrium are well preserved. The central apse has preserved the steps leading up to the bishop's throne. The church had mosaics with geometric designs and representations of birds and fishes, and mosaics of four animals – a boar, a bear, a lion and a bull – can still be seen in the atrium.

North-west of the atrium is a smaller church – probably a baptistery, since there is a large immersion font on the south side.

Péyia; basilica complex of Ayios Yeóryios

Lara Bay, which has a beautiful sandy beach, is reached on a difficult unsurfaced road running north to the Akámas peninsula. Here the Cypriot fishery authorities have been running a project, started in 1976, for protecting the turtles which are now an endangered species.

Lara Bay

Peristeróna   E 6

Περιστερώνα
Altitude: 200m/660ft
Population: 1200

28km/17 miles west of Nicosia on the road to Tróodos is Peristeróna, a village which was a place of some importance in the Middle Byzantine period. In the 12th century it belonged to Kýkko Monastery, and later was handed over to the Frankish Counts of Jaffa in Palestine. The main feature of interest is the church of SS Hilarion and Barnabas (key from coffee-house next to the church).

Situation and characteristics

★Church of SS Hilarion and Barnabas

The multi-domed church of SS Hilarion and Barnabas – a type rarely found in Cyprus – is one of the most important examples of 11th century architecture on the island. The two saints to whom the church is dedicated are not to be confused with the well known Cypriot saints Barnabas, first bishop of Cyprus, and the hermit Hilarion. These were two young men of Cappadocia (in eastern Anatolia), officers in the Roman army in the time of Theodosius II (5th c.), who on becoming converts to Christianity retired from the army, gave all their possessions to the poor and thereafter lived a life of great piety. Their remains were mysteriously brought to Cyprus, where a church was built in their honour.

Foundation legend

The church is of imposing effect with its domes and bell-tower (a later addition). The five domes are arranged in a cruciform formation over the aisles (cf. the church of Ayía Paraskeví at Yeroskípos: see entry). The lateral aisles are separated from the central aisle (nave) by massive piers linked by arches.

The church

Little survives of the original interior. The only relics of the Byzantine period are a 12th century painting of the Mother of God on the north-east pier and the wooden door of the west doorway. The other paintings (e.g. the figure of David on the north-east pier) date from the 16th century.

In the narthex at the west end of the church – a later addition – are two funerary monuments. Since the burial of the dead within a church was usual only in the Roman Catholic church, it seems that this church was also

Interior

187

Church of SS Hilarion and Barnabas

used by the Franks. This is suggested also by the marble holy-water stoup in the church.

Icons

On the 16th century iconostasis are icons of the 16th and 17th centuries. The most notable is an icon of the Presentation in the Temple (1520), with an inscription naming the donor as Zaphiris, who is depicted kneeling before the high priest. In the north aisle are icons of the 15th and 16th centuries depicting St Paul, the Mother of God, Christ and St Barnabas.

Phikárdhou   F 7

Situation and characteristics

9km/6 miles north-west of Makherás Monastery (see entry) the picturesque little hill village of Phikárdhou has authentic village architecture, ranging in date between the 18th and early 20th centuries. This led the Department of Antiquities in 1978 to designate it as an ancient monument with statutory protection. Since then the village has been systematically restored in co-operation with the house-owners. Phikárdhou takes its name from a noble family of the medieval period which had connections with the English court about the year 1500.

Village life

In 1946 the village had a population of 120: now it has fallen to 10, all of whom are old people, still working their land with wooden ploughs and sickles. They are mainly engaged in making wine and distilling brandy (*zivania*), though the grape juice is also used to make the sweets known as *kiofterka* and *soutzouko*. The village's narrow paved lanes are suitable only for pedestrians and animals; the local "transport system", therefore, consists of donkeys and mules, which are also used in agricultural work.

Village architecture

Most of the houses are two-storied, built of limestone and a local coarse stone called *sieropetra* on foundations of undressed stone. The rooms on

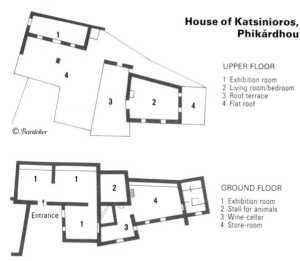

House of Katsinioros, Phikárdhou

UPPER FLOOR

1 Exhibition room
2 Living room/bedroom
3 Roof terrace
4 Flat roof

© Baedeker

GROUND FLOOR

1 Exhibition room
2 Stall for animals
3 Wine-cellar
4 Store-room

the ground floor are usually store-rooms and stalls for animals, and there is always a corner for a small wine-press. The flat roofs of the lower parts of the building also serve useful purposes (e.g. for the drying of grapes). They also serve as verandas, which can be entered from the living quarters on the upper floor. The upper floor usually consists of a single large room, which is divided up only by wooden piers. Attached to the house there is usually a small courtyard enclosed by a stone wall.

The two most important houses in the village, the Katsinioris House on the northern outskirts and the Achilleas Dimitri House beyond it, parts of which date from the 16th century, have been completely restored, and with their original furniture and furnishings, photographs and other exhibits offer a glimpse of traditional Cypriot village life (open: daily).

Rural Museum: Houses of Katsinioros and Achilleas Dimitri

Platanistása   F 6

Πλατανιστάσα
Altitude: 900m/2950ft

The village of Platanistása lies in the eastern Tróodos Mountains 30km/ 19 miles south-east of the little town of Tróodos. 5km/3 miles north-west of the village is the church of the Stavrós tou Ayiasmáti (key from the village priest).

Situation and characteristics

★ Church of the Stavrós tou Ayiasmáti

The church of the Stavrós tou Ayiasmáti (Holy Cross of Ayiasmáti) probably takes its name from the little town of Ayiasmáti in Asia Minor, for according to the local legend refugees from there came to Cyprus after the fall of Constantinople in 1453 and founded a monastery. This barn-roofed church (see Art and Culture, Byzantine Church Types) of the late 15th century has wall paintings showing western influence.

Inscriptions over the north and south doorways give the name of the donor as Peter, son of Peratis, and that of the painter as Philip Goul, who was also

189

responsible for the paintings in the church of St Mamas at Louvarás. On the outside of the south wall is a painting of the donor and his wife presenting a model of the church to Christ.

Wall paintings

The paintings in the interior of the church, which is single-aisled, are in two zones. In the upper zone are scenes from the life of the Virgin and the life of Christ; in the lower zone are figures of saints, notable among them St Mamas on his lion (see Sights in North Cyprus, Mórphou) and St George.

South wall

The New Testament cycle begins on the south wall, near the iconostasis, with Elizabeth and Zacharias (parents of John the Baptist), followed by the Evangelists Matthew and Luke, the Birth of the Virgin, her Presentation in the Temple, the Nativity of Christ, the Presentation of Jesus in the Temple, the Baptism of Christ, the Raising of Lazarus, the Entry into Jerusalem and the Transfiguration. An interesting feature is the inclusion of genre scenes, including the milking of the ewes, in the Nativity. A common detail in Byzantine representations of the Baptism is a figure personifying the river Jordan: here he is shown at Christ's feet pouring water from a jar.

West wall

On the west wall are the Crucifixion, the Descent from the Cross, the Last Supper, the Washing of the Feet, Christ in the Garden of Gethsemane, the Betrayal and Christ before Annas and Caiaphas.

North wall

The cycle continues on the north wall with Peter's Denial, Christ before Pilate, the Mocking, the Lamentation, Doubting Thomas, the Ascension, the Descent of the Holy Ghost (Pentecost), the Dormition of the Mother of God and the Evangelists Luke and John. The Dormition includes the figure of the Jew Jephonias, who tries to touch the Virgin's bier but has his hands cut off by the Archangel Michael.

In a recess on the north wall are ten small scenes depicting the discovery of the True Cross by Helen, mother of Constantine the Great. The series

St Mamas, patron of tax-evaders

Sacrifice of Isaac (Palekhóri)

begins with the declaration by a Jew named Judas that he has learned from his forefathers the whereabouts of the Cross. In the second scene he denies any knowledge, and is punished by being confined for three days in a dry well. In the third scene he is released after revealing where the Cross is hidden. The next scene shows him praying on Golgotha and being told in a divine revelation the exact position of the relics (including the other two crosses). The sixth scene depicts the discovery of the relics, which are then taken to St Helen in a triumphal procession. In the eighth scene the True Cross is identified by a dying woman. Judas, converted to the Christian faith, is appointed bishop of Jerusalem. He discovers the nails used in Christ's crucifixion, and in the last scene he is shown taking them to Helen, who sinks to her knees in reverence.

In the conch of the apse is the Mother of God Blacherniótissa with her hands raised in prayer, flanked by the Archangels Michael and Gabriel. Below this are the Communion of the Apostles and eight prelates.

Apse

Surroundings of Platanistása

See entry

Lagoudherá

Palekhóri

10km/6 miles south-east of Platanistása, in the picturesque little village of Palekhóri, is the church of the Metamórphosis tou Sotíros (the Transfiguration; key held by priest). The walls of this single-aisled church of the early 16th century are completely covered with paintings which show affinities with the paintings in the churches of Platanistása and Louvarás and the church of the Archangel Michael in Galáta. Here too western influence can be detected.

Church of Metamórphosis tou Sotíros

In the upper zone of the walls are New Testament scenes, in the lower zone figures of saints.

The cycle begins on the south wall with the death of St Mary the Egyptian, a repentant harlot who after her conversion to Christianity lived as a hermit in the desert. This is followed by the Three Youths in the Fiery Furnace, the Nativity of Christ, the Presentation in the Temple, the Baptism of Christ, the Raising of Lazarus, the Entry into Jerusalem and the Transfiguration. In the Baptism figures personifying the river Jordan (a bearded man) and the sea (a woman riding on a fish) are seen at Christ's feet, fleeing before him (cf. the church of Ayía Paraskeví, Yeroskípos).

Paintings in naos

On the west wall the cycle in the upper zone begins with the Last Supper, the Washing of the Feet, Christ on the Mount of Olives and the Betrayal. Below this is Christ before Annas and Caiaphas, followed by Christ before Pilate, Peter's Denial and the Mocking.

In the conch of the apse is the Mother of God with her hands raised in prayer, flanked by the Archangels Michael and Gabriel. Below this is the Communion of the Apostles, with Judas (far left) spitting out the bread, and below this again are fathers of the Church. On the side walls are the Sacrifice of Isaac and the Hospitality of Abraham.

Paintings in bema

In the main street of the village can be found its principal church, the small three-aisled basilica of the Panayía Chrysopantanássa, which also dates from the 16th century. The wall paintings are poorly preserved and unrestored. They include scenes from the life of the Virgin, a figure of St Nicholas and the story of the discovery of the True Cross.

Church of Panayía Chrysopantanássa

Pólis

Πόλις
Altitude: sea level
Population: 1800

Situation and characteristics

The little town of Pólis ("City") lies in Khrysókhou Bay on the north coast of Cyprus, on the site of the ancient city-kingdom of Márion. It has beautiful beaches along the coast, but its remote situation has largely preserved it from the high-rise hotels and the swarms of tourists of the more easily accessible resorts. The visitors who come here are mostly backpackers, who can find cheap accommodation in private houses, or the campsite north of the town close to the beach. To the east of Pólis are the old copper-mines, long since closed down.

History

The ancient settlement of Márion is believed to have been founded in the Late Bronze Age by Achaean incomers. By around 1000 B.C. a city-kingdom had been established here, though one of no great importance. In the 5th century, however, copper-mining brought the town a degree of prosperity.

During the conflict between Greeks and Persians Márion was at first on the Persian side, but in the 4th century, together with other city-kingdoms, it ceased to pay tribute to the Persians. During the fight for the succession of Alexander the Great Márion supported Antigonus, and after the victory of his rival Ptolemy I, at the end of the 4th century, the town was razed to the ground. It was later rebuilt by Ptolemy II and renamed Arsinoe.

In Byzantine times the town became known as Pólis tis Khrysókhou, the City of the Land of Gold.

During the fighting between Greeks and Turks in the 1960s Pólis suffered severe damage in Turkish air attacks.

In the sleepy little town of Pólis

Surroundings of Pólis

A few kilometres west of Pólis is the village of Lakhí, which has a pictur-   Lakhí
esque little fishing harbour and with its brightly coloured boats and baskets
preserves a corner of the old, unspoiled Cyprus.

To the west of Pólis is the Akámas peninsula, with the most north-westerly   Akámas
point on the island, Cape Arnaúti. The peninsula takes its name from   peninsula
Akámas, son of Theseus, who is said to have landed here on his way back
from Troy. This uninhabited area, one of the most beautiful parts of Cyprus,
with ideal walking country, was declared a nature reserve in 1989; but since
it is used by the British forces on Cyprus as a training area it is from time to
time closed to the public. On the peninsula, near the Baths of Aphrodite, are
two nature trails (the "Aphrodite" and the "Adonis" Trails) laid out by the
Cyprus Tourism Organisation (CTO).

8km/5 miles north-west of Pólis are the Baths of Aphrodite (Loutra Aphro-   ★Baths of
ditis). From a shady recess in the rock fresh water flows into a small pool   Aphrodite
where, it is said, Aphrodite used to bathe under a fig-tree. Here she was
surprised one day by Theseus's son Akámas and the two fell in love; but
they were discovered and betrayed by an old woman, and Aphrodite was
forced to return to Olympus.

In a sandy bay 8km/5 miles beyond the Baths of Aphrodite in the direction   Fontana Amorosa
of Cape Arnaúti is the Fontana Amorosa, Aphrodite's Fountain of Love.
According to the local tradition (though there may be some confusion here
with the Baths of Aphrodite) anyone who drinks from the spring will be
filled with youthful amorous ardour. The spring can by reached only on
foot or by boat from Lakhí. There is a beautiful footpath (especially in
springtime) from the Baths of Aphrodite (8km/5 miles).

Baths of Aphrodite

Droúsha

10km/6 miles south of Pólis on a minor road to Páphos, picturesquely situated on a hill (700m/2300ft), is Droúsha, an old village with houses in traditional style. From here there is a magnificent view of the bay in which Pólis lies.

Pyrgá – "Royal Chapel"   F 8

Πυργά
Altitude: 160m/525ft

Situation and
characteristics

In the village of Pyrgá 32km/20 miles to the west of Lárnaca near the Limassol–Nicosia motorway, is the so-called "Royal Chapel", a name of fairly recent origin (key available from the coffee-shop nearby).

The chapel, which is dedicated to St Catherine, was built during the period of Frankish rule, as is indicated by the Gothic architectural features, the Lusignan coats of arms on the ribs of the vaulting and the Frankish figures and French inscriptions in the wall paintings. The coats of arms and the figure of King Janus of Lusignan which appears in one of the paintings suggest that this was a royal foundation.

Built in 1421, the chapel has an aisleless rectangular ground-plan without an apse, with three doorways. Only fragments of the paintings which once covered the walls have been preserved. The figures of King Janus and his wife Charlotte of Bourbon appear in the Crucifixion scene. Below this is the Lamentation, in which a Latin bishop, presumably the second founder, appears. The paintings are still very much in the Byzantine style, but the representation of the Mother of God Hodigitría shows Italian features.

Surroundings of Pyrgá

Kórnos

To the west of Pyrgá, beyond the motorway, is the village of Kórnos, which is famed for its pottery, made by traditional methods. The coarse red ware with anthropomorphic designs is shaped on simple potters' wheels and fired in kilns reminiscent of Corinthian kilns of the 6th century B.C.

St Neóphytos Monastery   F 2

Μονή Αγίου Νεοφύτου
Altitude: 400m/1300ft

Situation and
characteristics

10km/6 miles north of Páphos, on the slopes of Mt Melissovounos, is the monastery of St Neóphytos. Outside the monastery are the cave and the cave-chapel (Enkleistra) hewn from the rock by St Neóphytos in the 12th century. A large monastery was built close to the Enkleistra in the 15th century, and the saint's remains were transferred to it in the 18th century. The monastery has extensive ranges of guest rooms, and attracts large numbers of visitors on holidays and feast days.

St Neóphytos

St Neóphytos was born in 1134 in Káto Drys near Léfkara and at the age of 18 became a novice in the monastery of Ayios Chrysóstomos, where he taught himself to read and write. A planned journey to the Holy Land ended with his arrest in the harbour of Páphos, and after his release he withdrew to the desolate hill region inland from Páphos, where he hewed a cell and a small chapel from the rock of the hillside. The piety and learning of the saintly recluse soon began to attract large numbers of pilgrims and disciples.

Monastery of St Neóphytos

Neóphytos wrote treatises on the Old and New Testaments, hymns and songs which mark him out as one of the great spiritual writers of the 12th century. He also composed a caustic account of the capture of Cyprus by the Crusaders. He died in 1214 at the age of 80 and was buried in the tomb which he had himself prepared in the Enkleistra.

★Enkleistra

Neóphytos founded a monastery in 1170 and drew up a Rule for it. He enlarged the cave chapel by the addition of a nave, the original chapel becoming the sanctuary of the church. The numbers of his disciples continued to increase, and in 1196 he withdrew to a new retreat above the church, from which he could listen to services through a hole in the roof of the church.

The Enkleistra is entered through the naos of the church, to the right of which, separated from it by the iconostasis, is the sanctuary (*bema*). In the bema is a small stone altar. Beyond this is the saint's cell, with a bench and a table hewn from the rock and the tomb which he had constructed for himself.

Wall paintings

The wall paintings in the Enkleistra were commissioned by the saint himself between 1170 and 1200. They are unique in showing Neóphytos among the saints while still alive. The earlier paintings were the work of Theodoros Apseudes; the painter of the scenes in the second phase, more than ten years later, is unknown.

Cella

Particularly notable are the paintings in the saint's cell, above his tomb. In the Descent into Hades (Anástasis) Christ is shown liberating Adam and Eve, watched by David and Solomon as representatives of the Old Testament. In the representation of the Deesis (the Virgin and St John interceding with Christ for mankind) Neóphytos is shown kneeling at Christ's feet.

The Enkleistra, with the saint's cell and rock-cut church

Bema

In the bema is a 16th century painting of Christ Pantokrator. Of particular interest is the representation of Neóphytos between the Archangels Michael and Gabriel. An inscription expresses his hope that he will be enrolled among the angels.

Naos

Some of the paintings in the naos were over-painted and renewed in the 16th century. They depict scenes from Christ's Passion – the Last Supper and the Washing of the Feet (both painted about 1503), the Betrayal, Christ before Pilate and the Crucifixion (all 12th century). The Hospitality of Abraham on the south wall dates from the 16th century.

Monastery church

The monastery church opposite the Enkleistra was built in the 15th century to replace the cave church, found to be too small. The nave is separated from the lateral aisles by large round columns with Corinthian-style capitals and roofed by a large dome. The saint's remains are in a wooden sarcophagus to the left of the iconostasis; his skull is preserved in a silver reliquary. On the 16th century iconostasis is a 19th century icon of St Neóphytos holding a silver cross.

Wall paintings

The surviving paintings date from the first half of the 16th century, when Cyprus was under Venetian rule. In the south aisle are scenes from the life of Anne and Joachim, who are shown presenting gifts to the high priest, Zacharias, in the hope of fulfilling their desire for a child.

In the north aisle is the cycle of the Acathist Hymn, 24 scenes dedicated to the life and glorification of the Virgin. The hymn is thought to have been composed by the Patriarch of Constantinople in the 7th century. Among the scenes depicted are the Annunciation, the Visitation, the Nativity and the Flight into Egypt.

Wall paintings in the cave chapel

Stavrovoúni Monastery   F 8

Μονή Σταυροβουνίου
Altitude: 690m/2265ft

Stavrovoúni, the richest in tradition of all Cyprus's monasteries and the most austere, is reached by turning off the Limassol–Nicosia motorway shortly before Kórnos and continuing on a steep and winding road which passes the monastery of St Barbara (Ayía Varvára), now an annexe of Stavrovoúni. Beyond this, visible from a long way off – a landmark even for passing ships – is the monastery of Stavrovoúni, perched like an eagle's eyrie on a conical crag. From the monastery there are breathtaking views of the Tróodos Mountains, the south coast of Cyprus (Lárnaca) and in clear weather of Nicosia. The monastery's name, Hill of the Cross (from *stavrós*, "cross", and *vounó*, "hill"), refers to the relics of the True Cross which led to the foundation of the monastery.

Situation and characteristics

Only men are permitted to enter the monastery.

In this arid region the supply of water is a problem. In earlier times the monastery depended on water collected during the winter in four underground cisterns. Water is now pumped up from a spring at the foot of the hill.

According to its legend the monastery was founded in the 4th century at the behest of St Helen, mother of Constantine the Great. When returning from the Holy Land in A.D. 327 with the relics of the True Cross she was driven ashore on Cyprus by a storm. The site of the present monastery was then occupied by a pagan temple of Aphrodite. An angel told Helen in a dream to build a church on Cyprus. Then when she awoke on the following morning the relics had disappeared and the pagan altar on the hill was engulfed in flames. The relics were found in the fire, unscathed: whereupon Helen

Foundation legend

197

Royal Chapel, Pyrgá (see p. 194)

Stavrovoúni Monastery

resolved to found a monastery on the spot and left it some of the relics. Thereafter, it is said, a long period of drought on Cyprus came to an end.

History
During the period of Lusignan rule the monastery was occupied by Benedictine monks. In the 15th century it was pillaged by the Mamelukes, who are thought to have been responsible for the disappearance of the relics of the True Cross (some fragments of which are said to be preserved in a silver cross in the church). The present fortress-like monastery was built in the 17th and 18th centuries on the remains of earlier buildings.

The monastery
The domed church, in the centre of the ranges of cells, contains a valuable 15th century wooden cross decorated with scenes from the life of Christ. On the north side of the monastery was discovered a secret crypt in which the monks took refuge in times of danger. It now contains a chapel dedicated to SS Constantine and Helen.

Tamassós
E 7

Ταμασσός
Altitude: 150–200m/490–660ft

Situation and characteristics
20km/12½ miles south-west of Nicosia, at Politikó, are the excavated remains of ancient Tamassós (Latin Tamassus), one of the oldest city-kingdoms in Cyprus (open: June 1st–Aug. 31st, Tues.–Sun. 9am–noon and 4–7pm; Sept. 1st–May 31st, Tues.–Sun. 9am–1pm and 2–4.30pm).

The road approaching the site runs past curious table-like hills, bearing witness to the copper-mining which once brought the city wealth and power. Two tombs and the remains of a temple are all that can be seen today.

The site was first investigated by a German archaeologist, Max Ohnefalsch-Richter, in the 19th century. Systematic excavations were begun in 1970 by a team from the German university of Giessen.

Tombs of the 3rd millennium B.C. give evidence of the earliest occupation of the site, and other finds have shown that it was continuously inhabited in later millennia. In the "Odyssey" (I,184) Athena speaks to Telemachus of a city named Temesa which could be reached by sea where she desired to exchange iron for copper. This was probably the Cypriot town of Tamassós, which was known in Homer's time for the mining and processing of copper. In the 7th century B.C. the town enjoyed its first great period of prosperity.

At the beginning of the 5th century B.C. Tamassós was destroyed, probably as a consequence of its involvement in the Ionian rebellion against the Persians. Thereafter it was rebuilt and established trading contacts with mainland Greece. There is historical evidence for the cult of Aphrodite, Zeus, Dionysus and Heracles and of the building of temples to these divinities. In the 4th century B.C. King Pasikypros sold Tamassós to the city-kingdom of Kítion (Lárnaca). After the expulsion of the Persians the city was again destroyed, probably during the fighting between Alexander the Great's successors.

After being once again rebuilt Tamassós had a further period of prosperity. In the 1st century A.D. Paul and Barnabas came to Tamassós in the company of Heraclidius (see below), a Cypriot, who then became the first bishop of Tamassós. There is believed to have been a bishop of Tamassós in the Middle Ages, but thereafter the town declined into insignificance.

History

Sights

The two large dromos tombs of the 7th century B.C. which have been found at Tamassós are thought on the basis of their rich grave goods to have been the tombs of the local kings. The decorative stone mouldings and the roof structure point to an imitation of the timber buildings which were then normal.

★**Royal tombs**

The first tomb is approached by a narrow stepped dromos. On either side of the entrance are half-columns topped by carved capitals with volutes. The tomb chamber containing the sarcophagus is entered through a pedimented doorway in which the stone is cut to resemble wooden panels.

Tomb 11

The second tomb is also entered by a stepped dromos, the walls of which are faced with finely dressed stone. The doorway of the tomb chamber is richly decorated in the same way as a house or temple, flanked on both sides by pillar-like blocks of stone in which are carved large capitals with volutes. Over the doorway is a frieze of dentils, another imitation of timber construction.

The doorway leads into an antechamber with recesses carved from the rock in the likeness of doors, blind windows and friezes of volutes and palmettes. The antechamber and the tomb chamber both have gabled roofs, with stone beams again imitating timber prototypes.

Tomb 5

Some 200m/220yd south of the royal tombs are the scanty remains of a sanctuary whose origins go back to the Archaic period. The excavators interpreted this as a temple of Aphrodite, together with dwelling-houses and copper-working workshops. Here as at Kítion (Lárnaca) cult and copper-working were closely associated. The temple consisted of a forecourt, the main temple and the holy of holies.

Temple of Aphrodite

Surroundings of Tamassós

Monastery of St Heraclidius (Ayios Iraklidhíos)

Situation and characteristics

1.5km/1 mile west of Tamassós, at Politikó, stands the monastery of St Heraclidius. The monastery, which was founded about 400, was abandoned in the 18th century, but in 1962, on the initiative of Archbishop Makarios III, was reoccupied by a community of nuns.

Legend of St Heraclidius

St Heraclidius, the son of a pagan priest, accompanied the apostles Paul and Barnabas on their missionary journey to Tamassós, and on the way there was baptised in the river Pedhiéos. After thorough instruction he was appointed by Paul to be the first bishop of Tamassós. There he served the large Jewish community, together with "Mnason of Cyprus, an old disciple" (Acts 21,16), and built a small basilica.

Heraclidius is credited with numerous miracles, including the raising of the dead and the control of floods. During the absence of St Mnason he suffered a martyr's death in the market square of Tamassós and was succeeded as bishop by Mnason.

History

About A.D. 400 a three-aisled basilica was built over the graves of the two saints. Remains of mosaics, columns and capitals from this church can be seen in the present monastery. The original church was destroyed by the Arabs in the 9th century and later replaced by a new one. The present two-aisled church was built in the 15th/16th century on the ruins of its three-aisled predecessor.

The monastery

In the south aisle of the church, which is dedicated to St Heraclidius, are pillars and wall paintings of the 10th/11th century from the earlier churches.

In the monastery of St Heraclidius

In the 17th and 18th centuries the monastery had a great reputation as a school of icon-painting, and a number of 18th century wall paintings in the church are by a monk named Philaretos who worked in this school. The iconostasis in the south aisle is 18th century. The north aisle was added in the 16th century and became an independent church dedicated to the Trinity. Its iconostasis is 17th century, as are the icons of Christ, the Mother of God and John the Baptist.

The church's greatest treasure is the skull and a bone from the hand of St Heraclidius, which are wrapped in cloth of gold.

On the south side of the church is a small domed chapel built in the 14th century over the supposed tomb of the saint. It contains a number of stone sarcophagi of the Roman period. Built into the high stone iconostasis are fragments with early Christian designs and symbols. In the 15th century the iconostasis was painted with figures of saints; it was restored in the 18th century.

Reliquary chapel

To the east of the church are steps leading down to a burial vault, said to have been the first resting-place of the saint's remains.

Burial vault

See entry

Makherás

Tróodos Mountains   E–G 3–7

The Tróodos Mountains, which lie wholly within the Greek Republic of Cyprus and cover almost a third of the island's total area, have some of the most beautiful scenery in Cyprus. The successive ranges of hills within the massif are separated by deep valleys. To the west the mountains merge into an extensive upland region in which vines and fruit are grown. The

Situation and characteristics

A remote village in the Tróodos Mountains

northern part of the massif, in which there are many abandoned copper-mines, is almost empty of population. There are hotels in the little towns of Tróodos (see below), Páno Plátres, Pródhromos, Pedhoulás and Kakopetriá (see entry).

Mt Ólympos

The highest peak in the Tróodos range, and in the whole island, is Mt Ólympos (1951m/6401ft), on the summit of which is a British radar station. A viewing platform affords magnificent panoramic views of the range, extending in clear weather as far as the coast. Around Mt Ólympos are four waymarked nature trails (see below) laid out by the Cyprus Tourism Organisation (CTO).

On the east side of Mt Ólympos is Páno Amíandos, where until recently asbestos was mined in opencast workings. As a result of the publicity given in recent years to the carcinogenic qualities of asbestos the mine has now been closed down. In order to obviate the danger of soil erosion there are plans to plant two million trees in this area.

During the last ten years some of the remoter mountain villages have increasingly been abandoned as young people have left the country for the towns. Life returns to these villages only during the hot summer months, when relatives and friends come to visit the surviving villagers. The mountains are a popular holiday area with the people of Cyprus, who like to spend their holidays – almost invariably in August – in the cooler hill regions. Since the hotels are soon fully booked and there is only one camping site (at Tróodos), many Cypriots bring their tents and domestic equipment and camp on their own. Throughout the region there are beautifully situated and well maintained picnic areas.

Skiing on
Mt Ólympos

The good snow cover which can be expected on Mt Ólympos from January to March has promoted the development of skiing in this area. With

In the hill village of Khandriá: the ubiquitous donkey

Austrian help, four ski-lifts have been installed and a ski school established. In addition to short descents through the forests and some rather bumpy pistes there are two langlauf trails.

The slopes of the hills are mainly covered with Aleppo pines and at higher levels black pines. There are also cypresses, Cypriot cedars (Cedar Valley: see Kýkko Monastery, Surroundings), holm oaks, pines, strawberry trees and mulberries. Fruit-trees and vines grow up to 1200m/3900ft.

Flora and fauna

Of the hundreds of species of birds the most typical is the bare-necked griffon vulture. Walkers should beware of the adder and the green, black-spotted *koúfi* viper.

In the remoter mountain regions moufflon can occasionally be glimpsed. This "national animal" of Cyprus can be seen in the moufflon enclosure at the Stavrós tis Psókas forestry station (see Kýkko Monastery, Surroundings also Facts and Figures, Flora and Fauna).

Over many centuries the mountains offered hermits and monks the seclusion and solitude they sought, and as a result there are numbers of medieval monasteries in the Tróodos, for example Kýkko (see entry), Troodhítissa and Ómodhos (see below), and Makherás (see entry). Scattered about among the hills are nine small Byzantine barn-roofed churches, all included in UNESCO's list of world heritage sites. They are famed for their magnificent wall paintings (see Asínou, Kalopanayiótis, Kakopetriá, Lagoudherá and Platanistása).

★ Monasteries and churches

During the 1950s the mountains offered hiding-places for the EOKA "freedom fighters", who were able, with the support of the monasteries, to carry on their underground struggle against British colonial rule.

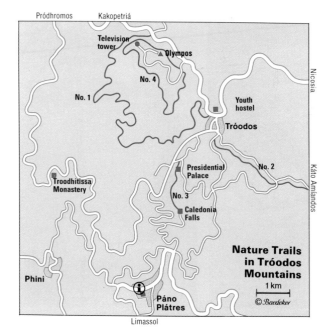

Nature Trails in Tróodos Mountains

★Walking in the Tróodos Mountains

On military grounds there are no walking maps of the Tróodos Mountains. Walkers should always carry a compass with them, since very few footpaths are waymarked: two exceptions are the walk in Cedar Valley (2 hours) and the path from Politikó to Makherás monastery (5 hours).

The four nature trails around Mt Ólympos all start from Tróodos. Each trail is numbered and given a name (see below). The paths are well made, with numbered signs drawing attention to particular species of plants. At each end of the trails, under the arched timber gateways, walkers can obtain leaflets describing the route; if stocks have run out, as they frequently do, the leaflets can be obtained from the CTO.

Nature Trail 1 ("Atalante")	The Khromion trail (9km/5½ miles) begins at a wooden gate near the post office in Tróodos (at the roundabout) and encircles Mt Ólympos at a height of about 1700m/5600ft to end on the Tróodos–Pródhromos road 4km/2½ miles north-west of Tróodos. It affords magnificent views of the mountains, extending down to the coast.
Nature Trail 2 ("Persephone")	The Makria Kontarka trail (3km/1¾ miles) starts from a wooden gate at the Civic Restaurant in Tróodos. It too offers magnificent views.
Nature Trail 3 ("Kaledonia")	The Krýos Potamós trail (2km/1¼ miles) begins 2km/1¼ miles south of Tróodos on the Páno Plátres road (near the Presidential Residence) and runs along a green and shady valley to the Kaledonia Falls, ending above Páno Plátres at the Psiló Déndro trout farm, where walkers can rest in the shade of tall trees and have a meal of freshly caught trout.
Nature Trail 4 ("Artemis")	The Khionístra trail (7km/4¼ miles), which is not yet completely waymarked, begins 1.5km/1 mile north-west of Tróodos on the road leading to

Nature trail on Mt Ólympos   *A weatherbeaten Tróodos pine*

Mt Ólympos, just after the turn-off for Pródhromos. At various points there are extensive views of the majestic mountain landscape.

Sights in the Tróodos Mountains

Tróodos, the highest town in Cyprus (1700m/5575ft) and an important road junction, lies below the summit of Mt Ólympos, 50km/30 miles from Limassol and 80km/50 miles from Nicosia. In actual fact the "town" consists solely of tourist facilities including grill restaurants, two hotels, souvenir shops, a filling station and a post office. Not surprisingly, therefore, it has a rather "deserted village" air in the off season, when no cars or tourist buses stop here. During the summer street traders and roadside stalls add to the bustle of activity in the town, and horses can be hired for treks in the surrounding area. All the nature trails described above start from Tróodos. There is also a very pleasant walk along the Krýos Potamós (Cold River) to the Kaledonia Falls, which are something of a miracle on this arid Mediterranean island. Tróodos is also a hive of activity when the skiing season begins in January (runs until March).

Tróodos

Outside the town on the Páno Plátres road is the summer residence of the President of Cyprus. On the palace, which was built for the British Governor of Cyprus in 1880, is a plaque recording that the French poet Arthur Rimbaud (then a deserter from the Dutch army) worked on the construction of the house.

7km/4½ miles south of Tróodos, on the southern slopes of the hills, is Cyprus's most popular mountain resort, Páno Plátres (alt. 1000–1200m/3300–3900ft; pop. 600), which is excellently equipped with facilities for visitors. In addition to numerous hotels, restaurants and coffee-houses there are many holiday houses belonging to wealthy Cypriots and Lebanese. Even the last king of Egypt, Farouk, had a sumptuous villa here. Through the town flows the Krýos Potamós (Cold River), the only watercourse in Cyprus which has a flow of water – though sometimes not very much – throughout the year.

Páno Plátres

On a hill (1300m/4265ft) 10km/6 miles north of Páno Plátres is the Troodhítissa monastery. Legend attributes its foundation in the 10th century to the discovery by two shepherds of the icon of the Mother of God of Tróodos, which had earlier been hidden by a monk to save it from the

Troodhítissa Monastery

Mother of God with her wonderworking girdle (main doorway of Troodhítissa Monastery)

iconoclasts. In later centuries the icon miraculously survived a series of fires. During the period of Turkish rule the monastery became a Christian school. It is now the summer residence of the bishop of Páphos.

The oldest part of the present monastery is the 18th century church, successor to an earlier church of the 13th century. As in the past, the monastery continues to attract large numbers of pilgrims to venerate the silver-plated icon of the Mother of God on the iconostasis and a wonderworking girdle which is believed to enable childless women to conceive. The monk in charge of the monastery shop, Barnabas, shows visitors photographs of happy couples from far and wide who have had their wish for a child fulfilled after a pilgrimage to Troodhítissa. This may be the reason for the name by which the monastery is also known, the Panayía Aphrodítissa.

Phiní

From Troodhítissa it is an hour and a half's walk to the hill village of Phiní (alt. 900m/2950ft), in a valley 6km/4 miles west of Páno Plátres. For centuries Phiní has been famed for its unglazed pottery – though here, as elsewhere in Cyprus, the traditional craft is slowly dying out. In the past the men of the village made *pitharia,* large storage jars for grain, wine or oil, between 1.5m/5ft and 2m/6½ft high, which were set into the floors of the village houses. The local pottery is now mainly made by women, who produce smaller pots of various kinds. There is a small museum displaying the different types of local ware.

Phiní also makes the finest hand-made basketwork chairs on the island, using branches from the local holm oaks.

Ómodhos

10km/6 miles south-west of Páno Plátres is the pretty hill village of Ómodhos (alt. 850m/2790ft), in which is the monastery of the Holy Cross (Stavrós). The village's main source of income is wine-producing, but the women also make beautiful lace.

According to the local legend the monastery was founded to house a fragment of the True Cross (brought to Cyprus by St Helen in the 4th century: see Stavrovoúni) and the hempen rope with which Christ's hands were bound, now preserved in two silver crosses on the iconostasis of the church. The monastery also possesses the skull of the apostle Philip, presented to it by one of the Byzantine Emperors, with the stamps of four Emperors to vouch for its authenticity.

The present monastic buildings are modern, with fine hand-carved cedar-wood ceilings, the ceiling of the former chapterhouse being particularly sumptuous. There is also a small EOKA museum, commemorating the underground movement for the liberation of Cyprus, which was supported by the monastery.

Yeroskípos

G 2

Γεροσκήπος
Altitude: 50m/165ft
Population: *c.* 1800

Situation and characteristics

4km/2½ miles south-east of Páphos lies the village of Yeroskípos, whose name is derived from the classical Greek Hierós Képos ("Sacred Garden"). In all probability this was the site of the gardens of the sanctuary of Aphrodite at Palaía Páphos (see Koúklia). The fragments of ancient masonry found scattered about the churchyard suggest that there may have been a small shrine of Aphrodite in Yeroskípos itself. The pilgrims who landed at Páphos no doubt made their way up through the sacred gardens to the much venerated sanctuary at Palaía Páphos.

Until the Second World War Yeroskípos, with its numerous mulberry trees, was a centre of silkworm culture. It owes its present prosperity to its proximity to the busy tourist centre of Páphos; it is famed for its pottery and for its Turkish delight (*loukoumia*), now sold all over South Cyprus.

★Church of Ayía Paraskeví

In the centre of the village is the little five-domed church of Ayía Paraskeví, which has 15th century wall paintings (key in the shoemaker's shop opposite the church). The church, which dates from the 10th/11th century, is one of only two five-domed churches in South Cyprus (the other being the church of SS Hilarion and Barnabas at Peristeróna: see entry). The model for the multi-domed church was provided by the 6th century church of St John at Ephesus. The church of Ayía Paraskeví, which is three-aisled, has three domes over the nave and one over each of the aisles. On the south side of the apse is a small domed chapel. The bell-tower was built in the 19th century, the western part of the church as recently as 1931.

Ayía Paraskeví ("St Friday"), to whom the church is dedicated, is credited with the power of curing eye complaints. Paraskeví is said to have been born on Cyprus in the 2nd century A.D. and to have been named Friday because she was born on that day to parents who had hitherto been childless. After the death of her parents she gave all her possessions to the poor, went to Rome and lived in a Christian community there. She was martyred during the persecutions in the reign of Antoninus Pius.

The wall paintings mostly date from the 15th century, but during restoration work paintings of the 10th and 12th centuries also came to light. In the east dome, over the altar, was found a cross with floral and geometric decoration, evidently dating from the iconoclastic period (8th/9th c.). The church must therefore be one of the oldest in Cyprus apart from the early Christian basilicas, now destroyed. Among the 12th century paintings is a representation of the Dormition of the Mother of God on the north wall, below the central dome, which was overpainted in the 15th century by a Crucifixion. The 15th century paintings depict scenes from the life of the Virgin and the life of Christ, with a profusion of figures reflecting western influence.

In the central dome is the Mother of God with her hands raised in prayer, in the western dome Christ Pantokrator. Particularly notable is the painting of the Baptism of Christ on the south wall, below the central dome. At Christ's feet is a small figure of a bearded man, a personification of the Jordan, who turns to flee before Christ. To the right is an old woman in a boat drawn by two sea monsters, representing the sea. The reference is to Psalm 114,3: "The sea saw it and fled: Jordan was driven back."

On the north wall of the nave, immediately in front of the painting of Ayía Paraskeví, is a double icon of the 15th century, hung behind glass, which was formerly on the iconostasis. On one side is the Mother of God with the Child, on the other the Crucifixion.

★Folk Art Museum

The little Folk Art Museum near the church in Athens Street illustrates the domestic life and folk art of the district of Páphos (open: Sept.–May, Mon.–Fri. 7.30am–2pm, Sat. 7.30am–1pm; June–Aug., Mon.–Fri. 7.30am–1pm, also Tues. 4–6pm).

It occupies the house of the British consul in western Cyprus, which was acquired by the Department of Antiquities in 1978. The house was built in

Church of Ayía Paraskevi . . .

. . . with wall paintings

Oil Press in the Folk Art Museum

1799 by Andreas Zimboulakis, an immigrant from Greece who became British consular agent.

The rooms of this typical Cypriot house are entered from a courtyard with a wooden gallery on the upper floor. The exhibits include a fully equipped kitchen, spinning and weaving equipment, agricultural implements and a wedding room with fine old chests, needlework, pottery and traditional costumes.

Sights from A to Z: North Cyprus

Bellapais/Bellabayıs

Altitude: 300m/985ft

Bellapais Abbey (open: daily 8am–5pm) lies at the foot of the Beşparmak Hills in the village of Bellapais, 6km/4 miles south-east of Kyrenia. The name of the abbey, one of the most beautiful Gothic monastic ruins in the Mediterranean area, is derived from the Greek *epískopos* ("bishop") by way of Lapais and Abbaye de la Paix (Abbey of Peace).

Situation and characteristics

The writer Lawrence Durrell lived in the village of Bellapais in the 1950s. In his book "Bitter Lemons" he describes the abbey in these words: "I was prepared for something beautiful, and I already knew that the ruined monastery of Bellapais (now Beylerbeyi) was one of the loveliest Gothic survivals in the Levant, but I was not prepared for the breath-taking congruence of the little village which surrounded and cradled it against the side of the mountain." He also refers to the "Tree of Idleness" in front of the abbey, which still survives. He was warned by one of his Cypriot friends, if he intended to try and work, never to sit under the Tree of Idleness: "its shadow incapacitates one for serious work."

Lawrence Durrell

The abbey, dedicated to Our Lady of the Hill, was founded in 1205 by Augustinian monks who had fled to Cyprus from Jerusalem after its conquest by Saladin in 1187, and the Lusignan king Hugo I granted it extensive properties. In the 13th century the abbey passed into the hands of Premonstratensian monks who had also fled from the Holy Land. Bellapais then became known as the White Abbey after the white habit of the Premonstratensians. The abbots were under the jurisdiction of the Archbishop of Nicosia, with whom they frequently came into conflict.

History

The present church was built in the reign of Hugo III (1267–84); the other buildings date from the 14th century. The king granted the abbot special privileges: he was permitted, for example, to wear an episcopal mitre during mass and when outside the abbey to wear a sword and gilded spurs. Thanks to generous gifts and donations the abbey grew rich and powerful.

Decline set in during the 16th century, when the strict Rule of the abbey was increasingly disregarded and the monks broke their vow of chastity. The Venetian authorities were about to take measures to restore order when Cyprus was captured by the Ottomans and the monks fled from Bellapais.

The ★★Abbey

In accordance with the usual layout of medieval monasteries, all the buildings are set at right angles to one another. The present entrance to the abbey is on the west side. It leads through a square courtyard into the narthex of the church (kept locked; the key is with the keeper). In the walls of the narthex are recesses for tombs, and there are remains of 15th century wall paintings. The church, which lies on the south side of the complex, has a wide nave and narrow lateral aisles, with a square choir at the east end. In the north wall of the church is a staircase leading up to the monks' dormitory (which no longer survives); the monks came down these stairs to attend services during the night. On the north side of the choir is a small sacristy.

Church

◀ *Kantara Castle*

Cloister

On the north side of the church is the cloister, in Late Gothic style (14th c.), with high pointed arches and the remains of beautiful Flamboyant tracery. On the lawn in the centre of the cloister are four tall cypresses.

Chapterhouse

At the south-east corner of the cloister stands the chapterhouse, with a single pier in the centre which supported the vaulting. The consoles on which the ribs of the vaulting rested show some remains of the former magnificent relief decoration. In this room was held the daily meeting of the monks presided over by the abbot.

Common room

The long room adjoining the chapterhouse was originally barrel-vaulted and is thought to have been the monks' common room, or possibly a scriptorium for the writing and copying of manuscripts. Over these two rooms was the monks' dormitory.

Refectory

On the north side of the cloister can be found the refectory. In front of the entrance is a Roman sarcophagus decorated with masks and genii carrying garlands, which was used to contain water. Over the doorway are the arms of the Lusignans as kings of Cyprus and Jerusalem.

The refectory, with a groin-vaulted roof, has been preserved intact. Measuring 30.40m/100ft by 11.50m/38ft by 11.50m/38ft high, it is one of the largest refectories of its period. On the north side steps lead up to a pulpit richly decorated with tracery from which one of the monks read sacred texts during meals. There are six windows, from which there are fine views of the town of Kyrenia on the coast below. Under the refectory was a store-room to which a staircase led down.

There are only scanty remains of the buildings on the west side of the cloister, probably the kitchen and other domestic offices.

Bellapais Abbey in sunshine . . .

. . . and under cloud

Surroundings of Bellapais

Vounoús/Taşkent

From Bellapais an unsurfaced road runs south through the hills, coming in 10km/6 miles to Vounoús/Taşkent, with the excavations of an Early Bronze Age necropolis. Here, in addition to a variety of pottery, were found the two famous clay models of a ploughing scene and a circular shrine in which some religious ceremony is being performed; both are now in the Archaeological Museum on the Greek part of Nicosia (see Sights in South Cyprus, Nicosia).

Buffavento Castle   D 8

Altitude: 954m/3130ft

Situation and characteristics

Buffavento Castle (the Italian name means "defier of winds") is perched on a precipitous crag in the Beşparmak Hills south-east of Bellapais. To reach it from Nicosia, take the Famagusta road and shortly before Trakhóni/Demirhan turn into a road on the left which runs up to a pass; then from the summit of the pass (view of Mt Pentadáktylos/Beşparmak, 740m/2428ft) take a dirt road on the left which comes in 6km/4 miles to a car park below the castle (28km/17 miles). From here it is a half-hour climb on foot to the castle. Buffavento can be reached from Kyrenia by leaving on the Famagusta road and at its highest point (view of the Mesaória plain) taking a road on the right (24km/15 miles).

In contrast to the two other castles in northern Cyprus, St Hilarion and Kantara (see entries), there are only slight remains of Buffavento. It does, however, offer superb views of the north coast (Kyrenia), the Mesaória plain and the castle of St Hilarion.

History

Like Kantara and St Hilarion, Buffavento was built in the 10th century and later was fortified by the Lusignans. Lying between the other two, it was an important link in the island's signalling system. The Lusignans also used it as a prison. At the end of the 15th century, after the Venetians gained control of Cyprus, the castle was demolished.

The castle

There are only scanty remains of the castle, which was built of undressed local stone. It consisted of a lower ward, the foundations of which can still be identified, and an upper ward some 20m/65ft higher up. The lower ward looks down on the Mesaória plain; from the upper ward, on the summit of the hill, there are wide panoramic views. The lower ward was occupied by the soldiers' living quarters and guard-rooms, stables and store-rooms. In the upper ward there are slight remains of a number of rooms facing west and two cellars.

The castle is in the present-day military zone and not often open to the public.

Surroundings of Buffavento

Monastery of Ayios Ioánnis Chrysóstomos

Below the castle, 3km/2 miles away, is the monastery of Ayios Ioánnis Chrysóstomos (St John Chrysostom; alt. 570m/1870ft), in which St Neóphytos is said to have become a novice at the age of 18 (see Sights in South Cyprus, St Neóphytos Monastery).

The monastery has two churches standing side by side. The older one, to the south, was originally built in the 11th century and was one of the few examples in Cyprus of a church with a dome carried on corner squinches, i.e. on an octagonal base. After its collapse it was replaced by a new church in the 19th century. The other church, which dates from the 12th century, has wall paintings of that period. Since the monastery lies in a military area and is used as a barracks, it cannot be visited.

Famagusta/Gazimağusa   E 11

Altitude: sea level. Population: 20,000

Famagusta (in Turkish Gazimağusa, or Mağusa for short), the second largest town in North Cyprus and formerly the island's principal port, lies 60km/37 miles south-east of Nicosia. The Greek name of the town, Ammóchostos ("buried in sand"), refers to its situation on the beaches of golden sand which extend along the east coast of Cyprus. It consists of two very different parts, the Old Town within the Venetian walls, which have been preserved intact, and the New Town (Yeni Mağusa or Maras) outside the walls. Before 1974 the Old Town was inhabited solely by Turks, the New Town (then known as Varósha or Maraş) by Greeks.

Situation and ★★ importance

Before 1974 Varósha was the tourist quarter of Famagusta, well equipped with high-rise hotels, banks, shops, markets and restaurants. Famagusta then had a total of some 10,000 hotel beds – more than the rest of the island put together. Varósha is now a depressing sight. The hotels, damaged by bombing in 1974, lie in a closed military area and are steadily falling into ruin. From the luxury Palm Beach Hotel, one of the few still open in Famagusta, there is a view of what is now a ghost town.

Varósha (Maraş)

The port of Famagusta, once the largest in Cyprus, has also declined. Before 1974 it was the only port in Cyprus with modern loading and discharging installations and accordingly handled most of the island's trade. Now it is one of only two commercial ports in North Cyprus the other being Kyrenia.

Port

The Eastern Mediterranean University, in which tuition is in English, was founded in 1986. It has departments of engineering and other voca-

University

Old Town of Famagusta, with St Nicholas's Cathedral

tional subjects. The Gothic church of Ayios Exorinós now serves as its Cultural Centre.

Tourism

Famagusta has begun to develop its tourist trade within the last few years, and is now the second most important tourist centre in North Cyprus. New hotels have been built on the beautiful sandy beaches north-east of the town, generally low-rise developments with their standard of amenity below that of the Greek Cypriot hotels. The efforts of the government of North Cyprus to boost the tourist trade have been effective with tourism becoming the fastest growing sector of the North's economy – a trend expected to continue.

Old Town

The Old Town with its narrow streets, ruined Gothic churches, street traders, fruit-stalls and shoeshine boys has a rather Oriental air. The many little shops and boutiques offer a tempting range of goods.

History

Foundation

The history of Famagusta begins in the 3rd century B.C. with the foundation by the ruler of Egypt, Ptolemy II, of the town of Arsinoe to the south of the ancient city of Sálamis (Constantia). In the 7th century A.D. the inhabitants of Constantia fled before the Arabs to the neighbouring town of Arsinoe, which had long been a city of ruins half buried under drifting sand. The town was now rebuilt and became known as Ammóchostos ("buried in sand"), since the new city was still threatened by the destructive power of the sand. It continued to be harassed by Arab raids, and achieved a measure of prosperity only in the 12th century, after an influx of Armenians. Then, following the conquest of Cyprus by Richard Coeur de Lion in 1191, Ammóchostos became known under the Lusignans as Famagusta.

Famagusta's medieval heyday

In 1291 Acre, the last Christian stronghold in the Holy Land, fell to the Muslims. Many crusaders, monks and merchants fled to Cyprus, bringing goods and money with them, and settled in Famagusta. The port became a

The ghost town of Varósha with its empty hotels

major centre of trade between East and West, and merchants from many countries set up their businesses in the town. In the 13th and 14th centuries it was one of the most flourishing and wealthiest towns in the whole Mediterranean area. The population grew to 70,000, and the streets were lined with sumptuous noble mansions. The kings of Jerusalem were now crowned in Famagusta, which was said to have more than 365 churches.

In 1374 there was a bitter dispute between the Genoese and the Venetians in Cyprus when the Genoese were denied their traditional privilege of holding the right-hand rein of the king's horse during the ceremonies of a royal coronation. They then captured and pillaged Famagusta and compelled the king to pay tribute. In 1489 the Venetians recovered the town and strengthened its defences in anticipation of a Turkish attack.

Venetian rule

In 1571, however, the Turks succeeded in taking the town after a ten-month siege. During the peace negotiations a dispute arose between the negotiators, and the Venetian commander, Marcantonio Bragadino, was killed for

Turkish rule

failing to honour his promise and not sparing the lives of fifty Turkish prisoners of war. The Christian population fled from Famagusta but were allowed to live outside the town. Since then the old town of Famagusta has remained Turkish, as the Turkish name Gazimağusa ("unconquered city") indicates.

19th and 20th centuries

After the Turkish conquest Famagusta declined into a town of little consequence, but in the 19th and 20th centuries its importance increased with the development of the port. The Turkish Cypriots continued to live in the Old Town, with Greeks and Armenians in the outer districts. In 1974, after heavy fighting, Famagusta fell to the Turkish forces.

Sights

Victory Monument

At a roundabout on the south side of the town, just outside the walls, is the Victory Monument erected by the Turks in honour of those who died in the civil war. It is a dynamic work of sculpture with scenes of battle and of flight, topped by the figure of Atatürk, the founder and first President of modern Turkey. Just beyond the roundabout a road on the left leads through the Land Gate (the Rivettina Bastion or Ravelin) into the Old Town.

Town walls

The walls of Famagusta, still excellently preserved, were built at the end of the 15th century on the remains of the older walls erected by the Lusignans. As the Turkish threat grew steadily greater the city commissioned a Venetian architect, Giovanni Girolamo Sanmichele, to build larger and stronger walls. The new walls, in the form of an irregular rectangle with a total circuit of 3.5km/2 miles, were 18m/60ft high and up to 9m/30ft thick. On the seaward side they were reinforced by the Diamond Tower, the Citadel ("Othello's Tower") and the Djamboulat Bastion. The land walls, which

Bastions of Famagusta's well-preserved town walls

were surrounded by a moat, were given additional protection by the Martinengo and Rivettina Bastions. There were originally only two entrances to the town, the Sea Gate and the Land Gate; others were opened up during the period of British colonial rule.

Lion of St Mark

The Citadel, popularly known as Othello's Tower (open: Mon.–Sat. 8am–5pm), is a square structure with fortified round towers at the four corners, built by the Venetians in 1492 on the remains of a smaller Lusignan citadel. Two sides are on the sea, while the two landward sides were given the additional protection of a moat. An inscription under the Lion of St Mark at the main entrance gives the date of construction and names the builder as Niccolò Foscarini. In the inner courtyard of the citadel can be seen the remains of a square Gothic tower and a large hall of the Lusignan period. Visitors can climb to the wall-walk, from which there are good views of the harbour and the Old Town with its numerous churches.

★ Othello's Tower/ Othello Kalesi

Since Shakespeare's "Othello" is set in a seaport in Cyprus, the Citadel has been identified as the scene of the drama and has become known as Othello's Tower. The Venetian vice-governor has been cast as the "Moor of Venice", since his name was Cristoforo Moro, in allusion to his dark skin. According to another theory Othello was Francesco di Sessa, who was exiled to Cyprus and, being also dark-skinned, was known as the "capitano moro". Shakespeare himself was never in Cyprus, but took his plot from a story by a Venetian writer, Giraldo Cinzio.

Othello

The Djamboulat Bastion (modern Turkish spelling Canbulat; open: Mon.–Fri. 8.30am–1pm and 2.30–5pm) now houses a small museum as well as the tomb of a Turkish cavalry officer, Canbulat Bey, who during the siege of Famagusta in 1570 rode his horse on to a wheel covered with knives with which the Venetians had protected the entrance and by his sacrifice enabled the Turks to take the town. His tomb is still honoured. The museum's collection includes Bronze Age pottery, Turkish domestic equipment and clothing (including wedding garb) and weapons of the 17th–19th centuries.
    Opposite the Djamboulat Bastion is a military cemetery commemorating the Turks who fell during the defence of Famagusta in 1963.

Djamboulat Bastion

The Martinengo Bastion, completed about 1550, is named after Hieronimo Martinengo, who died on his way to Cyprus to command the Venetian troops. The most massive of Famagusta's bastions, with walls up to 6m/20ft thick, it was designed to protect the town against attack from the landward side. Inside the bastion are two large underground chambers which offered shelter for 2000 men or could be used as ammunition stores.

Martinengo Bastion

Opposite Othello's Tower are the ruins of the little church of St George of the Latins, one of the oldest Gothic buildings in Famagusta, dating from the late 13th century. Richly decorated, in a style reminiscent of the Sainte Chapelle in Paris, it provided the model for St Catherine's Church in Nicosia.

Church of St George of the Latins

From the Land Gate Istiklâl and M. Ersu Streets lead to the ruined Gothic church of St George of the Greeks, built in the second half of the 14th century as the Orthodox counterpart to the Roman Catholic cathedral of St

Church of St George of the Greeks

Othello's Tower

Nicholas. The architectural decoration and the pointed arches show Gothic influence, while the domed roof of the nave recalls Byzantine models. In the choir apse there are remains of wall paintings. Unfortunately much of the church was destroyed over time.

Ayios Nikólaos and Ayía Zóni

To the east of St George of the Greeks are two small Orthodox churches. The two-aisled 15th century church of Ayios Nikólaos is now a ruin. Adjoining it is the well preserved Byzantine domed cruciform church of Ayía Zóni (the Holy Girdle of the Mother of God), which dates from the 14th century (no access).

★★St Nicholas's Cathedral/ Lala Mustafa Pasa Mosque

From St George of the Greeks Naim Efendi Street runs north-west to St Nicholas's Cathedral in Namık Kemal Square, which dominates the skyline of Famagusta. This Roman Catholic cathedral is one of the best preserved Gothic buildings on the island. It was begun in 1298 under the direction of Baudouin Lambert and consecrated in 1326, at the same time as St Sophia in Nicosia. This was the coronation church of the kings of Jerusalem – for the Lusignans were not only kings of Cyprus and Armenia but also nominally kings of Jerusalem, though that city was now held by the Turks. The last Lusignan queen, Catherine Cornaro, signed her abdication document here, and her husband James II was buried in the cathedral.

St Nicholas's Cathedral, the most Gothic church in Cyprus, shows affinities with the French cathedrals in the Île de France. When it was converted into a mosque in the 16th century the sculpture was removed and the paintings covered with whitewash, and a small minaret was built on the north tower of the façade.

Façade

The façade, which is preserved up to the third stage of the tower, is a masterpiece of Gothic architecture. The three doorways are topped by

The ruined church of St George of the Greeks

crocketed pediments with delicate tracery, extending above the horizontal cornice of the upper storey. The second stage has a large and beautiful rose window flanked by two blind windows. The towers, now reduced to stumps, have Gothic windows crowned by pediments. The walls of the church are supported by massive buttresses. At the left-hand and right-hand ends of the façade are two small polygonal staircase towers giving access to the external gallery on the west front, on which the kings showed themselves to the people after their coronation.

Interior

The church, which is three-aisled and five bays long, has an interior length of 55m/180ft and a width of 23m/75ft. The arches of the vaulting rest on massive columns; the clerestory has large Gothic windows. For its present function as a mosque the walls are whitewashed and the floor is covered

St Nicholas's Cathedral
Lala Mustafa Paşa Mosque

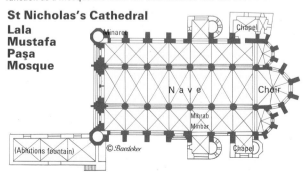

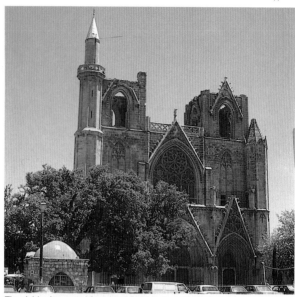

The richly decorated façade of St Nicholas's Cathedral

with carpets, and there are a mihrab and a minbar on the south side. At the east end of the nave is the polygonal apse; there is no ambulatory. The windows of the choir have fine tracery and externally are topped by pediments. The lateral aisles end in small apsidal chapels. In the apse of the north aisle (now the women's part of the mosque), set into the floor, is a medieval gravestone with a figure of St Nicholas with his episcopal mitre and crosier.

Loggia

On the south side of the square in front of the church are the remains of a Venetian loggia, now housing an ablutions fountain.

Ancient tree

In the square in front of the church is a 600-year-old mulberry fig-tree (*Sycomorus ficus*, a native of North Africa) planted during the period of Lusignan rule.

Other sights

Palazzo del Provveditore

In Namık Kemal Square, opposite the cathedral, are the remains of the Palazzo del Provveditore, the Venetian governor's palace. There was a royal palace here in the 13th century, in which the Lusignan kings resided after their coronation. The Venetians enlarged the palace, giving it a monumental Renaissance doorway, which still survives, together with some fragments of walls. The doorway, in rusticated stonework, has three arched entrances giving access to the interior of the palace, which is now a car park. In front of the doorway four large granite columns from ancient Sálamis support a cornice. Over the central round-headed arch can be seen the arms of the Venetian governor, Giovanni Renier (1552). Beyond the doorway, to the left, are the remains of a building which in Turkish times was used as a state prison. The Turkish national poet Namık Kemal was confined here from 1873 to 1876 for writing a play which was considered to be seditious. There is a monument to him on the north side of the square in front of the cathedral.

To the north of the Palazzo del Provveditore stand the ruins of a Gothic church belonging to a Franciscan friary founded by the Lusignan king Henry II in the 13th century. It now houses the Old Town Discothèque.

Church of St Francis

Round the apse of the church is a disused public bath-house built in 1601 by the Turkish governor, Cafer Paşa, who also constructed an aqueduct to bring water to Famagusta. In Namık Kemal Square is the Cafer Paşa Fountain.

Cafer Paşa Baths

From Namık Kemal Square Abdullah Paşa Street leads to the Early Gothic church of SS Peter and Paul, built in the 14th century at the expense of Simone Nostrano, a wealthy merchant, for the use of the merchants' guild.

Church of SS Peter and Paul

This three-aisled basilican church, excellently preserved, is a building of clear Gothic forms. The nave is separated from the narrow aisles by low pointed arches borne on stout columns and is lit by simple clerestory windows. The nave leads directly into the apse, and there are two small lateral apses at the east ends of the aisles. The nave and aisles are spanned by groined vaulting with carved bosses.

After the Ottoman conquest in 1571 the church was converted into the Sinan Paşa Mosque, and thereafter was used as a potato and grain store. After renovation in the 1960s it now houses the Municipal Library.

Continuing along Abdullah Paşa Street to the town walls and turning right, we come to the Nestorian church of Ayios Yeóryios Exorinós, built in 1359 by one of the wealthiest merchants in Cyprus. The original church was single-aisled, three bays long, with a semicircular apse, but soon after it was built it was enlarged by the addition of two short aisles, only two bays long, ending in small apsidal chapels. In Turkish times it was used as a camel stable, but in the early 20th century it was taken over by Orthodox Christians and dedicated to Ayios Yeóryios Exorinós (St George the Exile).

Ayios Yeóryios Exorinós

The church has remains of wall paintings (which originally covered the whole of the interior) and inscriptions dating from its occupation by the Nestorians. It now houses the Cultural Centre of the Eastern Mediterranean University.

An Armenian church dedicated to the Mother of God, a Carmelite church and the little church of St Anne all lie within a military area near the old town walls and cannot be visited. Also within the prohibited zone is an icon museum (ask outside the area).

Other churches

Icon Museum

Surroundings of Famagusta

See Sálamis

Énkomi/Tuzla, Alasia

See Sálamis

Monastery of St Barnabas

See entry

Sálamis

Kantara Castle

C 11

Altitude: 680m/2230ft

Kantara Castle is reached from Nicosia by taking the road which runs via Kythréa/Değirmenlik and Lefkóniko/Geçitkale to Tríkomo/Iskele and then turning left into a road signposted to Árdhana/Ardahan (86km/53 miles). From Famagusta take the coast road; then at Perivólia/Bahçeler turn left into the road to Tríkomo/Iskele and continue from there to Kantara (43km/27 miles).

★Situation and characteristics

Kantara (= "bridge, arch") is the most easterly of the three castles in the Beşparmak Hills built in the Middle Ages to defend the island from attack.

Church of the Panayía Kyra, Livádhia

with the paintings in Asínou church. The surviving paintings depict scenes from the life of the Virgin; in the dome is Christ Pantokrator.

Livádhia/
Sazlıköy
(38km/24 miles)

From the turn-off for Tríkomo the coast road continues to Ayios Theódhoros/Çayırova, from the far end of which a road goes off on the left to Livádhia (3km/2 miles). In this village, opposite the mosque, a narrow dirt road goes off on the left to the abandoned church of the Panayía Kyra, standing by itself in a field. This little domed cruciform church was built in the 10th/11th century on the remains of an early Christian basilica and originally belonged to a monastery. Before 1974 there was a mosaic of the Mother of God in the apse (see Art and Culture, Cyprus's Threatened Cultural Heritage).

Lythrángomi/
Boltaşlı
(56km/35 miles)

The main road continues to Leonárisso/Ziyamet, from which a road on the right leads to Lythrángomi, with the fine church of the Panayía Kanakariá, which originally belonged to a monastery. This three-aisled domed church was built in the 12th century on the remains of an early Christian basilica of the 6th c.; the south aisle with its doorway was added in the 13th c.

The apse of the original church survived down the centuries, with a fine 6th century mosaic of which fragments were still in position in 1974. Thereafter it was stolen and disappeared from sight for some time, finally turning up in the United States (Indianapolis) in 1989. An American art dealer had bought the mosaic from a Turk for 1.2 million dollars and offered it to the Getty Museum in Malibu, California, for 20 million dollars. When the Church of Cyprus heard this it claimed the mosaic as church property, and an American court finally directed that it should be returned to Cyprus. The mosaic has been restored and is now on show in the Icon Museum in Nicosia (see South Cyprus, Nicosia).

The church contains badly damaged remains of wall paintings of the 10th–16th centuries. South of the church are ruins of the monastery buildings which are now used as stables.

From the turn-off for Lythrángomi the main road continues to Yialoúsa/Yenierenköy, where a road goes off on the right to Melánarga/Adaçay. The first little road opening off this road on the left leads to the village of Ayía Triás/Sipahi, at the far end of which, on the left, are the remains of the early Christian church of Ayía Triás. In this large excavation site can be seen the foundations of a three-aisled basilica of the 7th century, with a few columns and column bases indicating its ground-plan. There is a well preserved mosaic pavement with geometric patterns. Associated with the church was an extensive complex of buildings, including a small baptistery with a baptismal chapel on the south side of the apse containing an immersion font for the baptism of adults.

Ayía Triás/ Sipahi
(65km/40 miles)

Rizokárpaso, the most easterly village on the peninsula, was the see of an Orthodox bishop in the 13th century. The former cathedral of Ayios Synésios, now much altered, is still used by the Greek community living in Rizokárpaso.

Rizokárpaso/ Dipkarpaz
(86km/53 miles)

30km/19 miles east of Rizokárpaso is the monastery of Ayios Andréas, which before 1974 attracted crowds of pilgrims every weekend; the key is held by the custodian, who lives in the cell block. According to the local legend the apostle St Andrew, while sailing along the coast of Cyprus, saved a ship's captain who was dying of thirst by directing him to a spring on Cape Andréas. The captain expressed his gratitude by the presentation of a valuable icon, to house which the monastery was founded. Thereafter St Andrew became the patron of seafarers.

Monastery of Ayios Andréas
(115km/71 miles)

The monastery buildings date from the 19th and 20th centuries. The monastery is still in Greek hands, and on special feast days like the

Monastery of Ayios Andréas

227

Ayios Phíon, a 10th century Byzantine church

Dormition of the Mother of God (August 15th) and St Andrew's Day a service is conducted by the Rizokárpaso priest.
There is a Turkish Cypriot police post here.

On the shore below the monastery is a small square Gothic chapel (15th c.) built over St Andrew's Spring, with a central column supporting the vaulting.

Cape Andréas

From the monastery it is another 5km/3 miles to the cape, on which the remains of a Neolithic settlement have been found. At the end of the 12th century Isaac Comnenus, fleeing from Richard Coeur de Lion (Richard the Lionheart), was taken prisoner here. Off the cape are the Klídhes ("Keys") Islands.

Ayios Phílon

On the way back from Cape Andréas, shortly before the church, take a road which runs up on the right and comes in 4km/2½ miles to the ruined church of Ayios Phílon, just above the coast. Near here was the ancient city of Karpasía, destroyed by the Arabs in the 9th century.

The church of Ayios Phílon was built in the 10th century on the remains of a small early Christian church. With its finely dressed stone and elegant mouldings round the doors and windows it is a magnificent example of 10th century Byzantine church architecture. The church is three-aisled, with a narthex and an atrium. On the south side are the baptistery, a cistern and a font.

Aphendriká

About 8km/5 miles east of Ayios Phílon are the three early Christian basilicas of Aphendriká – all that is left of a once important city destroyed by the Arabs. The churches were rebuilt in the 10th century. The best preserved of the three is the three-aisled church of the Panayía Asomatos.

Kyrenia/Girne   C/D 7/8

Altitude: 0–30m/0–100ft. Population: 7000

Kyrenia, on the north coast of Cyprus, is one of the most idyllic little towns on the whole island. The small horseshoe-shaped harbour with its yachts and fishing boats is surrounded by old houses and tavernas. Immediately south of the town are the Pentadáktylos Hills (Turkish: Beşparmak Dağları).
   Kyrenia is reached from Nicosia on an excellent new road (26km/16 miles). Coming from Famagusta, turn off the Nicosia road just after Demirhan into a road on the right (73km/45 miles).

★Situation and characteristics

Kyrenia is now the principal tourist centre in North Cyprus, with beautiful sandy beaches to east and west of the town and good walking in the nearby Beşparmak Hills. The majority of North Cyprus' hotels are situated in or around Kyrenia. Small hotels and guest houses, such as the long-established Dome Hotel, are located in the centre of town or on the harbour while larger hotels are slightly away from the town centre. Most of the visitors come from Turkey. There are also some British-owned holiday and retirement houses in and around Kyrenia, which was a favourite British resort during the colonial period.

Tourism

The little harbour, dominated by the massive bulk of the Castle to the east, is suitable only for small boats. In the centre of the harbour basin is a small medieval tower, from which a chain could be spanned to the shore to close the harbour to an enemy. Beyond the Castle is a modern harbour (military port) used by freighters and ferries.

★Harbour

Kyrenia has a well preserved Old Town of narrow streets and handsome houses with romantic balconies. Notable features are the Cafer Paşa Mosque and the neighbouring Turkish baths (still in use). The ground floors of many of the old houses on the harbour have been converted into attractive restaurants which tempt the visitor to linger.

Old Town

The area was first settled in Neolithic times. In the Bronze Age the population increased, and there were close contacts with the coast of Asia Minor. After the Hellenisation of the island by the Achaeans Kyrenia

History

Ancient times

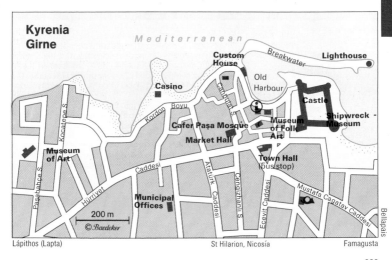

The harbour of Kyrenia, one of the principal attractions of North Cyprus

became one of the Cypriot city-kingdoms, which in 312 B.C. came under the control of the powerful city of Sálamis. At the end of the 4th century B.C. Kyrenia, in common with the other cities of Cyprus, was incorporated in the empire of the Ptolemies. In the 4th century A.D. it became the see of a bishop.

Middle Ages

The town suffered repeatedly from Arab raids and in the 7th century, when the Roman fortifications were still standing, the Byzantines supplemented them by a citadel at the harbour entrance. When the harbour was again fortified in the 10th century the work was confined to the enlargement and strengthening of the citadel, and the town walls were abandoned.

During the conflict between the Emperor Frederick II and the Cypriot nobility in the early 13th century the imperial forces entrenched themselves in the castle but were compelled in 1233 to surrender. Thereafter the castle was rebuilt, and in the 14th century it became the favourite residence of the Lusignan king James I.

In 1460 Kyrenia was the scene of a struggle for the succession between the heiress to the throne, Carlotta, and John II's illegitimate son James the Bastard, who claimed the throne for himself. The conflict was won by James, who starved Carlotta out in Kyrenia and later married Caterina Cornaro, the last Lusignan queen of Cyprus.

During the period of Venetian rule the castle was much altered. After the Turkish conquest of Nicosia in 1570 Kyrenia surrendered without more ado.

Sights

★ Castle

The Castle (open: Mon.–Sat. 8am–1pm and 2–5pm) lies in the north-east of the town, protecting the entrance to the harbour. Its origins go back to the citadel built in the 7th century, which was enlarged and strengthened

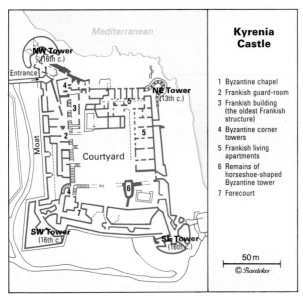

Kyrenia Castle

1 Byzantine chapel
2 Frankish guard-room
3 Frankish building (the oldest Frankish structure)
4 Byzantine corner towers
5 Frankish living apartments
6 Remains of horseshoe-shaped Byzantine tower
7 Forecourt

Mediterranean

NW Tower (16th c.)

Entrance

NE Tower (13th c.)

Moat

Courtyard

SW Tower (16th c.)

SE Tower (16th c.)

50 m

© Baedeker

in the 10th century. The Lusignans made great changes in the structure, and the north and east wings were completely rebuilt. The Venetians reinforced the castle still further by building stronger towers. In 1570 it passed into the hands of the Turks. During the period of British colonial rule it was used as a prison. In 1959 it was assigned to the Department of Antiquities, and it now houses the Shipwreck Museum (see entry).

The castle, roughly square in plan, is flanked by three large corner towers. Within the castle are some remains of its Byzantine predecessor, a rectangular structure with small round towers. A 12th century Byzantine chapel dedicated to Ayios Yeóryios (St George) has also been preserved. Behind this is a large circular bastion built by the Venetians. From the Frankish period dates the guard-room in the western range of buildings, which now contains the tomb of Sadık Paşa, commander of the Turkish fleet, who was killed in 1570. There are fine views of the harbour and the hills from the walls, which mostly date from the Frankish period.

On the east side of the castle is a range of Frankish living apartments, two of the apartments are now occupied by the Shipwreck Museum (see entry). From the wall at the south end there is a view down into the courtyard, at the south-east corner of which can be seen the remains of a horseshoe-shaped Byzantine tower.

The castle

In the Shipwreck Museum, which was opened in 1976, are displayed the remains of an ancient cargo-ship of the 4th century B.C. with its complete cargo. A series of photographs document the recovery of the ship by a team of American archaeologists in 1968. The wreck, lying 1.5km/1 mile off the coast at a depth of 33m/110ft, was discovered by a sponge-diver. It is one of the oldest wrecks ever found in the Mediterranean. The archaeologists were able to trace the course of the ship's voyage, from Samos by way of Kos and Rhodes to Cyprus. The ship, which was 80 years old when it went down, was 14m/45ft long, built of timber from Aleppo pines, using copper nails. The cargo included over 400 amphoras, 29 millstones and

Shipwreck Museum

Kyrenia Castle, with the Shipwreck Museum

numbers of jars containing almonds. Among the other objects found were four wooden spoons and cups, suggesting that the vessel had a crew of only four men, who lived on the fish they caught and the almonds they carried with them.

In the early 1960s a group of archaeologists from Texas built an exact replica of the ship, "Kyrenia II", which in 1986 sailed along the coasts of Cyprus.

Museum of Folk Art

On the harbour is the Museum of Folk Art (open: Mon.–Sat. 8am–1pm and 3–5pm), in a traditional Cypriot house of the 18th century. The basement, which is divided into two by an arch, originally served as a barn and a granary. On the first floor are displayed agricultural and domestic equipment, including oil-presses, ploughs and weaving looms; on the second floor is the old living room; and on the third floor is a display of crochet work and embroidery.

Cafer Paşa Mosque

In the street immediately behind the harbour front is a mosque built by Cafer Paşa in 1580 and restored in the 1970s. The minaret is a picturesque landmark on the town's skyline.

Fine Arts Museum

To the west, a little way from the town centre, can be found the Museum of Art (open: Mon.–Sat. 8am–1pm and 2–5pm), with a collection of European paintings, Chinese and European porcelain and needlework from the Far East.

Byzantine harbour

A road which goes off on the left from the Famagusta road just before the hospital leads to an ancient quarry and the Byzantine harbour (beyond which is the new naval harbour). Here can be seen remains of dressed stones and a rock-cut Byzantine chapel.

Remains of the ancient ship   *Oil-press in Museum of Folk Art*

Surroundings of Kyrenia

10km/6 miles east of Kyrenia is Ayios Epíktitos/Catalköy. In the Club Acapulco holiday village is a Neolithic settlement excavated by British archaeologists in 1969–73.

Ayios Epíktitos

Farther east a road branches off the coast road on the right shortly before Ayios Amvrósios/Esentepe and runs south to the ruined Armenian monastery of Sourp Magar (alt. 500m/1650ft; 35km/22 miles from Kyrenia). The monastery, dedicated to the 4th century hermit Makarios, was founded by Copts in the 12th century and taken over by the Armenians in the 15th century. In the 19th century it became a place of refuge and an orphanage for the Armenian community in Turkey. The present church dates from that period. The monastery is still a favourite place of pilgrimage for Armenians living in Cyprus.

Sourp Magar monastery

From Ayios Amvrósios a road goes south-east to the beautifully situated Antiphonitis monastery (30km/19 miles from Kyrenia), now abandoned, which dates from the 12th century. The church is the last surviving example in Cyprus of the type with a dome carried on corner squinches, i.e. on an octagonal base. The narthex was added in the 14th century, the loggia on the south side in the 15th. There are some remains of the wall paintings with which the walls were once covered.

Antiphonitis monastery

10km/6 miles south-west of Kyrenia lies the pretty village of Kármi/Karaman. Mainly consisting of new houses, it is a holiday resort and retirement retreat for many British people. Just before the village are the excavations of a Bronze Age cemetery of chamber tombs.

Kármi/ Karaman

8km/5 miles west of Kyrenia on the Mórphou road, on the right, is the Peace and Freedom Museum. In the courtyard of the museum are military vehicles and armour captured from Greek Cypriot troops. The museum itself

Peace and Freedom Museum

displays a series of photographs illustrating the intervention of Turkish troops in 1974 and commemorating those who fell. Unfortunately all the labels and explanations are in Turkish.

A short distance farther along the road is the monumental concrete Peace Memorial, commemorating the Turkish intervention on July 20th 1974.

Lamboúsa

10km/6 miles west of Kyrenia, at the village of Karavás/Alsancak, are the excavated remains of ancient Lamboúsa, which lie in a closed military area and cannot be visited. In the 8th century B.C. Lamboúsa was a splendid royal capital. In early Christian times it was a place of considerable importance, the see of one of the leading Cypriot bishops, but in the 7th century it was destroyed by the Arabs. Here in the 1960s was found the famous hoard of early Christian silver, part of which can now be seen in the Archaeologial Museum in Nicosia (see Sights in South Cyprus, Nicosia).

Lápithos

A few kilometres inland from Lamboúsa is Lápithos/Lapta, the site of an ancient city founded in Achaean times where there is said to have been a sanctuary of Aphrodite. Excavations have brought to light geometrically shaped tombs.

Mórphou/Güzelyurt   D 5/6

Altitude: sea level. Population: 12,000

Situation and characteristics

The little town of Mórphou, which means "beautiful country" in Turkish, lies 50km/30 miles from Kyrenia at the western tip of the Turkish part of Cyprus, in a fertile alluvial plain bordering the wide sweep of Mórphou Bay. The town's economy depends mainly on the huge plantations of citrus

Church of St Mamas, now a Museum of Greek Orthodox Art

fruits which surround it. The agricultural development of this area began in the Frankish period, when the Lusignans promoted the growing of sugar-cane and cotton.

Until 1974 the mines at Skouriótissa and Mavrovouní also made a contribution to the town's economy, producing copper, iron ore and pyrites. Nowadays the soft drinks industry is of some importance.

The Mórphou plain was first settled during the Bronze Age. Material recovered by excavation in this area suggest that it was occupied by incomers from western Anatolia. Down the centuries Mórphou Bay always played an important part in the economy. The town established here, however, never developed into a large city-kingdom, no doubt because it was overshadowed by its powerful neighbour, Sóloi/Soli.

History

Sights

The church of St Mamas (key in adjoining Archaeological Museum) was built in the 18th century, the successor to earlier Byzantine and Frankish churches and probably also to an ancient temple of Aphrodite. Since 1974 it has been a Museum of Greek Orthodox Art.

Church of St Mamas

The interior of the church, which is three-aisled, with a high dome, incorporates fragments of Gothic work. The columns in the nave have Gothic ornament, and the two small marble columns in the west window and the tomb of St Mamas are other relics of the medieval building. The north and south doorways also show Gothic features.

Interior

The carving on the iconostasis is 17th century work, and in the lower part is finely carved relief decoration of the Venetian period (16th c.). The royal doors in the centre of the iconostasis are flanked by two small marble columns with Gothic capitals. On the columns at the east end of the nave are paintings of SS Peter and Paul.

On the north wall, under a Gothic arch, is the Byzantine sarcophagus of St Mamas, and above it is a series of painted scenes from his legend. The story they tell is that the saint's sarcophagus was washed ashore in Mórphou Bay, found by a peasant and, in accordance with instructions given in a vision, taken to a particular spot where a monastery was built in the saint's honour.

St Mamas, one of the saints most venerated in Cyprus, gained the reputation of a "tax rebel" and now ranks as the patron saint of tax-evaders. He is said to have lived as a hermit in a cave near Mórphou. The Byzantine governor called on him to pay his taxes, and when Mamas refused he sent two soldiers to bring him to the capital, Nicosia. On the way there they encountered a lion, which Mamas tamed, and he then rode into the town on the lion. The governor was so impressed that he exempted Mamas from payment of any taxes in future.

Legend of St Mamas

The former residence of the Orthodox bishop of Mórphou is now occupied by the small Museum of Archaeology and Natural History (open: daily 8am–6pm). The ground floor is mainly devoted to natural history, with a collection of stuffed animals, including many species of birds, fishes, turtles and tortoises, snakes and foxes.

Museum of Archaeology and Natural History

On the upper floor are pre-Christian antiquities from private collections, including material from the excavation of a Bronze Age settlement at Toúmba tou Skoúrou (near Mórphou), pottery of the Bronze Age and the Geometric and Archaic periods, idols and Hellenistic and Roman oil lamps, as well as Byzantine pottery. The most interesting exhibit is a statuette of

Museum of Archaeology and Natural History, Mórphou

the Ephesian Artemis – with her numerous breasts evidently a fertility symbol – which was recovered from the sea off Sálamis in 1980.

Surroundings of Mórphou

Ayía Iríni/
Akdeniz

23km/14 miles north of Mórphou are the excavations of Ayía Iríni/Akdeniz. The site (in an area which is sometimes closed to the public on military grounds) is reached by turning off the main road to Kyrenia at Dhióris/Tepebaşı into a minor road heading towards the coast.

In a sanctuary on this site were found 2000 terracotta figures of varying size dating from the Archaic period, some of which can now be seen in the Archaeological Museum in Nicosia (see Sights in South Cyprus, Nicosia).

Mýrtou-Pighádes

15km/9 miles north-east of Mórphou is the Bronze Age shrine of Mýrtou-Pighádes, which is reached by taking a road on the right 1km/¾ mile beyond Mýrtou/Çamlıbel. Here in a courtyard can be seen a stone altar with large bulls' horns. Evidence was found of connections with Minoan Crete during this period, so it seems likely that the bull cult was taken over from there.

Philiá/
Serhadköy

At Philiá, 10km/6 miles east of Mórphou, are the excavated remains of an Early Bronze Age settlement. Pottery found here pointed to connections with western Anatolia. This is regarded by archaeologists as a site of particular importance in the chronology of early Cypriot cultures.

Sóloi/Soli

See entry

Vouní/Bademlıköy

See entry

Kyrenia Gate

Nicosia/Lefkoşa   D/E 7/8

Altitude: 165m/540ft. Population: 45,000

On the situation and importance of Nicosia, the Green Line through the
divided city, the frontier crossing point, the history of the city and the
Venetian walls (see Sights in South Cyprus, Nicosia).
    The Turkish part of Nicosia can be reached either by way of the frontier
crossing point at the old Ledra Palace Hotel (see Practical Information on
South Cyprus, Frontier Crossing) or by travelling direct to North Cyprus by
way of Turkey.

Situation and
★importance

Sights in Northern Nicosia

The Kyrenia Gate, formerly known as the Porta del Provveditore, is a short
distance from the frontier crossing point along Selim II Street. The gate,
built in the 16th century at the same time as the walls, is the most northerly
of the three original gates. The square tower on top of the gate was added
during restoration work in 1821. During the British colonial period the
central opening was closed and traffic was directed to left and right of the
gate.

Kyrenia Gate

At the near end of Girne Caddesi (Kyrenia Street), which runs south from
the Kyrenia Gate, is the Museum of Turkish Folk Art (open: Mon.–Sat.
8am–1pm and 2–5pm), which since 1963 has been housed in the former
monastery (tekke) of the Whirling Dervişhes. The order of Whirling Dervişhes, founded in the 13th century by Mevlâna Jelâleddin Rumi (1202–73),
was banned by Kemal Atatürk in 1925 on account of its reactionary views.
The dervishes sought by dancing and singing to achieve a state of ecstasy
which would bring them closer to Allah. In the former prayer hall are

Mevlevi Tekke/
Museum of
Turkish
Folk Art

View of Nicosia from the south

displayed traditional dervish costumes and musical instruments (red flutes, small drums, etc.), precious fabrics, pewterware, furniture and illustrated manuscripts of the Koran. In a long corridor roofed with domes are sixteen completely identical sarcophagi belonging to leaders of the dervish community. In the courtyard are Ottoman gravestones.

Venetian Column

Girne Caddesi leads into Atatürk Square, in the centre of which stands the tall Venetian Column. This grey granite column was brought to Nicosia from ancient Sálamis in the 16th century, set up on a hexagonal base and decorated with the coats of arms of leading Venetian families. The Lion of St Mark which originally topped the column was replaced during the British colonial period by a copper globe.

Sarayönü Mosque

To the west of the Venetian Column, beyond a row of houses, can be seen the minaret of the Moorish-style Sarayönü Mosque, built in 1820, in the time of Ali Paşa, as a prayer hall for the Turkish governors. At the beginning of the 20th century, after its destruction in an earthquake, it was restored by a British architect. The interior has horseshoe arches in stones of different colours. Since 1964 the mosque has been used only for marriages.

Ground-plan of Sarayönü Mosque

© Baedeker

Arab Ahmet Mosque

From Atatürk Square, Sarayönü Street to the right, runs into Mahumet Paşa Street. Along this street to the left is the Arab Ahmet Mosque, built in the

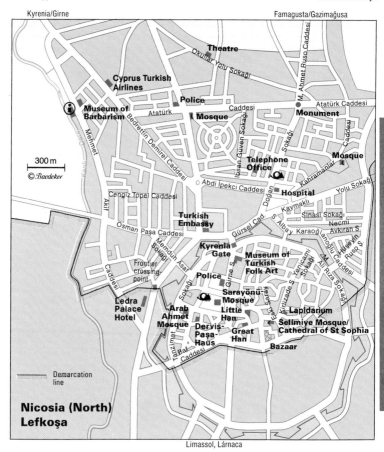

Kyrenia/Girne   Famagusta/Gazimağusa

Nicosia (North)
Lefkoşa

Demarcation line

Limassol, Lárnaca

17th century in honour of Arab Ahmet, a general who had distinguished himself during the conquest of Cyprus in the 16th century. The mosque, which was restored in 1845, is the only domed mosque in Nicosia. It is set in beautiful gardens, originally an Islamic cemetery. It contains a number of historic tombs, including that of Grand Vizier Kamil Paşa (1833–1913), the only Cypriot to attain that rank.

From here Salahi Sevket Street joins Beliğ Paşa Street, along which to the left is the recently restored House of Derviş Paşa (open: Mon.–Sat. 8am–1pm and 2–5pm). This 19th century mansion in what was formerly the Armenian quarter of the town was built by Derviş Paşa, publisher of the first Turkish Cypriot newspaper, "Zaman" ("The Times"), which began to appear in December 1891.

House of Derviş Paşa Ethnographic Museum

This two-storey house is in a style typical of the houses of well-to-do Turkish families in the 19th century. The ground floor is built in stone, the

239

upper floor in sun-dried brick. The ground floor rooms, with the servants' quarters and the kitchen, open off the central courtyard; they now display domestic equipment, porcelain and weaving looms. The decoration and furnishings of the family rooms on the upper floor, including the bride's room, the bedrooms and the dining room, have been preserved in their original condition, and with their display of costumes and fabrics give an interesting picture of Turkish life in the 19th century.

★Büyük Han
(Great Han)

From Beliğ Paşa Street Kyrenia Street (Girne Caddesi) leads to Arasta Street, in which is the Büyük Han (Great Han), an old caravanserai. Built by Mustafa Paşa in the 16th century, it provided accommodation for travelling merchants. In the 19th century, under British colonial rule, it was used as a prison, and was later occupied by poor Turkish families. Its most striking features are the octagonal chimneys. In the centre of the spacious inner courtyard is a small Islamic chapel (*mescit*), a prayer hall for the merchants. On the ground floor were stables and store-rooms, on the upper floor living rooms and bedrooms.

The building is at present being restored to house a Museum of Turkish and Islamic Art.

Büyük Hamam
(Great Baths)

In a narrow side street off Asma Altı Street is the Büyük Hamam (Great Baths). The entrance to this Turkish bath-house, which is still in use, is through the doorway of the 14th century Gothic church of St George of the Latins, which stood in the old market square but after the conquest of Cyprus gave place to Turkish buildings. The doorway has delicate sculptural decoration of high quality.

Kumarcılar Han
(Little Han)

On the right-hand side of Asma Altı Street is the 17th century Kumarcılar Han ("Gamblers' Han") or Little Han, now occupied by the Turkish Cypriot Office of Antiquities. It is laid out round a courtyard with a lawn surrounded by flower-beds. The former guest rooms are on the upper floor.

Little Han, now occupied by the Office of Antiquities

Cathedral of St Sophia

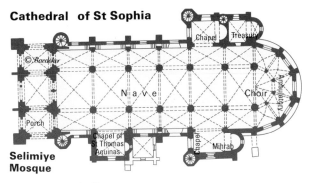

Selimiye
Mosque

Asma Altı Street runs into Arasta Street, which leads direct to the former
Cathedral of St Sophia, now the Selimiye Mosque. The largest Gothic
church in Cyprus, in which the Lusignan kings were crowned, it was built in
the 13th century on the remains of an earlier church. The foundation stone
was laid in 1209 by Alice de Champagne, wife of King Hugo I, and the
church was consecrated in 1326; the west front was completed only in the
mid 14th century. In the 15th century the church was pillaged by raiding
Mamelukes and damaged by earthquakes.

★★ Cathedral of
St Sophia/
Selimiye Mosque

After the Turkish conquest in 1571 the cathedral was converted into the
Aya Sofya Mosque. The unfinished west towers were topped by minarets,
the Gothic sculpture was removed and the paintings in the interior covered
with whitewash. The medieval gravestones set into the floor are now
covered by carpets, and a mihrab (prayer niche) marks the direction of
Mecca. The mosque was renamed the Selimiye in 1945 in honour of Selim
II, Sultan at the time of the conquest of Cyprus.

This three-aisled basilica, measuring 66m/217ft by 38m/125ft, is rather
squat in appearance, but in architectural structure is reminiscent of the
French Gothic cathedrals. Like Reims and Amiens Cathedrals, it has an
ambulatory round the choir, but it lacks the ring of choir chapels, the
transept and the triforium of the French cathedrals.

The church

The groined vaulting of the nave is borne on large round columns. The
ribs of the vaulting end at the imposts of the columns and are not carried
down to the ground in the usual manner of the French cathedrals. In the
polygonal apse are four antique columns. The clerestory has large quadri-
partite windows.

In the second bay on the south side is the Chapel of St Thomas Aquinas,
who dedicated his work "Of the Rule of Princes" to one of the Lusignan
kings. The porch at the west end of the church, with its slender columns and
beautiful capitals, is wholly in line with French models. Here can be seen
the remains of figures of kings and saints destroyed by the various con-
querors. Over the porch is a gallery on which kings and great personages
received the homage of the people.

The nave and aisles have the flat roofs typical of Cyprus. Great buttresses
help to withstand the thrust of the vaulting and the walls.

The custodian of the Bedesten, the Ottoman Library, the Lapidarium and
St Catherine's Church can be found in a small room adjoining the Library or
in the Office of Antiquities in the Little Han.

To the south of the Selimiye Mosque are the ruins of the Bedesten (Covered
Market), originally the church of St Nicholas of the English, which shows
both Byzantine and Gothic features. Of the original church built in the 12th
century there survive the two aisles on the south side and wall paintings
depicting St Andrew. In the 14th century the church was enlarged. A north

Bedesten

Cathedral of St Sophia, now the Selimiye Mosque

aisle was added, the nave was reroofed with a dome borne on a drum, the choir was extended by a five-sided apse and the large and richly decorated doorway on the north side was surmounted by a pointed pediment. Over the doorway are a statue of a saint and six coats of arms added in the Venetian period. On a small subsidiary doorway is a relief of the Dormition of the Virgin.

The church contains medieval gravestones and reliefs. During the period of Venetian rule it was the seat of an Orthodox bishop. In the Turkish period it was used as a grain store and later as a cloth market. Facing the church on the south side is the present-day market hall.

Archbishop's Palace

On the north side of the Selimiye Mosque stands the former palace of the Roman Catholic archbishop, built in 1329, which was connected with the cathedral of St Sophia by an underground tunnel. After the Turkish conquest the upper floor was rebuilt in Turkish style. In 1821 it became the official residence of the Turkish governor, and during the British colonial period it was used as a school. It is now the headquarters of the Association of Turkish Cypriot Municipaliities.

Chapterhouse

At the south-east corner of the mosque the medieval chapterhouse now houses a collection of firearms and Turkish gravestones.

Ottoman Library

To the east of the mosque can be found the Ottoman Library, built in 1829 in honour of Sultan Mahmut II (1784–1839), which has a valuable collection of old Turkish, Persian and Arabic books and manuscripts (open: Mon.–Sat. 8am–1pm and 2–5pm). Many of its treasures came from the palace library in Istanbul. Above the bookcases, in gold letters, is a poem by the Mufti of Cyprus, Hilmi Effendi, addressed to the Sultan.

★Lapidarium

50m/55yd east of the mosque is the Lapidarium, also known as Jeffery's Museum after its founder. Housed in a 15th century Venetian building, this

Lion of St Mark, in the Lapidarium

lapidary museum displays a collection of medieval architectural fragments, gravestones and furniture. A large Late Gothic traceried window is said to have come from the palace of the Lusignan kings. Of particular interest are a sarcophagus of the Dampierre family and the gravestone of the Frankish general Adam of Antioch.

From the Lapidarium Kirlizade Street leads to the church of St Catherine, the most important Gothic church in Nicosia after the cathedral of St Sophia. Built in the 14th century, it probably belonged originally to a monastery. This narrow church has an aisleless nave with delicate groined vaulting and a triangular apse. After the Turkish conquest in 1571 it was converted into a mosque (named after a noted Turkish general) and equipped with a minaret.

St Catherine's Church/Haydar Paşa Mosque

Outside the Venetian walls, in Mehmet Akif Street (the road to Kyrenia), is the Museum of Barbarism (open: Mon.–Sat. 8am–1pm and 2–5pm). The museum occupies an old Turkish house in which the wife and three children of a Turkish doctor and officer, Nihat Ilhan, were murdered in December 1963 by Greek EOKA/B fighters. Photographs document the atrocities committed by Greeks during the Cypriot civil war in the 1960s.

Museum of Barbarism

Surroundings of Nicosia

15km/9 miles north-east of Nicosia, near the road to Famagusta, is the town of Kythréa/Değirmenlik, on the site of ancient Chytri, which according to legend was founded in the 12th century B.C. by Chytros, son of Akamas. Excavations here brought to light a Bronze Age necropolis and slight remains of the acropolis and a temple of Aphrodite. The finding of a bronze statue of the Emperor Septimius Severus (see Sights of South Cyprus,

Kythréa

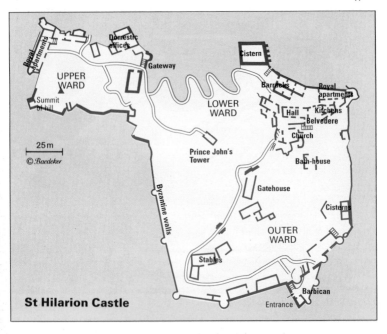

St Hilarion Castle

Nicosia, Archaeological Museum) shows that the site was continuously occupied into the Roman imperial period.

Nearby is the spring of Kephalovryson, from which a 60km/37 mile long aqueduct carried water to ancient Sálamis.

St Hilarion Castle   D 7

Altitude: 721m/2366ft

★Situation and characteristics

St Hilarion Castle (open: daily 8am–5pm) is reached from Kyrenia by taking the new road to Nicosia and turning into a road on the right shortly before the summit of the pass (11km/7 miles). The road runs through a military area in which photography is forbidden.

St Hilarion, the most westerly and the best preserved of the castles in the Beşparmak Hills, is perched on a rocky crag with twin peaks, affording magnificent views of the hills, extending down to Kyrenia on the coast. The ruins bear witness to the one-time splendour of this "castle of the thousand rooms", as it is popularly known.

History

Foundation

The castle is named after St Hilarion, a 6th century Syrian hermit who spent the last years of his life in a cave in the Beşparmak Hills. A chapel was built in his honour and then, in the 10th century, a monastery. In the 11th century the Byzantines built a castle on the site, into which they incorporated the monastic buildings; remains of the 10th century church can still be seen. Under the Lusignan kings the castle was strongly fortified and was given the name of Dieu d'Amour, a garbling of the Greek word *Didymoi* ("Twins") – referring to the twin peaks of the hill.

Ruins of St Hilarion Castle   *The castle gateway*

In the 13th century the castle played an important part during the conflict between the Cypriot nobility and the Emperor Frederick II, who claimed possession of the island. Frederick's forces withdrew to the castle but in 1232, after a long siege, were obliged to surrender it to the Lusignans, who thereafter made it their summer residence.

Frankish rule

In the 14th century St Hilarion was again involved in a conflict for control of Cyprus. When the Lusignan king Peter I died in 1369 his son Peter was not recognised as his successor by the nobility, who preferred his uncle, Prince John of Antioch. Peter I's widow Eleanor of Aragon mustered her forces against Prince John, who sought safety in St Hilarion. Then, doubtful of the loyalty of his own Bulgarian bodyguard, he had them thrown from a tower of the castle to their death. Finally, however, he lost the struggle for the throne, and Peter II succeeded his father.

The present ruins date mainly from a further rebuilding of the castle in 1391. In Venetian times St Hilarion was abandoned.

Sights

The castle is in three sections: the outer, lower and upper wards. The outer ward is entered through a double gateway with a barbican, from which a stepped path leads up to the outer ward, passing a large cistern, stables and living quarters for the garrison.

Outer ward

Passing through a gatehouse, once approached by a drawbridge, we enter the lower ward. Beyond this is the 10th century Byzantine church which is the only relic of the former monastery. The church originally had a dome carried on corner squinches, i.e. on an octagonal base. To the north of the church are steps leading down to a large hall, probably the former refectory. To the east is the Belvedere, a vaulted loggia. Adjoining this are the

Lower ward

apartments in which the royal family lived before the completion of the upper ward.

Prince John's Tower

To the left of the path leading to the upper ward, standing by itself, is Prince John's Tower, from which John of Antioch is said to have had his body-guard thrown to their death.

Upper ward

The upper ward, entered through an arched gateway, had a double ring of fortifications. To the north are domestic offices, to the west the royal apartments. The richly traceried Gothic windows with their stone benches give some idea of the former splendour of these rooms. From the "Queen's Window" on the west side there is a superb view of the surrounding area.

Sálamis   D 11

Situation and ★★importance

8km/5 miles north of Famagusta, on the coast, are the excavations of ancient Sálamis, once the most important city-kingdom on the island (open: daily 8am–7pm, in winter to 5pm). There are two entrances to the site, one on the main road, the other on the seaward side. The various features of interest can be seen by car.

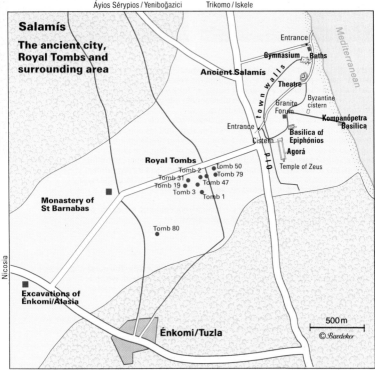

Palaestra, Sálamis

The city of Sálamis is said to have been founded in the 12th century B.C. by   **History**
Teukros (Teucer), a hero of the Trojan War, son of the Greek king Telamon of
Sálamis. In the 11th century Sálamis took the place of the neighbouring city
of Alasia (see Surroundings of Sálamis), which was destroyed in an earthquake, and thereafter became, economically and politically, one of the
leading cities in Cyprus, with a population in its heyday of 100,000. It owed
its predominance to its excellent situation in a large bay within easy reach
of the East and to the quality of its kings.

In the 8th century B.C. Sálamis was the most powerful city-kingdom in
Cyprus, with trading contacts with Cilicia, the Phoenicians and Egypt.
Outside the city was a large necropolis. At the end of the 8th century,
however, Sálamis together with the rest of Cyprus was compelled to pay
tribute to Assyria. Under Egyptian rule Sálamis became predominant over
the other city kingdoms. The first coins minted in Cyprus were issued by
King Euelthon of Sálamis (560–525). During the struggle between the
Greeks and the Persians there were repeated rebellions in Sálamis. The
expansionist urge of King Euagoras I in the 5th century B.C. brought Sálamis into conflict with the Persians, but in 323 B.C., with the help of Alexander the Great, the city broke free from Persian control.

In the Ptolemaic period the city-kingdoms of Cyprus were dissolved, and
thereafter Sálamis lost its predominant position to Páphos. In the 4th
century A.D. the city, now largely Christianised, was devastated by an
earthquake and a tidal wave, after which it was rebuilt and renamed Constantia. In the early 5th century Constantia became capital of the island.
Then in the 7th century, after continuing Arab raids, the town was abandoned and the new city of Ammóchostos (later Famagusta) was founded a
few kilometres to the south.
    The surviving remains of ancient Sálamis date mainly from late antiquity
and the Byzantine period.

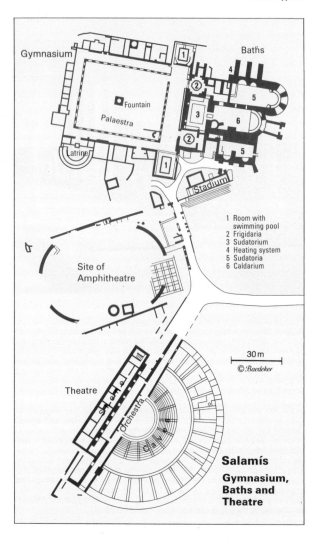

1 Room with
  swimming pool
2 Frigidaria
3 Sudatorium
4 Heating system
5 Sudatoria
6 Caldarium

30 m
© Baedeker

Salamís

**Gymnasium,
Baths and
Theatre**

Sights

To the right of the seaward entrance to the site are the gymnasium and the
baths.

Gymnasium

The gymnasium, which was discovered in 1882, dates from the 4th century
A.D. It replaced an earlier building destroyed in the earthquake.

In ancient times this was a place of both physical and intellectual training.
Physical exercises were practised in the palaestra, an open court, originally
sanded, measuring 53.5m/176ft by 39.5m/130ft. In the centre was a foun-

tain basin, and later also a statue. Round the court were four porticoes, off which opened various rooms – changing rooms, work rooms and other rooms in which philosophical conversations and discussions were held. At both ends of the east portico were pavilion-like annexes containing rectangular pools.

At the south-west corner of the Gymnasium is a communal latrine with 44 seats. In Roman times the latrine had a clear view of the palaestra, but in the Christian period it was closed off by a wall.

Latrine

The annexes to the east portico house a small museum displaying sculpture found during the excavations. Some of the antique statues lack their heads, struck off in Christian times.

Museum

From the east portico we enter the baths. The first room is one of the two frigidaria (cold baths), with an octagonal pool in the centre. Between this and the other frigidarium is the sudatorium (sweat-bath), with a recess containing a painting which shows Hylas, Heracles' companion, raising his spear against a water nymph.

Baths

To the east of this is the caldarium (hot room), with remains of the hypocaust (heating system) and a number of small basins. To right and left of the caldarium are two other sudatoria.
    In the southern sudatorium are remains of a mosaic showing Apollo and Artemis killing Niobe's children. Another mosaic depicts the old river god Eurotas watching Zeus approaching Leda in the form of a swan.
    South-east of the gymnasium was the stadium, of which some remains of the seating survive. In a depression between the gymnasium and the theatre is the site of the amphitheatre.

The theatre, built in Augustan times, was badly damaged in the 4th century earthquake and thereafter was used as a quarry of building stone. It was restored in the 1960s. It was one of the largest theatres in the Mediterranean area, with seating for 17,000 spectators.
    In the semicircular orchestra was a small altar on which offerings were made before a performance. The cavea, originally 20m/65ft high, had 50 tiers of seating, divided by stairways into nine segments. The stage wall was originally 40m/130ft long and decorated with paintings.

Theatre

In this area also was the forum, the city's market square and meeting-place, which was completely destroyed in the earthquake. The columns of pink Egyptian granite lying about the site give some indication of its former splendour.

Granite Forum

To the south of the forum is the Basilica of Epiphánios, the largest basilica in Cyprus (58m/190ft by 42m/138ft), which dates from the end of the 4th century A.D. It is named after St Epiphánios, bishop of Sálamis in the 4th century. The ground-plan is seven-aisled, with two very narrow outer aisles. In the central apse are the remains of the benches for the clergy. At the east end of the south aisles is another small church, probably of the 7th century. Under this was found a tomb, presumably that of Bishop Euphánios. In the 7th century a wall was built round the church and the adjoining residential area for protection against Arab raids. The basilica remained in use into the Middle Ages.

Basilica of
Epiphánios

Farther along the road is a cistern, the largest such structure of the Byzantine period in Cyprus. Three rows of columns originally supported a vaulted roof. An aqueduct brought water from the Beşparmak Hills to a tank on the city walls, from which it was piped to the cistern, which was half above and half below ground level.

Cistern

Adjoining the cistern is the Agora or Stone Forum, built in the Augustan period – one of the largest forums in the Roman world (55m/180ft by

Agora
(Stone Forum)

228m/750ft). On the north side was a long colonnaded portico, which was
originally lined with shops.

Temple of Zeus

On the south side of the Agora was the temple of Zeus, a small podium
temple which was presumably dedicated to Zeus Salaminios. It was
approached by a broad flight of steps and surrounded by colonnades. The
slight remains of the podium date from the Augustan period.

Kampanópetra Basilica

Unusually, the Kampanópetra Basilica (open: daily 8am–5pm) has two
atria (forecourts). The larger of the two is at the west end, leading into the
narthex, which has an apse at each end. The smaller atrium at the east end
opens on to the seashore. In the west atrium is an octagonal fountain for
ritual ablutions before services. Flanking the lateral aisles of the basilica are
katekhouména for the catechumens, the unbaptised members of the
community.

★Royal Tombs

Situation and characteristics

The Royal Tombs (open: daily 8am–4pm) lie a few hundred metres west of
Sálamis on the road to the monastery of St Barnabas. The ticket kiosk is on
a side road to the left.

The necropolis of Sálamis, the largest cemetery area on the island,
extending for a total length of 5.2km/3¼ miles, dates from the 7th/6th
century B.C. In this area the kings and nobles of Sálamis were buried in
underground chambers, some of which have been preserved.

All the tombs are of the same type. A long walled dromos (entrance
passage) ran down to the tomb, widening as it approached the entrance.
From the end of the dromos steps led down to the propylon, a paved
forecourt on the far side of which was the doorway of the tomb chamber.
After the burial the dromos was filled in and a mound was built up over the
grave.

The rich grave goods found in the tombs, as well as demonstrating the
wealth of their owners, yielded information on burial rites. In the forecourt
of several graves were the skeletons of horses and human skeletons,
suggesting that the dead man's servants were sometimes sacrificed as well
as his horses. Beside the skeletons were items of harness, a chariot and
vessels filled with food for the dead man. Many of the grave goods show
Assyrian or Egyptian influence.

Tomb 50 (reconstruction)

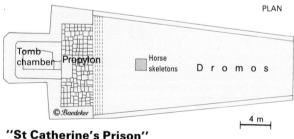

"St Catherine's Prison"

Tomb 50, "St Catherine's Prison"

The finest of the tombs is No. 79, in which were found horse skeletons, remains of chariots, two thrones decorated with ivory, a bed 1.89m/6ft 2in. long by 1.11m/3ft 8in. wide and two bronze cauldrons with animal protomes in Egyptian style – all now in the Archaeological Museum in Nicosia (see Sights in South Cyprus, Nicosia).

Tomb 79

Lying near the road is Tomb 50, known as St Catherine's Prison, its vaulted roof (added in Roman times over the original gabled roof) visible from a long way off. It was used in early Christian times as a prison, and seems later to have been a chapel dedicated to St Catherine: hence its name.

Tomb 50

Tomb 3, on the other side of the access road, is covered with a high tumulus which attracted 19th century tomb-robbers. It is approached by a dromos 24.60m/81ft long and 5.20m/17ft wide, lined by walls of sun-dried brick. The tomb chamber itself is built of dressed stone. Here too were found horse skeletons and the remains of chariots. Traces of a funeral pyre on the floor of the dromos point to a fire burial.

Tomb 3

Near the royal tombs is the Cellarka complex of simple shaft tombs belonging to humbler members of the community. Something like a hundred of these tombs, which lie just below the surface of the ground and have short dromoi, have been excavated. Many are evidently family tombs, separated from their neighbours only by a low wall.

Cellarka tombs

Surroundings of Sálamis

Monastery of St Barnabas

2km/1¼ miles west of the Sálamis excavations lies the former Monastery of St Barnabas (open: daily 8am–4pm). In 1992 the church was restored, the

Situation and characteristics

altar rebuilt and the interior walls decorated with icons. Around the inner courtyard in the former communal rooms of the monastery there is an archaeological museum (with among other things, finds from Sálamis).

Legend of St Barnabas	St Barnabas is the patron saint of Cyprus. A native of the island, he sailed to Cyprus with the apostle Paul and helped him in his missionary activity. During a later visit to Cyprus he was stoned to death near Sálamis by the Jews. He was buried by a companion, but the place of his burial remained unknown until the 5th century, when Archbishop Anthemios of Cyprus, guided by a vision, found the saint's tomb and thus enabled the Church of Cyprus to attain autocephaly (see Facts and Figures, Religion).

The monastery The monastery built over the saint's tomb in the 5th century was destroyed by the Arabs. A new multi-domed church was built in the 10th century, and its ground-plan is preserved in the present church, built in 1756. The bell-tower was added this century.

Interior The chapel to the right of the apse has modern wall paintings depicting the finding of the saint's tomb in four sequences: from left to right Anthemios's dream, the finding of the tomb and the Gospel which it contained, Anthemios presenting the Gospel to Emperor Zeno, the recognition of the Church of Cyprus as autocephalous and the presentation of the new privileges. On the walls of the church, which is otherwise without sculptural decoration, are antique capitals.

Burial chapel Separate from the church is a modern chapel containing the tomb of St Barnabas (key from custodian of monastery).

Alasia (Énkomi/Tuzla)

Situation and characteristics A few kilometres south of the monastery of St Barnabas (10km/6 miles north-west of Famagusta), near the village of Énkomi/Tuzla, are the excavated remains of ancient Alasia, whose origins go back to the 2nd millennium B.C. The earliest evidence of settlement at Alasia dates from the 17th century B.C., when the town began to grow wealthy through the working and export of copper. Between the 15th and 12th centuries Alasia played an important part as an intermediary in trade between the Middle East and the Aegean, and Minoan merchants, later followed by Mycenaeans, came to Cyprus. Opposite Alasia on the coast of Syria was the city of Ugarit, where excavations have brought to light a Cypriot quarter with goods from Alasia.

Copper-working In its heyday the city was surrounded by walls and had a population of between 10,000 and 15,000. As at Kítion (Lárnaca) there was a close association between cult and copper-working. The smelting ovens lay within the bounds of the city, frequently near temples.

Excavations The excavations have revealed the foundations of the ancient city of the 13th and 12th centuries B.C. A main street traversed the settlement from north to south, with side streets dividing it into separate quarters. Remains of the town walls, dwelling-houses and a number of temples were also discovered. The first excavators found skeletons and rich grave goods: gold jewellery, ivories, bronze and silver objects, pottery and the famous 12th century statue of a horned god now in the Archaeological Museum in Nicosia (see Sights in South Cyprus, Nicosia).

Sóloi/Soli   E 4

Altitude: 30m/100ft

Excavations of ancient Sóloi

Swan mosaic in the early Christian basilica

The excavations of ancient Sóloi (open: daily 8am–6pm, in winter to 5pm) lie on the slopes of a hill above Karavostási ("landing-place", in Turkish: Gemikonağı), which in antiquity was the port of Sóloi. The harbour was used in this century for the shipment of ore from copper-mines at Skouriotissa, which is now on the other side of the Green Line. The disused conveyor belts for loading the ore still reach far out to sea.	Situation

The ancient myth recounts that Sóloi was founded by Akámas, son of Theseus and the lover of Aphrodite. According to Strabo (64/65 B.C.–A.D. 23) the city was rebuilt on its present site about 600 B.C. on the advice of Solon, one of the Seven Sages. In gratitude for this excellent advice King Philokypros named the new city after Solon.

History

Foundation

At the end of the 6th century B.C. Sóloi ranked after Koúrion and Amathoús as one of the leading city-kingdoms on the island. Herodotus (V,115) tells us that the city distinguished itself in repeated rebellions against the Persians. The palace of Vouní (see entry) was built by the pro-Persian king of Márion (Pólis), Doxandros, to give him better control of Sóloi. In Roman times Augustus granted the copper-mines of Sóloi to Herod the Great, king of Judaea, and many Jews came to Sóloi to work in the mines. In the 7th century Sóloi suffered from repeated Arab raids. In spite of this the remains of temples and houses seem to have survived into the 18th century. Thereafter the site was used as a quarry of building stone.

City-kingdom

Excavation of the site began in the 1920s, revealing remains of a Roman theatre and an early Christian basilica.

Excavations

Sights

The theatre of Sóloi (reconstructed), which dates from the 2nd century A.D., is considerably smaller than the theatres of Koúrion and Sálamis. The cavea is 52m/170ft in diameter, the semicircular orchestra 17m/55ft. From the theatre there is a magnificent view of the sea (though in ancient times this would be blocked by the stage wall).

Theatre

Remains of a temple of Aphrodite were found on the hill behind the theatre. A number of cemeteries round the site bear witness to a large population in the Geometric period, continuing into Roman times.

Temple of Aphrodite, cemeteries

The excavations of the site brought to light the famous marble statue, the Aphrodite of Sóloi, which is now one of the principal treasures of the Archaeological Museum in Nicosia (see Sights in South Cyprus, Nicosia).

Aphrodite of Sóloi

At the foot of the hill are the remains of a 5th century Christian basilica, some 30m/100ft long, with three apses at the east end, on the foundations of which a new church was built in the Middle Ages. Excavations in 1966/67 revealed early Christian mosaic pavements which originally covered the whole area of the basilica. A number of representations of animals have survived, including in particular a fine swan.

Early Christian basilica

See entry

Vouní/Bademlıköy

Vouní/Bademlıköy   E 4

Altitude: 255m/835ft

◀ *Monastery of St Barnabas*

Remains of the palace of Vouní

Situation and characteristics

5km/3 miles from Sóloi, at the western tip of North Cyprus, are the remains of the palace of Vouní (open: daily 8am–4pm). A winding road leads up to the top of the hill (*vouní*), from which there are fine views of the coast. The palace, excavated by Swedish archaeologists from 1928 onwards, lies on the highest point of the hill.

History

The palace of Vouní had only a short life. Built in the early 5th century B.C., it was destroyed by fire about 380 B.C. It is believed to have been built by the pro-Persian King Doxandros of Márion to control the pro-Greek city of Sóloi.

Three building phases have been identified, suggesting that the palace was altered and enlarged by different owners at different times. Above the palace are a temple of Athena and treasuries of the 5th century B.C.

Sights

First phase

Approaching the palace from the south, we come into a long room divided into three sections, presumably the entrance hall. From here a flight of steps leads down to a courtyard surrounded on three sides by porticoes. In the centre of the courtyard are the remains of a cistern, with a stele on the east side which would have supported a windlass for raising water.

Around the courtyard are living apartments, some of them originally two-storied. The arrangement is reminiscent of the Persian type of liwan house. To the east are the remains of baths, which are among the oldest to have survived from antiquity.

Second phase

During the second phase various store-rooms were added on the east side of the palace, laid out round a courtyard containing a well.

Palace of Vouní

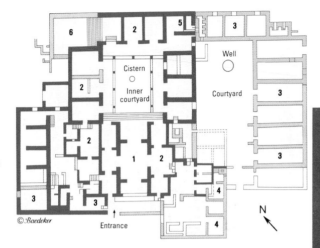

1 Entrance hall
2 Living apartments
3 Domestic offices
4 Kitchens
5 Bath-house
6 New entrance in 3rd phase

 1st phase
2nd phase
3rd phase

© *Baedeker*

In the final phase the original entrance was walled up and a new one built on the north side of the palace, on the pattern of the Greek megaron house.

Third phase

On the southern slopes of the hill (the side opposite the custodian's house) are the remains of a temple of Athena. Here was found the famous Cow of Vouní, a small bronze statuette which is now in the Archaeological Museum in Nicosia (see Sights in South Cyprus, Nicosia).

Temple of Athena

Practical Information from A to Z: South Cyprus

Accommodation

See Camping and Caravanning, Hotels, Youth Hostels

Airlines

21 Alkeos Street, Nicosia;
tel. (02) 44 30 54

Cyprus Airways

203 Archbishop Makarios III Avenue, Limassol;
tel. (05) 37 37 87

37 Gladstone Street, Páphos;
tel. (06) 23 35 56

Lárnaca Airport;
tel. (04) 64 32 88

British Airways

Antiques

Antiques may be exported only with an authorisation from the Ministry of Transport. The export of old icons is prohibited.

The only officially licensed antique dealers are Petros Colocassides, 3 Onasagoras Street, Nicosia; tel. (02) 47 55 21, and Sothebys, Nicosia from whom visitors can buy antiques authorised for export.

Banks

There are both local and international banks in Cyprus. Travellers' cheques, Eurocheques and credit cards are accepted (see Currency).

Banks are open Mon.–Sat. 8.30am–1.30pm. In the larger towns they are frequently open also in the afternoon for the benefit of visitors: May to September 4–6.30pm, October to April 3–5.30pm.

Opening times

Beaches

The coast of Cyprus consists mainly of shingle beaches, small sandy bays and bizarrely shaped cliffs. The most beautiful beaches and the finest sand are in the south-east of the island at Ayía Nápa. The west coast has a mixture of sand and shingle beaches and rocky coasts. A well-known sandy beach is the Lady's Mile Beach to the west of Limassol. Popular bathing beaches are the Ayía Nápa beaches in the south-east and Koúrion Bay and Coral Bay on the west coast. Pólis Bay, in the north-west of the island, has shingle beaches with areas where nude bathing is tolerated. Topless bathing is now allowed on many beaches, particularly hotel beaches.

◀ *Religious procession on the feast of the Epiphany*

The bathing season begins in April and lasts until the end of November. Even in winter the temperature of the water never falls below 16°C/61°F. Water quality is in general excellent.

Many beaches belong to hotels and are closed to non-residents. They are well maintained and equipped with all necessary facilities. On popular beaches not belonging to hotels – including particularly the beaches outside Ayía Nápa and on the coast to the west of Páphos and Pólis – there is usually a restaurant which hires out sun umbrellas and loungers.

The following is a selection of the best known bathing beaches.

Lárnaca	Beach below the seafront promenade (usually overcrowded) Mackenzie Beach, at the airport Beaches to the east of the town (mainly hotel beaches) Cape Kíti, 17km/10½ miles west via Perivólia (sand and shingle)
Limassol	Town (Dassoudi) beach, opposite the Municipal Gardens Lady's Mile Beach, to the south-west, beyond the new harbour (sand and shingle) Governor's Beach, 22km/14 miles east, just beyond the road to Ayios Yeóryios monastery (sand and shingle)
Pissoúri	Pissoúri Beach, a beautiful sandy beach reached from the road to Columbia Pissoúri Beach Hotel
Páphos	Tourist Beach, to the south of the town, a well cared for beach run by the Cyprus Tourism Organisation (can also be reached from Yeroskípos) Timi, a long sandy beach south of Páphos Coral Bay, 10km/6 miles north, a popular bathing beach with tavernas Pétra tou Romíou, 21km/13 miles south, a shingle beach near the Rock of Aphrodite
Pólis	Lakhí, 5km/3 miles west of Pólis, with sand and shingle beaches extending to the Baths of Aphrodite.

Bookshops

Books in Cyprus tend to be expensive. In some of the larger towns there are bookshops with books in English, French and German:

Limassol	K. P. Kypriacou, 57 Anexartisia Street; tel. (05) 3 75 11 A. Ioannides & Co., 30 Athens Street; tel. (05) 36 22 04
Nicosia	MAM (The House of Cyprus Publications), Laïkí Yitoniá; tel. (02) 47 27 44 (archaeology and art) Bridgehouse, Shop 13, Byron Avenue; tel. (02) 44 32 97

Business Hours

Banks	See entry
Chemists	See entry
Government offices	In summer government and local government offices are open Mon.–Fri. 8am–2pm; in winter 7.30am–2.30pm, Thur. 8am–6pm.

In summer, Mon.–Sat. 8am–1pm and 4–7pm; in winter 8am–1pm and   Offices
2.30–5.30pm; closed Wednesday and Saturday afternoons.

See Sights from A to Z   Museums

See Petrol   Petrol stations

See Post, Telephone, Telegraph   Post offices

In summer (May to September) shops are usually open Mon.–Sat.   Shops
8am–1pm and 4–7pm, in winter (October to April) Mon.–Sat. 8am–1pm
and 2.30–5.30pm. Shops are closed on Wednesday and Saturday afternoons and on Sundays.
   In the villages opening times may vary according to the shopkeeper's
habits and moods. Shops are frequently open on Sundays.

See entry   Public holidays

Camping and Caravanning

"Wild" camping is prohibited and those who engage in it risk prosecution.
Official camping and caravanning sites (below) are equipped with sanitary
facilities, shops and tavernas.

Agía Nápa Camping lies to the west of the town.   Ayía Nápa
Open: March to October. Tel. (03) 72 19 46

Forest Beach Camping, 8km/5 miles east on the beach   Lárnaca
Open: April to October. Tel. (04) 62 24 14

Governor's Beach Camping, 20km/12½ miles east   Limassol
Open: throughout the year. Tel. (05) 63 23 00

Feggari Camping, 13km/8 miles north near Coral Bay, at Pegeia   Páphos
Open: throughout the year. Tel. (06) 62 15 34

Yeroskípou Zenon Gardens Camping, 3km/2 miles east of Páphos harbour,   Yeroskípou
east side of Yeroskípou Tourist Beach
Open: April to October. Tel. (06) 24 22 77

Pólis Camping lies in a eucalyptus grove on the beach   Pólis
Open: March to October. Tel. (06) 32 15 26

In a pinewood 2km/1¼ miles from Tróodos Hill Resort on the Kakopetriá   Tróodos
road   Mountains
Open: May to October (weather permitting). Tel. (05) 42 16 24

Car Rental

Since most visitors to Cyprus come by air, a rented car is a good way of
getting around. There are offices or agencies of car rental firms in all the
larger towns and at Lárnaca airport. In addition to the well known international firms (Avis, Hertz, Europcar, Budget) there are numerous local
firms from which cars, motorcycles, mopeds and even bicycles can be
hired.

The driver of a rented car must possess a national driving licence and be at
least 21 years old. The wearing of seat-belts is obligatory for drivers and
front-seat passengers, with a substantial fine for non-compliance. (See
also Motoring in South Cyprus).

Car rental firms at Lárnaca airport:
Avis; tel. (04) 64 31 120
Budget; tel. (04) 62 91 70
Europcar; tel. (04) 64 55 90 (in the town); 51 51 57 (airport)
Hertz; tel. (04) 64 33 88 (airport); 65 51 45 (town)

Chemists

There are chemists' shops (Greek *pharmakíon*) in all towns of any size. They are identified by a red cross on a white ground and, usually, the English word "Pharmacy". Most of the usual international medicines and drugs are available in Cyprus.

Opening hours

Mon.–Fri. 7.30am–1pm and 3–7pm, closed Wed. and Sat. afternoons.

Out-of-hours
service

Medicines can be obtained outside the normal hours by dialling 192 or the emergency number 199. The addresses of chemists providing out-of-hours services on a rota basis are shown on a notice in the window of all chemists' shops and are listed in newspapers.

Currency

The Cypriot unit of currency is the Cypriot pound (C£), also called the lira, which is divided into 100 cents.
   Cypriots frequently still count in shillings (*sillíngia*), of which – as in pre-decimal British currency – there were 20 to the pound; a shilling is thus equivalent to 5 cents.
   There are banknotes for 1, 5, 10 and 20 pounds and coins in denominations of 1, 2, 5, 10, 20 and 50 cents.

Exchange rates

These are subject to fluctuation. They can be obtained from banks and tourist offices and are also published in national newspapers.

Changing money

It is advisable to change money in Cyprus itself, where the exchange rates are better than outside the country.

Import and
export of
currency

There are no restrictions on bringing in foreign currency in banknotes or travellers' cheques, but sums in excess of 1000 US dollars or the equivalent in other currencies must be declared on arrival. There is a limit of C£50 on the amount of Cypriot currency which may be brought into or taken out of the country.

Travellers'
cheques,
Eurocheques and
credit cards

Travellers' cheques and Eurocheques are accepted by all banks. The main international credit cards (Visa, Diners' Club, American Express, Access, Eurocard) are accepted by most shops, restaurants and hotels.

Customs Regulations

In addition to personal effects visitors may take the following items into Cyprus duty-free: 200 cigarettes or 250 grams of cigars and tobacco; 75 centilitres of wine; 1 litre of spirits; 30 centilitres of perfume and toilet water and other goods to the value of C£50 (excluding jewellery). They may also take their own car without payment of duty for three months (possibly extendable).
   The import into Cyprus of drugs, weapons, plants (flowers, fruit, bulbs, seed) and live bait is prohibited.

Cypriot banknotes

Cycling

Most airlines will carry bicycles within the normal free baggage allowance of 20 kilograms (45 pounds).

In the major tourist centres bicycles can be hired from hotels or from car and motorcycle rental firms (see Car Rental).

Cyclists exploring the country by bicycle should be prepared for some rough riding since the minor country roads on which there is less motor traffic tend to be hilly and are usually unsurfaced.

The Cyprus Cycling Federation, 20 Ionos Street, P.O. Box 4572, Nicosia; tel. (02) 45 63 44, is glad to help visiting cyclists with advice and information. It also runs cycle races in spring and autumn.

Cyprus Cycling Federation

Diplomatic and Consular Offices

Offices of the Republic of Cyprus

High Commission of the Republic of Cyprus
93 Park Street, London W1Y 4ET. Tel. (0171) 499 8272/4

United Kingdom

Embassy of the Republic of Cyprus
2211 R Street North West, Washington DC 20008. Tel. (202) 462 5772/0873

United States

In Cyprus

British High Commission
Alexander Pallis Street, Nicosia. Tel. (02) 47 31 31/7

United Kingdom

United States   Embassy
Metochiou and Ploutarchou Streets
Nicosia
Tel. (02) 47 61 00

Distances

The distances, in kilometres, between towns in the Greek part of Cyprus are shown in the following table:

Distances in km between towns in South Cyprus							
	Nicosia	Limassol	Páphos	Lárnaca	Tróodos	Ayía Nápa	Pólis
Nicosia	–	86	163	51	77	88	205
Limassol	86	–	77	69	46	123	106
Páphos	163	77	–	146	120	182	42
Lárnaca	51	69	146	–	123	37	160
Tróodos	77	46	120	123	–	160	104
Ayía Nápa	88	123	182	37	160	–	197
Pólis	205	106	42	160	104	197	–

Electricity

Electricity is 240 volts AC. Power sockets in most new buildings take British-style three square-pin plugs. Almost all hotels have 110 volt sockets for electric razors.

Emergencies

In the larger towns dial 199 for police or fire or ambulance services. For police telephone numbers in smaller towns, see Police.

Pharmacy out-of-hours service: dial 192.

Events

See Public Holidays and Festivals

Excursions

Many travel agencies in Cyprus operate coach tours (usually half day or day trips) taking in the most interesting sights – archaeological, artistic or scenic – on the island, with a knowledgable English-speaking guide. They also organise walking tours and boat trips. Excursions can be booked either in the agencies themselves or in hotels, which will have posters advertising the various agencies' programmes.

Food and Drink

Lunch is eaten between 12.30 and 2pm. Dinner does not usually begin before 8pm, though hotels have adjusted to the habits of foreign visitors and often serve dinner earlier.

Hotel restaurants offer a predominantly international cuisine, adapted to British and French tastes, but Greek Cypriot cooking can be found in the tavernas. Cypriot dishes are tasty and substantial, highly spiced but not sharp. Much use is made of parsley, garlic, coriander and lemon juice. The sweets show Arabic influence.

Mezedhes

Characteristic of the Greek Cypriot cuisine are the *mezedhes* (singular *mezé*) – a choice of appetisers or hors d'oeuvre offered as an accompaniment to a drink or at the beginning of a meal. They may amount to a meal in themselves, with anything from 16 to 32 different items, either hot or cold. The following are some of the things that may be included:

dolmádhes = stuffed vine-leaves
féta = ewes'-milk cheese
haloúmi = a hard, salty goat's milk cheese which may be eaten raw, roasted
   or fried
hiroméri = smoked ham
houmous = a purée of chick peas, sesame, olive oil and lemon
loúnza = smoked pork tenderloin
manitária = mushrooms
marídhes = fried whitebait
tahina = sesame paste
talattoúri, tsatzíki = sliced cucumber and garlic in yoghurt
taramosaláta = a pink "dip" made from cod's roe

Other Dishes

horiátiki = a "country" salad of cucumbers, tomatoes, greens, olives and
   féta
kapári = tender caper shoots in salt and wine vinegar

Mezedhes (appetisers) in a Cypriot bar

melintzanosálata = aubergine salad
patatasaláta = potato salad

Soups (soúpes)	psarósoupa = fish soup soúpa avgolémono = chicken soup with egg and lemon juice soúpa hoúmi = chick pea soup

Meat dishes
(kréata)

afélia = cubes of pork stewed in red wine with coriander
arní me fasólia = lamb with beans
keftédhes = fried meat balls
kléftiko = lamb roasted in aluminium foil in a sealed oven or earthenware
  pot
kotópoulo lemonáto = chicken boiled in a lemon sauce
kounéli stifádo = rabbit stew with onions
koupépia or dolmades = vine-leaves stuffed with rice and minced meat
moussaká = layers of fried aubergine and fried sliced potatoes interspersed
  with minced meat and covered with a bechamel sauce
paidákia = grilled lamb cutlets
pastítsio = noodles with minced meat and potatoes
piperés yemistés = stuffed peppers
pítta = flat unleavened bread, often filled with kebabs of shredded veal
sheftaliá = grilled spice sausage
soúvla = large pieces of grilled meat (usually lamb)
souvlákia = kebabs of lamb or pork grilled on a spit
stifádo = beef stew with onions
tavás = lamb or beef cooked in a sealed
  earthenware pot with onions
tomátes yemistés = stuffed tomatoes

Fish (psária)

astakós = lobster	oktapódhi = octopus
barboúnia = red mullet	péstrofa = trout
garídhes = prawns	tónnos = tunny
kalamári = squid	

Vegetables
accompanying
meat

Potatoes (patátes) are almost invariably served with meat, often in the form
of chips. Rice (rísi) may be served as an alternative. A particular speciality is
sweet potatoes (kolokási).

Sweets
(glyká)

baklavá = layers of filo pastry filled with ground almonds in a cinnamon-
  flavoured syrup
dáktyla = a finger-shaped filled pastry
flaoúnes = small Easter cakes filled with cheese and peppermint
loukoumádhes = honey puffs
skámali = semolina pudding sprinkled with almonds
soutzoúko = almonds soaked in grape juice
vasilópitta = a New Year cake containing a coin which brings luck to the
  finder

Recipes

Soúpa
avgolémono

Ingredients (for 6 to 8 people): 8 cupfuls of chicken stock, 1 cupful of rice,
6 egg yolks, half cupful of lemon juice, salt and pepper to taste.
  Boil the rice in the chicken stock until cooked. Remove from the heat.
Whisk the egg yolks with the lemon juice, slowly adding 1 or 2 cupfuls of the
stock. Then gradually pour the eggs into the stock and continue to stir. Add
salt and pepper to taste.

Dolmádhes

Ingredients: 300 grams of fresh or dried vine-leaves, 1½ cupfuls of oil,
3 cupfuls of finely grated onions, 2 cupfuls of rice, 2 cupfuls of water, half
cupful of pine kernels, 3 tablespoonfuls of finely chopped dill, 3 tablespoonfuls of parsley, half teaspoonful of finely grated mint, salt, pepper,
1 teaspoonful of sugar, 2 lemons, 2 cupfuls of boiling water.

Lightly brown the onions in half the oil, add the rice and cook slowly for 10 minutes in a closed pan. Add the hot water, pine kernels, herbs and spices. Steam in a closed pan until the water has evaporated. Take off the cooker and allow to cool. Wash the vine-leaves and boil for 2–3 minutes in salted water until they are soft; then stuff them with rice, put them in a pan and pour the rest of the oil, the lemon juice and the boiling water over them. Cover with a plate, put the lid on the pan and steam for 45 minutes.

Minced meat may be added to the rice if desired.

Ingredients: 1 kilogram beef, ½ kilogram of small peeled onions, 4 finely chopped cloves of garlic, 1 cupful of oil, 3 laurel leaves, black pepper, cinnamon, ½ kilogram of grated tomatoes, 2 cupfuls of hot water, half cupful of vinegar, salt and pepper.   **Stifádo**

Cut the meat into small pieces. Lightly brown the onions in a casserole; then take out the onions and cook the garlic in the casserole until it is soft. Brown the meat on a low heat, and add the vinegar and, when this is boiling, the tomatoes, salt, pepper, laurel leaves, cinnamon and hot water. Cook for about 2½ hours on a low heat, and thirty minutes before the meat is done add the onions.

(The last two recipes are from the book by Nearchos Nicolaou, "Dishes from Cyprus, the Island of Aphrodite").

Drinks (potá)

A Cypriot meal always ends with a cup of coffee. Cypriots usually drink mocha coffee, either without sugar (kafés skéttos), with a little sugar (kafés métrios) or very sweet (kafés glykós). Tea (tsái) is also a popular drink.   Coffee, tea

Popular non-alcoholic drinks are milk (gála), orange juice (portokaláda), almond juice (soumáda) and other soft drinks common to the western world.   Soft drinks

See entry   Wine

Oúzo (an aniseed-flavoured spirit), brandy and sherry are made in Cyprus. Country people make a marc brandy (dzivaniá), the sale of which is officially prohibited.   Fortified drinks and spirits

A favourite long drink in Cyprus is brandy sour, which also appeals to visitors. This refreshing drink is a mixture of brandy, lemon juice, angostura and soda water.   Brandy sour

A local firm, Keo, brews a light and digestible beer. Carlsberg beer is also brewed locally.   Beer (bíra)

Frontier Crossing

Visitors to the Greek part of Cyprus can (though this is not encouraged by the Cypriot government) make day trips into the Turkish-occupied area in the north between the hours of 8am and 6pm (sometimes only 4.30pm). The only frontier crossing point is in Nicosia, at the end of Markos Drakos Avenue. There, by the old Ledra Palace Hotel, is the Greek passport control, and between this and the Turkish frontier control is the United Nations buffer zone. At the Turkish control point a one-day visa costing C£1 will be issued. It is not permitted to spend the night in the Turkish zone or to take a car over the frontier.

For an excursion into North Cyprus visitors can either rent a car or use public transport; but in view of the short time allowed the best plan is to see the principal sights by taxi. A reasonable price for the day can be negotiated. Visitors must be sure to return to South Cyprus by 6pm at latest.

Visitors to North Cyprus are not allowed to cross into the Greek Republic of Cyprus. (See Sights A to Z South Cyprus, Nicosia.)

Getting to South Cyprus

By air
The quickest and easiest way to get to Cyprus is by air. Cyprus is linked with the international network
of air services, and in recent years has increasingly become a junction point for connections with the Middle East and the Gulf states.

Direct flights from London to Lárnaca International Airport are operated by British Airways and Cyprus Airways. The airport at Páphos is used mainly by charter flights.

The flight from London to Lárnaca takes around 4½ hours.

A second airport at Páphos caters for charter flights.

By car
The journey from Britain to Cyprus by car, involving two ferry crossings, is long and expensive. A car may be imported for a period of up to three months. Drivers must carry a national or international driving licence and their car registration document and must be covered by third party insurance.

By sea
There are services throughout the year from Athens (Piraeus) to Limassol via Iraklion (Crete) and Rhodes; the journey takes about two days. During the summer there are services from Ancona and Brindisi. Cyprus also has connections with Israel (Haifa), Syria (Latakia), Lebanon (Beirut) and Egypt (Alexandria).

Shipping lines in Greece
POSEIDON Lines Shipping Co. S.A.
in Piraeus: Akiti Miaouli Street 35–39
Tel. (01) 4 29 20 46, fax (01) 4 29 20 41

SALAMIS Lines Ltd.
in Piraeus: Filellinon Street 9
Tel. (01) 4 29 43 25, fax (01) 4 29 45 57

Shipping lines in Cyprus
POSEIDON Lines (Cyprus) Ltd.
Franklin Roosevelt Street 124, Limassol
Tel. (05) 74 56 66, fax (05) 74 55 77

SALAMIS Lines Ltd.
28th October Avenue, Limassol
Tel. (05) 35 55 55, fax (05) 36 44 10

Guides

In Cyprus there are licensed guides qualified to take visitors around archaeological sites and other places and features of interest. Information about such guides can be obtained from the central organisation to which all licensed guides belong:

Cyprus Tourist Guides Association, P.O. Box 4942, Nicosia.
Tel. (02) 45 77 55.

Hotels

In general hotels in Cyprus are of high quality, in line with international standards. The main tourist centres – Ayía Nápa, Lárnaca, Limassol and

Páphos – have large numbers of hotels, and the hill regions and the smaller towns along the coast are well equipped with accommodation.

Hotel standards are monitored by the Cyprus Tourism Organisation (CTO), which annually fixes minimum and maximum tariffs for the different categories of hotels and approves the tariffs of individual hotels, having regard to the standard of comfort and amenities provided.

CTO

Hotels in Cyprus are divided into five categories, being awarded from one to five stars according to comfort and amenity. The rates for each room must be displayed in the room.

Categories

Hotel apartments, tourist apartments and tourist villas (self-catering) are divided into three categories, from A to C. Establishments below these categories are called "hotels without a star" and guest houses. There are no "bed and breakfast" rooms in private houses.

Hotel apartments

The price ranges per person for a double room with breakfast in the various categories of hotel are as follows:

Tariffs

★★★★★ C£55–80
★★★★ C£30–60
★★★ C£17–33
★★ C£16–22
★ C£10–17
For unclassified hotels the rate is below C£10.

For apartment hotels in category A the price range is between C£20 and C£30, in category B between C£15 and C£20 and in category C between C£8 and C£18. In the off season (Nov. 1st to Mar. 31st in the coastal regions, Oct. 1st to June 30th in the hills) prices are between 20% and 50% lower, the biggest reductions being in January and February.

During the holiday season it is difficult to find a room: advance booking is therefore advisable. Information about hotels and complete hotel lists can be obtained from the Cyprus Tourism Organisation (see Information).

Hotels in South Cyprus (a selection)

★★★Rodon, tel. (05) 52 12 01
★Vlachos, tel. (05) 52 13 30
Unclassified: Meteora, tel. (05) 52 13 31

Agrós

★★★★★Alion Beach, tel. (03) 72 29 00; Grecian Bay, tel. (03) 72 13 01
★★★★Asterias Beach, tel. (03) 72 19 01; Dome, tel. (03) 72 10 06; Florida, tel. (03) 72 18 21; Grecian Sands, tel. (03) 72 16 16; Nissi Beach, tel. (03) 72 10 21
★★★Anonymous Beach, tel. (03) 72 13 20; Bella Napa Bay, tel. (03) 72 16 01; Christofinia, tel. (03) 72 16 10; Marina, tel. (03) 72 17 21; Napia Star, tel. (03) 72 15 40; Nissi Park, tel. (03) 72 11 21; Pavlonapa Beach, tel. (03) 72 24 00; Sungarden Beach, tel. (03) 72 10 00
★★Anesis, tel. (03) 72 11 04; Chrysland, tel. (03) 72 13 11; Cornelia, tel. (03) 72 14 06; Pambos Magic, tel. (03) 72 12 14; Voula Beach, tel. (03) 72 13 30
Hotel apartment: A Androthea, tel. (03) 72 11 11; Anthea, tel. (03) 72 14 11; Euronapa, tel. (03) 72 24 44; Kermia Beach, tel. (03) 72 14 01; Napiana, tel. (03) 72 17 26; Nissiana, tel. (03) 72 12 24
B Alexia, tel. (03) 72 19 50; Castalia, tel. (03) 72 11 06; Eleana, tel. (03) 72 16 40
C Agrino, tel. (03) 72 12 50; Tsokkos Holiday No. 2, tel. (03) 72 12 11

Ayía Nápa

Droushia Heights, tel. (06) 33 32 51

Droúsha

Galáta

★Rialto, tel. (02) 92 24 38

Kakopetriá

★★★Hellas, tel. (02) 92 24 50; Makris Sunotel, tel. (02) 92 24 19
★★Hekali, tel. (02) 92 25 01
★Kifissia, tel. (02) 92 24 21; Krystal, tel. (02) 92 24 33
Unclassified: Loukoudi, tel. (02) 92 24 32

Kalopanayiótis

Unclassified: Drakos, tel. (02) 95 26 51; Heliopoulis, tel. (02) 95 24 51; Kastalia, tel. (02) 95 24 55; Loutraki, tel. (02) 95 23 56

Káto Pyrgos

★Pyrgiana Beach, tel. (06) 52 23 22; Pyrgos Bay, tel. (06) 52 20 01; Tylo Beach, tel. (06) 52 23 48

Lakhí

★Latsi, tel. (06) 32 14 11

Lárnaca

★★★★★Golden Bay, Lárnaca–Dhekélia road, tel. (04) 64 54 44
★★★★Lordos Beach, Lárnaca–Dhekélia road, tel. (04) 64 74 44; Palm Beach, Lárnaca–Dhekélia road, tel. (04) 64 45 00; Princess Beach Sunotel, Lárnaca–Dhekélia road, tel. (04) 64 55 00; Sandy Beach, Lárnaca–Dhekélia road, tel. (04) 64 63 33; Sun Hall, Athens Avenue, tel. (04) 65 33 41
★★★Beau Rivage, Lárnaca–Dhekélia road, tel. (04) 64 66 00; Faros Village, Perivólia (14km/8½ miles south), tel. (04) 42 21 11; Flamingo Beach, Piale Pasha Street, tel. (04) 65 06 21; Four Lanterns Sunotel, 19 Athens Avenue, tel. (04) 65 20 11; Henipa, Oróklini road, tel. (04) 64 60 22; Karpasiana Beach Sunotel, Lárnaca–Dhekélia road, tel. (04) 65 50 01; Sveltos, Oróklini road, tel. (04) 64 71 00
★★Arion, 26 Galileo Street, tel. (04) 65 02 00; Baronet, Makarios III Avenue, tel. (04) 63 61 11; Eva, Lárnaca–Dhekélia road, tel. (04) 64 51 00; I. B. Sandbeach Castle, Piale Pasha Street, tel. (04) 65 54 37
★La Maison Belge, 103 Stadiou Street, tel. (04) 65 46 55; Pavion, St Lazarus Square, tel. (04) 65 66 88; Tefkros, 11 Tefkros Street, tel. (04) 65 37 27
Rainbow Inn, Zenon Kitieus Street, tel. (04) 65 58 74
Hotel apartment: A Atrium Zenon, Zenon Pierides and Kitieus Streets, tel. (04) 62 01 00; Michael's Beach, Lárnaca–Dhekélia road, tel. (04) 64 46 00; Stavros, Lárnaca–Dhekélia road, tel. (04) 64 60 00; Sunflower, 69 Makarios III Avenue, tel. (04) 65 01 11
B Acropolis, G. Afxentiou Avenue, tel. (04) 62 37 00; Adonis Beach, Piale Pasha Street, tel. (04) 65 66 44; Boronia, Lárnaca–Dhekélia road, tel. (04) 64 62 00; Lucky, Lárnaca–Dhekélia road, tel. (04) 64 72 22; Tofias, Lárnaca–Dhekélia road, tel. (04) 64 58 00
C Chryssopolis, 1 Kimon Street, tel. (04) 62 84 44; Fairways, 44 Makarios III Avenue, tel. (04) 65 05 30; Sussex, Lárnaca–Dhekélia road, tel. (04) 65 12 11

Limassol

★★★★★Amathus Beach, Amathoús (9km/5½ miles east), tel. (05) 32 11 52; Apollonia Beach, Potamos Yermasoyias, tel. (05) 32 33 51; Le Méridien Limassol, Amathoús (12km/7½ miles east), tel. (05) 32 70 00; Limassol Sheraton, Amathoús (12km/7½ miles east), tel. (05) 32 11 00; Poseidonia Beach Sunotel, Amathoús (6km/3½ miles east), tel. (05) 32 10 00
★★★★Churchill Limassol, 28th October Street, Ag Athanasios, tel. (05) 32 44 44; Curium Palace, 2 Byron Street, tel. (05) 36 31 21; Elias Beach, Amathoús (11km/7 miles east), tel. (05) 32 50 00; Limonia Bay, Amathoús (11km/7 miles east), tel. (05) 32 10 23; Miramare, Potamos Yermasoyias, tel. (05) 32 16 62
★★★Alasia, 1 Haydari Street, tel. (05) 33 20 00; Aquamarina, 139 Spyros Araouzos Street, tel. (05) 37 42 77; Ariadne, 333 28th October Street, tel. (05) 35 96 66; Atlantica, Potamos Yermasoyias, tel. (05) 32 11 41; Crusader Beach Sunotel, Potamos Yermasoyias, tel. (05) 32 13 33; Elena Beach, 39 Amathoús Avenue, tel. (05) 32 28 55; Kanika Pantheon, 28th October and I Metaxa Streets, tel. (05) 34 26 42
★★Continental, 137 Spyros Araouzos Street, tel. (05) 36 25 30; Pefkos, 86 Kavazoglou Street, tel. (05) 37 70 77

★Le Village, 220 Leontios A' Street, tel. (05) 36 81 26; Limassol Palace, 97–99 Spyron Araouzos Street, tel. (05) 35 21 31; Panorama, 36 Pavlos Melas Street, tel. (05) 36 46 67

Unclassified: Acropole, 21 G. Malikides Street, tel. (05) 36 27 06; Astoria, 13A G. Malikides Street, tel. (05) 36 27 08; Metropole, 6 Iphigenia Street, tel. (05) 36 26 86

Hotel apartment: A Balmyra Beach, 76 Georgios A' Street, Potamos Yermasoyias, tel. (05) 32 26 00; Castle, 2 Prof. Elias Street, tel. (05) 32 14 50; Ermitage Beach, Potamos Yermasoyias, tel. (05) 32 32 30; Pegasus, 78 Georgios A' Street, Potamos Yermasoyias, tel. (05) 32 13 20

B Azur Beach, Potamos Yermasoyias, tel. (05) 32 26 67; Bertha, Amathoús (9km/5½ miles east), tel. (05) 32 23 24; Demero, Georgios A' Street, Potamos Yermasoyias, tel. (05) 32 23 31

C Estella, 2 Kranos Street, Potamos Yermasoyias, tel. (05) 32 19 22; Mylos, 1 Ambelakion Street, Potamos Yermasoyias, tel. (05) 32 17 77; White Arches, Amathoús (9km/5½ miles east), tel. (05) 36 46 65

★★★★★Cyprus Hilton, Archbishop Makarios III Avenue, tel. (02) 37 77 77   **Nicosia**

★★★★Churchill Nicosia, 1 Achaeans Street, tel. (02) 44 88 58; Ledra, Grivas Dighenis Avenue, Engomi, tel. (02) 35 20 86; Philoxenia, Eylenja Avenue, Eylenja, tel. (02) 49 97 00

★★★Cleopatra, 8 Florinis Street, tel. (02) 44 52 54; Europa, 16 Alkeos Street, Engomi, tel. (02) 45 45 37; Kennedy, 70 Regaena Street, tel. (02) 47 51 31

★★Asty, 12 Prince Charles Street, Ag Dometios, tel. (02) 47 30 21; Averof, 19 Averof Street, tel. (02) 46 34 47; Lido, 6–8 Philokypros Street, tel. (02) 47 43 51

★Carlton, 13 Princess de Tyras Street, tel. (02) 44 20 01; City Sunotel, 215 Ledra Street, tel. (02) 46 31 01; Regina Palace, 42–44 Regaena and Fokion Streets, tel. (02) 46 30 51; Venetian Walls, 38 Ouzounian Street, tel. (02) 45 08 05

Unclassified: Delphi, 24 Pantelides Avenue, tel. (02) 47 52 11; Royal, 17 Euripides Street, tel. (02) 46 32 45; Sans Rival, 7C Solon Street, tel. (02) 47 43 83

Guest House: Alasia, 23 Pygmalion Street, tel. (02) 45 43 84

Hotel apartment: B Lordos, 18 Sina Street, Engomi, tel. (02) 44 10 39

C Excelsior, 11 25th March Street, tel. (02) 31 74 00

★★★★★Annabelle, Poseidon Avenue, tel. (06) 23 83 33; Imperial Beach,   **Páphos**
Poseidon Avenue, tel. (06) 24 54 15

★★★★Alexander The Great, Poseidon Avenue, tel. (06) 24 40 00; Cypria Maris, Poseidon Avenue, tel. (06) 23 81 11; Ledra Beach Sunotel, Poseidon Avenue, tel. (06) 24 48 48; Páphos Beach, Poseidon Avenue, tel. (06) 23 30 91

★★★Aloe, Poseidon Avenue, tel. (06) 23 40 00; Cynthiana Beach, Kisonerga (8km/5 miles north), tel. (06) 23 39 00; Dionysos, 1 Dionysos Street, tel. (06) 23 34 14; Kissos, Vereniki Street, tel. (06) 23 61 11; Paphiana, Konia (4km/2½ miles north), tel. (06) 23 52 52; Theofano, Danae Street, tel. (06) 23 36 66

★★Apollo, Apostle Paul Avenue, tel. (06) 23 39 09; Kings, Tombs of the Kings Road, tel. (06) 23 34 97

★Agapinor, Nikodimos Mylonas Street, tel. (06) 23 39 26; Kinyras, 91 Makarios III Avenue, tel. (06) 24 16 04; Pyramos, 4 St Anastasia Street, tel. (06) 23 51 61

Guest House: Pelican Inn, 102 Apostle Paul Avenue, tel. (06) 23 28 27; Trianon, 99 Makarios III Avenue, tel. (06) 23 21 93

Hotel apartment: A Daphne, 3 Alkmini Street, tel. (06) 23 35 00; Helios Bay, Chlorakas (6km/3½ miles north), tel. (06) 23 56 56; Rania, Poseidon Avenue, tel. (06) 23 54 44

B Hilltop Gardens, off Tombs of the Kings Road, tel. (06) 24 31 11; Mirofori, Constantia Street, tel. (06) 23 43 11; Theseas, 1–3 Iason Street, tel. (06) 23 55 11

Imperial Beach Hotel, Páphos . . .   *. . . and its lobby*

C Aloma, 5 Klytemnistra Street, tel. (06) 23 74 00; Evelyn, 3 Thalia Street, tel. (06) 23 22 22; Fikardos, Tefkros Street, tel. (06) 23 75 25

Paralímni/
Protarás

★★★★Capo Bay, Protaras, tel. (03) 83 11 01; Golden Coast, Protaras, tel. (03) 83 13 66; Sunrise Beach, Protaras, tel. (03) 83 15 01; Tsokkos Protaras, Protaras, tel. (03) 83 13 63; Vrissiana Beach, Protaras, tel. (03) 83 12 16
★★★Kapetanios Bay, Protaras, tel. (03) 83 11 70; Pernera Beach, Pernera, tel. (03) 83 10 11
★★Cristalla, Protaras, tel. (03) 83 14 60
★San Antonio, G. Afxentiou Street, tel. (03) 82 15 61
Hotel apartment: A Flora, Protaras Road, tel. (03) 83 12 34; Kokkinos, Protaras Road, tel. (03) 83 14 44; Paramount, tel. (03) 83 14 00
B Andreotis, tel. (03) 83 12 50; Crest, Protaras Road, tel. (03) 83 14 66; Oasis Park, 187 Protaras Street, tel. (03) 82 25 01
C Sinoro, Kaparis, tel. (03) 82 27 77

Pedhoulás

★★★Churchill Pinewood Valley, tel. (02) 95 22 11
★★Marangos, tel. (02) 95 26 57
★Jack's, tel. (02) 95 23 50
Unclasssified: Central, tel. (02) 95 24 57; Christy's Palace, tel. (02) 95 26 55; Elyssia, tel. (02) 95 26 59
Guest House: Kallithea, tel. (02) 95 22 94

Péyia

★Yeronisos, Ayios Yeóryios, tel. (06) 62 10 78
B Christina, tel. (06) 23 37 42; Euronest, tel. (06) 62 11 21

Pissoúri

★★★Columbia Pissouri Beach, tel. (05) 22 12 01
★Bunch of Grapes Inn, tel. (05) 22 12 75

★★★★Forest Park, tel. (05) 42 17 51; Pendeli, tel. (05) 42 17 36
★★Edelweiss, tel. (05) 42 13 35; New Helvetia, tel. (05) 42 13 48
★Kallithea, tel. (05) 42 17 46; Minerva, tel. (05) 42 17 31; Mount Royal, tel. (05) 42 13 45; Splendid, tel. (05) 42 14 25
Unclassified: Lanterns Cottage, tel. (05) 42 14 34
Hotel apartment: B Paul's, tel. (05) 42 14 25

Plátres

★★Marion, tel. (06) 31 12 16
Unclassified: Akamas, tel. (06) 32 13 30
Hotel apartment: B N. Stratis, tel. (06) 32 18 94

Pólis

Unclassified: Alps, tel. (05) 46 21 81

Pródhromos

★★★Troodos Sunotel, tel. (05) 42 16 35
★★Jubilee, tel. (05) 42 16 47

Tróodos

Information

Information about Cyprus can be obtained from the following offices of the Cyprus Tourism Organisation (CTO):

Cyprus Tourist Office
213 Regent Street
London W1R 8DA
Tel. (0171) 734 9822

United Kingdom

Cyprus Tourism Organisation
13 East 40th Street
New York NY 10016
Tel. (212) 683 5280

United States

CTO Offices in Cyprus

Leof Lemesou 19; tel. (02) 33 77 15
Laiki Yitonia; tel. (02) 44 42 64

Nicosia

15 Spyros Araouzos Street; tel. (05) 36 27 56
35 George I Street, Patomos Yermasoyias; tel. (05) 32 32 11
Harbour; tel. (05) 34 38 68

Limassol

Vasileos Paulou Square; tel. (04) 65 43 22
Airport; tel. (04) 64 30 00 (24 hour service)

Lárnaca

3 Gladstone Street; tel. (06) 23 28 41
Airport; tel. (06) 42 28 33

Páphos

In summer: tel. (03) 72 17 96

Ayía Nápa

In summer: tel. (05) 42 13 16

Plátres

Information about events, theatre programmes, festivals and sporting occasions is published in the Cyprus Tourist Organisation's "Diary of Events" or "Monthly Events", or "Cyprus Time Out", "Nicosia This Month" and "Seven Days in Cyprus".

Publications

Insurance

Visitors are strongly advised to ensure that they have adequate insurance cover including loss or damage to luggage, loss of currency and jewellery. As Cyprus is not a member of the European Union it is also advisable to take out adequate medical insurance before leaving home.

Language

As a result of Cyprus's 80 years of British colonial rule visitors will usually be able to find local people with some knowledge of English; but in the remoter parts of the country it is helpful to have at least a smattering of modern Greek.

Modern Greek

Modern Greek is considerably different from ancient Greek, though it is surprising to find how many words are still spelled the same way as in classical times. Even in such cases, however, the pronunciation is very different.

The Greek Alphabet

		Ancient Greek	Modern Greek	Pronunciation
A	α	alpha	alfa	a, semi-long
B	β	beta	vita	v
Γ	γ	gamma	ghamma	g; y before e or i
Δ	δ	delta	dhelta	dh as in English "the"
E	ε	epsilon	épsilon	e, open, as in "egg"
Z	ζ	zeta	zita	z
H	η	eta	ita	ee, semi-long
Θ	φ	theta	thita	th as in "thin"
I	ι	iota	iota	ee, semi-long
K	κ	kappa	kappa	k
Λ	λ	lambda	lamvdha	l
M	μ	mu	mi	m
N	ν	nu	ni	n
Ξ	ξ	xi	xi	ks
O	o	omicron	ómikron	o, open, semi-long
Π	π	pi	pi	p
P	ρ	rho	rho	r, lightly rolled
Σ	σ	sigma	sigma	s
T	τ	tau	taf	t
Y	υ	ypsilon	ípsilon	ee, semi-long
Φ	ψ	phi	fi	f
X	χ	chi	khi	kh, ch as in "loch"; before e or i, somewhere between ch and sh
Ψ	ψ	psi	psi	ps
Ω	ω	omega	oméga	o, open, semi-long

There is no recognised standard system for the transliteration of the Greek into the Latin alphabet, and many variations are found.

Accents

The position of the stress in a word is very variable, but is always shown in the Greek alphabet by an accent. In the past there were three accents – acute (´), grave (`) and circumflex (^) – but since there was no difference in practice between the three only the acute accent is now used.

The "breathings" over a vowel or diphthong at the beginning of a word, whether "rough" (') or "smooth" ('), are not pronounced and are now little used.

The diaeresis (¨) over a vowel indicates that it is to be pronounced separately, and not as part of a diphthong.

Punctuation

Punctuation marks are the same as in English, except that the semicolon (;) is used in place of the question-mark (?) and a point above the line (·) in place of the semicolon.

Numbers

0 midhén	30 triánda	Cardinals
1 énas, myá, éna	31 triánda énas, myá, éna	
2 dhyó, dhío	40 saránda	
3 tris, tría	50 penínda	
4 tésseris, téssera	60 eksínda	
5 pénde	70 evdomínda	
6 éksi	80 oghdhónda, oghdhoínda	
7 eftá	90 enenínda	
8 okhtó	100 ekató(n)	
9 ennyá	101 ekatón énas, myá, éna	
10 dhéka	153 ekatón penínda tris, tría	
11 éndheka	200 dhiakósi, dhiakósyes,	
12 dhódheka	dhiakósya	
13 dhekatrís, dhekatría	300 triakósi, -yes, -ya	
14 dhekatésseris, dhekatéssera	400 tetrakósi, -yes, -ya	
15 dhekapéndhe	500 pendakósi, -yes, -ya	
16 dhekaéksi, dhekaáksi	600 eksakósi, -yes, -ya	
17 dhekaëftá, dhekaëpta	700 eftakósi, -yes, -ya	
18 dhekaokhtó, dhekaoktó	800 okhtakósi, -yes, -ya	
19 dhekaënnyá, dhekaënnéa	900 ennyakósi, -yes, -ya	
20 íkosi	1000 khíli, khílyes, khílya	
21 íkosi énas, myá, éna	5000 pénde khilyádes	
22 íkosi dhyó, dhío	1,000,000 éna ekatommíryo	

1st prótos, próti, próto(n)	10th dhékatos, dhekáti	Ordinals
2nd dhéfteros, -i, -o(n)	11th endhékatos, endhekáti	
3rd trítos, -i, -o(n)	20th ikostós, -i, -ó(n)	
4th tétartos, -i, -o(n)	30th triakostós, -i, -ó(n)	
5th pémptos	100th ekatostós, -i, -ó(n)	
6th éktos	104th ekatostós prótos	
7th évdhomos, evdhómi	124th ekatostós ikostós tétartos	
8th óghdhoos	1000th khilyostós	
9th énatos, enáti		

½ misós, -i, -ó(n), ímisis	¼ tétarton	Fractions
⅓ tríton	¹⁄₁₀ dhékaton	

Days of the Week, Months, Festivals

Sunday	Kiryakí	The week
Monday	Dheftéra	(evdhomádha)
Tuesday	Tríti	
Wednesday	Tetárti	
Thursday	Pémpti	
Friday	Paraskeví	
Saturday	Sávato(n)	

January	Yanuáryos, Yennáris	Months
February	Fevruáryos, Fleváris	(mines)
March	Mártyos, Mártis	
April	Aprílyos	
May	Máyos, Máis	
June	Yúnyos	
July	Yúlyos	
August	Ávghustos	
September	Septémvryos	
October	Októvryos, Októvris	
November	Noémvryos, Noémvris	
December	Dekémvryos	

Festivals	New Year's Day	Protokhronyá
	Easter	Páskha, Lámbra(i)
	Whitsun	Pendikostí
	Christmas	Khristoúyenna

Everyday Expressions

General	Good morning, good day!	Kaliméra!
	Good evening!	Kalispéra!
	Good night!	Kalí níkhta!
	Goodbye!	Kalín andámosi(n)!
	Do you speak	Omilíte
	English?	angliká?
	French?	galliká?
	German?	yermaniká?
	I do not understand	Dhen katalamváno
	Excuse me	Me sinkhorite
	yes	nè, málista (turning head to side)
	no	ókhi (jerking head upwards)
	please	parakaló
	thank you	efkharistó
	yesterday	khthes
	today	símera, símeron
	tomorrow	ávrio(n)
	Help!	Voíthia!
	open	aniktó
	closed	klistó
	when?	poté?
	single room	dhomátyo me éna kreváti
	double room	dhomátyo me dhío krevátya
	room with bath	dhomátyo me loutro
	What does it cost?	Póso káni?
	Waken me at 6	Ksipníste me stis éksi
	Where is	Pu inè
	the lavatory?	to apokhoritírion?
	a pharmacy?	éna farmakíon?
	a doctor?	enas yatrós?
	a dentist?	énas odhondoyatrós?
	. . . Street?	i odhós (+ name in genitive)?
	. . . Square?	i platía (+ name in genitive)?

Travelling	aerodrome, airfield	aerodhromyon
	aircraft	aeropláno(n)
	airport	aerolimín
	All aboard!	Is tas thésis sas!
	arrival	erkhomós
	bank	trápeza
	boat	várka, káiki
	bus	leoforíon, búsi
	change	allásso
	departure (by air)	apoyíosis
	(by boat)	apóplous
	(by train)	anakhórisis
	exchange (of money)	saráfiko
	ferry	férri-bóut, porthmíon
	flight	ptísis
	hotel	ksenodokhíon
	information	pliroforía
	lavatory	apokhoritírion
	luggage	aposkevá
	luggage check	apódiksis ton aposkevón

non-smoking compartment	dhya mi kapnistás
porter	akhthofóros
railway	sidhiródhromos
restaurant car	vagón-restorán
ship	karávi, plíon
sleeping car	vagón-li, klinámaksa
smoking compartment	dhya kapnistás
station (railway)	stathmós
stop (bus)	stásis
ticket	bilyétto
ticket-collector	ispráktor
ticket window	thíris
timetable	dhromolóyion
train	tréno
waiting room	éthusa anamonís

address	dhiéfthinsis	At the post office
air mail	aeroporikós	
express	epíghousa	
letter	epistolí	
letter-box	ghrammatokivótio(n)	
package	dhematáki	
parcel	dhéma, pakétto	
postcard	takhidhromikí kárta	
poste restante	post restánt	
post office	takhidhromíon	
registered	sistiméni	
stamp	ghrammatósimo(n)	
telegram	tileghráfima	
telephone	tiléfono(n)	
telex	tilétipo(n)	

Maps and Plans

The Cyprus Tourism Organisation supplies, free of charge, a map on the scale 1:400,000 (not entirely accurate). Among maps available outside Cyprus are the following:
Bartholomew's Holiday Map, 1:300,000, with town plans
Hallwag, 1:300,000, with town plans
AA/Macmillan Traveller's Map, 1:275,000, with town plans and map of Tróodos Mountains, 1:80,000
Freytag & Berndt, 1:250,000, with town plans
Geo Project, 1:250,000, with town plans
Hildebrand, 1:200,000

Road maps

Other maps available in Cyprus (and possibly through specialised map shops outside Cyprus) include the following:
A road map on the scale 1:250,000, with contours (but no town plans) published by the Department of Lands and Surveys (not always up-to-date);
Four sheets covering the whole of Cyprus on the scale 1:100,000, also published by the Department of Lands and Surveys;
Cyprus Topographical Map, 1:100,000 (available from MAM bookshop in Nicosia).
Other maps may be found in petrol stations, bookshops and souvenir shops in Cyprus.

On grounds of security no detailed maps for walkers are available.

Walking maps

Medical Assistance

Medical care	Since there is no medical school in Cyprus all Cypriot doctors have been trained in Europe or America, and most of them speak English. For inpatient treatment there are state-run general hospitals, in which emergency treatment is free. For serious illnesses, however, it is advisable to go to private hospitals, which have a better clinical reputation. Bills for medical treatment, either by general practitioners and specialists or in private hospitals, and the cost of medicines usually have to be paid on the spot. It is essential, therefore, to take out temporary medical insurance before leaving home.
Consulting hours	Mon.–Sat. 9am–1pm and 4–7pm
Emergencies	Dial 199
Hospitals	Lárnaca: Lárnaca Hospital, Grigoris Afxentiou Avenue/Markos Drakos Street, tel. (04) 65 20 07 or 63 03 22 New Hospital, Mystras Street, tel. (04) 2 79 99 and 2 81 11 Limassol: Lendios Street, tel. (05) 33 01 56 Nicosia: General Hospital, Homer Avenue, tel. (02) 45 11 11 Makarios Hospital, tel. (02) 49 36 00 Páphos: Neophytos Nikolaides Street, tel. (06) 24 01 11 Paralímni: tel. (03) 82 12 11 Pedhoulás: Health Centre, tel. (02) 95 24 59 Plátres: Health Centre, tel. (05) 42 13 24 Pólis: tel. (06) 32 14 31
Chemists	See separate entry

Motoring in South Cyprus

Road network	Cyprus has an excellent network of roads serving all its towns and villages, but outside the main tourist areas many of the roads are unsurfaced. In the hills the roads are often narrow and winding, calling for great care in driving. Most signposts and road signs are in English as well as in Greek. On dirt roads, however, they are sometimes only in Greek. Drivers should note that there is a move to change the spelling of some place names, eg. Lárnaca becoming Larnaka, however most changes are not significant enough to cause confusion. Some 6918km/4320 miles of the roads are asphalted. There is a four-lane motorway from Nicosia to Limassol and Lárnaca. A wide, well engineered road runs along the coast from Páphos to Ayía Nápa, and a good asphalted road runs through the Tróodos Mountains from Nicosia via Tróodos and Plátres to Limassol.

Vehicles travel on the left, as in Britain. On roundabouts traffic coming from the right has priority. Road traffic regulations are in line with international custom.

Speed limits are 40km/24 miles an hour in built-up areas, 75km/46 miles an hour on main roads and 100km/62 miles an hour on motorways and expressways, where the **minimum** speed limit is 65km/40 miles an hour.

Seat belts must be worn in the front seats of a car; the penalty for not doing so may be a quite considerable fine. Children under five must not sit in the front seats.

It is an offence, with heavy penalties, to drive with a blood alcohol content of over 90 milligrams to 100 millilitres.

Rented cars always have a red number plate; ordinary private cars have yellow or white plates. Official cars have green plates, United Nations vehicles blue ones.

Filling stations are open on weekdays from 6am to 6pm. On Saturdays they close at 4pm. Lists of petrol stations open on Sundays from 6am to 6pm are given in the newspapers. In Nicosia and all the coastal towns there are coin-operated petrol pumps available for self-service 24 hours a day.

The Cyprus Automobile Association (CAA), which is associated with the AA, provides 24-hour breakdown assistance, patrol and towing service: for help, telephone (02) 31 31 31. The Association's head office is at 12 Chrysanthou Mylonas Street, Nicosia, tel. (02) 31 32 33. Visitors driving their own car can obtain information from the Association on the third party insurance required (see also Getting to South Cyprus – By Car).

However much care is taken accidents can happen. If involved in an accident do not get angry; be polite and keep calm. Then take the following action:

1. Warn oncoming traffic by switching on the car's warning lights and setting a warning triangle some distance before the scene of the accident.

2. Look after anyone who has been injured, calling an ambulance if necessary.

3. Inform the police.

4. Record full particulars of the accident. Draw a sketch of the accident and if a camera is available take photographs of the scene.

5. Write down the names and addresses of witnesses (independent witnesses are particularly important).

6. Fill in a European Accident Statement (this is supplied by most insurers).

Make no admission of responsibility for the accident, and above all do not sign any document in a language you do not understand.

On returning home report the accident to the insurance company and send them the European Accident Statement.

Museums and Archaeological Sites

The opening times of museums and archaeological sites vary: see individual entries in the "Sights from A to Z" section of this guide. The major archaeological sites, as well as the principal museums in Nicosia, Limassol and Páphos are open on most public holidays; but all museums and archaeological sites are closed on great religious festivals and national holidays (e.g. Christmas Day, New Year's Day and Greek Orthodox Easter Sunday).

Photography

Written permission must be obtained for taking photographs in museums.

Night Life

Among the most popular places of entertainment for visitors are the bouzouki bars where performances of folk music and dancing can be enjoyed. These are to be found in the four large towns and in some of the smaller tourist centres like Plátres and Pólis. In addition there are discothèques, night bars and cabarets in Nicosia, Limassol, Lárnaca, Páphos, Ayía Nápa and Pólis.

Information about what is on in Nicosia can be obtained from "Nicosia This Month" (available only in Cyprus).

The following is a selection of bouzouki bars, discothèques and cabarets:

Nicosia
Bouzouki bars

Elysee, Evagoras Avenue, tel. (02) 47 37 73; Kapello, Laiki Yitonia, tel. (02) 45 00 80; Neraida, Dhigenis Avenue, tel. (02) 44 59 76; Varonos, Dhigenis Avenue, tel. (02) 44 34 04.

Discothèques

(Almost all the discos are in the Engomi district). Galaxy, Patatsos Street, tel. (02) 45 81 84; Africana Disco, Michael Parides Street, tel. (02) 45 64 95; Rollingstones Disco, Ipsilandis Street, tel. (02) 45 92 60.

Cabarets

(Almost all the cabarets are in Regaena Street and side streets opening off it). Casanova Night Club, 31 Archbishop Makarios III Avenue, tel. (02) 46 50 82; Maxim Cabaret, 14 Princess de Tyras Street, tel. (02) 44 56 79; Trocadero, 1 Pantelides Avenue, tel. (02) 47 78 71.

Limassol
Bouzouki bars

Alexandra, Amathoús (near Sheraton Hotel), tel. (05) 32 17 70; Salamandra, near Limassol–Nicosia road, opposite Poseidonia Hotel, tel. (05) 33 42 00; Klapsides, near the old harbour, tel. (05) 32 00 22; Archontissa, 103 Makarios III Avenue, tel. (05) 33 77 88 (night club, music); Le Panache, Makarios III Avenue; tel. (05) 36 75 43 (night club, music).

Discothèques

There are many discos in the Potamos Yermasoyias hotel district. Lazer's Disco, 89 George I Street, tel. (05) 32 13 50; Malibu Disco, Ambelakia Street, tel. (05) 32 25 00; Caribbean Disco, 91 George I Street, tel. (05) 32 18 68.

Lárnaca
Bouzouki bars

Gold Fish, Lárnaca–Dhekélia road, near Palm Beach Hotel; Fantasia, Timayia Avenue, tel. (04) 45 53 92; Nostalgia, Timayia Avenue, tel. (04) 43 65 50; Golden Night, 25 Galileo Street, tel. (04) 45 27 30.

Discothèques

Casablanca, Artemis Avenue, tel. (04) 62 32 80; Discobolos Dancing Centre, Artemis Avenue; Lazer's Disco, Makarios III Avenue; Spilia Disco, Lord Byron Street.

Cabarets

Acapulco, Hermes Street; Byzantion Night Club, Artemis Avenue, tel. (04) 62 32 80; Dolce Vita, Timayia Avenue, tel. (04) 62 31 30.

Páphos
Bouzouki bars

Demokritos, Dionysos Street, tel. (06) 23 33 71; Ifigenia, Poseidon Avenue, tel. (06) 23 41 67; Hippopotamas, Poseidon Avenue, near Cypria Maris Hotel, tel. (06) 23 74 27; Odyssee Disco, 16 Ayios Antonios Street, tel. (06) 23 86 44; Eros Disco, Ayia Anastasia Street, tel. (06) 23 46 35.

Plátres
Bouzouki bar

Mandra, on road to Káto Plátres, near church.

Discothèques

Satisfy Disco; Andy's Disco.

See Restaurants   Tavernas

See entry   Theatres

Nudism

Nudism is officially prohibited, and offends Cypriot ideas of morality, which visitors should respect. Unofficially, there are a number of small beaches (e.g. in Pólis Bay) where visitors can get an all-over sun tan. Topless bathing is now widely tolerated.

Opening Times

See Business Hours

Photography

Archaeological sites and places of historical and artistic interest can usually be photographed, but flash photography is forbidden in some of the Byzantine churches in the Tróodos Mountains and in most museums (though photography may be allowed in a museum on written application for permission).

Permission should always be asked before photographing people. Most Cypriots do not mind being photographed.

It is strictly forbidden to take photographs of military installations, the demarcation zone between the Greek and Turkish parts of Cyprus and guard posts on the Green Line.

The usual international brands of film can be bought all over Cyprus, though prices are rather higher than at home. It is advisable, therefore, to take sufficient films for the holiday. Photographic shops in the large towns can supply spare parts and carry out repairs to cameras.

Police

In all the larger towns dial 199 for the police.   Emergencies

Nicosia: tel. (02) 30 51 15   Police stations
Lárnaca: tel. (04) 63 02 00
Limassol: tel. (05) 33 04 11
Páphos: tel. (06) 24 01 40

Smaller places with their own numbers:
Agrós: tel. (05) 52 11 36
Ayía Nápa: tel. (03) 72 15 53
Paralímni: tel. (03) 82 12 11
Pedhoulás: tel. (02) 95 26 48
Plátres: tel. (05) 42 13 51
Pólis: tel. (06) 32 14 51

Post

There are post offices in all the larger towns and villages. Opening times   Opening times
are Mon.–Fri. 7.30am–1.30pm, also Thur. 3–6pm (not in July and August),
Sat. 7.30am–noon.

Pillar-box – a relic of colonial times

Some of the larger post offices are also open in the afternoon (except Wed. and Sat.), 3.30–5.30pm from October to April, 4–6pm from May to September.

Head post offices
Nicosia: Central Post Office, Eleftheria Square; tel. (02) 30 32 31
Limassol: Central Post Office, Gladstone Street and Themis Street; tel. (05) 33 01 90
Lárnaca: Post Office, Zenon Kiteus Street; tel. (04) 63 01 81
Páphos: Post Office, Apostolos Pavlos Avenue; tel. (06) 24 02 23

Public Holidays and Festivals

Official holidays
On the following public holidays shops (except in resort areas) and banks are closed:
January 1st: New Year's Day
January 6th: Epiphany
March 25th: Greek Independence Day
April 1st: Cypriot National Day (the beginning of the fight for independence from British rule)
May 1st: Labour Day
August 15th: Dormition of the Mother of God
October 1st: Independence Day (foundation of the Republic of Cyprus)
October 28th: Greek National Day ("Ókhi Day", commemorating Greece's "No" to the Italians in 1940)
December 25th/26th: Christmas

Movable festivals
"Green Monday" (Monday of Shrovetide): Carnival (great Carnival parade in Limassol). Festival of St Lazarus in Lárnaca, when the icon of the saint is carried through the town during Holy Week.

Easter: On Good Friday shops are closed in the afternoon; on Easter
  Saturday, Easter Day and Easter Monday they are closed all day.
Whitsun: Kataklysmos festival in Lárnaca on Whit Monday, 50 days after
  the Orthodox Easter (all shops closed).

See also Facts and Figures, Folk Art and Traditions, Religious Festivals

January 17th: St Anthony's Day (Nicosia and Limassol)   Local religious
January 24th: St Neophytus' Day (monastery of St Neóphytos)   festivals
February 2nd: Presentation of the Virgin in the Temple (festival in Chrysor-
  royiátissa monastery)
April 23rd: St George's Day (Lárnaca)
June 29th: SS Peter and Paul (solemn religious service in Káto Páphos,
  with the Archbishop of Cyprus)
September 14th: Festival of the Holy Cross in Stavrovoúni and Ómodhos
October 4th: Festival of St John Lampadistes in Kalopanayiótis
October 18th: Festival of St Luke in Nicosia and Palekhóri, Koúklia

May: Anthestiria Festival (Flower Festival) in Lárnaca, Limassol, Páphos   Other festivals
  and Paralímni
July: Limassol Festival (folk events, exhibitions, circus, drama)
Beginning of August: Pampaphia Folk Festival in Páphos
End of August/beginning of September: Dionysia (wine festival, with music and dancing) at Stroumbí, near Páphos
Beginning of September: Limassol Wine Festival, a twelve-day event held
  in the Municipal Gardens which attracts thousands of visitors, who on
  payment of a small entrance charge can sample all the wines of Cyprus.
September/October: "Cypria" International Festival in Nicosia (music,
  dance, theatre)

Public Transport

The forms of public transport available in Cyprus are buses, "service taxis"
(shared taxis) and ordinary taxis. There are no railways or tram services.

Service buses – the cheapest form of transport in Cyprus – operate be-   **Buses**
tween towns and villages and also between the larger towns and nearby
beaches. There is usually only one bus a day to villages in the hills, and the
buses do not always keep to their timetable. Services between villages are
mostly run by old Bedford buses which carry mail and luggage as well as
passengers. Each village has its own bus to take people to work and
children to school.
  Most bus services are run by four large companies, Kallenos, Kemek,
EMAN and Costas. Information about services can be obtained from local
bus offices and tourist information offices.

Nicosia–Lárnaca: Lefkaritis, 6 Stasinos Avenue; tel. (02) 44 25 66   Services from
Nicosia–Limassol: KEMEK, 34 Leonidas Street; tel. (02) 46 39 89   Nicosia
Nicosia–Plátres, Kalopanayiótis, Pedhoulás: KEMEK, Leonidas Street/
  Homer Avenue; tel. (02) 46 39 89
Nicosia–Tróodos and Kakopetriá: Solea Bus, Costanza Bastion, near Elef-
  theria Square
Nicosia–Kýkko Monastery: Kambos Bus, Leonidas Street/Homer Avenue

Lárnaca–Nicosia, Limassol: Lefkaritis, Athens Street; tel. (04) 62 54 40   From Lárnaca
Lárnaca–Ayía Nápa: EMAN, Athens Street, opposite Sun Hall Hotel
Lárnaca–Paralímni (via Dherínia): Paralímni Bus, Athens Street
Lárnaca–Léfkara: St Lazarus Square
Lárnaca–Airport: Athens Street, at Four Lanterns Hotel, Bus 21
Airport–Lárnaca: Bus 21

Old Bedford buses

From Limassol	Limassol–Nicosia, Páphos: KEMEK, Enosis Street/Irene Street; tel. (05) 36 32 41

From Limassol
Limassol–Nicosia, Páphos: KEMEK, Enosis Street/Irene Street; tel. (05) 36 32 41
Limassol–Lárnaca: Lefkaritis, Spyros Araouzos Street/Hadjipavlou Street; tel. (05) 36 26 70
Limassol–Plátres: Karydas, 21 Thessaloniki Street; tel. (05) 36 20 61
Limassol–Plátres: Plátres Bus, 50 Eleftheria Street; tel. (05) 36 29 07
Limassol–Plátres, Pródhromos, Pedhoulás: G. Demos, Enosis Street/Irene Street
Limassol–Agrós: Agros Bus, Enosis Street/Irene Street

From Páphos
Páphos–Pólis: Fontana Amorosa Bus, Pallikarides Street; tel. (06) 23 67 40
Páphos–Limassol: KEMEK, Fellahoglou Street; tel. (06) 23 42 55
Páphos–Pyrgos: Pyrgos Bus, Karavella car park, Pallikarides Avenue
Páphos–Coral Bay: ALEPA Bus, Karavella car park, at Zena cinema (near Ev. Pallikarides Avenue)

From Pólis
Pólis–Páphos: Fontana Amorosa Bus; tel. (063) 21 11 15

Service taxis
Service taxis (shared taxis) are large Mercedes taxis which can seat up to seven people. They run at half-hourly intervals on fixed routes between the larger towns, from 6am to 6pm (7pm in summer).
    Service taxis can pick up passengers by arrangement at any particular point on their route and will drop them at any desired point at their destination.

Fares
The fares are reasonable, normally ranging between C£1 and C£1.50. The fare is the same whatever the number of passengers.

Offices
Nicosia–Lárnaca: Acropolis, 9 Stasinos Avenue; tel. (02) 47 25 25
Nicosia–Lárnaca, Limassol: Kyriakos, 27 Stasinos Avenue; tel. (02) 44 41 41
Nicosia–Lárnaca: Makris, 11 Stasinos Avenue; tel. (02) 46 62 01

Nicosia–Limassol: Karydas, 8 Homer Avenue; tel. (02) 46 22 69
Nicosia–Limassol: Kypros, 9 Stasinos Avenue; tel. (02) 46 48 11

Lárnaca–Limassol, Nicosia: Acropolis, Kalogreon Street/Makarios Avenue; tel. (04) 65 55 55
Lárnaca–Limassol, Nicosia: Makris, 13 King Paul Street; tel. (04) 65 29 29
Lárnaca–Nicosia: Kyriakos, 2 Hermes Street; tel. (04) 65 51 00

There are no service taxis to Ayía Nápa, into the Tróodos Mountains (except Limassol–Plátres) and to the airport. For Páphos, change in Limassol.

Limassol–Nicosia, Páphos: Karydas, Thessaloniki Street; tel. (05) 36 20 61
Limassol–Nicosia, Páphos: Kypros, 49 Sp. Araouzos Street; tel. (05) 36 39 79
Limassol–Nicosia, Páphos: Kyriakos, Thessaloniki Street; tel. (05) 36 41 14
Limassol–Lárnaca: Makris, 166 Hellas Street; tel. (05) 36 55 50
Limassol–Lárnaca: Acropolis, 49 Sp. Araouzos Street; tel. (05) 36 67 66

Páphos–Limassol: Karydas, 29 Ev. Pallikarides Street; tel. (06) 23 24 59
Páphos–Limassol: Kypros, 134 Makarios Avenue; tel. (05) 23 23 76
For Lárnaca or Nicosia, change in Limassol

The ordinary taxis have meters. Fares, which are fixed by the government, **Taxis** are reasonable. The charge is increased by about 10% for journeys outside the towns. For journeys at night (between 11pm and 6am) there is approximately a 15% increase. There is no charge for the first piece of luggage, but for more than one item, weighing over 13 kilograms (28½ lb), there is a supplementary charge.

Radio and Television

The Cyprus Broadcasting Corporation (CyBC) transmits programmes in   Radio
English daily, from 10–10.30am, 1.30–2.30pm and 7.30–9pm (Programme 2, 498m/693KHz and 91.1MHz VHF). On the same channel a tourist programme – "Welcome to Cyprus" – is broadcast between 8 and 8.30am Monday to Friday.

The British Forces Broadcasting Service (BFBS) transmits programmes 24 hours a day (Channel 1, 99.6, 92.1 and 89.7MHz VHF; Channel 2, 95.3, 89.9 and 91.9MHz).
   A private station, Radio One, broadcasts in English.
   The BBC World Service can also be heard on 127MHz VHF.

The CyBC has two television channels, broadcasting in the evening. Pro-   Television
grammes are mainly in English.

Restaurants (see also Food and Drink)

Cypriots like eating out in parties of family and friends. Not surprisingly, therefore, Cyprus is particularly well equipped with restaurants and eating-places in every category of price and quality, ranging from sandwich stalls by way of modest tavernas to speciality restaurants serving French cuisine. Even in remote little villages there are modest but excellent family-run tavernas, and there are bars and pubs in all places of any size.

The local coffee-house (kafenion) is a popular meeting-place and social   Coffee-house
centre. In addition to coffee and other drinks it serves a variety of   (kafenion)
sweets.

Prices   Prices are controlled by the Cyprus Tourism Organisation (CTO), and res-
                          taurants are required to display their tariffs. Value added tax (VAT) at a rate
                          of 8% plus a service charge of 10% is included in the bill.

Menus   Menus are usually written in English as well as in Greek.

Restaurants and Tavernas (a selection)

Nicosia   Acropolis Restaurant, 12 Leonidas Street; tel. (02) 46 48 71
                          Athineon Restaurant, 30B and 32A Ippocratous Street, Laïkí Yitoniá; tel.
                              (02) 44 47 86
                          Royiatico Restaurant, Laiki Yitonia; tel. (02) 45 50 81
                          Tembelodendron, 48 Kefallinia Street; tel. (02) 33 06 13
                          Ten Lanterns, 5 Kefallinia Street; tel. (02) 42 14 10
                          Aegeon Tavern, 40 Hector Street; tel. (02) 34 75 22
                          Classic Tavern, 2 Erechtheion Street; tel. (02) 35 26 28 (with live music)
                          Faros Tavern, 48 Archbishop Makarios III Avenue; tel. (02) 43 76 68
                          Greek Tavern, 46 Grivas Dhigenis Avenue; tel. (02) 44 55 56 (with live music)
                          Plaka Tavern, 8 Archbishop Makarios III Square, Engomi; tel. (02) 44 64 98
                          Skaraveos Fish Tavern, 4 Nikokreon Street; tel. (02) 46 49 95
                          Psarolimano Fish Tavern, 55 28th October Avenue; tel. (02) 35 09 90

                          Other restaurants in Nicosia are listed in "Nicosia This Month" (obtainable
                          only in Cyprus).

Limassol   Klima Tavern, Potamos Yermasoyias; tel. (05) 32 15 66
                          Old Harbour (Ladas), Sýntagma Square; tel. (05) 36 57 60
                          Fish Tavern, 217 Franklin Roosevelt Street; tel. (05) 39 42 44
                          Kolossi Steak House, Kolóssi; tel. (05) 23 25 70
                          Assos Restaurant, old Limassol–Nicosia road; tel. (05) 32 19 45

                          Arab cuisine: Al Kaima (live Oriental music); Shahrazad Restaurant (live
                          Cypriot and Oriental music), tel. (05) 32 16 09.

                          There are numerous restaurants in the hotel district and on the seafront
                          promenade, and many modest little tavernas round the old market hall. It is
                          also worth going out to the village of Yermasóyia for the sake of its friendly
                          tavernas.

Lárnaca   Alakati Restaurant, 71 Athens Avenue; tel. (04) 65 30 42
                          Archontissa Restaurant, Athens Avenue (with live music)
                          Sokrates Restaurant, Lárnaca–Dhekélia road
                          Stani, 5A Kotyia Tepe Street; tel. (04) 62 38 10
                          Varos Restaurant, corner of Hermes Street and Dhigenis Akritas Street

                          There are other good restaurants on the harbour promenade.

Páphos   Avgerinos Restaurant, Minos Street; tel. (06) 23 29 90
                          Jason Steak House Restaurant, Jason Street; tel. (06) 24 24 58
                          Kyklamino Restaurant, Pyramos Street; tel. (06) 23 77 66
                          Demokritos Restaurant, Dionysos Street; tel. (06) 23 33 71 (with live music)
                          Chez Alex; tel. (06) 23 47 67 (fish taverna)

                          There are other fish restaurants on the harbour.

Plátres   Psilodendro Restaurant, Trout Farm; tel. (05) 42 13 50
                          Mandra, on the road to Káto Plátres (live music)

Shopping, Souvenirs

In the towns there are shops of all kinds selling both home-produced and imported goods, and in the old quarters of Limassol and Lárnaca visitors will still find old craftsmen's workshops selling their own products. Prices are, in general, fixed, though in individual cases there may be scope for bargaining.

Shoes are a particularly good buy, since Cyprus has a considerable local shoemaking industry. Textiles and leather goods can also be bought at very reasonable prices. Silver jewellery, often based on ancient models, can be found in Limassol, Nicosia and Páphos and in the little village of Léfkara. Lace made in traditional fashion can be bought not only in Léfkara and Ómodhos where it is made but also in all tourist centres. Páphos is famed for its woven fabrics.

Clothing, jewellery, lace

Pottery and basketwork are produced in the Páphos area, and the villages of Kórnos and Phiní are also noted for their pottery. Natural sponges are fished off the west coast near Páphos; they are relatively dear, since they are now found only in areas difficult of access. Various kinds of sweets, in particular Turkish delight, are popular souvenirs of a visit to Cyprus, and Cyprus brandy and Commandaria, the sweet dessert wine which is one of the oldest wines in the world, also offer good value.

Pottery, sponges, sweets, drinks

In order to promote the production and sale of traditional craft goods the Cyprus Handicrafts Service has established handicraft centres in a number of towns in which visitors can buy a range of traditional articles like pottery, embroidery, leather, copper and batik work.

Handicraft centres

There are handicraft centres (open: Mon.–Fri. 7.30am–2.30pm, also Thur. 3–6pm) in the following towns:

Nicosia: 186 Athalassa Avenue; tel. (02) 30 50 24; Laïkí Yitoniá; tel. (02) 30 30 65

Limassol: 25 Themidos Street; tel. (05) 33 01 18
Lárnaca: 6 Kosma Lysioti Street; tel. (04) 63 03 27
Páphos: 46 Apostle Paul Avenue; tel. (06) 24 02 43

Sport

Bicycles can be rented in all the larger towns and in tourist centres (see also Cycling).

Cycling

There are excellent diving grounds off the coasts of Cyprus, particularly in a number of small bays on Cape Gréco, near Ayía Nápa. Diving equipment can be hired in the main tourist centres.
    Information can be obtained from the following organisations:

Diving

Cyprus Federation of Underwater Activities, P.O. Box 1053, Nicosia; tel. (02) 45 46 47
Cyprus Sub-Aqua Club, P.O. Box 3547, Nicosia; tel. (02) 45 46 47

Lárnaca Sub-Aqua Club, P.O. Box 1503, Nicosia; tel. (04) 47 77 57
Sun Fish Diving Centre, 26 Archbishop Makarios Avenue, Ayía Nápa;
    tel. (03) 72 13 00
Aloe Divers, Aloe Hotel, Páphos; tel. (06) 23 40 00

Fishing

A number of private lakes and artificial lakes are stocked with freshwater fish such as trout, carp and grayling. Fishing permits can be obtained from the Head Office Fisheries Department, 13 Aiolou Street, Nicosia, tel. (02) 40 35 26. Angling equipment can be bought in the large towns, and there are now also hotels which hire out equipment. There are no restrictions on sea fishing, and deep-sea angling is a popular sport.

Golf

There are two golf courses: Tsada Golf Club at Páphos, tel. (06) 64 27 74 and the Elias near Limassol, tel. (05) 32 50 00.

Riding

Although riding is not a widely popular sport in Cyprus a number of riding clubs have been established in recent years.

Nicosia

Lapatsa Sports Centre, Dhefterá (12km/7½ miles outside town on the Tseri–Dhefterá road); tel. (02) 62 10 21

Limassol

Elias Horse Riding Centre, on Limassol–Nicosia road; tel. (05) 32 50 00

Lárnaca

Flamingos Riding Club; tel. (04) 65 56 60

Páphos

Riding Centre, near the Tombs of the Kings; tel. (06) 63 39 66

Sailing

There are boating harbours at Lárnaca, Limassol, Páphos and Ayía Nápa; the most modern of these, the Lárnaca Marina (tel. (04) 65 31 10), has moorings for 400 boats. The Limassol Sheraton Pleasure Harbour at Limassol (tel. (05) 32 11 00) has 227 moorings and facilities for boat hire.

Skiing

Skiing is possible in the Tróodos Mountains in winter. There are four ski-lifts on Mt Ólympos. The Cyprus Ski Club, P.O. Box 2185, Nicosia, tel. (02) 36 53 40, hires out equipment and has a number of skiing instructors. See Sights in South Cyprus, Tróodos Mountains.

Tennis

There are public tennis courts in all the larger towns, and many hotels and apartment complexes have courts (the majority flood-lit) on which non-residents can also play.
Cyprus Tennis Federation, P.O. Box 3931, Nicosia; tel. (02) 36 68 22 (morning only).

Nicosia

Champs Elysées, Archangel Street; tel. (02) 35 31 88
Eleon Tennis Club, 3 Plutarch Street, Egkomi; tel. (02) 44 99 23
Field Club, Egypt Avenue; tel. (02) 45 20 41
Lapatsa Sporting Centre, Dhefterá (11km/7 miles outside town on the Tseri–Dhefterá road); tel. (02) 62 12 01
Engomi; tel. (02) 44 99 23

Limassol

Limassol-Famagusta Tennis Club, 3 Mesaoria Street; tel. (05) 33 59 52
Limassol Sporting Club, 11 Olympion Street, Tsiflikoudia;
    tel. (05) 35 98 18

Lárnaca

Lárnaca Tennis Club, 10 Kilkis Street; tel. (04) 65 69 99

Páphos

On Yeroskípos Tourist Beach (3km/2 miles east of harbour);
    tel. (06) 23 45 25

Walking

Cyprus offers ideal walking country. In the Tróodos Mountains and on the Akámas peninsula at the Baths of Aphrodite there are nature trails laid out by the Cyprus Tourism Organisation. Other nature trails in the ammochostas (Famagusta) area, the Páphos Forest and near Argos village have been laid-out by the Forestry Department.

Stout footwear is advisable, since many paths are narrow and stony; it also provides protection against snakes.

Walking tours are organised by various travel agencies.

Many hotels and private agencies offer facilities for various water sports, including wind-surfing, water-skiing and surfing.

Wind-surfing, water-skiing

Equipment for all kinds of water sports can be hired from Jalos Sports in Pólis.

Telephone, Telegraph

Post offices do not provide telephone or telegraph services, which are handled by the Cyprus Telecommunications Authority (CYTA). International telephone calls can also be made from telephone kiosks, with payphones operated by coins or phonecards ("telecards") (obtainable from post offices, the CYTA, banks, souvenir shops or kiosks). All telephones have subscriber trunk dialling.

CYTA offices in the larger towns:
Nicosia: 1 Museum Avenue
Limassol: Athens Street (corner of Markos Botsaris Street)
Lárnaca: Lord Byron Street
Páphos: Grivas Dighenis Street

To Cyprus:
from the United Kingdom: 00 357
from the United States or Canada: 011 357

International dialling codes

From Cyprus:
to the United Kingdom: 00 44
to the United States or Canada: 00 1

Nicosia: 02
Ayía Nápa: 03
Paralímni/Protaras: 03
Lárnaca: 04
Limassol: 05
Plátres: 05
Páphos: 06
Pólis: 06

Local dialling codes

When telephoning from abroad to Cyprus (or to the United Kingdom) the initial zero of the local code should be omitted.

Theatres

For theatre-lovers the best place to go in Cyprus is Nicosia, which offers a varied programme of performances, mostly in Greek but sometimes also in English.

Municipal Theatre (1200 seats)
Museum Street
tel. (02) 46 30 28

Nicosia

Anglo-Cypriot Theatre
Chantelais House, Chr. Sozos Street
tel. (02) 45 78 60

289

Satirico Theatre
Athens Street, Strovolos
tel. (02) 42 16 09

New Theatre
Chantelais House, Chr. Sozos Street
tel. (02) 45 78 62

ENA Theatre
4 Athens Street
tel. (02) 34 82 03

In summer there are performances in the open-air theatre at the Famagusta Gate.

Limassol   Pattcheion Theatre, Ayia Zoni Street (performances in Greek only)

Koúrion   Performances are given during the summer in the Roman theatre of Koúrion.

Time

Cyprus observes Eastern European Time, two hours ahead of Greenwich Mean Time. Summer Time, three hours ahead of GMT and two hours ahead of British Summer Time, is in force from the last weekend in March to the last weekend in September.

Tipping

Hotel and restaurant bills include a 10% service charge, plus 8% Value Added Tax (VAT). In addition waiters expect a further tip, as do taxi-drivers.

Trade Fairs and Exhibitions

The Cyprus International (State) Fair, held annually in May and June, in Nicosia, displays the products of Cyprus and neighbouring countries, as well as Europe, the Middle East, China and Japan.

Information:
Cyprus State Fairs Authority, P.O. Box 3551, Nicosia.

Travel Documents

Visitors from the United Kingdom, the United States, Canada and many other countries require only a passport, without visa, for a stay of up to three months. For a stay longer than three months a permit must be obtained from the Migration Department in Nicosia.

Visitors with a North Cyprus stamp in their passport will not be admitted to the Republic of Cyprus. If visiting North Cyprus however, you can ask to have the stamp put on a form separate from the passport.

Weights and Measures

Although Cyprus adopted the metric system in 1987, there are still instances where old British Imperial measures are used (particularly outside the main towns). Petrol is often still sold by the gallon rather than the litre, distances given in miles, weights measured in okes (2.8 pounds/1.268kg) and temperatures in Fahrenheit.

When to Go

Cyprus has some 340 sunny days in the year (see Facts and Figures, Climate). It gets very hot in summer, with temperatures ranging between 30°C/86°F and 40°C/104°F on the coast and in inland areas, but visitors who are not afraid of heat will enjoy a bathing holiday during the summer months. Only in the hills is it rather cooler.

Summer

The most pleasant months are in spring (April to the end of May) and autumn (September to the end of November). During these months it is not so hot, while with Cyprus's perennially mild climate the water is still warm enough for bathing. In spring the island is covered with trees in blossom and is particularly attractive for walkers. There may be occasional light showers of rain both in spring and in autumn.

Spring and autumn

In the mild winter months Cyprus is a good place for a restful holiday, without the hustle and bustle of the main holiday season. Since the temperature of the sea never falls below 16°C/61°F, bathing is still possible. In winter there is snow in the hills, and modest facilities for skiing on Mt Ólympos (four ski-lifts).

Winter

Wine

Cyprus is one of the oldest wine-producing countries in the world, and still occupies a leading place world-wide in terms of production per head. Its success in maintaining this position over the last twenty years is largely due to the introduction of modern wine-making techniques.

A third of the agricultural population is engaged in viticulture. The most important wine-producing areas are the relatively rainy southern slopes of the Tróodos range, followed by the coastal plains.

The native types of grape – never affected by phylloxera – are Mavron, Maratheftiko and Ophthalmo (black) and Xynisteri and Alexandria Muscatel (white).

Types of grape

Chrysorroyiátissa wines

The oldest wine on the island was first made by the Knights of St John in the 12th century and named Commandaria after their commandery of Kolóssi (see Sights in South Cyprus, Kolóssi). Commandaria is made from the black Mavron and white Xynisteri grapes in the proportion of nine to one. The heavy sweetness of this dessert wine is the result of the sun-drying of the grapes. Eleven villages, including Yerasa and Kalokhoria, are entitled to call their wine Commandaria.

Commandaria

The bulk of Cyprus's wide range of white wine (áspro krasí), red wine (kókkino krasí) and sherry-type wines comes from four large wineries in Limassol – Keo, Sodap, Etko and Loel. Visits to these, and other wineries, are possible.

Wineries

The country wines made by the growers themselves are also of good quality, and as a

Country wines

291

rule rather heavier. The villages of Ómodhos, Plátres and Kiláni are noted for their wine. Chrysorroyiátissa Monastery also produces excellent white and red wines.

White wines
Among the best known dry white wines are Aphrodite, Palomino, White Lady, Keo Hock, Thisbe and Arsinoe 62. Rather sweeter are St Hilarion and Blonde Lady.

Red wines
The most popular dry red wines are Othello, Afames, Keo Claret, Dark Lady, Hermes, Negro and Olympus.

Youth Hostels

Youth hostels in Cyprus are open to holders of the International Youth Hostel Association card; non-members are also accepted, they are issued with a guest card upon arrival at a hostel. Beds can be booked in advance through the Cyprus Youth Hostel Association, P.O. Box 1328, Nicosia; tel. (02) 4 20 27.

Youth hostels
Nicosia: 5 I. Hadjidaki Street; tel. (02) 44 48 08
Ayia Nápa, Dionysios Solomos Street; tel. (03) 72 31 13, (02) 44 20 27
Lárnaca: 27 Nikolaos Rossos Street; tel. (04) 62 11 18
Páphos: 37 Eleftherios Venizelos Avenue; tel. (06) 23 25 88
Tróodos: in the pinewoods; tel. (05) 42 24 00
Stavrós tis Psókas Forest Station; tel. (06) 33 21 44, (06) 72 23 38

Practical Information from A to Z: North Cyprus

Accommodation

See Camping and Caravanning, Hotels

Airlines

See Getting to North Cyprus

Antiques

The export of antiques from North Cyprus is prohibited.

Banks

Banks in North Cyprus will change cash, travellers' cheques and Euro-cheques. Many shops, restaurants and hotels accept credit cards (Euro-card, Visa, Diners' Club).

Mon.–Fri. 8.30am–noon (winter), 8am–2pm (summer).   Opening times

Beaches

Some of the finest beaches on the island are in North Cyprus, such as the wide bays with beaches of fine sand at Famagusta and the little sandy and shingle bays at Kyrenia.
  Beaches belonging to hotels are equipped with sun umbrellas and loungers and can be used by non-residents on payment of an admission charge.

Beach on the south side of the town, at the Palm Beach Hotel   Famagusta
Long beaches to the north of the town
Sálamis Beach, at the excavations of ancient Sálamis

Beautiful lonely sandy beaches   Karpasía
                                                                      peninsula

(Many of the beaches to the west of Kyrenia belong to hotels.)   Kyrenia
Riviera Beach, 4km/2½ miles west: good for snorkelling
Golden Rock Beach, 8km/5 miles west (restaurants)
Mermaid Beach, to the west of the town, at the Deniz Kızı Hotel
Mare Monte Beach, 12km/7½ miles west, at the Mare Monte Hotel
Karakum Beach, 4km/2½ miles east
Acapulco Beach, at the Club Acapulco holiday village
Twelve Mile Beach, 20km/12½ miles east: the longest sandy beach on the
  coast.

There are other beaches in Mórphou (Güzelyurt) Bay.

Bookshops

There are two bookshops in North Cyprus selling foreign (mostly English) books: Rüstem's Bookshop (Rüstem Kitabevi), 26 Girne Caddesi, Nicosia (near Atatürk Square, opposite the Saray Hotel); tel. 207 14 18.

Business Hours

Banks	See entry
Chemists	See entry
Government offices	Open: Mon.–Fri. 7.30am–2pm in summer; 8am–1pm and 2–5pm in winter.
Museums	See Sights from A to Z
Post offices	See Post, Telephone, Telegraph
Shops	In summer (May to September) shops are open Mon.–Sat. 7.30am–1pm and 4–6pm. In winter (October to April) they are usually open Mon.–Sat. 8am–1pm and 2–6pm. In the country many shops stay open later in the evening and are also open on Sundays. In some tourist areas shops do not close for lunch and may even open until 8pm.
Public holidays	See entry

Camping and Caravanning

"Wild" camping is permitted, but the local people should always be asked for permission.

There are three official camping sites with sanitary facilities:
Onur Camping, to the north of Sálamis, opposite the Gıranel Bay Hotel
Riviera Camping, 6km/4 miles west of Kyrenia (restaurant, private beach)
Lara Camping, 15km/9 miles east of Kyrenia

Car Rental

The driver of a rented car must possess a national or international driving licence and be 25 years or over with at least 2 years driving experience.

Rental charges in North Cyprus are very reasonable, and are reduced still further in the off season. The charge usually includes third party insurance and unlimited mileage.

Chemists

The word for a chemist's shop is Eczane. Since not all internationally available medicines can be obtained in North Cyprus visitors who require particular drugs should take a supply with them.

Opening hours   Mon.–Sat. 8am–1pm and 2–6pm (winter), 7.30am–1pm and 4–6pm (summer).

Currency

The currency of North Cyprus is the Turkish lira (TL). There are banknotes for 20,000, 50,000, 100,000, 250,000, 500,000, 1 million and 5 million TL and coins in denominations of 50, 100, 500, 1000, 2500, 5000, 10,000, 25,000 and 50,000 TL.

The Turkish lira is subject to rapid inflation. It is advisable, therefore, to check up on the current exchange rate through a bank or travel agency shortly before leaving home and to change only as much money as is likely to be required for immediate needs.

Exchange rates are better in Turkey or in North Cyprus itself than in other countries. Major European currencies and the US Dollar, travellers' cheques and major credit cards are also welcome.

See entry   Banks

Customs Regulations

In addition to personal effects visitors may take into North Cyprus, duty-free, 2 bottles of wine or 1.5 litres of spirits, 400 cigarettes or 500 grams of tobacco.
    The export of valuable antiques is strictly forbidden.

Cycling

Hitherto there have been practically no facilities for hiring bicycles in North Cyprus. As part of the effort to promote tourism, however, a bicycle hire agency has recently been opened on the harbour promenade in Kyrenia.

Diplomatic and Consular Offices

North Cyprus is not recognised officially, and the only diplomatic mission is the Turkish embassy. To look after the interests of British residents, however, the British High Commissioner or his representative attends at a small office behind the post office in Kyrenia (Girne) on Saturday mornings, and the consular section of the High Commission maintains an office in the former High Commissioner's residence in Mehmet Akif Street, Nicosia (open: Mon.–Fri. 7.30am–1pm; tel. 227 49 38).

For United States citizens there is the American Centre in Güner Türkmen Street (open: Mon.–Fri. 8am–5pm; tel. 227 24 43).

Distances

The distances, in kilometres, between towns in the Turkish part of Cyprus are shown in the following table:

Distances in km between towns in North Cyprus						
	Nicosia	Famagusta	Mórphou	Kyrenia	Rizokárpaso	Sóloi
Nicosia · Lefkoşa	–	61	40	26	123	54
Famagusta · Gazimağusa	61	–	94	73	80	108
Mórphou · Güzelyurt	40	94	–	48	158	12
Kyrenia · Girne	26	73	48	–	133	60
Rizokárpaso · Dipkarpaz	123	80	158	133	–	184
Sóloi · Soli	54	108	12	60	184	–

Electricity

Electricity is 240 volts AC. Power sockets take British-style plugs, usually three-pin.

Emergencies

Medical aid   See entry

Police   Nicosia/Lefkoşa: Atatürk Square, Girne Caddesi; tel. 228 34 11
                Famagusta/Gazimağusta: at St Nicholas's Cathedral and in Ilker Karter
                    Caddesi; tel. 366 53 10

                Kyrenia/Girne: at Castle; tel. 815 22 66
                Mórphou/Güzelyurt: tel. 714 21 40
                Léfka/Lefke: tel. 728 74 23
                Tríkome/Iskele: tel. 371 23 33
                Lápothos/Lapta: tel. 821 85 12

Events

See Public Holidays and Festivals

Excursions

Local travel agencies operate coach tours (usually day trips) to the main sights in North Cyprus, with English-speaking guides. They also organise walking tours and boat trips. Excursions can be booked either in the agencies themselves or in hotels.

Food and Drink

The food and drink of North Cyprus are broadly similar to those of the Greek part of the island, though some dishes have different names and show the influence of mainland Turkey. Meze is also popular in North Cyprus, but exclude the flesh of the pig in any form.

The times of meals are as in South Cyprus. The hotels also generally serve international cuisine; many tasty local dishes, however, can be found in Turkish restaurants.

North Cypriot   Balık = fish
dishes   biber dolması = green peppers stuffed with rice
                    biftek = beefsteak
                    cacık = cucumber salad with yoghurt and garlic (Greek tsatzíki)
                    ekmek = bread
                    günür çorbası = soup of the day
                    imam bayıldı = "The imam fainted": aubergines with onions and tomatoes
                    köfte = meat balls
                    lahmacun = Turkish pizza with highly spiced minced meat
                    omlet = omelette
                    piliç = chicken
                    pirzola = lamb chop

Turkish sweets

Outdoor oven at a taverna

şeftali = a spicy lamb sausage
şiş kebab = pieces of meat grilled on the spit
tarama = a paste made from spiced cod roe
tavuk = chicken
yaprak dolması = stuffed vine leaves
yeşil salata = green salad

Since practically no grapes are grown in North Cyprus most of the wine (şarap) in this part of the island is imported from Turkey. Well-known brands are Villa Doluca and Kavaklıdere (both red and white). Selim and Son's winery produces a dry white wine named Aphrodite.

Drinks

Raki is a spirit similar to the Greek ouzo.

Beer (bira) also comes from Turkey. Two popular light beers are Turkish-brewed Efes and Tuborg. A locally brewed beer is called Gold Fussel.

Coffee (kahve) and tea (çay) are drunk in the coffee-houses. As in South Cyprus there are three degrees of sweetness – sweet (şekerli), medium sweet (orta) and without sugar (sade).

A favourite non-alcoholic drink is ayran (yoghurt diluted with water).

Ingredients: 2 onions (chopped), 3 spoonfuls olive oil, 2 tomatoes (diced), 2 spoonfuls chopped parsley, garlic, the juice of half a lemon, salt, 3 aubergines (medium size), 2 cupfuls water.

Recipe:
Imam bayıldı
("The imam
has fainted")

Preheat the oven to 180°C/356°F. Cook the onions in oil for 5 minutes and pour them into a dish with the tomatoes, the garlic, the parsley and the lemon juice. Add salt and stir well. Cut the stalks off the aubergines. Peel half of each aubergine with a potato knife, leaving the other halves in their skins, and lightly cook them in the oil from the onions. Then cut the aubergines lengthwise, take out the flesh and fill them with the tomato, onion and parsley stuffing. Cook for 45 minutes in an ovenproof dish, and garnish with parsley.

Frontier Crossing

Visitors to North Cyprus cannot enter the Greek part of Cyprus, which regards a visit to the Turkish part of the island as an illegal act. Visitors to South Cyprus may, however, make day trips into the Turkish area – though this is not encouraged by the Greek Cypriot authorities (see Practical Information on South Cyprus, Frontier Crossing).

Getting to North Cyprus

Visitors can travel to North Cyprus either by air or by sea, but entering it from South Cyprus is subject to restrictions of the Greek Cypriot authorities (see Frontier Crossing).

By air

Since the Turkish Republic of North Cyprus is not recognised under international law, no international airlines fly to North Cyprus apart from Turkish Airlines, Cyprus Turkish Airlines, Istanbul Airlines and Onur Airlines, which use the Turkish Cypriot airport of Ercan (24km/15 miles east of Nicosia). These airlines cannot fly direct to Ercan from Britain and other countries, and flights therefore always make an intermediate stop in mainland Turkey (usually Istanbul); there are also flights from Izmir, Ankara, Antalya and Adana. Visitors can of course fly to Istanbul by other airlines and get a connecting flight from there to Ercan on one of the Turkish airlines.

The flight from Britain, allowing for the stop in mainland Turkey, takes about 6 hours.

By sea

The only shipping services to North Cyprus are from the Turkish ports of Taşucu (west of Silifke), Mersin, Antalya and the Israeli port of Haifa.

From Taşucu the fast MV "Barbaros" (the Kıbrıs Express) sails daily (except Saturdays) in summer to Kyrenia (Girne); the crossing takes 2–3 hours. The "Fatih Feribotu" sails three times weekly between Taşucu and Kyrenia, the "Girne Sultan" four times weekly, taking about 8 hours in each case.

Shipping offices:
Taş Tur, Atatürk Caddesi 82, Taşucu; tel. 324 13 34
Sea Bird Co. Ltd, Iskenderun Caddesi 40/4, Girne; tel. 581 5 35 54

From Mersin there is a ferry to Famagusta three times weekly. The crossing takes about 10 hours.

Shipping offices:
Turkish Maritime Lines, Liman Binası, Kat 2, Mersin; tel. 324 2 31 88 28
Çelebi Han, Istiklâl Caddesi 127, Sok. 2, Mersin

By car

It is worth while taking a car only if it is proposed to spend some time in North Cyprus. Supplementary third party insurance must be taken out, either on the ferry to Kyrenia or at the customs office on arrival in Famagusta. A car can be taken into North Cyprus for a period of up to three months (renewable up to one year) without payment of duty.

N.B.

On arrival in North Cyprus it is advisable to ask the immigration officer not to put a stamp in your passport (request a separate entry visa to be stamped instead), since this would make it difficult on a future occasion to enter South Cyprus and would be likely to cause difficulty in entering Greece.

Hotels

North Cyprus has a range of accommodation for holidaymakers including hotels, bungalows, hotel-apartments, holiday villages, motel-camping and bed and breakfast, covering a wide range of quality and price categories (from one to five stars). The Hotels Board of North Cyprus supervises hotel standards and tariffs. The following is a selection of hotels for visitors entering North Cyprus from Turkey.

Categories

★★★Saray Hotel, Girne Caddesi (Atatürk Square), tel. 020 7 11 15
★★Sabri's Orient (outside the town on the Kyrenia road), tel. 020 7 21 62

Nicosia/ Lefkoşa

★★★★★Palm Beach, Kemal Servet Sokağı (Maras), tel. 366 20 00/2
★★★★Park Hotel (at Sálamis excavations), tel. 378 82 13; Sálamis Bay (at Sálamis), tel. 378 81 11
★★★Boğaz Hotel, tel. 371 26 59; Cyprus Gardens, tel. 371 27 22; Mimoza Hotel, tel. 378 82 19
Apartment Hotels: Sea Side, tel. 378 82 39; Sema, tel. 366 12 22
★★Old Town Hall, tel. 366 34 64
Apartment Hotels: Dagli, tel. 378 82 11; Laguna Beach, tel. 366 65 02/4
★Panorama Hotel, tel. 366 58 80; Portofino Hotel, tel. 366 43 62

Famagusta/ Gazimağusa

★★★★★Celebrity (14km/8½ miles west), tel. 081 87 51/3
★★★★Dome Hotel (in town centre), tel. 815 24 53/7
Apartment Hotel: Jasmine Court, tel. 815 14 50/20; Holiday Village: The Olive Tree, tel. 824 42 00
★★★Dorana (in town centre), tel. 815 35 21/2; Grand Rock Hotel, tel. 815 22 38; Deniz Kizi Hotel about 10km/6 miles west), tel. 821 87 10/1; Kyrenia Oscar Hotel, tel. 815 48 01; Hotel Liman (on harbour), tel. 815 20 01/2
Holiday Villages: Acapulco, tel. 824 41 10; Ambelia, tel. 815 21 75

Kyrenia/Girne

The lonely sandy beach of the Palm Beach Hotel, Famagusta

★★Atlantis, tel. 815 22 42; Bellapais Gardens, tel. 815 60 66; Hotel British (on harbour), tel. 815 22 40; Golden Bay (10km/6 miles west), tel. 821 85 40; Kings Court, tel. 821 84 99; Pia Bella Hotel, tel. 815 53 21/3; Sammy's Hotel, tel. 815 62 79; Socrates Hotel, tel. 815 21 57

Information

Tourist information about North Cyprus (brochures, map, list of hotels and tour operators, etc.) can be obtained from the Tourism Counsellor, Office of the London Representative, Turkish Republic of Northern Cyprus, 28 Cockspur Street, London SW1Y 5BN, tel. (0171) 930 5069 and (0171) 839 4577. Tourist information may also be obtained from other representatives offices.

In the USA you may write to:
Office of the Representative
Turkish Republic of Northern Cyprus
821 United Nations Plaza, 6th Floor
New York N.Y. 10017
New York. Tel. (212) 5575612

Office of the Representative
Turkish Republic of Northern Cyprus
1667 K. Street, Suite 690
Washington D.C. 20006
Washington. Tel. (202) 4625772

In Canada you may write to:
Dr Ezel Örfi (Honorary Representative)
The Office of The Honorary Representative in Canada
of the Turkish Republic of Northern Cyprus
300 John Street, Suite 330
Thornhill, Ontario, L3T 5W4
Canada. Tel. (416) 905 8848604

In North Cyprus   Ministry of Tourism and Social Assistance
Mersin 10, Nicosia/Lefkoşa

Tourist offices:
Nicosia/Lefkoşa: Mehmet Akif Caddesi (outside town walls),
    open: Mon.–Fri. 8.30am–noon and 2–4pm
Famagusta/Gazimağusa: Fevzi Çakmak Caddesi (in New Town),
    open: Mon.–Fri. 9am–noon and 2–4pm
Kyrenia/Girne: on harbour promenade (below the mosque),
    open: Mon.–Fri. 9am–12.30pm and 1.30–5pm
Ercan Airport: tel. (371) 47 03

Language

The official language of North Cyprus, and the language spoken by most of the population, is Turkish. In the tourist centres, however, many people speak English.

Turkish	Pronunciation	
a	a	Alphabet
b	b	
c	j	
ç	ch as in "church"	
d	d	
e	e	
f	f	
g	g (hard, as in "gag")	
ğ	(barely perceptible; lengthens preceding vowel)	
h	h (emphatically pronounced, approaching c in "loch")	
ı	a dark uh sound, as in the last syllable of "over"	
i	i	
j	zh as in "pleasure"	
k	k	
l	l	
m	m	
n	n	
o	o	
ö	eu, as in French "deux"	
p	p	
r	r	
s	s	
ş	sh	
t	t	
u	u	
ü	as in French "une"	
v	v	
y	y, as in "yet"	
z	z	

Number	Turkish	
0	sıfır	Numbers
1	bir	
2	iki	
3	üç	
4	dört	
5	beş	
6	altı	
7	yedi	
8	sekiz	
9	dokuz	
10	on	
11	on bir	
20	yirmi	
21	yirmi bir	
30	otuz	
40	kırk	
50	elli	
60	altmış	
70	yetmiş	
80	seksen	
90	doksan	
100	yüz	
200	iki yüz	
1000	bin	
2000	iki bin	

½	yarım	Fractions
¼	çeyrek	

	English	**Turkish**
Useful words and expressions	good morning	günaydın
	good day	merhaba
	good evening	iyi akşamlar
	good night	iyi geceler
	goodbye	Allah aısmarladık
	Have a good trip	güle güle
	yes	evet
	no	hayır
	please	lütfen
	thank you	mersi
	open	açık
	closed	kapalı
	exit	çıkıs
	Is there . . .	Var mı . . . ?
	There isn't any . . .	Yok . . .
	What does it cost?	Bu kaça?
	where?	nerede?
	when?	ne zaman?
	men	erkekler
	women	kadınlar
	letter	mektup
	chemist's shop	eczane
	bookshop	kitapçi
	post office	postahane
Topographical terms	island	ada
	garden	bahçe
	town hall	belediye
	petrol station	benzin istasyonu
	street, road	cadde(si)
	mosque	cami(i)
	market	çarşı(sı)
	fountain	çeşme
	hill, mountain	dağ
	sea	deniz
	house	ev
	bath-house	hamam
	inn, caravanserai	han
	castle, fortress	hisar
	landing-stage	iskele
	gate	kapı
	caravanserai	kervansaray
	direction of Mecca	kıble
	church	kilise
	bridge	köprü
	pavilion, kiosk	köşk
	village	köy
	tower	kule
	library	kütüphane
	liman	harbour
	square	meydan(ı)
	prayer niche in a mosque (marking the direction of Mecca)	mihrab
	pulpit in a mosque	minber
	museum	müze(si)
	room	oda
	school	okul
	bus stop	otobüs durağı
	park	park

English	Turkish
beach	plaj
police	polis
ablutions fountain	şadırvan
palace	saray
town	şehir
street	sokak (sokağı)
water	su
repair garage, workshop	tamirhane
dervish convent	tekke
hill	tepe
tomb	türbe
ship	vapur
road	yol

Maps and Plans

Most of the maps of Cyprus (see Practical Information on South Cyprus, Maps and Plans) give only the Greek names of places in North Cyprus which now have Turkish names. The AA/Macmillan Traveller's Map of Cyprus (1:275,000), however, gives both Greek and Turkish names.

There is also a free North Cyprus Tourist Map (1:325,000), obtainable from the Offices of the Representative, Turkish Republic of Northern Cyprus (see Information), and at tourist offices in North Cyprus.

Medical Assistance

Since there is no medical school in North Cyprus, all the doctors have been trained in other countries, most of them in Turkey. Many doctors speak English.

There are both state-run hospitals and private clinics. Visitors receive free emergency treatment in state hospitals; otherwise hospital treatment must be paid for. It is therefore advisable to take out temporary medical insurance before leaving home.

Hospitals

The following are the largest hospitals:

Kyrenia/Girne: Cumhuriyet Caddesi; tel. 081 5 20 14
Mórphou/Güzelyurt; tel. 071 4 21 25
Famagusta/Gazimağusa: Polatpaşa Bulvarı; tel. 036 6 28 76

Nicosia/Lefkoşa; tel. 020 7 14 41 or 7 39 71
Kyrenia/Girne; tel. 081 5 22 66
Famagusta/Gazimağusa; tel. 036 6 53 28
Tríkomo/İskele; tel. 037 1 23 19
Léfka/Lefke; tel. 078 1 77 57
Karavostási/Gemikonağı; tel. 077 1 73 22 or 1 73 51
Lápithos/Lapta; tel. 028 1 83 22

Emergency aid

Motoring in North Cyprus

North Cyprus has an excellent road network, enabling all the towns and villages to be reached by car. All the main roads between the larger towns are asphalted. Only minor roads, for example on the Karpasía peninsula or in the hills, are unsurfaced, though they can easily be negotiated by cars.

Road network

Nicosia is connected with Famagusta and Kyrenia by new, well engineered roads.

Traffic
regulations

Road traffic regulations are in line with international standards. Vehicles travel on the left, with overtaking on the right; vehicles on roundabouts have priority.

Distances on signposts and road signs are given in miles.

The speed limit in towns is 48kmph/30mph, outside built-up areas it is 80kmph/50mph.

Petrol

Petrol is still sold by the gallon in North Cyprus. Standard grade petrol is not available: only premium and diesel. It is considerably cheaper than in western Europe.

Petrol stations, generally located in town centres, are open daily from 6am to 6pm (sometimes later).

Museums

The opening times of museums and archaeological sites vary from place to place (see Sights from A to Z). On great religious festivals like the Sugar (Eid-I Fitr) Festival and the Festival of Sacrifice museums and sites are closed.

Photography is permitted in most museums.

Night Life

There are a number of discothèques, bars and casinos in the three principal towns of North Cyprus.

Discothèques
Nicosia

Picnic Hotel, outside the Old Town
Saray Hotel, Girne Caddesi (Atatürk Square)

Famagusta

Palm Beach Hotel, Kemal Servet Sokağı
Old Town Disco and Pub, west of St Nicholas's Cathedral

Kyrenia

Dome Hotel, in the town centre by the sea
Rooks, opposite the Dome Hotel
Moonlight Disco, on the Famagusta road
Hippodrome, in the town centre, opposite the Town Hall

Casinos

There are casinos in Nicosia (Sabri's Oriental Hotel), Famagusta (Sálamis Bay Hotel, Palm Beach Hotel) and Kyrenia (Hotel Liman, Dome Hotel, Celebrity Hotel). French and American roulette, baccarat and blackjack are played under international rules. The casinos are usually open from 9pm to 4am.

Nudism

Topless bathing and nudism are permitted in North Cyprus.

Opening Times

See Business Hours

Photography

It is forbidden to take photographs of military installations, but there is no difficulty about photographing features of tourist interest. Photography is also permitted in most museums. Before photographing people you should take care to ask their permission.

Films are expensive in North Cyprus, and not all brands are available. It is advisable, therefore, to take an adequate supply of films from home.

Post

There are post offices in all towns of any size. Mail addressed to western Europe is likely to take at least 8–10 days to arrive. Mail for places in the Turkish part of Cyprus should not be addressed to North Cyprus, which is not internationally recognised, but should bear the code Mersin 10, Turkey (a town in mainland Turkey) after the name of the town.

Postal services

Post offices are open Mon.–Fri. 7.30am–2pm and 4–6pm, Sat. 7.30am–2pm.

Opening times

Nicosia: Sarayönü Sokağı, near Atatürk Square
Famagusta: near St Nicholas's Cathedral
Kyrenia: Cumhuriyet Caddesi

Head post offices

Public Holidays and Festivals

Since Atatürk's reforms in the 1920s the weekly day of rest in Turkey has been Sunday and not, as in other Islamic countries, Friday. The holidays and festivals celebrated in North Cyprus are broadly the same as in Turkey. On both fixed holidays and movable festivals all shops and public institutions are closed.

Official holidays

January 1st: New Year's Day
April 23rd: National Sovereignty Day and Children's Day
May 1st: Labour Day
May 19th: Youth and Sports Day, Atatürk Memorial Day
July 20th: Peace and Freedom Day (anniversary of the landing of Turkish troops in 1974)
August 1st: TMT Day (Turkish Endurance Organisation)
August 30th: Victory Day (commemorating Turkey's victory in the war with Greece in 1922)
October 29th: Turkish National Day (commemorating the proclamation of the Republic of Turkey in 1923)
November 15th: Proclamation of the Turkish Republic of Northern Cyprus, 1983

Muslim religious festivals are determined by the Islamic lunar calendar, and move back ten days each year (i.e. occur ten days earlier) in the Gregorian calendar.
Ramadan is the month of fasting (February/March). The 24th day of the month is a public holiday.
Şeker Bayramı (Eid-l Fitr Festival): a three-day festival at the end of Ramadan, when gifts of sweets are exchanged.
Kurban Bayramı (Festival of Sacrifice; May/June): a four-day festival (Mohammed's birthday) on which lambs are sacrificed and shared with the poor (see Art and Culture, Folk Art and Traditions).

Movable festivals

Local festivals   Mid July: Festival of Tourism in Kyrenia/Girne
                   May/June: Orange Festival in Mórphou/Güzelyurt
                   Mid July: Festival of Tourism in Famagusta/Gazimağusa
                   Beginning of August: Wine Festival in Famagusta/Gazimağusa

Public Transport

Buses   Service buses run regular services, usually at hourly intervals, between all
                   the places of any size in North Cyprus; fares are low. The timing of services
                   can be found by enquiry at bus stations.

Nicosia   The bus station is in Kemal Aşık Caddesı. From here there are buses and
                   service (shared) taxis to Kyrenia, Famagusta and Mórphou/Güzelyurt.
                   There are also buses to Kyrenia starting from Girne Caddesi (in front of the
                   Museum of Turkish Folk Art in the Mevlevi Tekke).

Famagusta   The bus station is outside the town walls in Mustafa Kemal Bulvarı (Lev-
                   koşa Yolu), near the Atatürk Monument.

Kyrenia   The bus station is in the town centre, at the point where the Nicosia road
                   begins.

Radio and Television

                   The Bayrak Broadcasting and Television Corporation (Bayrak Radio ve
                   Televizyon, BRT), with two radio and television channels, transmits brief
                   news bulletins in English.
                   Greek Cypriot and British Forces programmes and the BBC World Ser-
                   vice can also be received in North Cyprus.

Restaurants

Nicosia   There are a number of restaurants offering local specialities in Girne
                   Caddesi.

Famagusta   There are good restaurants near the Palm Beach Hotel. An excellent restau-
                   rant in the town centre is the Viyana Restaurant on the north side of the
                   Cathedral. On the road to Sálamis is the Dernek Restaurant. The Petek
                   Pastanesi is a cake shop near Othello's Tower with a tempting assortment
                   of cakes, pastries, etc.

Kyrenia   There are a number of good eating-places around the harbour, including
                   the Set Restaurant (fish), the Harbour Club Restaurant (French cuisine) and
                   the Set Restaurant near the mosque (Italian dishes).
                   5km/3 miles east of Kyrenia is the Lemon Tree Restaurant (fish dishes;
                   live music). In the ruins of Bellapais Abbey is the Kybele Restaurant.

Shopping, Souvenirs

                   In the larger towns leather goods and items of clothing can be bought at
                   reasonable prices. Popular souvenirs are beautiful woven fabrics and
                   basketwork, pottery, alabaster and copper articles. A wide range of gold
                   and silver jewellery can be seen in Kyrenia and Famagusta.

Harbour-front restaurant, Kyrenia   *Country taverna near Mórphou*

Sport

North Cyprus, like the southern part of the island (see Practical Information on South Cyprus, Sport), caters for a wide range of sports. Many hotels have their own tennis courts and facilities for a variety of water sports.

Lack of wind in summer months and military restrictions around parts of the coastline make sailing difficult. The old harbour of Kyrenia provides moorings.

Sailing

Dolphin Sailing, operates sailing, para-sailing, speed boat and aquarocket trips from Deniz Kızı beach (Kyrenia) from May to October. Sailing dinghies and catarmarans can also be hired from Palm Beach and Sálamis Bay Hotels in Famagusta.

Water skiing is operated from hotels Club Acapulco, Chateau Lambousa and Mare Monte in Kyrenia; Deniz Kızı, Palm Beach and Salámis Bay in Famagusta.

Water Skiing

Windsurf boards can be hired from hotels Celebrity, Club Kyrenia, Chateau Lambousa and Mare Monte in Kyrenia; Palm Beach, Park, Sálamis Bay, Cyprus Gardens, Long Beach and Mimoza in Famagusta.

Wind-surfing

Cyprus Diving Centres:

Diving

Kyrenia Diving Centre
21 Philecia Court, Kyrenia. Tel. 815 60 87

Fred Dive Ltd
7 Kemal Aşık Caddesı, Nicosia. Tel. 815 17 43

Tennis	In Kyrenia there are tennis courts at the Celebrity, Chateau Lambousa, Mare Monte and Club Acapulco hotels, Jasmine Court Hotel Apartments, L.A.S. Holiday Centre, Olive Tree Holiday Village and Riverside Holiday Village.
	In Famagusta the Cyprus Gardens, Palm Beach, Park, Sálamis Bay and Sea Side hotels have tennis courts.
Riding	3km/2 miles west of Kyrenia, at Karaoğlanoğlu, is the Tunal Riding Club (a stud).
Walking	The Beşparmak Hills are good walking country. There are no waymarked routes.
Beaches	See entry

Telephone, Telegraph

Telephone	Telephone calls can be made from hotels, telephone kiosks or telegraph offices. Payphones are operated by tokens (jeton), obtainable in post offices and telegraph offices.
	All international calls are routed via Mersin in Turkey.
Telegraph offices	Nicosia: Telecommunication Office, in the Yenişehir district
	Famagusta: Polatpaşa Bulvarı
	Kyrenia: Cumhuriyet Caddesi
International dialling codes	North Cyprus to the United Kingdom: 00 44
	North Cyprus to the United States or Canada: 00 1
	United Kingdom to North Cyprus: 00 90 392
	United States or Canada to North Cyprus: 011 90 392
	When telephoning to the United Kingdom from North Cyprus the zero of the local dialling code should be omitted.

Time

See Practical Information on South Cyprus, Time

Tipping

It is customary to give a tip of about 10% in hotels and restaurants, also to hairdressers and taxi drivers.

Travel Documents

Visitors to North Cyprus must have a passport valid for at least six months from their date of arrival; no visa is required for visitors from western countries. The passport will be stamped by the North Cyprus immigration officers on entry and exit; but since a North Cyprus stamp in a passport will normally prevent the holder from entering the Greek Republic of Cyprus, and possibly also from visiting Greece, it is advisable to ask to have the stamps put on a form separate from the passport.

Weights and Measures

As in South Cyprus (see Practical Information on South Cyprus, Weights and Measures)

When to Go

See Practical Information on South Cyprus, When to Go

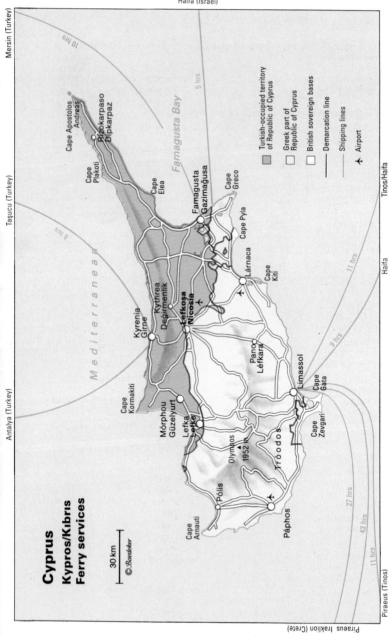

Cyprus
Kypros/Kibris
Ferry services

30 km

© Baedeker

Legend:
- Turkish-occupied territory of Republic of Cyprus
- Greek part of Republic of Cyprus
- British sovereign bases
- Demarcation line
- Shipping lines
- ✈ Airport

Mediterranean

Famagusta Bay

Tróodos

Olympos 1952 m

Places:
- Cape Apostolos Andreas
- Rizokarpaso Dipkarpaz
- Cape Plakoti
- Cape Elea
- Famagusta Gazimağusa
- Cape Greco
- Cape Pyla
- Lárnaca
- Cape Kiti
- Kythrea Değirmenlik
- Lefkosa Nicosia
- Kyrenia Girne
- Pano Léfkara
- Limassol
- Cape Gata
- Cape Kormakiti
- Mórphou Güzelyurt
- Lefka Lefke
- Cape Zevgari
- Pólis
- Cape Arnauti
- Páphos

Routes/destinations:
- Haifa (Israel)
- Mersin (Turkey)
- Taşucu (Turkey)
- Antalya (Turkey)
- Piraeus (Tinos)
- Piraeus Iraklion (Crete)
- Tinos/Haifa
- Haifa
- 10 hrs
- 5 hrs
- 8 hrs
- 11 hrs
- 9 hrs
- 27 hrs
- 43 hrs
- 11 hrs

Index

Principal Sights of Tourist Interest

South Cyprus

(*continued on page 316*)

Principal Sights of Tourist Interest

(*continued from page 316*)

North Cyprus

Imprint

188 illustrations, 21 ground-plans, 9 town plans, 9 drawings, 9 general maps, 5 situation plans, 2 tables, 1 large map of Cyprus at the end of the book

Original German text: Astrid Feltes, Barbara Peters, Prof. Wolfgang Hassenpflug
Editorial work: Baedeker-Redaktion (Astrid Feltes)
General direction: Rainer Eisenschmid, Baedeker Stuttgart

Cartography: Gert Oberländer, Munich; Hallwag AG, Berne (large map of Cyprus)

Source of illustrations: Archaeological Museum, Nicosia (4); Couteau (1); Feltes (116); Guenther (6); Hartmann (2); Historia (2); Lade, Helga (1); Louis Cruise Lines (1); Peters/Strub (45); Pierides Museum (1); Schuster (1); Troodhítissa Monastery (1); Ullstein (5); Zavallis (1).

English language edition: Alec Court
Original English translation: James Hogarth

Revised text: Wendy Bell, Margaret Court

3rd English edition 1997

© Baedeker Stuttgart
Original German edition 1996

© 1997 Jarrold and Sons Limited
English language edition worldwide

© 1997 The Automobile Association
United Kingdom and Ireland

Published in the United States by:
Macmillan Travel
A Simon & Schuster Macmillan Company
1633 Broadway
New York, NY 10019–6785

Macmillan is a registered trademark of Macmillan, Inc.

Distributed in the United Kingdom by the Publishing Division of the Automobile Association, Fanum House, Basingstoke, Hampshire RG21 2EA

Licensed user:
Mairs Geographischer Verlag GmbH & Co.,
Ostfildern-Kemnat bei Stuttgart

Printed in Italy by G. Canale & C.S.p.A – Borgaro T.se –Turin

ISBN 0 7495 1529 5 UK

Notes